FAITH AND PHILOSOPHY IN THE
WRITINGS OF PAUL RICOEUR

Loretta Dornisch

Problems in Contemporary Philosophy
Volume 29

The Edwin Mellen Press
Lewiston/Queenston/Lampeter

B
2430
.R554
D67
1991

Library of Congress Cataloging-in-Publication Data

This volume has been registered with The Library of Congress.

This is volume 29 in the continuing series
Problems in Contemporary Philosophy
Volume 29 ISBN 0-88946-737-4
PCP Series ISBN 0-88946-325-5

A CIP catalog record for this book

is available from the British Library.

Copyright © 1990 Loretta Dornisch

All rights reserved. For information contact

The Edwin Mellen Press
Box 450
Lewiston, New York
USA 14092

The Edwin Mellen Press
Box 67
Queenston, Ontario
CANADA L0S 1L0

The Edwin Mellen Press, Ltd.
Lampeter, Dyfed, Wales
UNITED KINGDOM SA48 7DY

Printed in the United States of America

FAITH AND PHILOSOPHY IN THE WRITINGS OF PAUL RICOEUR

TABLE OF CONTENTS

INTRODUCTION

One of the thinkers of the twentieth century who has struggled with the questions of human life is Paul Ricoeur, philosopher of faith. As one who seeks to read the signs of his times, Ricoeur is a leader and mentor for many thinkers who find his insights helpful in their search for meaning. That he calls himself a philosopher of faith indicates that he chooses to ask the philosophic questions from a particular focus and within a particular framework. This focus is one which grew out of Ricoeur's own search for meaning in the times, events, and intellectual currents in which he found himself, which included war, death, the tension of faith and ideology, and attempts to account for evil in human experience.

This book is an introduction to Ricoeur's work for those who, like Ricoeur, are concerned about the human questions. Because the human experience is often opaque, it calls for an interpretation which makes meaning possible.

The book also provides a way of seeing a larger perspective of Ricoeur's work which is voluminous. This introduction, of course, cannot comprehend the total work, but it can reflect some of the major themes as well as some of the relationships in order to provide a perspective.

Ricoeur has been described as eclectic because his searchings and his topics are far-ranging and involved in dialogue with many other thinkers of the twentieth and earlier centuries. Rather than saying he is eclectic, however, we should rather say that he is a thinker who through study enters into dialectic. For example, when he wanted to write On Interpretation: Essays on Freud, in spite of having already studied Freud intensively, he decided to retranslate Freud from the German and to use that as his text.

Similarly, when he came in contact with the English and American schools of literary or language study, the dialogue led to his being invited to lecture in departments of literature.

Formally Ricoeur is neither theologian nor biblical researcher. Nevertheless, the biblical texts are of prime importance for him. Coming from a liberal Protestant background, he experienced in 1936, when he was twenty-three, the "Barthian shock" of the power of the Word in the scriptures; he was nourished on the Word theologies of Ebeling and Fuchs, and has reflected all his life on the meaning of the word in the scriptures. So there is in his writings frequent reference to kerygma, that is, the message, the proclaiming of the good news of Jesus Christ. Besides scattered allusions to the scriptures in many of his works, there are substantial sections of his books as well as many articles on aspects of the Bible. It is not surprising, then, that he is invited, not only to theological centers, but also to centers which specialize in biblical research. It is especially in the areas of symbol, of language, and of interpretation theory that Ricoeur has much to offer.

This book, however, is not intended as a book for specialists. Ricoeur offers much to any person who seriously asks the questions: Why do we so often feel divided within ourselves? Is there any meaning in suffering and death? What is guilt? What is the power of the subconscious within the human experience? What is the power of language and symbol in the way we interpret our human experience? What is the power of the human will to create new worlds, new meanings, new actions, new societies?

The book is arranged in seven sections focused on some major interests which pervade Ricoeur's work:

    I.   Ricoeur and the Human Questions
   II.   Ricoeur and the Challenge of Faith
  III.   Ricoeur and the Christian Tradition
   IV.   Ricoeur and the Crises of Society
    V.   Ricoeur and the Problem of Interpretation
   VI.   Ricoeur and Biblical Research
  VII.   Ricoeur, Language, and Interpretation Theory

These themes are united by an emphasis on interpretation theory and symbol, and each one grows out of, but still includes the previous theme. In other words, we start with the questions pertaining to what it means to be human. These questions remain as nucleus for an examination of the problem of faith. Faith will then be put in the context of the Christian tradition, which in Ricoeur's view is inseparable from the problems of human society. But all of this is structured by our experiences as symbolic beings, by the language which we are given and which we create, and by the ways we interpret the signs about us. In each section, we will gradually enlarge the horizon, starting from a narrower focus, and then extending that focus to include the larger structures of our human experience.

The style of the study is descriptive and interpretive, with critical analysis left to others except incidentally where such analysis proves helpful in understanding the flow of the work. Some biographical and anecdotal references are included when they can illustrate the point at hand. It is hoped that others will assume the tasks of a careful biography and of critical analysis. Since Ricoeur's work is still incomplete, it is too soon for a definitive study, although a number of studies on aspects of Ricoeur's work have begun the process. Nevertheless, a thematic study can make clear that Ricoeur's work calls for hope, courage, and a search for meaning, qualities which make possible a journey toward freedom.

PART I.   RICOEUR
         AND THE HUMAN QUESTIONS

CHAPTER ONE

Why Philosophy?

In seeking wisdom, the philosopher asks the human questions. He or she seeks to find meaning in human life, to find out what it means to be a human being. Personally and professionally, Ricoeur has been asking these questions all his life, with friends, family, other teachers, students. The task of asking questions and seeking answers has been his continuing philosophical thrust.

We will look at three moments in which he summarized his searching and use these as focal points for describing his philosophical journey. The first is an address published in Montreal in 1968, as part of a conference entitled Why Philosophy? The second was prepared in 1971 at the request of his colleagues in the Divinity School at the University of Chicago when he was asked to speak about the problems he had been working with during the 1960's. The third was written in 1978 for The Iliff Review to summarize his relation to the history of philosophy. In these three articles we can see three different facets of Ricoeur's work as philosopher. Each will provide some key points for reflecting, not only on Ricoeur's task as philosopher, but also on the task of those who with him want to ask the human questions.

WHY PHILOSOPHY?

Why philosophy? Why ask about the meaning of human life? At the beginning of western philosophy, Socrates drew out of his own reflection the insight that the life which is not examined is not worth living. Today we may modify that to: the life which is not examined and found meaningful is not worth living.

Ricoeur sees every philosopher as one who like Socrates
stands confronting his times. He is not an escapist.
He tries to avoid illusion. He attempts to see things
as they are.

When the world was confronted with the Jonestown
massacre in Guyana in 1978, Time magazine asked Ricoeur
about the problem of evil in our times. He answered:

> What I fear is that everyone will try
> to disconnect themselves from
> Jonestown. [It is too easy to say,]
> "We are the good people. This cannot
> happen to us."[1]

Ricoeur does not absent himself from the times in which
he lives. On the contrary, like Socrates, he confronts
his times. He opens himself to the questions raised in
his existential situation, and he seeks for meaning.

Ricoeur sees the philosopher's task as meaningful
on three levels: the level of daily life, the level of
the scholarly life, and the level of the reflective
life.

The Level of Daily Life

For Ricoeur, the philosophic task is congruent
with the living out of daily life. Each person's existential situation is interwoven with the events of his
time. The unfolding of the early part of Ricoeur's
personal and professional life was interwoven with the
unfolding of the events in France preceding, during,
and in the aftermath of World War I. That war raised
the questions, not only of the meaningfulness of his
father's death, but of the problems of peace and war.
His father had been killed in the early part of that
war. Certainly, he thought, his father had died for a
good cause, but the proprietor of the apartment house
where Ricoeur lived with his grandparents felt that
France had been in error. In the proprietor's view,
the war had been a mistake. Ricoeur came to believe
that history is violent, but that we must nevertheless
always strive toward peace.

In contrast to the reflections on death and war,
Ricoeur's schooling during the 1920's and early 1930's
provided the joy of discovering the great classical
thinkers of the western world. The reading of essays,
poetry, novels, philosophy raised new questions and

supplied new patterns to try out in the lived
situation. Enthusiastic teachers, colleagues, and
students added the excitement of debate and appreciation. Among them were three persons who stand out as
indicative of the directions which Ricoeur would follow: Emmanuel Mounier, Roland Dalbiez, and Gabriel
Marcel.

Three Early Philosophic Influences

A Philosophy of Personalism

Emmanuel Mounier called himself a philosopher, and
later wrote a philosophy of personalism, although he
had chosen not to complete his degree, and even to
dissociate himself from the university world, which to
him seemed removed from society.

Unlike Mounier, Ricoeur opted to stay in the
university setting. The university provides for him a
milieu, a place, an extended family. The university is
not separated from daily life; on the contrary, academic thought has often transformed the world. What
began in Plato as looking beyond sense impressions made
possible mathematics and measurement, the development
of physics, and, in fact, some of the dominant characteristics of our technological world (History and
Truth, 4). In other words, theory and action cannot be
separated: each affects the other (5). We cannot
speak correctly of those who are committed and of those
who are uncommitted. Words are not separate from
action. On the contrary, they have the power to change
the ways we understand and they have the power to
change the heart. They create, reinforce, or modify
meaning, and thereby create our worlds of meaning and
action.

Ricoeur believes that his work as a university
professor affects daily life. Just as in physics
energy is never lost but only transformed, so the power
of the word reverberates to other places and times from
the reflective thought brought to expression in the
university or in the marketplace. Word calls for action and action leads to word.

Ricoeur admires "the word which reflects
efficaciously and acts thoughtfully" (5). He calls us
to an integrity of word and action, an integration of
thought and action contrary to the fragmentation
characteristic of many aspects of modern life. He

reminds us that what happens at Harvard, or at the
University of Chicago, or at the University of California affects the unfolding of our civilization, and, in
turn, what happens on the streets of Boston or New York
or Los Angeles affects the theorizing of the reflective
persons in our society.

A bronze sculpture marks the former place of the
Shedd fieldhouse on the campus of the University of
Chicago where Fermi and others produced in the secrecy
of the early days of World War II the first controlled
sustained nuclear reaction. This was the culmination
of the work of generations of theorists whose works
seemed to most persons removed from everyday life.
That reaction radically reoriented our history, including the dramatic events of Hiroshima, the technological
and political aspects of nuclear energy, as well as the
development of nuclear medicine.

But although Ricoeur chose to remain in the
university setting, at the same time he chose to remain
associated with Mounier as a member of Esprit, the
movement and journal Mounier founded in 1930 out of a
vision of a civilization called personalist to designate the civilizing task of creating a civilization.
In this context, personalism refers to the "first investigations of the review Esprit and of some allied
groups concerned with the political and spiritual
crisis which was then breaking out in Europe." The
movement hoped to affect history "by a certain type of
combative thought" (135).[2]

After Mounier died in 1950, Ricoeur's tribute in
Esprit included this evaluation of personalism:

> Its main contribution to contemporary
> thought has been to offer a philosophi-
> cal matrix to professional philoso-
> phers, to propose tonalities to them,
> theoretical and practical holding notes
> containing one or several philosophies,
> pregnant with one or several philo-
> sophical systematizations. For many of
> us, this is our true debt to our friend
> (136).

Ricoeur admired the unusual balance Mounier had
maintained between "the virtue of confrontation, and
generosity or abundance of heart" (161). Confrontation
provides strength but generosity provides grace. The

two create an alliance of the ethical and of the
poetic.

Ricoeur not only remained a member of Esprit, but
he also published articles in the journal regularly,
and, with his family, joined those members living in
the Esprit community at Chatenay Malabre when he returned to Paris in 1958. In other words, Ricoeur has
always identified himself with the tasks of civilization.

Paradoxically, although Ricoeur has always taken a
leadership role in the political, familial, and academic communities of which he has been a part, nevertheless, he views philosophy, in the last analysis, as
a work of one person. A philosopher works in relationship, but not on a team. ("Dimensions d'une recherche
commune," 837). Such a paradoxical relationship of the
individual and the community will continue to be part
of Ricoeur's life. He is always involved in community
and communities. Yet he writes as an individual.

The Freudian Influence

Another aspect of the effect of philosophy on
daily life is reflected in Ricoeur's relationship with
Roland Dalbiez, his first philosophy teacher. In his
late teens Ricoeur took from Dalbiez a pre-university
course in which the human questions were raised in the
context of the western philosophic tradition, but also
within a contemporary orientation. What does it mean
to be a human being? What does it mean to be free?
How can we discern what is true and what is false?
What is the relationship of the individual to society?
What is the power and authority of the state? These
are the questions the early Greek philosophers
Socrates, Plato, and Aristotle asked, but they are also
the questions asked by contemporary philosophers and
other reflective persons. Dalbiez was familiar not
only with the French neo-Kantianism of the time, but he
was influenced also by the insights of Freud, about
whom he later wrote a book. Dalbiez raised questions
and pointed directions for Ricoeur within the tradition
of western philosophy, but also in dialogue with modern
disciplines such as psychoanalysis, psychology, sociology, and cultural anthropology. For Dalbiez, however, as well as for Ricoeur, the human questions are
raised in the context of a philosophical anthropology,
that is, in the context of the western European tradition of asking, "What is human being?"

A Philosophy of Mystery, Incarnation,
and Reconciliation

Besides Mounier and Dalbiez, a third person who
indicates a direction Ricoeur will take is his "great
teacher," Gabriel Marcel.

> What I liked in Marcel was his Socratic
> method of teaching. Every Friday eve-
> ning in his home Gabriel Marcel brought
> together twenty or so of his disciples
> and friends; we tried never to cite
> ready-made analyses or interpretations.
> Instead, we were required to think on
> the basis of fresh examples, whether
> real or imaginary, investigating the
> ontological implications of the situa-
> tion under consideration, exploring new
> avenues, taking chances, using the
> resources of our dialogue alone. In
> this way we participated to a greater
> or lesser extent in developing and
> discussing the great themes familiar to
> readers of Gabriel Marcel: existence
> versus objectivity, the critique of the
> pretensions of the Cogito, the primacy
> of "I am," concrete being and dialogue,
> death, betrayal, despair, fidelity,
> hope, ... The desire for this con-
> crete ontology has never left me ("My
> Relation to the History of Philosophy,"
> 5).

Through the questioning, the risk taking, the
discussions, Ricoeur made some key questions his own:
How much can we know of human life? How much remains
mystery? The mystery of being is one of Marcel's favorite themes. It becomes foundational for Ricoeur
also, but is transformed for him by his studies of the
language of symbol and the fullness of language. The
study of the mystery of being is also considerably
modified by the particular direction of Ricoeur's care-
fulness of method and by his deep respect for systematic analysis. While respecting the complexity of
human life, Ricoeur will not use complexity as an ex-
cuse for avoiding analysis or for avoiding the hunger
to know.

For Marcel and for Ricoeur, human existence is
incarnate, in-the-flesh, in-the-body. This seems obvious, but is too often ignored or distorted in human

life. Existence is always concrete existence,
existence in the here-and-now.

Marcel unfolded his ideas, not only in his
Metaphysical Journal of 1927 and in his proposal in
1933 for a concrete approach to the mystery of being,
but also in his plays and essays embodying his additional themes of presence, fidelity, hope, freedom,
ambiguity, and the call to believe. In a series of
published conversations, Ricoeur summarizes his remembrance:

> Let me recall, Mr. Marcel, that time
> when as students we used to come to
> your home. We met in the hopes of
> getting to the very quick of experience
> and exploring its meaning . . . .
>
> You are of the same breed as Péguy,
> Emmanuel Mounier, and all those who
> have grasped the profound unity of the
> body and the spirit. All your thought,
> despite the fact of the inhuman we were
> speaking about in an earlier conversa-
> tion, testifies to the extreme proxim-
> ity, the strict continuity between
> incarnation, which is like the basso
> continuo of all our wanderings and
> quests, and hope, which is nothing
> other than a continual getting underway
> again (Tragic Wisdom and Beyond, 218,
> 256).

But, at the same time that he was learning so much
from his "great teacher" Marcel, Ricoeur was also looking for a more systematic method of examining the philosophic questions. He was beginning to find such a
method in the phenomenology of Husserl.

Toward a Phenomenology

What does Ricoeur's research at this point tell us
about human existence? It points the direction and
outline of a philosophical anthropology that affects
daily life. It makes clear that human being is complex. The existence of human being is incarnational,
in-the-body, here-and-now, in this time and place. A
person's experience is always in relation to other
beings. While there is no simple explanation for persons and for the culture of which they are a part, yet

the things themselves call for efforts to know more about the things. Such efforts open up the question of knowledge. Somehow we know other things and other persons, and through knowing others and knowing self as other, we somehow know ourselves. Philosophy searches for knowledge, but in that search, philosophy aims at a unity of knowledge, a system, or at least an understanding of relationships. In a similar way, human beings seek knowledge of relationships and meaning, and ultimately even unity and system.

But human learning takes place, not only in the presence of the "thing itself," but also in dialectic, in placing one thing next to another. Besides being known through its own phenomena, an apple is also known in relationship to an orange, or perhaps in relationship to another apple. The self is also known in relationship to another; moreover, part of the self is known in relationship to another part, as Freud discovered in his analysis of the unconscious.

But persons are not only in relationship to others. They are also within a civilization. Any seeking for wisdom, any philosophy, seeks a vision of a civilization dedicated to the human person. In Marcellian or Ricoeurian terms, such vision will include concern for the problems of "concrete being and dialogue, death, betrayal, despair, fidelity, hope," freedom, love ("My Relation to the History of Philosophy," 5).

These same concerns were not just abstract words for Ricoeur during the 1930's. He had pursued the human questions formally in Brittany at the University of Rennes, from which he received a first academic degree. After teaching Greek and philosophy at Saint-Brieux for a year, he went up to Paris.

> That was the thing to do. Everything
> was going on there, I was a socialist
> then, you know. We thought socialism
> would solve the problems (Conversation,
> Jan., 1979).

He enrolled at the Sorbonne at the University of Paris in 1934, when he was twenty-one. The next year he received the Agregation, the certificate qualifying him to teach at the university level. In the same year he married Simone Lejas, whom he had long known in Brittany. Their first three children were born in the years before World War II. Two more children were born after the war.

The thirties saw the growing power of Hitler, with
all the personal, social, political, and philosophic
questions which the Nazi movement raised. Like many
other Frenchmen, Ricoeur was mobilized and served as an
officer in the French army during World War II. He was
captured and spent five years in a prison camp.
"Death, betrayal, despair, fidelity, hope," freedom,
love, became the realities of everyday life.

Questions and attempts at answers are not just
parts of an abstract philosophy. They are the substance in some way of every human life, of every person
who asks about the meaning of his or her experience in
relationship to others and to society.

After World War II, the questions would be raised
in the context of the Algerian or South Asian wars, or
in the context of civil rights, of nuclear power or
ecology, or of contemporary problems of economic and
political oppression. In each context, the questions
are new, but there is at the same time a pattern of
continuity because the questions are about the human
situation.

The Level of the Scholarly Life

Philosophy, then, is justified on the level of
daily life. It also has value on the level of the
scholarly life. Etymologically, the word scholar is
related to the word school. Ordinarily, a scholar is
one who has been formally trained in a school of some
kind. Today we think of a scholar as one who has
achieved mastery in a particular discipline and who is
then able to contribute to the continuing growth of
that discipline. It is generally assumed that a
scholar uses a scientific methodology, that he or she
is in dialogue with other scholars, is seeking knowledge, and is accountable for the research pursued.

The Scientific Attitude

As a scholar, the philosopher is always in
dialogue, not only with other philosophers and humanists, but also with persons in the sciences ("Interrogation philosophique et engagement," 9-17). This is
especially important today when science is a dominant
mode of thought, and when in many quarters the scientific world view is equated with reality. Ricoeur
describes three characteristics of the scientific

attitude prevalent among scholars in the twentieth
century.

Model of Exactitude: First is a striving for
exactness, for accuracy. Scientific models, precise
accuracy in measurement, accounting for loose ends,
statistical probability and predictability are de-
manded. What is the relationship of a philosopher to
this model of exactitude? What is the relationship of
one who seeks wisdom to those scientists who prize the
statistically accurate? Does the philosopher emulate
those in the exact sciences and even try to exceed them
with system, taxonomies, and statistics? Or, at the
opposite end, does the philosopher ignore the sciences
or see them as unrelated to philosophic work? Each of
these positions is held by some philosophers, and each
position is tempting especially in this era of emphasis
on science. Ricoeur sees either extreme as erroneous.
Instead, the reflective philosopher attempts to appre-
ciate the exactness of the scientific model, but also
to point out its limitations.

This position of Ricoeur has been evident in his
dialogue with structuralists, especially Lévi-Strauss,
the founder of French structuralism as applied to anthropology. Ricoeur has not only appreciated the
striving for system and exactness, but has recommended
incorporation of scientific findings into philosophic
endeavors, as well as response to scientific critique.
Nevertheless, the philosopher stands in a position also
to point out the limitations of a model of exactitude.
A system that is too neat does not recognize its own
limitations. It is blinded by reason of its own implicit ideology. Thomas Kuhn's book The Structure of
Scientific Revolutions[3] illustrates how difficult it is
sometimes for those within an accepted conceptual world
to recognize the time limits of that world and Kuhn
makes clear the impossibility of fully standing outside
that world. The strength of the philosopher is that
tradition has trained him or her precisely to ask the
questions which open cracks in the world view or in the
ideology and which raise the possibility of other perspectives. In other words, the philosopher can critique the absoluteness of science as idol or as Truth.
We do not think of our world view or "Truth" as ideology. On the contrary, we are tempted, as Ricoeur says,
to name as ideology, not our own thought, but the
thought of our adversaries.

> [Ideology] is the thought of the other.
> He does not know, but I know . . . .

> To this pretension is joined another:
> not only, one says, does there exist a
> point of view that is not ideological,
> but such a point of view is that of a
> science comparable to that of Euclid
> for geometry and that of Galileo and of
> Newton for physics and cosmology. It
> is remarkable that this pretension
> . . . is exactly that which Aristotle
> condemned among the Platonists of his
> time in the matter of ethics and of
> politics, and to which he opposed the
> pluralism of methods with degrees of
> rigor and of truth ("Science et
> idéologie," 330).

The philosopher is one who asks questions about both
scientific principles and scientific method. From the
position of questioner, he can point out the limitations of a science which perhaps may not acknowledge
its own limitations. Reciprocally, of course, the
scientist is in an excellent position to perform a
comparable service for the philosopher. Concretely,
current studies of death--whether philosophic, speculative, medical, or ethical--show the practicality of the
relationship between a discipline such as philosophy
and a practical science such as medicine. No discipline is sufficient of itself to provide a model of
truth.

In a similar way, Ricoeur recognizes the insights
and scientific endeavor of a structuralist way of analyzing a text or a section of the Bible, but he is also
able to point out the limitations of an absolutizing
approach.

Fragmentation of knowledge: The appreciation of a
model of exactitude is the first characteristic of the
prevalent scientific attitude. A second characteristic
is the fragmentation of knowledge.

The Renaissance human being, thought to be
educated to be conversant with "all knowledge" is no
longer possible, and perhaps never was. This first
became clear in the growing specialization within the
scientific world when persons within one speciality
were no longer able to understand persons in another
specialty. However, specialization has now accelerated
so much that fragmentation is more and more characteristic of persons in their everyday relationships, and
even in the various roles they play in their lives. A

Nobel prize winner gave a mind-stretching lecture
describing the magnificence of the cosmos and included
a statement that as a scientist, of course, he knew
there was no God in that cosmos. To the surprise of
his audience, however, he concluded his remarks by
saying, "You know, I'm a Bible reader . . ."

Whatever the integration this particular speaker
may have attained for himself within these two separate
roles, it is common today to find not only scholars,
but also persons in all walks of life, who are fragmented by the diverse worlds in which they walk.

Extension of the human sciences to all areas of
human experience: At the same time, paradoxically, the
human sciences have been extended into all areas of
human experience. Religion, love, sex--all are presumed subordinate to the dominant scientific attitude.
While we may agree that all aspects of human experience
are legitimate objects for scientific study, at the
same time, we have to insist that the limits of methodology can lead to distortion. A dying patient is more
than a scientific study can adequately describe. When
a person is dying, we are in the realm of mystery and
of person. Such a realm defies statistical analysis.

It is here that philosophy has much to offer in
the human quest for knowledge and wisdom. The philosopher seeks to heal the fragmentation of knowledge by
striving toward a reflection of the fullness of language and the fullness of human experience. Human
beings are not only subjects or objects to be studied,
whether by psychological, psychoanalytical, sociological, or cultural models, but human beings are also
subjects in the active sense of the word, in the way we
speak about subjective feelings or insights, that is,
in those feelings and insights which come from us as
autonomous, acting, integrating persons. A human being
is the place where the subjective and the objective
exist together in the paradox of a person who can say,
"I'm not the kind of person who does that--and yet I
did that." In other words, we can perceive ourselves
as both subject-acting and as object-acted-on. Our
language reflects this dichotomy: "I gave myself a
haircut." "I said to myself: you had better go."

Yet some aspects of science, in striving for
objectivity, have denied the subjective as real, and
thereby have absolutized the objectifying attitude to
such a degree that workers in a business, patients in
a hospital, or poor persons in a society can be

quantified, manipulated, and fragmented as objects so
much that they are no longer respected as human beings.
Against such a tendency, the philosopher strives for
wholeness, for a recognition of the dichotomy within
human beings. The philosopher strives toward a respect
for the person, not only as actor in his or her own
story, but as one acted on, both by self, by others,
and by social structures.

The Level of Reflective Life

Philosophy is needed, then, on the level of daily
life and on the level of scholarly life. What of the
level of reflective life? To reflect is to hold up a
mirror for our thoughts, to think over, to ponder. To
reflect is to seek for meaning. We may speak of the
reflection of the newspaper columnist or of the writer
of editorials. The sidewalk philosopher of the
California docks Eric Hoffer reflected on the world he
witnessed. A modern philosopher such as Ricoeur reflects on his world.

As he seeks for meaning, the philosopher must at
the same time strive to avoid illusion. Rather than
succumbing to false simplicity, he will expect a complexity correlative to the various manifestations of
truth, wherever it is found. Insofar as possible, he
will avoid the temptations implicit in personal, academic, political, or cultural defense mechanisms. He
will respect the autonomy of scientific research and
the value of quantitative probability, but he will also
recognize the sometimes stronger value of qualitative
probability. In other words, there are aspects of
human life which do not lend themselves to quantitative
measurement. In spite of its dominance in our culture,
a dollar-cost analysis is not necessarily the best way
to measure a human being who is a patient in a hospital. Quality of life is not in one-to-one correspondence with that which can be quantitatively measured.
One then works to evaluate quality: quality of verification, of truth, of value, of life. Then one may be
in a position to judge meaning on the basis of
qualitative probability.

But meaning is always historically conditioned.
In the complexity of human life and human history,
there is no absolute of a one-way totally exclusive of
other ways. Nor is meaning cumulative in a linear
sense. Nevertheless, as a Christian, Ricoeur sees the
symbol of the End Time as a symbol of the unity of

truth for which human beings, including philosophers,
strive. Human knowledge is always heuristic, open-
ended, reaching for more.

Lastly, in his search, the philosopher seeks for
meaning which he can appropriate for his own life,
which can constitute his world, that is, the world in
which he lives. A characteristic of many persons in
scholarly, academic, and technological areas today is
that they have found specialized knowledge, but not
sufficient human meaning. Thus the astronaut turns to
politics or to religion. The paleontologist turns to
philosophy. The philosopher turns to gardening. The
theologian turns to medicine or to law.

Ricoeur constantly calls persons to seek meaning
which they can make their own, which they can appropriate in order to make their lives more human and
thereby achieve greater freedom not in a falsely indi-
vidualistic sense, but in the sense of persons in relationship within a civilization.

For Ricoeur, the question of reflection, of
meaning and non-meaning, is ultimately the question of
the sacred, of the holy. And, of course, what is holy,
what is sacred, is life.

> Heidegger says somewhere that a poet
> sees the Holy, and a thinker sees
> Being. They stand on different moun-
> tains, but their voices echo one an-
> other (The Religious Significance of
> Atheism, 93).

Although the question of meaning and non-meaning
brings differences of opinion, the philosopher reflecting on his world cannot avoid the issues. On the contrary, he must seek to clarify, even though this may
bring conflict. In fact, in the tradition of Pascal's
wager, with all its potential for risk, the philosopher
is called to choose among the interpretations, to seek
meaning although the meaning remains open-ended. The
philosopher is called to witness. So are other human
beings.

Philosophy, then, has value on three levels: the
level of daily life, the level of scholarly life, and
the level of reflection. In spite of the difficulties,
the human questions deserve to be pursued. Integral to
the human condition is the questioning, the seeking,
the desire, the hunger to be called to meaning.

CHAPTER TWO

The Call to Meaning

The second moment we will use as focal point for
describing Ricoeur's philosophical journey is an
address he gave in 1971 at the invitation of his colleagues in the Divinity School at the University of
Chicago. Ricoeur had been appointed John Nuveen Professor in the Divinity School and the Department of
Philosophy at the University of Chicago, the chair
previously held by Paul Tillich. In this address, he
summarized and evaluated in the context of his on-going
philosophical task some of the problems he had been
working on during the 1960's. Over a period of thirty
years Ricoeur has moved from existentialism to a philosophy of language with many steps along the way and
with a cumulative integration that assimilates each
step into the next one, so that there is a surprising
continuity in what may superficially appear fragmented.
We will correlate this second focal point with the
third, an article published in the fall of 1978, in
which Ricoeur summarizes his relation to the history of
philosophy ("My Relation to the History of Philosophy"). It is necessary first, however, to ask what
directions Ricoeur had been pursuing earlier.

Early Influences

For most Americans, philosophy is not an important
discipline, so it may be somewhat difficult to understand, for example, European university students coming
together at a German cafe, and asking, among the first
questions, "Who is your philosopher?" Americans generally are not aware of following a particular philosopher or philosophy, although as Robert Bellah has

demonstrated, there may well be in America a shared
"civil religion" which provides a context of common
values. Early in this century, John Dewey articulated
for Americans a philosophy of pragmatism, and today we
may well theorize about contemporary capitalism as a
way of life, but Americans are more used to perceiving
differences of world view in terms of profession:
business, education, military service, engineering,
medicine, law; or of religious background: Methodist,
Episcopalian, Roman Catholic, Jewish, Baptist; or of
social classes: jet set, blue collar workers, un-
skilled laborers, hippies; or of color/ethnic group-
ings: Chicanos, Blacks, Wasps, Middle Class.

While there are similar perceptions in Europe, the
educational system there, at least until the 1960's,
usually gave to those who were university educated an
acquaintance with philosophy which provided a shared
group of questions, a shared tradition of intellectual
history, and a roster of intellectual heroes, predominantly German, French, or English. The traditions,
rooted in the Greek world which centered around
Socrates, Plato, and Aristotle, provided a line of
thought which continued with modifications through the
Roman world, through the medieval synthesis, and then
into the modern world through Kant and Hegel, Locke and
Hume, and through all those others who continued asking
the questions and posing answers.

This was the tradition which attracted Ricoeur
when he was a young student at the University of Paris
engaged in "studies which were influenced much more by
French neo-Kantianism than by Bergsonianism" (5),
studies building on Aristotle and Kant, the "great
architects of the Treatises on the Categories." Nevertheless,

Upon completion of my studies at the
University of Paris . . . I found myself confronting simultaneously the
thought of Gabriel Marcel and that of
Husserl. This conjunction is typical
of the sort of dichotomic influences
which under varied and at times strik-
ingly different forms have never ceased
to put me to the test. Each of these
two influences was a break with neo-
Kantianism, though in entirely different ways (5).

Phenomenology: To the Things Themselves

What was the impact of Husserl on Ricoeur? As
"father of Phenomenology," Husserl developed a philosophy which attempts to go "to the things themselves,"
relying on evidence rather than only on abstract theory. Husserl gave importance to perception in the broad
sense of the perceiving by the human being of the phenomena in the world. He developed this model of the
life-world, of the person perceiving the phenomena in
his or her life world. Especially in Germany some
followers of Husserl have continued the tradition in
terms of a "transcendental idealism," which emphasizes
ideas, and a human consciousness which transcends or
goes from the perceiving subject to the object perceived.

Other followers of Husserl, many of them French,
wanted to emphasize the whole of concrete human existence, and were therefore called existentialist phenomenologists or simply existentialists. Sartre and
Merleau-Ponty are often placed in this group. The
labels are misleading, yet helpful to those unfamiliar
with the individual philosophers. Especially in the
1940's and 1950's the term "existential philosophy" was
used to refer to those trying to describe or to analyze
their existential situations. Sartre, through his
philosophy and plays, Camus through his novels, and
Merleau-Ponty through his philosophy of perception,
provided vocabulary and models for their generation.
Ricoeur's own work was in this context. He was asking:

> How is it possible to introduce within
> the framework of a philosophy of the
> will, on which I had written ten years
> earlier, some fundamental experiences
> such as guilt, bondage, alienation, or,
> to speak in religious terms, sin? As
> such this problem could be expressed in
> terms of an existential philosophy. All
> existential philosophies of the forties
> and fifties had met this problem. We
> may speak of inauthentic life with
> Heidegger, or boundary situations (Grenz-
> situationen) with Jaspers, or of Being
> and Having and of despair with Gabriel
> Marcel. My problem belonged to this
> sphere of questions with a somewhat
> more specific interest. My problem was
> to distinguish between finitude and
> guilt (Philosophy of Paul Ricoeur, 86).

Yet these were intellectual developments which had
and still have little direct impact on Anglo-Saxon
countries, where philosophers group "Kant and Hegel,
Husserl and Heidegger, Gabriel Marcel, Sartre and
Merleau-Ponty, and finally Gadamer . . . ,--all lumped
together" under the term "'Continental' philosophy"
("My Relation to the History of Philosophy," 10-11).
Ricoeur himself, of course, is also placed in this
group.

It was partly his study of Husserl which gave
directions to Ricoeur which have continued throughout
his philosophic journey.

> [My] desire for systematism in
> philosophical method I found in
> Husserl, more precisely, in the <u>Ideas</u>
> (which I was to translate into French
> several years later). In Husserl I
> admired not only the care taken in his
> descriptions but the way they were
> linked together. Some of Husserl's
> theses could be made, without distort-
> ing them too much, to agree with the
> thought of Gabriel Marcel: the central
> nature of the question of meaning, the
> subordination of the linguistic and
> propositional level to the fundamental
> sense of experience itself (5).

But the idealism of Husserl was in conflict with
the concrete ontology of Marcel:

> This conflict explains why I have
> always tried to separate . . . the
> phenomenological <u>method</u> of description
> from the idealist <u>philosophy</u> (6).

For Ricoeur, however, none of this exploration was
an ivory tower experience. On the contrary, it was
undertaken in the whirlwind situation preceding, during, and immediately after World War II. From the
Friday evening conversations in Marcel's home, preceding World War II, where Ricoeur and twenty or so others
had shared their experiences and their philosophizing,
the scene shifted for Ricoeur to the French army and
then, after Ricoeur was captured, to a German prison
camp on the Polish front. There he shared a small room
with Mikel Dufrenne, another French philosopher.

By giving the guards American cigarettes received
through the Red Cross, Ricoeur and Dufrenne were able

to get books from the nearby university library. A
small table with a candle, the precious book, a philosopher seated on either side, one studying the left
page, the other the right, taking notes on pieces of
butcher paper, then reversing positions in order to
study the other page--this was the setting for
Ricoeur's continuing to pursue the human questions in
his philosophic journey.

How was it possible to hope in such a situation?
Ricoeur answers, "Mikel Dufrenne was the eternal optimist! We were always going to be liberated next week!"
(Conversation, Jan., 1979). And in the meantime, they
would study, translate, and write philosophy.

Jaspers: A Philosophy of Existence

Ricoeur had been introduced to the thought of
Heidegger and Karl Jaspers in Gabriel Marcel's circle
of friends and students. The "forced leisure" of the
prison camp allowed him "to read all that was available
of each of them before 1945" (6). Ricoeur was attracted
to the work of Jaspers, whose writings seemed to him
close to that of Marcel.

There were many things about Jaspers which
appealed to Ricoeur in his human search. Unlike
Heidegger, who had capitulated for a while to the Nazi
illusion, Jaspers had stood as human being and as confronting citizen against the Nazi maelstrom (7). But
it was not only the man, it was also the philosophy of
Jaspers which was more congenial to Ricoeur's. A number of themes were particularly appealing:

1) Symbol. Jaspers had formulated a theory of
symbol related to language which Ricoeur found very
helpful in developing his own theory of symbol. Symbols are the "scripture of an Other" which I must decipher (Karl Jaspers, 65). But what are symbols? From
its root meaning, symbol suggests that two or more
things are thrown together, and from this juxtaposition
or intermingling there arises a new meaning which is
greater than or different from either or any of the
parts. For example, if I make a poster with a beauti-
ful picture of mountains and then add the words of the
psalm, "I lift up my eyes to the mountains," I have
symbolized a relationship of mountains and of a person's religious experience which is essentially positive. But if, instead of the words of the psalmist, I
substitute a picture of rusty beer cans, old tires, and

other debris, I have changed the symbolization to
communicate an ecological position and a more negative
experience. All human experiences are complex processes of similar symbolic perceptions.

Jaspers, then, compared symbol, the complex object
of our perceptions, to writing or to a scripture of an
Other. Why capitalize Other? To an English-speaking
person, the capital letter suggests deity, God. But
Jaspers, in spite of a rather traditional Christian
upbringing, had rejected the accepted ideas of God. He
uses Other here in a way which reminds us of Rudolf
Otto's treatment of the Holy as the unknown which is at
the same time attractive and enlightening, but also
terrifying or awe-inspiring. Both Jaspers as expressed
unbeliever and Ricoeur as expressed believer belong to
a philosophic tradition which continues to ask the
ultimate questions, including the one about the Being
of all beings, called by Lonergan the known unknown.
Somehow we know that which we do not know.

These "symbols are the scripture of an Other which
I must decipher." The last four words call for explication. By reason of being, these symbols require a
reaction from me. I am called to decipher them, to
interpret them. They call me into relationship. It is
through these symbols that "transcendence is announced
to me" and I become hearer.

Like the word Other, the word Transcendence is
often capitalized. The two words are not disparate.
Transcendence is "a stepping across" from our own perception to a relationship with another. As symbol of
the Other, the noun Transcendent is often capitalized
as well, and in a believer's context may be a philosophic name for the deity. But there is something far
more profound here than just a philosophic language for
items of belief. On the contrary, the philosophic
language is asking the questions which belong to all
times and places, to all cultures. What is the universe and what is my relationship within it? This can
never be other than a human question. It is the question Job asked, and when he heard in the voice which
came out of the whirlwind the "scripture of an Other"
which he had to decipher, his attempts led him to sit
with his hand over his mouth--in silence. The symbols
call me to listen. They call me to wonder.

If we try to translate the symbol into objective
language, we lose the full meaning. How often we have
returned from a peak experience,--for example, a

vacation with spectacular views of ocean or mountains,
--overflowing with words. We may talk for as long as
anyone will listen, but conclude by saying, "But I
really can't put it into words." Words fall short of
the symbolic experience.

In this sense, everything is able to be symbol--
the birth of a baby, falling in love, a cloud, a storm,
a wildflower, a play or a poem--and as symbol each
thereby manifests transcendence.

> Being-there and being-symbol are two
> dimensions of the same world, the one
> for consciousness in general, the other
> for existence, and in the symbol, the
> object disappears as object, in such a
> way that Transcendence appears in it,
> without one being able to separate the
> symbol from the being which it signi-
> fies (Karl Jaspers, 291).

The symbol has a totality which is not
comprehended by analysis or synthesis. Though we try,
and it is a useful exercise, we really cannot take
symbol apart without destroying or radically transforming its meaning. In a similar way, we can separate the
hydrogen and oxygen which constitute water, but we no
longer have water. Nor can we summarize symbol anymore
than we can summarize a poem. In the process we have
lost the symbol or the poem. Such is the expression of
the human face which truly wishes to communicate with
another. Here existence speaks to existence.

> The symbol . . . announces being; it
> seems to speak, but it is a transcen-
> dent silence . . . . One is not able
> to appraise these symbols, but to be-
> lieve them and to live them (Gabriel
> Marcel et Karl Jaspers, 426).

2) Limit-situations. Another aspect of Jaspers'
existentialist philosophy which appealed to Ricoeur and
which is finding renewed interest in contemporary
American thought is Jaspers' description of limit-
situations. Limit-situations are experiences on-the-
edge, at the boundary-line, where we are stretched to
our limits. Like the symbolic experience, they are
thick with meaning, so much so that they challenge but
also defy thought and expression. With Jaspers,
Ricoeur will often say that they are opaque. But in
spite of being thick and opaque, these limit-situations
call for action.

Jaspers lists four limit-situations: death, suffering, struggle, and fault. They are ones that he himself knew personally, and ones which Ricoeur came to know, especially in the context of war. To experience the death of comrades, to face death oneself, to see bodies piled up for mass burial is to make philosophy concrete.

Suffering comes in many forms: the anguish of everyday life described by Heidegger, separation from family and friends, the absurdity of personal and structural oppression. The personal and cultural contexts change but the human thread continues and crosses temporal and cultural boundaries. It affects our bodies, our feelings, our knowledge, our actions.

Death and suffering are the extreme forms of that on-going struggle to become who we will become: the struggle, perhaps, to get up each day, to build a marriage, to find meaning, to integrate personality, to build a civilization, to survive. Struggle often becomes combat and confrontation. In American experience the struggle of the bus boycott became for Martin Luther King, Jr. the combat of civil rights and the confrontation which led to his death. For Ricoeur, as for many of us in one degree or another, the struggle has been the day-to-day combat and confrontation in the political, educational, academic, philosophic, and personal spheres.

The last limit or boundary situation which Jaspers describes is fault. It is this last which becomes so important for Ricoeur, especially in his studies which led to The Symbolism of Evil, one of his most widely received books. In French, as well as in English, the word fault has a double or multiple connotation. It suggests not only a wrong committed by a human being-- "It is my fault"--, but also a rift, a geologic fault, a cleavage which has destroyed the integrity of the original and which, like the San Andreas fault in California, is always subject to tremor, destruction, and chaos.

For Ricoeur, fault is the most troubling of the limit situations, even more than suffering, struggle, and death, because it is in the relationship of me with myself (Karl Jaspers, 190). This importance of the fault pervaded many of Ricoeur's studies for the succeeding eighteen years, at least until he had finished writing Freud and Philosophy, which is an examination of the deep rifts within the unconscious and subconscious discovered by Freud.

But it is not just tragic situations which take us
to the edge. There is joy in the birth of a child.
There is the peak experience, the moment of insight.
There is the mastery and beauty we find in a symphony
of Mahler, a poem of Hölderlin or of Rilke, or in the
leap of a ballet dancer or a skater. These too may be
at the limit, experiences which break our boundaries.

3) Paradox. A third idea from Jaspers which
becomes very important for Ricoeur and which appeals to
many Americans faced with the incongruities of modern
life is the notion of paradox. Like many persons in
the latter half of the twentieth century, Ricoeur has
often been faced with contradictions. This view contradicts that one. This philosophy is the opposite of
that one. This part of me is the opposite of that part
of me. One can understand why Jaspers' philosophy of
paradox, then, had strong appeal for Ricoeur.

The concept of paradox permeates Jaspers'
philosophy but is especially brought to the fore in
what he calls the attitudes of existence before Transcendence. The believer may see this as human being
before God, but Jaspers intends it in a much larger
sense. We may think of an individual person as an
existence which is constantly overflowing into and
touching other existences, but especially as that which
is not limited by concrete existence. This is an insight similar to that of Eastern thought systems which
perceive the individual as part of a larger whole, the
All. No woman or man is an island. There is not an
individual existence of and by itself.

The attitudes of such an existence may be
characterized according to Jaspers by four paradoxical
relationships:

(1) Nearness and distance. The fully human, the
"divine," seems so near and yet so far. Happiness is
always just out of our reach. As Otto tells us, the
holy is tremendens fascinans. Psychologists also speak
of the attraction-avoidance conflicts within our personalities.

(2) Fall and elevation. "Sometimes I'm up,
sometimes I'm down," is the line from a traditional
spiritual. It registers a trait of common experience.
We fall out of favor, with ourselves or with someone
else, and then sometimes we are just as suddenly restored. "Lord, you have cast me down, but then you
have lifted me up," is the line written by the psalmist

to express his similar experience. Paul wrote, "In
Adam all fell, in Christ all were lifted up." There is
a rhythm here, whether it is bio-rhythm or cosmic
rhythm, which seems to pervade human life.

(3) <u>The challenge to overcome and the temptation
to give up</u>. "Try again," the mother will say to the
child. So will the Olympic coach who helps the com-
petitor continue through years of grueling practice and
training in spite of defeat or victory.

(4) <u>The orderly law of the day and the disorderly
passion of the night</u>. This phrase reflects the
Freudian and Jungian studies related to conscious existence as contrasted with the unconscious, subconscious,
and intuitive aspects of our existence. We are reminded of the yin-yang diagram of eastern thought, as
well as of the long tradition of western literature
which pictures mystery and chaos in the dark forest or
in the long nights.

Today we may feel much more positively toward the
night side of our personalities. In fact, some people
are "night" persons. Moreover, studies on intuition
and the right side of the brain reveal how neglected
these areas have been in much of western thought. What
is symbolized by day and night, however, is the apparent order as contrasted with apparent disorder. Order
signifies that which we can understand, that over which
we have control, that to which we give meaning. Disorder is that which defies ordering, which doesn't fit,
which dissolves limits and bursts boundaries, which
leaves us "out of control" and, like Job, either raving
against injustices, or sitting silent with our hands
over our mouths.

> [Karl Jaspers'] thought possessed an
> architecture [which] I found most attrac-
> tive . . . the majestic composition of
> the three volumes of his <u>Philosophy</u>:
>   Orientation in the World
>   Illumination of Existence
>   Metaphysics . . .
> Upon our return from captivity, I along
> with Mikel Dufrenne, my friend and
> companion in misfortune, made a sort of
> synopsis--more systematic than usual!--
> of the thought of Jaspers, while at the
> same time paying my first debt to
> Husserl by translating the <u>Ideas</u> ("My
> Relationship to the History of Philoso-
> phy," 6).

The Drama of Human Freedom

The quotation above does not communicate the drama
of the human enterprise involved. Not only had Ricoeur
and Dufrenne studied the materials under the difficulties of the prison camp, but the notes had been carried
out of the camp under dramatic circumstances. Toward
the end of the war, as the inevitability of German
defeat became clear, the prison system broke down, so
that, finally, the guards looked the other way or left,
and, with other prisoners, Ricoeur and Dufrenne started
walking west. On one level, the disorder of the night
was giving way to the order of the day and the possibility of freedom.

> After 1945 I worked at coming to terms
> with (in the sense of the German
> Auseinandersetzen) my two masters,
> Marcel and Husserl, all the while
> orienting myself within the rich philo-
> sophical constellation of post-war
> France marked by existentialism and
> marxism, before the surge of the
> Nietzschean and psychoanalytic tide
> (6).

It was, indeed, a very rich time in post-war
France. There was the opportunity to build everything
anew. Political liberation had come. The task remained to extend that freedom into all aspects of life.
There were reunions with family and friends, the seemingly infinite possibilities of building a new France
and a new Europe. Existentialism and marxism came into
the marketplace. With existentialism, persons could
seek freedom here and now. They could take responsibility for their lives. With marxism, they had the
tools for a critical analysis of the social, political,
and economic structures which might bring about a more
just and egalitarian society. As there were many forms
of existentialism, so there were many forms of marxism,
and the lines between forms were frequently blurred.
In addition, names and labels were inadequate. Nevertheless, some patterns emerge; some names stand out.

Sartre and Merleau-Ponty

Two philosophers who stand out especially in post
World War II France are Sartre and Merleau-Ponty.
Sartre became the center of a flow of thought emphasiz-
ing freedom, nothingness, the absurd, and at the same

time, political equality, especially as it was being
sought by French communists.

Merleau-Ponty was emphasizing perception as a key
to understanding,

> developing [his thought] somewhere
> between concrete ontology and phenomen-
> ology, that is, in a region where I
> wanted to situate myself and to pro-
> ceed. Most of all, [Merleau-Ponty's]
> The Phenomenology of Perception was for
> me the model of the phenomenological
> work whose conception and method I was
> hoping to extend in the field of The
> Voluntary and the Involuntary (6-7).

Heidegger

We cannot leave this section without some mention
of Heidegger, who was a student of Husserl and who
became one of the seminal philosophers of the twentieth
century. Although there are many similarities between
the ways Heidegger and Ricoeur have investigated the
human questions, there are more differences. Ricoeur
had studied Heidegger's works in Germany, and had recognized the radical character of his thought. Nevertheless:

> My respect for Heidegger, although it
> has never ceased to grow to this very
> day, has always been marked by certain
> ever increasing reservations. So,
> while the careful and frequent reread-
> ing of Sein und Zeit has always filled
> me with great admiration, I have
> remained hostile to the critique of
> humanism, in particular in the Letter
> on Humanism (7).

Ricoeur has also been critical of Heidegger's
"contributing to the collapse of the questions of the
subject." Although this collapse is probably the opposite of Heidegger's intention, it has, ironically,
"played into the hands of the new scientism represented
by structuralism" (7). This scientism is the absolutizing of that which is perceived or evidenced, without
the acknowledgement of the subjective character of all
knowledge. In this way, "science" becomes "truth."

So we may think of the period from 1936 through
1949 as a period of initial exploration for Ricoeur
which was within the parameters of an

> existential phenomenology, although at
> the time I did not dare call it pheno-
> menology for I did not wish to cover my
> own attempt with the authority of
> Husserl, whom I was translating into
> French. It was phenomenology, however,
> in the sense that it tried to extract
> from lived experience the essential
> meanings and structures of purpose,
> project, motive, wanting, trying, and
> so on (PPR, 87).

Ricoeur was asking the human questions, analyzing,
reflecting, writing. He published two books, one co-
authored with Mikel Dufrenne: Karl Jaspers; the other
written alone: Gabriel Marcel et Karl Jaspers, sub-
titled Philosophy of Mystery and Philosophy of Paradox,
the first phrase referring to Marcel, the second to
Jaspers. Before 1950, he had published more than
twenty articles on philosophic, political, and Christian topics, and had begun major translations into
French of Husserl's writings.

At the same time, he taught for three years at
Collège Cevenol, a Quaker affiliated college in the
mountains of eastern France, where he recovered his
health which had been ravaged by the war, and where he
reflected on and was active in building relationships
again between French and German persons. Among the
dominant topics were the problems of violence and
reconciliation, topics which recur in his writings
especially during the 1950's.

Through the sponsorship of the French National
Center of Scientific Research and of UNESCO, Ricoeur
became involved in many projects pertaining to French
philosophy, including the project of translating
Husserl's works into French. This involvement continues and has produced a number of important studies,
for example, Main Trends in Philosophy.

The human questions do not have a privileged time
and place. They can emerge in university study, in the
relationships involved in raising a family, in the
interactions of friendship, in facing our own falli-
bilities, in the struggles related to war, violence and
peace, alienation and reconciliation, death and life.

They may be articulated in a poem, a conversation, a
symphony, or a philosophic essay. Their place may be a
teacher's home on Friday evenings, the small room of a
prison camp, the college classroom, or a ski slope.
They are the questions in which we are all involved as
we work for meaning, joy, and love.

We have seen some of the ways in which Ricoeur
explored the human questions during this first period
centering in an existential phenomenology. The foundations had been laid. The time was ripe for expanding
the horizon. This expanding would center around the
beginning of the project of a Philosophy of the Will.

CHAPTER THREE

The Life Project: A Philosophy of the Will Begins

"The good that I will to do, I don't do. But the
evil I don't will to do I do" (Romans 7.19). In this
sentence, Paul captures the experience we feel as human
beings, of being pulled in different directions. He
describes the split we feel within ourselves when, with
one part of us, we are drawn to one action while another part of us is pulled in another direction. Shall
I choose this course or that? buy a car or save my
money? develop a friendship with this person? break off
this relationship? Such is the dualism we feel within
ourselves, a dualism which is universal to the human
condition.

THE VOLUNTARY AND THE INVOLUNTARY

The tension is an ancient problem. Aristotle
defined it in words which have become classic in philosophy and which have through the centuries been part
of our common language. The voluntary somehow describes that which we choose to do, or the power of
making such choice. The involuntary is that which we
do not confirm with our free choice, or that power over
which we do not seem to have control.

> Since that which is done under
> compulsion or by reason of ignorance is
> involuntary, the voluntary would seem
> to be that of which the moving princi-
> ple is in the agent himself, he being
> aware of the particular circumstances
> of the action (McKeon, ed., Introduc-
> tion to Aristotle, 351).[1]

The terms have been taken up in a variety of
contexts and fields. Physiology uses them to describe

two different kinds of muscles in the body, those which
we voluntarily or consciously move, and those which
move involuntarily or in ways not subject to our conscious control.

Many insights of this century have blurred the
lines between the two concepts. Freud's researches
into the unconscious raised serious questions through
experiential data about the characteristics of each
idea and their interrelationships. Freud was supplying
new insights to an ancient debate: that of free will
versus determinism. Most serious thinkers have dealt
with the problem: Do I have control over my actions?
Or are there forces beyond my control which determine
what I do?

The question is also key in religious traditions.
Job raised it in the context of his life. Augustine,
Aquinas, and Luther offered differing solutions. In a
religious world view, the problem is entangled with the
problems of gift or grace. "How much is God involved
in what I do? In what way are my actions from his
power or from mine?"

Those scientists who see themselves as a-religious
and sometimes as anti-religious take different positions depending on the traditions out of which they are
working. One of the better known positions in America
is that of B. F. Skinner who denies the possibility of
the voluntary.[2] On the contrary, he says, we are conditioned to the actions we perform much as Pavlov's
dogs were conditioned to salivate, or as Skinner's
pigeons were conditioned to turn full circle in order
to obtain food.

The problem has been a classic one in philosophy
for twenty-five hundred years. In his study of
Husserl's Ideas I Ricoeur had noticed that at several
points, Husserl had suggested that the problems of the
will should be reexamined using a method of intentional
analysis such as he had used to examine perceptual
consciousness (Husserl, 213).

Moreover, Ricoeur's study of Jaspers had made him
aware of the paradox involved in willing: at the very
moment that I choose limited ends or goals, I realize
that these goals are relative. I am never satisfied.
Somehow, within the finite or the limited, the infinite
or the unlimited is present (Karl Jaspers, 146). Already in Gabriel Marcel et Karl Jaspers, Ricoeur was
looking for the elements of a phenomenology or a

description of willing (207), although he was aware of
the limits of such a phenomenology.

The Background of the Study

It is interesting to sketch the background against
which these studies were taking place. The studies had
begun in the Parisian situation of the 1930's described
above, including the Friday evening exchanges in
Marcel's home. But the Husserl commentaries were
chiefly accomplished in the small room Ricoeur shared
as prisoner-of-war for five years with Mikel Dufrenne.
The notes were written in the margins of the book. The
study Karl Jaspers was written with Ricoeur and
Dufrenne sharing one book and exchanging "sides" as
described above. The questions about freedom were
meditated on in the context of being a prisoner in the
no-man's land between Germany and Poland, where
Dufrenne, the "eternal optimist," expected liberation
to take place each new week that rolled by. The questions about will were raised in a situation dominated
by the involuntary tasks of prison life, brought about
paradoxically by the "Will to Power," and the
Nietzschean Superman context out of which Hitler's rise
to power came. These are the same questions of freedom
and will which were raised again for the persons involved in the Algerian War and in the wars of southeast
Asia.

As indicated earlier, Ricoeur felt closer to
Merleau-Ponty than to Sartre. Merleau-Ponty's work was
in an area where Ricoeur wanted to place himself and
proceed, "somewhere between concrete ontology and phenomenology." Concrete ontology is the thrust Ricoeur
had adopted from Marcel, of trying to place being in a
concrete, "incarnational" situation, rather than in the
abstract, idealistic framework characteristic of many
philosophies. He wanted to describe the phenomena
carefully and objectively; that is, he wanted to use
the phenomenological method he had learned from Husserl.

Merleau-Ponty's masterpiece The Phenomenology of
Perception became a model for Ricoeur. He wanted to
extend that conception and method into the field of
The Voluntary and the Involuntary (MRHP, 7). In 1950
Ricoeur published a book with that phrase as title.
The English translation highlights the modern existen-
tial thrust with the title Freedom and Nature: The
Voluntary and the Involuntary. In his Introduction,
Ricoeur places this study of the relations between the

Voluntary and the Involuntary as the "first part of a
more extensive whole" with the "general title Philosophy of the Will."[3] This is the life enterprise in
which Ricoeur is still engaged.

Threefold Task of a Phenomenology of the Will

        In the next year after this major publication,
Ricoeur read a paper at the International Colloquium on
Phenomenology in Brussels (referred to in The Voluntary
and the Involuntary, xi), in which he outlined the
"Methods and Tasks of a Phenomenology of the Will." It
would include three parts: 1) an eidetics, or "pure
description," 2) an empirics (the empirical, the daily
and universal experience), including the problem of the
fault, the limitations of freedom, and 3) a poetics.

        Like the terms voluntary and involuntary, the
poetics has its roots in Aristotle. In the Greek,
poetics refers to creativity, the concept of making
new, of bringing forth to being.

        The poet's function is to describe, not
        the thing that has happened, but a kind
        of thing that might happen . . . a kind
        of thing that might be . . . . (Under-
        lining mine. McKeon, ed. Introduction
        to Aristotle, 635-636).

        For Aristotle, as well as for Ricoeur, "what
convinces is the possible." For Ricoeur, poetics is
related to "Transcendence, which hides within it the
ultimate origin" of the subject, of consciousness, of
the person creating (The Voluntary and the Involuntary,
3). The poet, the maker, has a much larger function
than that in ordinary usage today. The poet creates
the new, even a new world view. Ricoeur sees a poetics
of the will as a second Copernican revolution with the
possibility of rediscovering the desire for God.

        Life for us has a double meaning. We recognize
its limitations, but at the same time we recognize its
apparently limitless possibilities. We can envision
Viktor Frankl released from the concentration camp,
with all his family destroyed, yet walking down a coun-
try road, and falling on his knees to acknowledge with
gratitude the presence of life (Man's Search for Meaning).[4]

Free and Unfree: The Voluntary and the Involuntary

In The Voluntary and the Involuntary, Ricoeur
explores the basic questions: What is freedom? How
can we describe it? What are our problems of method in
description? What is our relationship with our bodies,
our motives, our actions?

The list of authors cited at the end of The
Voluntary and the Involuntary reveals the background
against which Ricoeur is writing. Of the more than one
hundred names in the list, most are philosophers, such
as Kant, Heidegger, Husserl, Marcel, Sartre, and
Merleau-Ponty. But a second group includes pioneers in
the study of psychology: Kurt Lewin, Koehler, and
other representatives of the early gestalt psychology
schools, as well as early American psychologists, such
as William James, Thorndike and Tolman, in addition to
Freud and others associated with psychoanalysis. A
third group are poets or poetic writers, including
Rilke, Valéry, Saint-Exupéry, and Camus.

The Voluntary and the Involuntary was published in
the series Philosophy of the Spirit, which includes
works by Marcel, Nedoncelle, Master Eckhart, Martin
Buber, Hegel, and Kierkegaard. This is a collection
and background foreign to much of contemporary American
psychology and philosophy, but one that continues to
have a strong impact on American theology, on humanistic philosophy, on counseling psychology, and on those
humanities which have kept contact with the European
community sometimes referred to as the Third Force.

What Method Shall I Use?

For phenomenologists and for any others who strive
to be scientific and to maintain scholarly standards,
the problem of method is important. What method shall
I use to seek knowledge, to strive for truth? Three
methods which are dominant in the contemporary American
academic world are: 1) scientific method which grows
out of and continues to be related to the natural
sciences; 2) pragmatic method which uses whatever
methods are "practical" and bring results; and 3) the
intuitional-artistic method which emphasizes "hunches"
and the process of discovery. What methods do we use
in our daily life as we strive to understand ourselves
and other human beings? That depends on our personalities and on what methods we may have consciously or
unconsciously learned as part of our education.

Through long meditation on Husserl, Ricoeur had
chosen the phenomenological method as his own. He
devotes the first chapter of his Philosophy of the Will
to the question of method of study. He is seeking two
things: to describe and to understand (The Voluntary
and the Involuntary, 3). He would like to make this
description and this understanding as pure as possible,
much as a natural scientist strives to work with pure
materials so as to eliminate extraneous variables. In
order to achieve such "cleanness" of approach, Ricoeur
sets aside or brackets for the present two extremely
important factors in the process of willing.

The Problem of the Fault

The first of these is the problem of the fault,
the internal weakness or fragility in human being which
is not logical, which constantly eludes our control,
and which is a continuing essential factor, not only in
the stories of individuals, but also in the stories of
societies, and, in fact, in universal history. This
problem of the fault will be the subject of Ricoeur's
second volume in his Philosophy of the Will, which he
will entitle Finitude and Culpability.

The Mystery of the Transcendent

The second factor which Ricoeur will set aside or
bracket until a later study is the problem of Transcendence (VI, 3). The word transcendent, whether capitalized or not, is subject to many definitions. It
suggests literally a "stepping across" or a "climbing
over." In the Kantian tradition, to think or to understand is to leap over the mere experience; so to transcend belongs to persons as rational beings by reason
of their ability to think.

On the other hand, for Kant, the ultimately real
world is for human beings unknowable: the Transcendent
which is beyond human being. Husserl, Marcel, and
Jaspers provide their own reflections on these concepts: 1) the transcendental as absolutely irreducible; 2) authentic transcendence as a going beyond the
objective; 3) the transcendent as in "free existence
and the figure (symbol) of the hidden divinity"
(Gabriel Marcel et Karl Jaspers, 64); or the transcendent in fidelity, hope, and love.

The transcendental as absolutely irreducible. In
other words, there is within human experience that

which doesn't reduce to words, to simple description,
or to simple analysis.

Authentic transcendence as a going beyond the
objective. The dominant scientific world view of our
societies, as well as of our education, usually encour-
ages us to be objective. Somehow, this is equated with
a greater approximation to truth. Ordinarily, of
course, this is good procedure. But to stop at the
objective is paradoxically often to miss the truth. An
objective description of the birth of a baby may well be
a distortion of the truth.

On the other hand, the scientific is essential in
our world. It serves as the diagnostic, which is extremely important. But the diagnostic cannot be an
end. A doctor should not diagnose simply for the sake
of diagnosis, but rather for the sake of healing. So,
too, we should not analyze human life or biblical studies or the universe only for the sake of an analysis
removed from the human. I have to participate actively
in my life as mystery. While aiming for objectivity, I
have to move from objectivity to existence. I have to
move from life as problem to life as mystery. If I
confine myself only to conceptual thought, I confine
myself to a loss of being. With Ricoeur, we want to
understand the mystery as a reconciliation and a restoration of our consciousness, our body, and our world.
Then an understanding of the voluntary and the involuntary will restore meaning, will restore life.

The transcendent as "free existence and the figure
(symbol) of the hidden divinity." In the tradition
from which Ricoeur comes, the Transcendent is associated with the questions of the Totally Other. At the
minimum, the term names the mystery which many persons
experience at the birth of a baby or on looking into
the apparent infinity of the universe, the known unknown. Since this is a realm beyond the provable, it
calls for the risk of belief or unbelief. Jaspers
chose the latter, Marcel opted for the former, and
Ricoeur opts, too, for the wager of belief. But such
belief is in terms of figure, symbol, configuration,
the patterning which human beings give to their experience.

The transcendent in fidelity, hope, and love.
These are words which Marcel brought to the existential
world and which in some areas became popular through
books such as his Creative Fidelity.[5] For Ricoeur,
too, these are aspects of human experience which defy

adequate logical description. They name leaps out of
our ordinary experience, leaps which we experience as
gift rather than as something attained or achieved.

But it is especially from Jaspers that Ricoeur
derived the linking of symbol and Transcendence. The
world is the symbol of Transcendence, of the Totally
Other. "To transcend is to lose the world as empiric
reality in order to reaffirm it as absolute object of
thought" (Karl Jaspers, 245). To transcend is to read
the figures, the symbols. "A true Transcendence is
. . . a presence which inaugurates a true revolution in
the theory of subjectivity; it introduces there a radically new dimension, the poetic dimension (Philosophie
de la volonté, Tome 1: Le volontaire et l'involontaire, 456, translation mine).

In many ways, Ricoeur's chapter on method in
Freedom and Nature: The Voluntary and the Involuntary
is a meditation on what it means to be a human being.
Ricoeur is continually in the process of developing a
philosophical anthropology, a long, many-faceted essay
on the perennial question: What is human being? Here
we will follow a few of his suggestions for meditation
by choosing some key concepts for elaboration.

What is the relationship of the voluntary and the
involuntary? Ricoeur recognizes that in psychological
studies, even when the terms voluntary and involuntary
are described, they are usually kept separate. Often
the involuntary systems are studied first, and the
voluntary are added afterwards. Ricoeur wants to make
clear a foundational principle: even though we distinguish two systems of the voluntary and the involuntary
for purposes of analysis, the separation suggests a
false dualism. The energies of the two systems are
reciprocal, that is, they mutually influence and interact with each other. But the will is pivotal: any
emotions or needs have human meaning only in relationship to the willed affirmation.

Ricoeur goes so far as to say that the involuntary
has no meaning of its own.

> Far from the voluntary being derivable
> from the involuntary, it is, on the
> contrary, the understanding of the
> voluntary which comes first in human
> being. I understand myself in the
> first place as one who says, "I will."
> . . . The will is the one which brings

order to the many of the involuntary
(Freedom and Nature: The Voluntary and
the Involuntary, 5).

At first sight, this seems a contradiction of what
we have learned from Freud and from social scientists
about influence outside our apparent autonomy. But
Ricoeur is countering the "I am not responsible" syn-
drome that has characterized much of twentieth century
society. He is calling, precisely, for responsibility
as a way toward freedom. Too often we are made to
believe that we have no power over our lives, that we
are ineffective reflections of involuntary energies.
Ricoeur is saying that, whatever the tensions and dual-
isms within the will, we cannot pretend the will is not
acting.

THREE MOMENTS IN THE ACT OF WILLING

As he analyzes the meaning of "I will," Ricoeur
finds three moments integral to the process. "To say
'I will' means first 'I decide,' secondly 'I move my
body,' thirdly 'I consent.'"

What does it mean to say, "I decide"?

> The willed is first of all that on
> which I decide, the project I form: it
> contains the direction of action to be
> done by me in accord with my abilities
> (7).

The roots of the words decide and project are of
interest here. To decide is literally to cut downward
or to cut off alternatives. To project is to throw
forward. So, like a fisherman throwing out a line, I
cut off alternative possibilities, at least for the
present, and throw my attention and energy in a certain
direction. The decision itself creates a particular
direction, generates action, and has an integral relationship with me and my abilities.

In order to describe what it means to decide,
Ricoeur looks first at those actions which are usually
called involuntary, but which are elusive even when
recognized. This is the impulsive thrust, which we
often feel is out of control. Yet here is precisely
the paradox. Either we resist the impulse, or we go
with it. In either case, we are willing in relation to
the involuntary. Though less under our conscious

control, nevertheless by default or by affirmation we
are deciding in a certain direction. "I am not the
kind of person who does that. But I did that. Therefore, I must be the kind of person who does that!"

Forces Which Affect Our Deciding

Most disciplines in the twentieth century
including biology, sociology, and psychoanalysis, have
shown us so many other forces affecting our decisions
that we have often eliminated from our considerations
the power of decision altogether. While there is no
question that we have discovered amazingly powerful
extraneous forces which affect us, and which it would
be an error to neglect, nevertheless it is also an
error to ignore the deciding which is integral.

Another view of the phenomenon of deciding may be
approached through looking at those moments of deciding
which are separable from their being carried out. In
other words, even though I may not be able to put a
decision into action, the decision is nevertheless
there. Ricoeur compares this to a charge in a battery.

> When I have decided to carry out a
> delicate proceeding I feel in a sense
> charged with it, in the way a battery
> is charged--the act is within my power,
> I am capable of it (39).

Action as the Test of the Decision

Whether the action was only daydreamed or actually
willed becomes clear as the intention is put to the
test. In other words, the proof of the decision is in
the action. In fact, we often only find out what we
have decided when we see the actions we have carried
out.

> There are even cases in which I remain
> uncertain of my own decisions until I
> have seen the action in practice, as
> the combat soldier who does not know of
> what he is capable . . . until he has
> received a baptism of fire (39-40).

We can better understand decision if we contrast it
with related phenomenon: the wish and the command.

> In both cases I can have a precise and
> even eager idea of what needs to be
> done, but the execution is not in my
> power, either because it depends
> strictly on events, as when I wish for
> the end of the war, or because it de-
> pends strictly on the will of someone
> else, as when I give instructions to
> subordinates (40).

The decision is somehow the intention, whether realized
or not.

We can learn much about deciding through looking
at our language. Most languages include an active
emphasis in the verbs and related structures which
communicate decision. Typical structures include:

> Subject -- Active Verb   -- Object
> I   -- decide to buy -- a car.

Some languages also include a reflective element: the
French "je me decide"--"I decide myself," as well as
the English "I make up my mind."

To Will Is to Think

Willing is not a separate power from thinking, as
some older philosophies or psychologies claimed. On
the contrary, "to will is to think" (41). My thoughts
turn toward a certain object. In some sense I become
what I see, what I imagine, desire, or will. When I
decide, somehow I turn myself toward a project.

An analysis of the word project is helpful here.
Ject is the root for throw, pro is forward. So to
project is to throw forward. A project is that which
we "throw forward." We can picture a mountain climber
who scans the rocks ahead, decides on a particular
direction, and throws his rope and hook in that direction. "A decision signifies, that is, designates in
general, a future action which depends on me and which
is within my power" (43).

The implications of such a simple description are
radical. At one blow I have eliminated the debilitat-
ing attitude of blaming others for my actions. I cannot blame my parents, my husband, or my wife. At the
same time, they cannot push responsibility for their
actions on to me or on to anyone other than themselves.

This is not to ignore or underestimate the power of
genetic, environmental, or political factors, of
course, but only to call back into play the power of
deciding.

Decision: Oriented toward the Future and the Possible

Because it is thrust toward a project, a decision
is oriented by necessity toward the future, toward the
possible, toward the power of creation. In a decision,
the present is linked with the future. At the same
time a metaphysical relationship between the present
and the future is put into operation. Finally, there
is opened up the power of creation.

The mountain climber again provides helpful
visualization. Though he stand at a particular place,
the mountain climber is perceiving and imaging possible
points for the next position, and that in relationship
to future positions. Some positions are impossible,
although that may not be clear until he has tried them.
Others the climber judges possible on the basis of
previous experience or other criteria. Like the swing-
ing and throwing of the rope and hook, the imagination
provides material out of which he makes a decision
which creates the power of a new position, first in
imagination, then in actuality. The power of the new
creation is actualized in the smaller triumphs of each
new position but symbolized dramatically in the con-
quest of standing at the top of Mt. Everest.

A Road Toward Freedom

When I decide, I start a way for being who I am,
what I am, and what I will become (63). My future, my
possibility, is rooted in my decision.

> Each decision I make uncovers a
> possible future, opens up some ways,
> closes others, and determines the out-
> lines of new areas . . . as a possible
> course for subsequent decision . . . .
> What I shall be is not already given
> but depends on what I shall do. My
> possible being depends on my possible
> doing . . . . The more I commit myself
> and the more I am able to do, the more
> I am possible (64).

Such direction is a road toward freedom.

CHAPTER FOUR

Our Motives and the Problem of Consent

Making a decision, of course, is related to motives. Why do I decide to do this rather than that? Motive is that which moves me. But the simplicity of the definition is deceptive. A motive is not a thing. It is not something. I cannot separate my motive from my decision, anymore than one can separate an incline from gravitational pull except for purposes of analysis. Motive is that which moves me, that which is integrally tied up with my deciding. Motive and deciding are moments in a process. Motive is related to decision only insofar as the deciding accepts the motive, wills it, makes it its own.

Much of our language and much of our psychology provide models which are often too neat in this regard: They suggest that the motive comes first, then the decision. One-two. Cause-effect. The simplicity is misleading. We require a different model, one that is more integral. Perhaps the relationship of inertia or the thrust of movement and the object in movement may be helpful. A ball hurtling through the air cannot be separated from the thrust which is keeping it in motion.

My Movements Reflect My Values

Just as deciding is related to motive, so motive is related to value. Our values take on flesh in our motives. Values enter into our stories through our motives which become concrete in our decisions. Our motives and values build first through the process of receiving praise or blame, satisfaction or dissatisfaction.

Such values are, of course, internalized, yet at
the same time they are identified with the project.
The project symbolically becomes the value. Our identity becomes linked with the project, so that a threat
to the project is a threat to our identity. On the
other hand, if we step back to evaluate the project,
that too is a risk because it calls not only the project, but also the value, into question.

Values and Ethics

What is the relationship of this valuing with
ethics? We may think of ethics as reflective or non-
reflective, that is, reflective as stepping back from
valued projects or actions in an attempt to evaluate
them, or non-reflective as not stepping back but identified with the project or action. Moral consciousness
is associated with the first kind, the reflective attempt to step back and evaluate the project (73). Such
moral consciousness makes a judgement through comparison. This is better than that. This is the best.
This is good. Just as in motives and valuation, in
ethics we try to give reasons. "I want to." "I like
this best." "I couldn't do that." "This is right."
"God says to do this." "Society says to do this or go
to prison."

We may think of groups or nations as networks of
such moral judgements which implicitly or explicitly
evaluate decisions, projects, and actions, and thereby
constitute the ethos of the group or nation. In his
description of a civil religion, Robert Bellah has
identified such an ethos for the American people.
Whether or not his analysis is correct, it seems clear
that there is a relationship between the ethos of a
group and its founding event.

The Power of a Founding Event

A founding event, such as the American Revolution,
calls into question previous value systems, previous
projects and sets of actions, and calls for a conversion or change to a new set of values and actions. If
successful, this constitutes a new orientation of the
ethos or ethics.

> [These] form, for a given consciousness
> at a given time of its development, a
> concrete, more or less ordained table,

> or better, a configuration or a
> constellation of fixed stars. These
> non-revaluated values form, so to
> speak, its ethical firmament, its . . .
> "horizon of value" (73).

The paradox of value is that it is related to my
story, my history. That is why we should not be surprised when a radical change in our own story brings
about a radical change in subordinate values, and even
in ones we thought primary. For example, as persons
grow older, they are surprised and sometimes shocked to
realize that their values have changed.

On the other hand, insofar as the good with which
we identify is a universal human good, the more universal will be our valuing and, therefore, perhaps, the
more lasting. The great religious leaders often discovered this in the process of their finding wisdom.
More often than not, they came to a simplicity of
values centering in love, justice, and the sacredness
of human life. Often in our lifetimes we come to know
individuals who have come to the same insights and who
live accordingly. We recognize them as good people who
have found a certain integrity within themselves, and
who are able to help others in their process toward
universal human values. Typically, it is not in their
articulation of such values, but in the way they live
their lives, in the motives, decisions, and actions of
their lives that we see what a human life can be.

Insight

The word insight points to another paradox
associated with our valuing. We are blind to a value
until we identify with it, at least vicariously. Insofar as we move from one value to another, we are shift-
ing our identity. It is a process filled with tension,
redescription, and new identities.

Conversely, when we have moved away from a
particular valuing, we can no longer "see" the one we
had previously championed, except by a conscious suspension of our present value and by a pseudo-adoption
of the previous value. We say about an action inconsistent with our current valuing, "I can't see that. I
used to, but I can't see it now." Since we do not
stand there, we are blind to its value. On the other
hand, when we are in conversation with someone advocating a value system different from our own, in our

tolerance we may often say, "I see." But even as we
say it, we are aware of the tension within us. If we
use the eyes of the other person, we see. But we do
not truly see with our own valuing eyes, because that
calls for at least a temporary overthrow of our own
valuing.

The Distance of Evaluation

The distance required for evaluation cuts out from
under us the foundation of our loyalties. It puts the
valuing with which we could or did identify outside our
present sphere of identity. Questioning can become the
primary value, but insofar as it does, it can militate
against a basic identity. Given that there aren't any
final answers in our finite situation, nevertheless,
there are patterns of meaning which can give configuration to our existence. Such configuration, while it
should be open to further development and further insight, is necessary for purposeful human living.

Ricoeur constantly calls us to a "recovery of
meaning," to a use of critical reflection and questioning without falling into the trap of making that the
end of our existence. We need to move through such
reflection and questioning to a post-critical "second
naiveté."

The Tension of Authority and Responsibility

Valuing has a tension-filled relationship with
authority on the one hand and with responsibility on
the other. This is a tension often first experienced
in relationship with parents. Inasmuch as I adopt
values different from those of my parents, I subvert
their authority and I am apparently lacking in responsibility to them. On the other hand, if I am to become
an adult, if I am to become an autonomous human being,
I have to see my own values, even if they differ from
those of my parents. There is then set up a conflict
of values as well as the correlated conflict of authority, responsibility, and identity. If I subordinate
mine to theirs, I never grow up. If I choose my own, I
create a new horizon, and, to some degree at least, a
new ethics. In such a situation, a parent often sees
the child as irresponsible. The correct adjective,
however, is often, not irresponsible, but responsible
to a different authority, a different set of values.

Our values, of course, are never entirely separate
from the group or groups with which we interact. New
value choices call for new community relations, and
reciprocally, new community loyalties call for new
values. A person entering military service opts for a
new value system, a new community, and a new authority.
A conscientious objector rejects those same premises,
and by his actions calls them into question.

In time of war, survival calls for the absolutizing of the group or national value. We can thereby
identify "we" and "they" in terms of "good" and "evil."
Our authority is the authority of the "good," of the
community with which we identify, and indeed, of our
own internalized identity. But the experiences in war
are not usually so neat. When the "killing of the
enemy" is perceived as the "killing of another human
being," the cluster of values is severely called into
question: the value of the authority--whether that of
the army, the nation, or the cause; the value of the
community supporting such an authority, and the value
of the individual who finds himself in a critical
situation where there is no one else who can answer for
him. The fragmented personalities which are part of
the fall-out of any war testify to the difficulty of
resolving this dilemma.

Responsibility and Mission

I can be not only responsible for . . .
but also responsible to . . . ; I am
responsible to those who in some sense
send me on a mission (82).

Responsibility and mission in their larger context
are terms relatively foreign to our present culture.
It seems reasonable to suppose a relationship between
their lack and some characteristics of the malaise of
our society. In our society there are many stimuli to
which we respond. But respond-ability to a stimulus is
not the same as responsibility for the self in relationship to society.

We respond to the stimuli provided by our
families, friends, newspaper headlines, economic rever-
sals, job opportunities. A certain assimilation or
avoidance takes place, but this is often along the
lines of the pseudo-scientific, subject-less, or behav-
iorist model, rather than in the full responsibility of
human action. It is little wonder that the opposite

pattern also emerges--persons who respond to nothing
but their own narcissistic thrusts. Self-satisfaction
and power override all other considerations. The lives
of many, of course, are alternatives of these patterns
or complex mixtures of the two.

But responsibility of the person within society
calls for a different model. Whereas the subject-less
model may be thought of as atomistic, fragmented, or
random, and the self-serving model may be thought of as
cancerous or destructive of the whole, the model of
responsibility of the person within society is one of a
complex tension between the one and the many. It is a
community model reflecting the community of the one and
the many, a community model reflecting the community of
human beings living in relationship with an earth and a
universe. No woman, man, child, animal, or tree, is an
island. To our regret, we have learned in this generation that polluting the air affects the breathing of us
all, that the destruction of the forests of the Amazon
will change the temperature as well as the air quality
of other parts of the world.

The Interdependence of All Things

The model of responsibility being called for is
one which recognizes the interdependence of all things,
and the responsibility of each individual within the
system of the universe as we know it. Concomitantly,
it is a false model to project ourselves as independent
of the universe, no matter how alienated our experiences may be. Responsibility and its correlative
freedom are possible only in the matrix of the total
universe.

Authority and Mission

Responsibility raises the question of authority
and mission. The word authority shares the same root
as the word author. We think of an author as someone
who writes. In a broader sense, an author is one who
initiates the new. As the initiator, the creator, the
author is responsible for that which she initiates. At
the same time, the initiating creates a mission and a
goal, as well as a relationship with those to whom the
authoring is directed.

As authors who initiate the new life of their
child, parents are responsible for what they have

begun.   They have the mission or goal of raising the
child.   In turn the child is called forth and yet,
simultaneously, the child calls the parents forth.   The
child's authoring, mission, and responsibility become
intertwined with that of the parents.   The initiating,
missioning, and responsibility intrinsically call forth
the same qualities in the child who, in turn, initiates, missions, and assumes responsibility.

The model may then be applied to those groups of
which we are members.

Group or   Initiating   Individual
Community   <——————————————>
                mission
                responsibility

Our social or religious group or community, our
culture, or our nation, precedes us.   Our birth is a
given.   It is a mystery that this is one topic on which
we could not have been consulted.   We are born as
American, Vietnamese, or African, with a particular
genetic, ethnic, economic, and cultural heritage.   But
we also choose groups which seem to call us forth to
the realization of our possibilities.   These groups are
responsible for us and to us.   In turn, we are responsible for and to the group, and that in a most radical
sense.

As we discover our abilities, our longings, our
needs, we reach out, looking for a possible goal, a new
frontier, a challenge worthy of our powers to initiate
and to respond.   Just as our heritage or our community
has sent us forth, has missioned us, has called us to
respond, so we discover a power in that mission that we
perhaps had not realized was there.   Classic examples
of such calling forth are religious vocations or the
vocations which respond to the needs of peace-making,
of politics, of war, of crises of all kinds.   The group
or the events call us forth and a new pattern of initiating, missioning, and responsibility is set up.

Authoring and Authority

It was Heidegger, among others, who called us
forth in this century to claim responsibility for our
own lives, to become authentic human beings, human
beings who author, who authenticate our own lives.
Jesus and other great religious leaders also call for
authentic responsibility.   Take hold of your life.
Become one who initiates.   Assume responsibility for

being sent forth and for sending forth. Recognize the
given of the universe, the given of the human condition
as authoring our existence. Know that we both call
forth and are called forth in responsibility to all
other beings in the universe, although, obviously,
there are degrees of responsibility.

It is valuing-willing which gives unity to this
process. My valuing becomes identified with the valuing of another or of others. For example, I fall in
love, or I join a religious group or a political party.
Values, at least for the present, are presumed as similar. My will then appears as one with that of the
other or of the community. Lovers perceive themselves
as one. The shared values effect similar willing. And
the increased power is immediately perceived. A new
strength is experienced, the strength of the other or
of the group. Lovers are often amazed to find in themselves new abilities. Those responding to a new political leader or to a religious group become new persons
to those who know them. New abilities are unleashed.
A liberation is evident. A new person is born.

When such a calling forth breaks through into a
relationship with the universe, with all human beings,
and with universal human values, we recognize a break-
through into wisdom, into love, that is at the same
time perceived as both universalized and particularized
to a marvelous degree. The one and the many are set
spinning in the dynamics of a centrifugal, centripetal
relationship, always in tension, but in the tension of
a spiral which is fundament and symbol of life.

Motives and the Body

My body is the most basic source of
motives . . . it is the initial exis-
tent, underivable, underivable, <u>involuntary</u> . . . .
My hunger, my thirst, my fear of pain,
my desire for music, or my sympathy all
refer to my willing in the form of
motives (85).

There is a circular relationship of my motives to
my projects which will satisfy or fulfill those motives. When I say, "I am hungry. I am going to have
something to eat," I am reflecting in discourse the
integral relationship of the involuntary and the voluntary. My body and my consciousness are not separable.

They move together in the process of my willing, of my deciding to have something to eat.

It follows that a simplistic stimulus-response model is inadequate. Our needs are more than sensations or reflexes. They are forces which can become motives. As such, they incline us but do not compel. That is why history as well as our own experience give us examples of persons who choose to "die of hunger rather than betray their friends" (93).

Our needs reveal values which are organic in a physiological as well as in a fully human sense. Pain and pleasure, good and evil, our needs and values, interact in complex ways we never completely sort out. Yet we can find a "crossroads of need and willing in imagination--imagination of the missing thing and of action aimed towards the thing" (95). As need becomes more specific, it involves the imagination, my power to create images. Need gives birth to an image which becomes a motive, and then a decision.

But all of this takes place within my own history, as well as in the history of those groups of which I am a member. My obligation, my attractions, my rejections --in other words, my process of willing is in the context of the histories of human beings. Nor is my process of willing separate from the story of all being. The hamburger which I choose to eat to assuage my hunger is part of the history of animals and grain, of economy and politics, of chemistry and physics. It is possible, in fact, to recognize all those relationships, and to choose to satisfy my hunger, not with a hamburger, but with a vegetarian meal. It is even possible to choose, as Gandhi did (93), not to eat in order to bring about a political change and a greater human good.

My body then is intimately involved with my motives.

> My body is the most basic source of
> motives, revealing a primordial stratum
> of values . . . . When I give preference
> to other values over these--when, as
> Plato puts it, I "exchange" my life for
> justice, for instance--I am no longer
> carrying on any purely academic debate.
> I really stake my existence, sacrifice
> myself. Thus all other values assume a
> serious, dramatic significance through
> a comparison with the values which
> enter history through my body (85).

From Hesitation to Choice

What is the story of a Decision? The movement is
from hesitation through a process of attention to the
choice itself which involves both determination and
indetermination. Strange as it may first seem, it is
in hesitation that we are seeking to make a choice. In
hesitation, we recognize, at least potentially, the
number of choices which are open to us. Hesitation
reflects that recognition and that potential. The fact
that we are hesitating indicates an ability to choose,
and a seeking to choose. At the same time, we know
that to make the choice is to will another step in our
life choices. We are choosing a particular mode of
being.

Hesitation as Chaos

On the other hand, as long as we hesitate we
remain in the chaos of our own powerlessness.

> I experience not my possibility, but my
> im-possibility. "I am not up to it."
> "I am losing my footing." "I am lost,
> swamped"--I feel powerless (138, trans-
> lation modified).

No wonder that indecision often characterizes neurosis
in our times. No wonder that so many people seek cults
in which all the decisions are made for them. Paradoxically, we long to make the decision or have it made
for us, but we hesitate, avoid, procrastinate--partly
because we recognize the power of the choice, partly
because we want to avoid taking responsibility for the
decision. For example, a woman lives in a hopeless
marriage for twenty years, dabbles in possible solutions, but hesitates to take the steps which involve
serious decision. Or a man hates his job for fifteen
years, complains, perhaps becomes an alcoholic, yet
avoids the decision. Part of the success of therapy is
precisely its ability to help people resolve the diffuseness of hesitation into the specificity of decision.

> I hesitate precisely because the world
> is an ironic question: and you, what
> will you do? Each tentative project is
> like a stammering response whose prog-
> ress is delineated by an outline of
> closed and open roads, of obstacles and
> implements, of openings and blank
> walls (139).

The Power of Time

Both hesitation and decision are involved in time.
Time does not stop because I hesitate. On the contrary, time and history go marching by. We are reminded of the maxim: He who hesitates is lost. Yet in
a state of hesitation, ironically we feel at home with
our old selves. There is a false comfortableness, an
inertia which we hesitate to interrupt. If, on the
other hand, we try out the possible roles, the possible
"me's" of the new project which the decision would call
for, we feel alien. We are not yet comfortable with
the new "I" which the decision would create. We would
like to have all options. In Kierkegaard's phrase we
are forced to "either/or." We are like children who do
not wish to let go of any of our toys, so we make impossible attempts to hold on to all of them, and consequently drop most, or else we frantically go from one
to another without enjoying or appreciating any one.

We are pulled in so many different directions.
Our family suggests one course, our profession another.
Culture, art, religion, athletics may all pull us in
different directions. They may "tear us apart so that
a person has to create his own unity, his independence,
his originality, and to dare his own style of life"
(148).

Choice and Attention

What is the relationship of choice and attention?
In a way, when we make a choice, we concentrate our
attention. We have thus far let our attention go from
one thing to another. Choice provides a centering, an
integration. It chooses a controlling symbol that
places other possibilities in relationship. It is
precisely here that the voluntary intersects with the
involuntary. In the diffuseness of the hesitation we
are more passive. We certainly don't feel free. We
feel we are victims of every stimulus or possibility
which comes along. When we start using our will, our
judgement, when we start making choices, then, contrary
to our expectations, we begin to feel free. The person
who decides to choose a new job, the student who chooses
a profession, experiences a surprising liberation,
often noticeable in the movement of body and spirit.
People remark, "You are so free, so happy." Dancing,
singing, and laughter are often some of the bodily
expressions.

Intellectualism or Irrationalism: A False Dilemma

In the context of attention and deliberation,
Ricoeur reminds us of the "false dilemma of intellec-
tualism and irrationalism" (156). Neither an excess of
reasons nor an excess of impulse will make us free.
History or culture tends to emphasize one or the other.
In earlier times of duty and obligation, we were oppressed by an over-rigidified system of reasons for
making decisions: "God says," "Teacher says," "Father
says," "the Bible says," "the Ten Commandments say,"
"the Church says,"--there was little room for spontaneity, insight, and the impulse of life. In many
societies, the pendulum has now swung in the opposite
direction. "Do whatever impulse suggests." "Try this.
Try that." As a result, we sometimes see walking our
streets the middle-aged dilettante whose childishness
is a burden for himself as well as for others. As his
life spins here and there, it seems to have sprung
loose from all mooring, and is therefore battered by
every wind and current which come along.

Choice as Event

Choice is an event. No wonder we often celebrate
it. Choice completes the process of focusing attention. It is "the peak of previous growth" and "the
surge" of newness" (164). It is a graduation, a step
completing what has gone before and inaugurating what
is to come. That is why it involves both determination
and indetermination. Paradoxically, a choice brings
about a particular determination toward a goal or a
project which at the same time frees to the fullness of
freedom involved in the infiniteness of the undeter-
mined. As long as we are hesitating we are in a chaotic indetermination which may be fruitful if it leads
toward decision, but which is paradoxically bounded by
horizons of randomness. Maybe this, maybe that. We
are a boat without a rudder. It is likely we will be
battered about and ultimately wrecked or washed up on
the shore. A free determination, on the other hand,
opens up horizons hitherto not perceived. I can choose
to remain in these waters, or to move into those.
Freedom leads through determination to a fuller indetermination which is heuristic, which opens up infinitely, which has horizons correlative to the horizons
of the universe and beyond.

The experience of freedom is in itself
a transitory experience which must

ceaselessly be recovered by <u>action</u> of
the self on the self (196).

In other words, freedom constantly requires choice.

Voluntary Movement and Human Capability

The Power of Action

Our actions prove or disprove whether our willing
is authentic. In our movement toward focusing our
attention in a particular direction, there is, of
course, the beginning of the action, but as long as the
projected willing is incomplete, it has not been put to
the test. It has not been verified (201). Will which
does not move to action is sterile, caught in the dol-
drums of wishing and dreaming. If we do not truly
carry through into action, we do not really will (201).

How Do I Act?

But how do I act? The organ by which I act is my
body. My body makes the action present. As an organ
it is extremely complex. All the human sciences are
engaged in the process of trying to name, describe, and
understand its complexity. We recognize within ourselves certain reflexes, which dramatically illustrate
the dualism we perceive within ourselves. "The reflex
is in me apart from me" (243). Yet, even in the realm
of controlling reflex action, for example, in using
biofeedback and self-hypnosis to control reflexes associated with blood pressure and digestion, there has
been enormous progress. The East also provides amazing
examples of holy men who have learned to control even
their breathing to a seemingly impossible degree.

Pre-formed Skills

Crucial in our ability to use our body for action
are what Ricoeur calls pre-formed skills, rather than
instincts or other related terms. Pre-formed skills
belong to primitive patterns of behavior of our human
development (232).

The infant knows how to follow an
object by moving his eyes and head.
. . . As soon as the world presents
itself to me, I know how to do something with my body (233).

Studies in linguistics by Chomsky and others suggest
that this is also true of language. Human being comes
with a basic potential for developing language.

Yet it is only gradually that we take possession
of our body, that we learn how to use it in a freeing
interaction of the voluntary and the involuntary. One
of the factors which is integrally involved with the
process is emotion which "appears as the province of
involuntary action," but which is so "interrelated with
habit" that these two can only be understood in terms
of each other (251). What is emotion? It is a movement which is part of the involuntary, but which, at
the same time, supports and accompanies voluntary action, because it precedes and limits the focus of the
action. Ricoeur discusses topics which are related to
emotion: surprise or wonder, joy and sorrow, love and
hate, desire and the key power of the imagination.

Wonder

Following Descartes, Ricoeur tells us that even
more basic than love and hate is the movement of admiration, wonder, or awe (253). This is the movement
called forth by what Rudolf Otto calls the Idea of the
Holy,[1] that which is at the same time both fascinating
and awe-inspiring. It is related to what Lonergan
describes as insight, and it is similar to Maslow's
"peak experience." Wonder is a "shock of knowledge in
a disturbance of the body (254) . . . . Through wonder, thought becomes in a sense physically imposed
. . . willing is surprised, . . . taken unawares" (255).
We know that we are being called or pushed to a new
dimension of being. As the roots of the word surprise
suggest, we are being "seized from below." The surprise may be pleasant or painful, but we know that it
is radical. It strikes at our roots, and we are wob-
bling from the impact. We can pretend it didn't happen
and try to suppress it. Or we can walk through as the
great literary heroes in the journey motif stories have
walked through to new knowledge.

Such insight touches all of our life. "Emotion is
rarely cerebral: it generally affects our body,
social, intellectual, spiritual, and other interests"
(256). The object of the wonder is initially perceived
as good or evil, or at least it is quickly accompanied
by such evaluation. As good, it draws forth love and a
desire for union; as evil it repels and pushes to separation or escape. If we find union with that which we

love, we are caught up in joy. On the contrary, if we
are separated from the good or we find it impossible to
escape the evil, we are overwhelmed by sorrow.

> In joy I am with my good, in sorrow I
> am with the evil: I have become that
> good and that evil. The good or the
> evil have become my mode of being. I
> am sad, I am happy: these expressions
> have an absolute meaning which we do
> not find in expressions like . . . "I
> love," or "I hate" (260).

Imagination and Desire

Imagination and desire play key roles in all these
movements. An image is a form of knowing. In an image
I somehow represent to myself that which is absent. In
a limited way, I make the absent present. But at the
same time, the presence of the image is unsatisfactory.
We want the fullness of presence. Our being becomes
desire. We move toward that which is loved, or that
which is perceived as the good.

> Desire is the body which dares and
> improvises, body brought to action
> pitch . . . . Desire is the initial
> thrust, body and soul, towards the
> object. That is why the full weight of
> ethics bears in the last instance on
> desire and on the means of controlling
> it (266. Translation modified).

Habits as Structures of Movement

When any of these movements has been learned or
acquired in such a way that it is habitual, we speak of
a habit that has been acquired. Through trial and
error, through custom or through discipline, we so
structure our movements that we do not have to think
about them. They move on a level which does not require our conscious thought. We look at the Olympic
skater or the ballet dancer and see movement that has
become habitual, yet which requires constant effort to
maintain. So it is possible to acquire a habit of
wonder and admiration, of love or hate, of joy or sorrow, of certain movements of imagination and desire.

But all description, of course, no matter how
technical or complex, belies the reality we experience.

The movements are multiple, they require effort. They
do not yield easily to an integration. They are multiple moments in willing which are straining for unity,
seeking a presence and a freedom so well symbolized by
the genius of the skater or the dancer.

Consent and Necessity

We decide on a project, we move to bring it about,
and finally we consent. The roots of the word con-sent
mean "to feel with," "to sense, together with." Consent is a problem. Shall we consent to the life we
have been given, to the universe as it is, or shall we
refuse to accept the givens, refuse to accept ourselves
as given, the universe as it is? No society or individual has solved the problem. "That's the way it is,"
we say. "Ce la vie!--That's life." But almost immediately the retort follows, "Yes, but . . . ." We
argue, we weigh. Perhaps, after our arguing, our weigh-
ing, our raging, we come to say, "Let it be.--Fiat."
This is consent.

Trying to be objective makes us dizzy. The
experience of my own personality, my unconscious, and
my biological life "is heavy, fleeting, or even empty"
(348. Translation modified). It is too easy to be
overwhelmed, to succumb to "fear and laziness" (349),
to yield to the temptation of non-being.

> My will is tied to the very general
> fact of growth,
> what I am I have become
> and I have been "a child before
> I became a man."

> Now childhood is the first dawn of
> consciousness;
> I proceed from this childhood.
> Finally all genesis leads back to an
> origin,
> growth to birth,
> The I who says "I" had been born one
> day;
> the I who claims to initiate acts
> does not initiate its own
> being.
> I have come forth from unknowns . . .
> I am no longer a being
> but an encounter among a
> considerable number of
> possible genetic combinations.

                And thus necessity has undergone its
                            last mutation
                    and won its last claim:
                it has become blind and absurd
                    chance (349. Linear arrange-
                    ment mine).

    Yet such necessity is the "locus of
responsibility" (351). It is where we will find our
freedom. "Freedom first says NO in wresting itself
from misfortune and absurdity . . . the yes of consent
is always won from the no" (354). Whatever my character, my personality structure, I have to "rescue" my
own freedom. Through the signs in my body and my
body's action, I have to wrestle with my conscious
being, my unconscious being, the totality of my life.
I have to walk through the stages of my development
from childhood through adolescence, maturity, and beyond. I have to come to terms with my own birth and my
own death.

Recognition Is Not Resignation

    But coming to terms is not acceptance. It is
wrestling. It is a refusal of non-being. It is a
recognition of the sadness of our own finiteness, our
fragility. But recognition is not resignation. Our
freedom answers back--we refuse the amorphous state of
non-being. Refusal avoids the aberrations of disillusionment on the one hand or the drama of suicide in its
various forms on the other hand. Refusal seeks an
alternative way:

            But suicide is not the only expression
            of refusal. There might be a courage
            to exist in the absurd and to face up
            to it, in comparison with which suicide
            itself would be only an evasion (466).

    Such refusal calls for a leap from existence to
transcendence. We learn to see ourselves and the universe as a symbol of Transcendence. "I become reunited
with my body through love of the Earth. It is this
detour which we shall try to understand as the road of
consent" (469). I am not the center of the universe.
I am one being among beings. I discover the wholeness
of the universe. I discover Transcendence, and I am
called to wonder, to contemplation. But my very act of
response reminds me that it is I who contemplate.
"Consent gives me to myself and reminds me that no one
can absolve me from the act of yes" (476).

Hope: A Move Toward Freedom

But consent is never far from the problem of evil
and suffering, so it must be through hope that it works
for and waits for something else.

> Admiration says, the world is good,
>   it is the possible home of freedom;
> I can consent.
> Hope says: the world is not the final
>   home of freedom;
> I consent as much as possible,
>   but hope to be delivered of the
>   terrible
> and at the end of time to enjoy
>   a new body and a new nature
>   granted to freedom (480.
>   Linear arrangement mine).

So we come to the conclusion: our freedom is only
a human freedom, incarnate, in-the-flesh, yet yearning
for the gracious freedom which we envision in the magnificence of a masterful skier or in the grace of a
superb dancer.   Such vision gives us a glimpse of a
Transcendence which is presence, a presence which revo-
lutionizes our idea of human being, which creates "a
radically new dimension, the poetic dimension" (486).

CHAPTER FIVE

Our Human Fallibility

In _Freedom and Nature: The Voluntary and the
Involuntary_, the first part of his _Philosophy of the
Will_, Ricoeur outlined the spheres of the most fundamental possibilities of human being, bracketing or
setting aside the phenomenon of human fallibility. The
first book was an _eidetics_ of the will, that is, a
"pure description" of the essential qualities, an abstract of human possibilities.

Now he turns to that which he had deliberately set
aside: the fallibility of human being, the capacity
for fault, the potential for brokenness and error.
This will be, not an _eidetics_, a pure description, but
rather, an _empirics of the will_, a study of the concrete expressions of an aspect of human being which is
opaque and absurd.

The fault or error of human being is called opaque
because it cannot be clearly seen; in fact, from a
rational point of view, it cannot be seen at all. It
does not make sense. It is absurd because it contradicts the logical. In ancient times, Job could not
account for it. Neither could Camus. Fault is possible because of human being's capacity for error. This
capacity is called fallibility, the ability to fail,
the ability to fall, to err. This is "the constitutional weakness which makes evil possible" (_Fallible
Man_, xix).

Ricoeur seeks to understand this weakness in the
disproportion characteristic of human being. Somehow
human being mediates between finitude or limitation and
infinitude or lack of limitation. We stretch for the
stars. We actually go to the moon. We send missiles
to outer space. At the same time, we murder and rape

and drop napalm in war. We are out of proportion. We reach for the infinitude of possibilities, but find ourselves slave to such finitude of weakness that we can only name it evil.

What is evil? We cannot say. We can give many examples, but we can move to tentative definition only through the concrete, the opaque. Evil shows itself in human existence. It is that which we discover, not knowing from where it comes. We can describe evil in relationship to the passions, to an enslaved will, to unconscious drives, to the problem of power. We can speak of evil as a "positive," a "something," a force too strong to be described as non-being. The "black holes" in the universe provide a useful model. They appear to be both the absence of cosmic forces, and, at the same time, the most intense concentrations of cosmic forces.

Ricoeur tries to understand evil by understanding it in relation to freedom. The effects of evil may be known by those who are innocent, but evil itself is known only in relation to deliberate choice. Ricoeur defines freedom as that which accepts responsibility. Therefore, freedom acknowledges that evil is committed, and that the responsibility of freedom, paradoxically, is to see that evil is not committed (xxv). Freedom begins with the recognition of the possibility of evil; that is, the acknowledgement of fault is "at the same time, the discovery of freedom" (xxvi).

But evil is a larger mystery than can be comprehended solely within the actions of human beings.

> Evil comes into the world insofar as
> human being posits it, but human being
> posits it only because he yields to the
> siege of the Adversary . . . by posit-
> ing evil, freedom is the victim of an
> Other . . . . Human being . . . appears
> no less a victim than guilty (xxix).

OUR HUMAN MISERY

As human being, we know that misery seems to be an integral part of the human condition. This state of being miserable involves our fragility and our inclination to make mistakes. Ricoeur begins with a working hypothesis that the idea that human being "is by nature fragile and liable to err is wholly accessible to pure

reflection" (3). This seems obvious; nevertheless, we
constantly fight against this fragility. We try to
cover it by cliché or avoid it by a false idealism.
The clichés are part of our language: "Well, that's
the way it is. C'est la vie." The false idealism is
just as much a part of our language, yet often a contradiction of reality. We say, "Everything will work
out," or "It will be all right tomorrow."

But in spite of our clichés and our false
idealism, we recognize a disproportion within ourselves. In the past, many thinkers have tried to situate this disproportion in an ontological region between
angel and animal, between being and nothingness. But
according to Ricoeur this is an error. Human being is
"intermediate within himself, within his selves" (6).
We are a mixture. We bring about mediations. Within
us and outside of us are many modalities and levels of
reality. Our existence and our actions provide the
mediation and the mixtures of many of these modalities
and levels of reality. This is the paradox of finite-
infinite human being.

Many philosophers of the twentieth century have
developed philosophies of finitude, of the limits of
human being. Certainly historical events provide a
background and a matrix for such philosophies of
limits. The holocaust, exploitation, continuing war
make dramatic our finitude. But implicit within such
finitude is a transcending of the limit, the transcending of finitude, that is, the thrust toward infinitude, toward a lack of limits.

> Human being is no less destined to
> unlimited rationality, to totality and
> beatitude than he is limited to a per-
> spective, consigned to death and
> riveted to desire (7).

A philosophical anthropology which includes this
relationship of finite and infinite requires a global
view of the whole of human being, a global view which
includes the rift we experience within, the disproportion with which we constantly wrestle, and the central
or mediating point at which we find ourselves.

Such a philosophical anthropology, however, will
not be just a subjective fantasy of human nothingness.
Rather, it will make use of a transcendental reflection, in which through imagination the misery of human
being will find its "synthesis" in its object, in that

which human being is studying. This will be a
philosophy of fallibility which links the misery which
we feel with the transcendental, and which thereby
recovers the object. The reflection moves from: 1)
the disproportion of knowing, to 2) that of acting, and
thence, to 3) that of feeling. Such reflection requires a progression which develops in "images,
figures, and symbols, and it is through these that
pathos reaches mythos, which is already discourse"
(12). In dialectic with Plato, Ricoeur explores the
theme of our human misery. We are a mixture, a field
of forces, drawn at the same time to the logical and to
the illogical, to the ordered and the disordered, to
the good and the wicked. We are wounded, but yearning
for healing. We feel pulled toward death, but struggle
to create new life. We are infinitely rich in the
earth and in the being that is ours, but also infinitely poor, empty, naked. We are beings of disproportion.

OUR DISPROPORTION IN KNOWING

We know only through the experience of the world
outside of us. Even when we know our own bodies, or
speak of knowing our own feelings, we are knowing them
as "object." We are making them object in order to
know them, in order to think about them, to talk about
them. By its nature, thinking transcends. That is, it
steps across from the subjective to the objective. It
goes out to the world to synthesize the meaning of that
world just as the baby's eyes and mouth and hands reach
out to know the world it inhabits. In fact, the baby
knows its mother before it knows itself, but one of the
earliest delights is to recognize its own hand, to see
it as it were for the first time.

A Limited Point of View

Paradoxically, reflection or knowing, as soon as
it reaches toward synthesis, toward giving meaning to
that which it perceives, is at the same time breaking
or fragmenting that which is known. We speak of not
being able to see the forest for the trees, or perhaps,
not being able to see the trees for the forest. If we
synthesize the idea of forest, we set aside the concept
of tree. If we look at the tree, we forget the forest.
As soon as we engage in reflection, we begin to divide
or separate the parts of that which is the object of
our reflection. As soon as we break it apart, we have
lost the whole.

It is in intuition that we can receive the
appearance of the whole. We "receive the presence of
things" (29).

> To receive is to give oneself
> intuitively to their existence; to
> think is to dominate this presence in a
> discourse which discriminates by denomi-
> nation and connects in articulate phras-
> ing (29).

But the whole is not the infinite. On the contrary,
since it is perceived only from our limited point of
view, it makes clear a finite perspective. At the same
time, nevertheless, it opens to an infinitude of possibilities. Recognition of the limits of the known makes
clear that there is an unknown. When an astronomer
gazes into space, she can see so far that the mind
quivers in awe. She seems to be seeing to infinity,
but it is precisely the apparent infinity which makes
her realize that the finite view is the one which is
only an opening out to the possibly infinite.

In other words, my body provides and conditions my
point of view. Nevertheless, I can place my body in
many different positions, each one making possible a
different point of view, a different perspective. In
each case, what I perceive is a world which is the
correlate of my view. "The world is not primarily the
boundary of my existence but its correlate" (31). I
recognize the limitation of my point of view by reflecting on the variety of points of view which are
open, not only to me, but to others. The broad and
multiple views make clear the finitude and limitation
of my own viewpoint at a particular time and place.

By changing my point of view in time and place, by
changing my bodily orientation, I make a change in the
world I perceive. The world is different to me. We
all have this experience when we move from one city to
another, or when we move from one stage of life to
another. We are surprised to realize that the world is
different. We recognize that our view of life while
living in one place is not the same as what it was when
we lived in another. We are confused, and, at least to
some degree, disoriented. We know that at least tem-
porarily part of our orientation to a world has died.
We confront our own limitations, our own finitude.

But an opposite effect may instead dominate our
perception. We visit Paris for the first time, and are

shocked by a reflective recognition of the limitations
of our previous point of view. How could I unconsciously have thought I knew the world when I didn't
know Paris? Again, we find ourselves a center of disproportion: the disproportion between our previous
narrow view of the world and the liberation we experience in a new world or a new way of life.

Sufficient mobility of my body gradually brings me
to a recognition of an "ultimate reference: the otherness that my free mobility brings into play is an otherness in relation to an initial position which is always
the absolute 'here'" (34). In other words, "it belongs
to the essence of perception to be inadequate" (35).
For Ricoeur this limited perspective or point of view
constitutes our "primal finitude" (37). This is the
basis for the disproportion between all our openness to
the possibility of infinity as opposed to the necessary
finiteness of our point of view, that is, of our
limited perspective.

Language Opens Us to the Infinite

It is amazing that as finite human beings we can
speak of our own finitude. Somehow we are able to
split our points of view so that we perceive finitely,
yet step outside ourselves to recognize the finiteness
of that perception. This apparent dichotomy is even
"quantitative: we only know a small number of things;
on the other hand, we hurry on to affirm many more
things than we know" (39). We experience our finiteness, yet at the same time we are moving to step out of
that finiteness, to transcend it. That movement out is
our intention to give meaning, or to signify. It is
the intention to express the point of view itself.

A child's early development in language and
perception provides interesting and basic examples of
this aspect of language. At a little more than one
year, a child points to a picture in a book and says,
"baby." She quickly generalizes so that she can point
to another child and say "baby." The next time she
looks into a mirror at herself, she says "baby." Each
is a finite perception of a picture, another child, of
the image of herself in the mirror. But through the
gift of language, she steps out of the limitations of
the finite perception to affirm the essential qualities
of "baby." Language opens her to the possibility of
the infinite.

> In being born I enter into the world of
> language which precedes me and envelops
> me. The mute look is caught up in
> speech which articulates the sense of
> it. And this ability to express sense
> is a continual transcendence, at least
> in intention, . . . of the perceived
> here and now (41-42).

Following Aristotle, Ricoeur finds in the verb the
power of affirming or denying, the power of the "yes"
or the "no." Such affirmation or denial may take the
form of a false negation, a false affirmation, a true
affirmation, or a true negation. In other words, when
we deny something, it may be either true or false. On
the other hand, when we affirm something, it too may be
either true or false. Such affirmation becomes assent
or choice, so that assent and the verb correlate with
each other. Such correlation becomes the correlation
of the understanding and the will in signifying meaning. But to signify meaning, that is, to use a verb,
is to transcend the limitation of a single point of
view. In each case mentioned above, the child was
signifying, "This is a baby that I see pictured in this
book." "This is a baby that I see opposite me." "This
is a baby that I see in the mirror." To affirm such
meaning is to transcend through language the limitation
of a single point of view.

The Middle Term: "Pure Imagination"

Our perspective, our point of view, is limited.
It reveals our finiteness. On the other hand, as we
have said, our ability to affirm, our use of a verb to
signify meaning, opens up the infinite. We are mediators of the disproportion between our finiteness and
the infinite. This disproportion "gives rise to the
problem of the third term, the intermediate term, which
we shall call pure imagination" (57). But this power
to imagine, this power to create the image, is much
more slippery than either the concept of the perception
or the concept of the transcendental quality of language. Such "pure imagination" is somehow in the correlation of our point of view and our language. It is
somehow in the synthesis of the two. Such synthesis
may then be called objectivity, or the unity between
the appearance and the expression. Our consciousness
becomes a mid-point between the unlimited and the
limited. It draws a model to say that things are "a
synthesis of meaning and presence" (59), "of meaning
and appearance."

Because our body opens onto the world, our
imagination, or our images, open out onto the world.
The synthesis of meaning and appearance, then, comes
through an image of openness or an image of light. We
do not see light, but "in the light. Light is thus the
space of appearance, but light is also a space of intelligibility" (62). But this mediating function which
embraces meaning and appearance escapes our empirical
study. It remains an enigma.

Following Kant Ricoeur pushes this mediating term
of the image back to a study of time. In other words,
when I recognize my perception, my limited point of
view, I recognize in some way the aspect of time. Now
I perceive this. Now I perceive that. One follows the
other.

Since one follows the other, I become aware of a
series, and of the limitation of each perception in a
series. This makes me aware also of the multiple quality of my perceptions, and thereby reinforces my awareness of the limitation of each point of view, but, at
the same time, also opens me out to infinite possibilities of perception. Whether it be awareness of time as
a series or an ordering, or time as somehow content and
scope, we are aware of an ordering which flows out of
our limitations, but which flows into an apparently
infinite series. "To know being is not merely to let
it appear, but is also to determine it intellectually,
to order it, to express it" (67). Our limited perception and our ability to reason and to give order join
our finite point of view and our openness to the infinite.

But the ordering does not come just from time
itself. The inadequacy of the concept of time led Kant
to what Aristotle had called the categories. But
Kant's exploration of the categories still does not, in
Ricoeur's view, solve the "enigma of the transcendental
imagination" (69). We have to presume such a power,
but we cannot prove it. It remains obscure and hidden.

The synthesis of appearance and meaning which the
imagination brings about Ricoeur calls consciousness
(70). It is "knowledge with." It is that realm of
"knowledge with" which looks to the object, which belongs to everyone who looks at that object and synthesizes appearance and meaning. It is the "I" of I think
which belongs to anyone who perceives the object and
synthesizes meaning. In this sense consciousness is
very different from self-consciousness, which is awareness of our own consciousness.

This transcendental stage of a philosophical
anthropology which is characterized by the disproportion of human being is necessary, in Ricoeur's view,
before one can go on to an analysis of myth and other
concrete expressions of the misery of human being.
Human beings are mid-way between being and nothingness
because they bring about mediations in things. Human
beings mediate the finite and the infinite in things.
At a first stage, this can be expressed in philosophic
discourse. It can be talked about logically. But the
merely logical discussion lacks the richness which myth
and other levels of language provide for human being.
In other words, there is a surplus of meaning in myth
and rhetoric which Ricoeur postpones for a later study.

OUR DISPROPORTION IN ACTING

Our disproportion is not only in our knowing. It
is not only in our finite perspective as contrasted
with our thrust toward a total view. It is not only in
the limitation indicated by the verbs we use to express
a finite point of view which at the same time implies a
thrust toward the infinite. Our disproportion is not
only in our imagination which somehow transcends our
finite perspective and our capacity for reaching toward
the universal. Our disproportion is also in our acting.

To the three focal points discussed as parts of
the Disproportion of Knowing correspond three focal
points in the Disproportion of Acting. To our limited
perspective corresponds the limited quality of our
"character." To the finite-infinite transcendence of
our verbs and our language, that is, to the finite-
infinite quality of our thrust toward meaning corresponds what we call our happiness. And third, to the
transcendental aspect of our imagination corresponds
the respect which is fundamental to our humanity.

The Disproportion of Our Character as Acting

"Character is, in a way, a totalization of all the
aspects of finitude" (FM, 77). Our character comes
out, first, from our body, from our sensory perception.
In our reflection, we see the relationships between our
sense perception, our motivations, and our acting. We
may see ourselves as threatened. In anger, controlled
or not, we act in a certain way. As we describe the
situation to a friend, we say we "see" why we acted in

such a way. We feel "inclined" to thrust back with
verbal or physical abuse, but a more dominant inclination to peace and control prevails, and we work through
the situation. We see the disproportion of our character in action.

My desires also show me the disproportion of my
character as acting. My desires draw me outside of
myself, to want to have this thing or that, to want to
do this action or that. My body often stands in sus-
pense: should I go out or stay in? Often I really
want to do both, but the concreteness of my body makes
it impossible to do both simultaneously. I feel myself
pulled in both directions but my finiteness allows only
one direction. I want both and often many more at the
same time. The disproportion cuts deeply into the
thrust of my desires.

In fact, I often don't even know what I desire. I
feel vaguely pulled toward certain actions, and vaguely
repelled by others, but often I don't even know what
they are. If I can write them out, or try to describe
them to a friend, sometimes they become clearer, and I
have given at least some proportion to the disproportion of my desires.

This disproportion of my sensory experience, my
motives, and my desires betrays itself in the variance
of my moods. My friend may be in a "good mood" when I
am in a "bad mood." My moods make clear how individual
I am. They reveal a continuing change within me. And
those changes often do not coincide with similar
changes in those around me. I may be "up" when they
are "down," or the converse may be true.

> We discover the feeling of the primal
> difference between the I and all
> others; to find oneself in a certain
> mood is to feel one's individuality as
> inexpressible and incommunicable. Just
> as one's position cannot be shared with
> another, so also the affective situa-
> tion in which I find myself and feel
> myself cannot be exchanged (85).

Pushed to its ultimate stance, this unique point
of view becomes self-love, an attachment to that point
of view which is unique to me. We want to preserve it,
so that, when severely threatened by sickness or death,
we transform the point of view into a radical will to
live, which may give us courage to survive, or which,

on the contrary, may push us to preserve our life over
that of another.

Such point of view, worked out in action, becomes
the style and the history of a particular way of life.
Our powers--whether bodily, psychical, or intellectual
--develop or do not develop in relationship to the
choices we make.   Choices build upon choices until a
particular characteristic action becomes habitual.   It
becomes a spontaneous way of acting.

> Habit is possible because the living
> person has the admirable power of
> changing himself through his acts.   But
> by learning, a person affects himself;
> his subsequent power is no longer in
> the situation of beginning but of con-
> tinuing; life goes on, and beginning is
> rare (87.   Translation modified).

Thus our original powers to do certain actions, as
well as our continuing modification of such powers
"shrink our field of availability; the range of the
possible narrows down" (88).   In other words, our original powers, and the powers we have developed which
then become habitual ways of acting, make clear the
finitude of our possibilities of acting.   At the same
time, to say that our possibilities are limited is to
say that all possibilities are unlimited.   Our finitude
calls for infinitude.   We recognize the disproportion
rooted within our powers.

Such disproportion keeps us on a tightrope between
spontaneity and inertia.   There is a "primordial inertia" by which we tend to go on in our existence, to
continue modes of acting which we have begun.   The
routine takes on a boring or deathly aspect, which lays
bare our finitude.   In fact, the word inertia denotes
an inability to move or to act or to change from a
course.   In contrast, the word spontaneity comes from
the root for free will or free choice of acting.   Once
more, we recognize ourselves as mediating a severe
disproportion between our tendency to continue in the
inertia of our present lack of power and our call to
act, to be.   Many persons become overwhelmed by the
everydayness of their continuing lives.   If they break
out of the oppression, either by acting freely to reaffirm their choices, or by spontaneously making new
choices, they experience the liberation of the free
movement of the will.   A person is tired out in the
experiences of the inertia of a marriage.   Through

counseling or through a change in some of the aspects
of that marriage, he may again freely choose the relationship. A contrasting form of action would be to
choose a new relationship, in which he might feel the
freedom of the new choice. Either choice makes him
aware of his finitude. Both are not possible at the
same time. The situation is essentially either/or.

Such finitude is inexorably tied up with time. We
can continue in the life we have been nursing and
"settle in," or we can become creators of time by the
way we structure it and make it new, by the way we
flesh out its meaning.

In the disproportion of our acting, then, there
are three aspects of our finiteness: the disproportion
within our perspective, the disproportion within our
self-love, and the disproportion within our inertia.
But these are not separate. They are part of a
totality which makes up my character, "my existence
taken as a whole" (89).

Our character is not something which can be
pictured from the outside. It has to be caught in our
expressions, in our actions, in the field of motivations and actions in which we operate. It is finite.
That is, our openness is limited by our field of motivations. It is a "finite manner of freedom" (93). It
is my foundational "accessibility to all values of all
persons in all cultures."

> My field of motivation is open to the
> whole range of the human. This is the
> meaning of the famous statement:
> "Nothing human is foreign to me." I am
> capable of every virtue and every vice;
> no sign of human being is radically
> incomprehensible, no language radically
> untranslatable, no work of art to which
> my taste cannot spread. My humanity is
> my essential community with all that is
> human outside myself; that community
> makes every person my like. My charac-
> ter is not the opposite of that
> humanity; my character is that humanity
> seen from somewhere (93).

My humanity partakes of the universal. By seeing
the characters of others who share this humanity, I
come to an awareness of the uniqueness of my share in
that humanity. My freedom is both an "unlimited

possibility and a constituted partiality" (94). In one
sense, I have "received" my character. I have inherited it. It is the fact of my existence. In another
sense I have constituted it by each of my choices
through life. Though finite, it opens on to the universal human condition. Though my existence provides a
narrow perspective, the correlate of that perspective
is my openness to the full spectrum of the possibilities of being a human being.

The Disproportion Between Our
Character and Our Happiness

Most of us have a naive idea of happiness. We
engage in a certain act. We experience what we call
happiness, a certain satisfaction or fulfillment. Our
act has achieved a certain result. We would like the
moment never to end. "I wish this day could last
forever," we say. Yet, at the same time, we often
recognize what a limited perspective this expression
reflects. For example, a woman's wedding day is sometimes the "happiest" day of her life. But even while
she is enjoying it and all that it symbolizes, she is
often aware, at least subconsciously, of the persons
who are not able to be there, or of those oppressed
women throughout the world whose children are starving
and who are themselves starving. For a moment or a
day, those aspects of unhappiness have been suppressed
or set aside, and a temporary act or state is assumed
to be eternal. The finite is assumed to be infinite.

In Ricoeur's view, this is a naive view of
happiness. Happiness is not an accumulation of satis-
fying acts. It is not finite, but it is "the horizon
from every point of view" (100). Happiness is not the
sum of pleasure, but the totality of meaning and fulfillment. Just as our particular limited perspective
leads us to the total possibilities of perception, so
our limited desire for fulfillment leads us to a global
view of the total possibilities for fulfillment.
Happiness is not the end of our individual desires. It
is, rather, that totality of meaning and contentment of
which we have a glimpse now and then. In one sense,
the joy of a woman's wedding day may symbolize this
totality of meaning and contentment because the community and joy of a small gathering may symbolize the
possibility of what we hunger for in regard to the
global community. The beatitude "Happy are they who
hunger and thirst for justice, for they shall be satisfied" seems to suggest this stretching for the horizon
of all possible meaning and good.

But the description of such a hunger only makes clearer the infinite distance between the desire and its realization. It makes clear the infinite gulf or disproportion between the finiteness of my viewpoint and the infinitude of what happiness really is.

> No act gives happiness, but the
> encounters of our life which are most
> worthy of being called "events" indi-
> cate the direction of happiness . . . .
> The events which bespeak happiness are
> those which remove obstacles and un-
> cover a vast landscape of existence.
> The excess of meaning, the overflow,
> the immense: that is the sign that we
> are "directed toward" happiness . . . .
> I am directed toward the very thing
> that reason demands. Reason opens up
> the dimension of totality, but the con-
> sciousness of direction, experienced in
> the feeling of happiness, assures me
> that this reason is not alien to me,
> that it coincides with my destiny
> (104-105).

Respect: the Fragile Synthesis

Can we bring together the finiteness of our point of view and the infinity of our thrust toward meaning and happiness? Yes, we can--in the synthesis of the person.

> The person is still a projected
> synthesis which seizes itself in the
> representation of a task of an ideal of
> what the person should be. The Self is
> aimed at rather than experienced (106).

This "person," as projected, is what Ricoeur refers to as humanity, not as a collective, but as that quality which belongs to each human being. In a person are brought together the uniqueness of a particular point of view and the thrust toward universal meaning. The uniqueness of character and the thrust toward happiness are synthesized in the individual human being. The synthesis is in the respect required for each human being, who is unique in a particular character, but who also signifies meaning in order to transcend the limi-tation of a single point of view. There is, then, an inner duality of respect which looks toward the unique character of the person, but also toward the universal

meaning and happiness which is the totality of all
perspectives, and which incorporates respect for each
of those other points of view which make up the totality. Such inner duality reflects the fallible structure of human being:

> All the aspects of finitude have been
> regrouped under the idea of finite
> perspective; all the aspects of in-
> finitude have been regrouped under the
> idea of meaning . . . . Thus, we can
> already say that respect is the fragile
> synthesis in which the form of the
> person is constituted (120-121).

OUR DISPROPORTION IN FEELING

The discussion of our disproportion in knowing and
our disproportion in acting lacks the richness and
depth of a discussion of our disproportion in feeling.
In another kind of terminology, it is a movement from
the disproportion in our theory, to the disproportion
in practice, to the disproportion in the affective
aspects of our humanity. In other words, "the third
step of an anthropology of fallibility is the 'heart,'
the Gemüt, Feeling" (124).

> The "heart," the restless heart, would
> be the fragile moment par excellence.
> All the disproportions which we have
> seen culminate in the disproportion of
> happiness and character would be inte-
> riorized in the heart (124).

The Relationship of Knowing and Feeling

What do we mean by feeling? The term covers many
words and concepts in our language. We may speak of
emotions, passions, intuitions, or affections. These
expressions are attempts to get at certain movements
within us which indicate the thrusts of our lives. We
speak of loving something or someone. We may experience hate. Some things seem to us good, others bad or
evil. Others give us joy or sorrow.

Our feeling is integrally related to our knowing.
Paradoxically, although feeling is something that
arises within us, and we often think of it as subjective, it is, at the same time "on" an object or a

"something." The intending or the moving on to the
object moves the feeling out of us in a certain way and
on to the object. "Our 'affections' are read on the
world they develop" (127).

Yet, it is not quite that simple. Especially two
disciplines in recent times have made it clear how
complex our feelings are: behavioristic psychology and
depth psychology. Since only the act is subject to
experimental description, behavioristic psychology
subordinates feelings to the external act. Ricoeur
replies that "feeling is not a part of the whole, but a
significant moment of the whole" (130). The physical
metaphors of equilibrium, tension, resolution are helpful in setting up models subject to experimental criteria, but, in Ricoeur's view, they miss the meaning of
the act, since they do not relate to the knowing and
the affective experience of the person whose act is
being described. Feeling reveals to us the intention
of the drives and tensions described by behavioristic
psychologists.

Besides behavioristic psychology, depth
psychology, whether that coming from Freud, Jung, or
someone else, has called our attention to the latent
meaning which is often hiding behind the manifest meaning. In some cases, in fact, as Freud has shown, the
latent meaning is the real meaning, and the apparent
meaning is only the symptom of what lies beneath. To
decipher the real meaning hidden in the surface meaning
requires a special kind of interpretation, a special
kind of hermeneutics. Any method of interpreting meaning always moves from a sense which may be less meaningful to a sense which adds to the meaning, or which
is the better meaning. It is part of the human quest
to strive for this fuller meaning which makes possible
a more authentic existence.

What else shall we say of the relationship of
feeling and knowing? First, that our feelings reflect
the choices we make which may bring about harmony or
disharmony with what we perceive as "good" or "bad."
Our choice may seem "natural" or not. We may feel a
"connaturality" between our acts and the movement of
other objects or beings in the universe. Such feelings
often involve some of the following movements: a movement by which we detach something or someone from
ourselves, which at the same time is to objectify the
thing or the person, and the opposite movement by which
we assimilate the thing or the person or make it our
own. In other words, by our feelings, we project on to

the object the qualities of that which is lovable or
hateful, desirable or repugnant, joyful or sad. Feeling is my bond to the world which I perceive, and, in
turn, that world which I have colored "is the sign and
symbol of my inwardness" (134).

Insofar as our feelings are expressions of our
intentions, we can objectify them or make them into
apparent objects. Ricoeur calls these values. Our
feeling-intentions reduce the object or thing to the
essence perceived as good or bad, suitable or harmful.
At the same time, the value is formed in relationship
to other values. This is here and now better than
that. Such acts of the mind, then, become not feeling
but "preferential intuition" (137).

> The pleasant and the unpleasant, met
> with on things, are not yet values;
> they only become so when they are re-
> duced to essence and confronted with
> other values in a preferential outlook
> (137).

What for example was the relationship between
feeling and knowing in a person in a Nazi concentration
camp? A person such as Viktor Frankl may have perceived certain objects, persons, or actions, which he
saw were good or bad, connatural or not, with his own
sense of being. He was pulled to a process of objectifying feelings or, on the other hand, of assimilating
them or making them his own. Certain things, persons,
or acts, became for him loveable or hateful, desirable
or repugnant, joyful or sad. Through a recognition of
such qualities, he was able to come to a better interpretation of his own internal workings. From the process, he affirmed or developed certain values, prefer-
ring one thing, person, or act to another. We can see
how different the process may be if we contrast the
feeling-intending-valuing of Frankl with that of
Goering, for whom the process was in many ways diamet-
rically opposed to that of Frankl.

Through Anguish to Joy

There is disproportion, not only in our knowing,
but also in our feeling. In Ricoeur's view, human
being is "stretched between the this-here-now," that
is, "the certainty of the living present, and the need
to complete knowledge in the truth of the whole" (139).
Our unique perception is always tied to our language

attempts to express meaning. This duality of knowing
is also reflected in the complex duality of our feelings. There is a polarity between our basic, almost
animal thrust toward life, and the "intellectual love"
or "spiritual joy" which is the thrust of another part
of our being. Somewhere in between is what we call our
"heart" (139).

This complexity or duality is, in turn, reflected
in the polarity of what we refer to as pleasure and
happiness. Pleasure is associated with finite acts
analogous to our finite perspective. Happiness is
related to a global perception of the whole, of which
my finite perception is a part. The relationship and
hierarchy of these two is revealed in our language and
the phenomena of a dualistic experience. We sometimes
recognize that we are suffering at the same time that
we are experiencing intense enjoyment, especially sensory enjoyment. On the other hand, a mother sacrific-
ing for her child and a Martin Luther King, Jr. provide
examples of persons rejoicing in their sufferings.

Pleasure is by nature finite. Whether it is the
pleasure of perceiving a work of art, of enjoying a
sexual relationship, of expending oneself in sport, or
of learning something new, the pleasure is still related to the finite. The pleasure is not infinitely
extendable.

Following Aristotle, Ricoeur builds the idea of
happiness, not on an extended idea of pleasure, but on
the radical principle of the act as good, and on the
essential dynamism of the human act. Fully human action relates to a way of life, to the style of a fully
human being acting out his or her way of living. In
such a way, happiness becomes the "highest form of the
pleasant" (148). When St. Augustine said, "Love God
and do as you will," he was expressing a similar idea.
If one is fully committed to God and the good, one's
actions flow out of the commitment and the life, and
happiness becomes related to the global perspective of
wisdom, of the totality. Particular pleasures may well
be even more intense within this totality, but the
totality is the source of happiness.

The totality is always related to reason and
meaning. Reason, our search for meaning, opens us to
the totality. At the same time, feeling searches for
fulfillment, and finds itself open to happiness.
"Feeling reveals the identity of existence and reason:
it personalizes reason" (155).

Our feelings are not satisfied with the finite.
Our dissatisfaction leads to extensions, models, or
schematizations which enable us to see the larger view.
One direction of such modeling is the model of inter-
human relationships.

> The infinitude of feeling emerges
> clearly from the fact that no orga-
> nized, historical community, no econ-
> omy, no politic, no human culture can
> exhaust this demand for a totalization
> of persons, of a Kingdom in which,
> nevertheless, we now are and "in which,
> alone, we are capable of continuing our
> existence" (156-157).

The other direction of such modeling is toward the
world of Ideas. We are in existence in relation to our
ideas, our ideas of "the world," of "the human community," of "We, the people." It is ideas or meaning
which gives a bond and a goal to a community. It is
ideas or meaning which provides the horizon for our
understanding of self, of feelings, and of community.
That is why Ricoeur can say:

> [The Heart's] fundamental openness or
> availability is always opposed to the
> greed of the body and living. Sacri-
> fice is the dramatic form which, in a
> catastrophe, takes on the heart's
> transcendence; sacrifice attests that,
> at the limit of life, to give one's
> life for a friend and to die for an
> idea is the same thing (157-158).

We are at the heart, once again, of the
disproportion within human being, the disproportion
between the limited perspective, and the thrust toward
totality. Human being is capable of joy, even in and
through anguish. By being human, a person is aware of
the finite perspective of his or her feelings, but at
the same time, is drawn in meaning toward a totality,
toward a universal view which transcends the finite.

Having, Power, and Worth

Pleasure and happiness are disproportionate. We
are fragile, and we experience the resultant conflict.
At the center of this conflict is the "human heart, the
heart's humanity" (162). Somehow this is the area

where we move between living and thinking, between life
and the word.

Ricoeur finds Thomistic and Cartesian treatments
of the passions inadequate because they miss this area
of the intermediate, of the "heart." Kant's
Anthropology goes further, but has the opposite difficulty. Because he starts with specifically human passions, Kant considers not the ideal, but the fallen or
broken forms of the feelings of human being. For his
philosophical anthropology, Ricoeur seeks the primordial for which the broken are the fragmented forms.
He organizes his search, therefore, around those three
human passions described by Kant which reflect typical
human situations embedded in culture and history. They
may be called possession, domination, and worth. More
usually, they are translated as having, power, and
worth. They correspond to the economic, political, and
cultural dimensions of our human worlds.

Having: We can hardly separate the "I" of who we
are from the "mine" of what we have. From the child
clinging to "my mother" or even to "my blanket," to an
older person clinging to a favorite chair, the relationship of who we are to what we have is symbolically
integral. We think we separate the two, but the loss
of a favorite article betrays how much our identity is
related to what we possess. If someone steals something from us, we feel that somehow our self has been
violated.

As human beings, a large part of our having is
related to our work, which is essentially our way of
producing or creating the things that we have. We move
through stages of acquiring things, of making them our
own, of possessing then ("sitting on them," as it
were), and preserving them, or "saving" them. In the
process, we experience both control and dependence. We
have control insofar as they are "ours." We are dependent insofar as they continue to be ours only in relationship to a complex of factors and persons beyond our
control. Once more we are in the middle of extreme
disproportion.

"Mine" and "yours" are part of the differentiation
of "you" and "I." No matter how much communion we move
toward in an ideal relationship, there still remains
the fact that my body, mind, and spirit define a basic
"I," inviolable as long as I remain human.

The fact that in community we move toward a "we"
does not contradict this basic having. It may

transcend it, but it still implies an identification of the "I" with the "we." Such an identification may generate a new polarity: "we" and "they." Or in a utopian model, the "we" may be universalized to include all human beings, in fact, all the universe.

Power: The relationships of having imply the relationships of power. The word power is used, in the first place, with a neutral connotation; that is, in itself, it is neither good nor bad. Nevertheless it denotes ordering, and, therefore, subordination. Even the "mine" and the "yours" set up such an ordering. Ordinarily the fact that something is mine sets that which is yours in subordination. With sufficient motivation, I may subordinate mine to yours, in which case I am identifying more with yours than with mine. Good friends, a married couple, or persons in a democratic society aim at reciprocal respect for the "mine" and the "yours" so that power is distributed. When power is distributed, then subordinating and commanding are also distributed.

In society it is difficult to maintain appropriate distributions of power. This is true in the simple society of the family. It is true in the complexity of the work experience, whether it is a home craft organization for work, or whether it is the work of the assembly line, or of international corporations. There is always the temptation of more power for the individual or for the institution with which certain persons identify.

> The fact remains that I could not understand power as evil if I could not imagine an innocent destination of power by comparison to which it is fallen. I can conceive of an authority which would propose to educate the individual to freedom, which would be a power without violence; in short, I can imagine the difference between power and violence; the utopia of a Kingdom of God, a City of God, an empire of minds or a kingdom of ends, implies such an imagination of non-violent power. This imagination liberates the essence; and this essence governs all efforts to transform power into an education to freedom (182).

Worth: By worth Ricoeur means honor or esteem. Ultimately, worth is synonymous with that which constitutes humanity. Worth reflects our desire to exist, our affirmation of self. In other words, it is not enough to have things. Neither is it enough to have power. We continually strive to exist, to affirm and build self through our desire for esteem. We want to be recognized or known. Through sociological studies we are aware of the devastation of a child who lacks such esteem. On the contrary, we read of human beings, who, although poor and apparently "powerless," are rich in self-esteem because of mutually reinforced affirmation within the family or group situation.

Nevertheless, such esteem is fragile, because it is based on opinions, our own and those of others. Brain-washing techniques of totalitarian governments or contemporary cults use our needs for esteem and worth as instruments of control. They are difficult to resist. In fact, those persons who were able to resist brainwashing in the Korean war imprisonment seemed able to survive precisely because their sense of self-esteem was so strong.

Mutual esteem is often strongest when it is developed as part of a common task and a common vision. Such task and vision help create a "we" which transcends individual opinion. Such task and vision may be distorted from a true esteem to a manipulation such as that which eventuated in the tragedy of the Jonestown mass suicide. But mutual esteem developed within a common task and common vision may also empower human beings to live as sisters and brothers in the same human family.

That is why true esteem must be linked to reason, ratio, appropriate relationships. What is our existence-worth? To affirm myself as autonomous, as end rather than as means to be manipulated is, at the same time, implicitly to affirm the other as autonomous, as end rather than as means to be manipulated. Such affirmation indicates that a human being is person, an end in herself or himself. I cannot use another, or I violate that person's integrity. Such quality of integrity and existence-worth is exactly what we mean by humanity. "I expect another person to convey the image of my humanity to me, to esteem me by making my humanity known to me" (187). Such images may be in one-to-one situations, but even these are part of the much larger economic, political, and cultural worlds, where economic systems, political institutions, works of art and literature, models of technology, environmental pollution or beauty, and other images of

humanity tell us who we are by affirming or denying our
worth.

> If humanity is what I esteem in another
> and in myself, I esteem myself as a
> thou for another. I esteem myself in
> the second person; in that case self-
> love, in its essential texture, is not
> distinct from sympathy . . . I love
> myself as if what I loved were another
> . . . worth is neither seen nor known
> but believed. I believe that I am
> worth something in the eyes of another
> who approves my existence (188-189).

It is precisely because esteem is experienced as
belief that it is so fragile. Again, we are at the
heart of our disproportion.

Fragility, Fallibility and the Possibility of Fault

Our disproportion in knowing, acting, and feeling
is the locus for our fragility. We are mixtures of the
limited and the unlimited, the finite and the infinite.
We are on a tight rope between extremes. That means we
are always subject to falling; we can err in one direction or another. To say we are always subject to falling is to say we are fallible.

But, in turn, what does Ricoeur mean to say that
we are fallible?

> Essentially this: that the possibility
> of moral evil is inherent in human be-
> ing's constitution . . . . Not just any
> limitation constitutes the possibility of
> failing, but that specific limitation
> which consists, for human reality, in not
> coinciding with itself. Human limitation
> [is] synonymous with fallibility (203-
> 205. Translation modified).

Drawing on Kant's categories of quality, Ricoeur
describes the categories of fallibility: 1) originating affirmation, 2) existential difference, and 3)
human mediation.

Originating Affirmation: "Originating" refers to
that which is at the beginning--foundational. "Affirmation" is the opposite of negation. To affirm is to

make a statement, to say yes, in this case, to posit
life. It is felt as the joy of existing, the joie de
vie. In Deuteronomy, the Hebrew people are urged to
"choose life."

Existential difference: But experience makes
clear to us that such affirmation is not our usual
existential situation. On the contrary, we are constantly confronted with our sadness, our finiteness,
our limitation. My perspective is one of negation.
Every birth implies a death. Every joy implies the
lack of that joy. No matter what my unity or harmony
with another, it is imperfect and open to the possibility of disharmony. No matter how great my love, it
is possible that such love can cease to exist. In
fact, it can even become hate. Such is the sadness of
my being finite.

Human mediation: But the dialectic of our
affirming life and yet recognizing the sadness of our
limitation makes clear that we stand in the middle. As
human beings, we are the mediators between the Yes and
the No. We ourselves are our fragility. We ourselves
are our limitation. "Human being is the Joy of Yes in
the sadness of the finite" (215).

In such a dialectic and mixture we can see the
"geologic fault" which is integral to human being. Our
fallibility makes clear that we are not what we affirm.
Somehow we are "already fallen" (219). But as soon as
we say "fallen," as soon as we suggest a capacity for
good or evil, we are no longer in a descriptive mode.
We require a "symbolics of evil" which is opaque, which
does not lend itself to usual philosophic discourse.
We are within the realm of a language of symbol and
myth. This is the subject of Ricoeur's next study:
The Symbolism of Evil.

But before we examine that development, we need to
examine a more fundamental question: What is the relationship of a philosophical anthropology to faith? Can
one consider human being without considering faith?
For Ricoeur these are not abstract questions. They are
questions with which he has struggled throughout his
life. They are questions which have challenged him as
philosopher and as human being. They are the subject
of the next section: Ricoeur and the Challenge of
Faith.

PART II. RICOEUR
AND THE CHALLENGE OF FAITH

CHAPTER ONE

Faith, Philosophy, and Religion

We have sketched the first part of Ricoeur's work of building a philosophical anthropology. We ask now: what is the relationship of a philosophical anthropology to faith? Is it possible to consider human being without considering faith? These questions have been and continue to be fundamental questions for Ricoeur as philosopher, as human being, and as person of faith.

We will first ask: what are the relationships of faith, philosophy, and religion? Secondly, we will look at faith and the problem of language, followed by the third topic, faith and ideology, and lastly by faith and interpretation.

Faith, Philosophy, and Religion

The relationships of faith, philosophy, and religion have been problems for Western philosophy for more than two thousand years. As the Greek philosophers developed their ways of thinking, they built methods of analysis which led to an autonomy of thinking not dependent on the gods. At the same time, the concurrently developing Hebrew traditions remained centered on the God of Abraham and on a tradition that presumed a faith. Because of the spread of Christianity out of Judaism to the nations, those who are heirs of the Christian tradition stand in two separate streams of thought which defy absolute integration. Ricoeur is part of this tradition and of these two separate streams of thought.

Ricoeur realizes that his position is one embracing a contradiction that can be mortal, but he

hopes to convert this into a living tension; he hopes
to live the contradiction, "to live Christian hope
philosophically." Although he hesitated to include the
essays "Christianity and the Meaning of History" and
"The Socius and the Neighbor" in his collection History
and Truth because of the explicitly Christian stance
which they assume, he felt that personal integrity
required him to deal directly with the issues. Ricoeur
believes he maintains this dynamic tension by separating the subjective motivation from the methodical
structure of the work in which he is engaged (History
and Truth, 7).

In "Interrogation philosophique et engagement,"
Ricoeur asks somewhat rhetorically, "If God is dead, is
human being possible?" To affirm God is not to limit
the existence of human being, but, on the contrary,
such an affirmation is "the power of human being's
power" (20-21).

> If there is an authentic problematic of
> faith, it pertains to a new dimension
> which I have previously described . . .
> as a "Poetics of the Will," because it
> concerns the radical origin of the I
> will, i.e., the source of effectiveness
> of the act of willing I
> describe this new dimension as a call,
> a kerygma, a word addressed to me. In
> this sense, I am in accord with the way
> in which Karl Barth poses the theologi-
> cal problem. The origin of faith lies
> in the solicitation of human being by
> the object of faith (Freud and
> Philosophy, 524-525).

The Problem of Faith

The problem of faith is woven as a strong part of
Ricoeur's lifetime of development. It was part of his
growing up in the reform tradition, as well as part of
his formal educational development. It was and is part
of his continuing philosophical search. While Barth
and other theologians provided for him theological and
faith nourishment, the philosophers Gabriel Marcel and
Karl Jaspers provided directions for relating faith to
philosophy and religion.

Ricoeur sees the work of the two philosophers as
complementary: Marcel's a philosophy of mystery and

Jaspers' a philosophy of paradox. The two philosophers
are similar because they ask the questions about "my
body and my history, me, and the other" which are the
"three peaks of the great triangle" of existential
reflection (Gabriel Marcel et Karl Jaspers, 18), but
they are different for a number of reasons including
their views on faith. Marcel's view is founded on
concrete existence which stretches or goes beyond to
the action of reconciliation. Such reconciliation is a
renewal of covenant, a seizing again of roots, a finding again of our sources. Such finding calls for a Yes
of Invocation (27). For Jaspers the paradox of our
human misery and the challenge of our liberty calls for
an affirmation of a Being which at the same time en-
velops and exceeds the misery of our human condition.

Faith and Philosophy

Faith and philosophy are often seen as contradictory. The apostle Paul perceived the difficulties. He
called for a wisdom which goes beyond philosophy, but
he recognized the truth of the unknown god of the
Areopagus.

The tradition of philosophy in relation to faith
has varied with the historical situation of the particular philosopher. For the world of faith of early
and medieval Christianity, faith embraced everything,
including philosophy which it imbued. Augustine wedded
neo-Platonism to his world of Christian faith. Aquinas
discovered in Aristotle a new framework for rethinking
Christianity. Implicit in each was the possibility of
separating faith from a rational, scientific, and eventually atheistic world view, examples of which we see
in the modern developments of philosophy and other
disciplines. Ricoeur is aware of the danger of such a
separation:

> The peril of an analytic account of
> this kind of philosophy is precisely
> that of separating a description of the
> human condition from a quest of being
> which is the true stake of reflection
> (34).

For each analysis, in other words, there is a
corresponding transcendental vision. The tragedy of
human existence which the philosopher reflects on implicitly calls for the search for the unity of being.
Existence is the "I." By positing such an existence, I

also posit the universe, Being, God, or the
Transcendent--the name depending on the world view of
which I am a part. The experience of our limited situation, whether in sickness or death, in struggle or in
joy, is experience of being on the edge, experience of
transcendence.

But to name transcendence is not to name the
solution. Although the philosopher is searching for
wisdom, philosophy is neither a system nor a solution.
It is a way of asking questions. Nor is the Being for
which the philosopher searches a totality. Being is
always the question mark. It is always the question of
why there is something rather than nothing. It is
always the question of why this universe rather than
another.

According to Jaspers one can think that there is
an unthinkable: such is the paradox. Jaspers concludes with a polarity of faith and non-faith, with
faith subordinated to philosophy. On the other hand,
for Marcel, non-faith is despair. Existence must always be seen in the face of the Transcendence.
Marcel's is not a philosophy of paradox, but one of
mediation and conciliation (43).

A Critique of Knowledge

Implicit in Marcel's concrete philosophy and in
Jaspers' philosophy of paradox is a critique of knowledge. The world of phenomena, of things as they appear
to us, is not the last word. Knowledge provides only
the illusion of a continuing peace. I may have the
illusion of being master, but on the day of my death,
if not before, I recognize my limitations.

We come then through existence to a recognition of
the limits of knowledge. Such recognition raises the
question of philosophic method. If existential philosophy cannot be system, can it nevertheless retain
the rigor of clarity of thought which provides the
foundation for the possibility of speaking of and
transmitting the experience of transcendence? How can
one avoid the extremes: on the one hand, the denial of
the experience of transcendence; on the other hand, a
fideism which denies the validity of reason? Ricoeur
is aware of the risks:

> On the one side, the experiences of
> existence risk collapsing into a weak

confidence which can be communicated.
On the other side, the experiences of
transcendence seem to incline to a new
fideism without criteria for truth
(74).

Jaspers and Marcel attempt to solve the problem
differently. Jaspers opts for a concrete dialectic in
which he acknowledges the density of the human situation, but at the same time recognizes the paradox of
the leap of liberty and the transcendent call. On the
other side, Marcel declares his method "hyper-
phenomenological." For him Being is less constituted
than recognized:

> And in this process, at the same time
> both active and submissive in the act
> of recognition, it is impossible to
> separate the raising up of my liberty
> which is awakened,--deciphered accord-
> ing to the measure of its faith and of
> its believing the meaning,--and the
> permeability of my attention which
> hears, encounters, discovers the mean-
> ing. It is here that to believe and to
> discover coincide (78).

Being exists for its own sake. It stands as an
Other than me. In spite of all my knowledge and de-
cipherment, it still remains way beyond me. In other
words, it remains mystery and paradox.

Philosophic Faith and Religious Faith

Faith is a set of beliefs. If one acknowledges
that being is mystery and paradox, that we cannot know
everything, that, in fact, we know very little compared
to all there is to be known, then we are faced with the
problem of faith. What shall I believe about those
things which I do not know?

I can say simply that I do not know, but that is a
basic statement of belief, belief that I do not know,
that I set aside those things which I cannot control by
knowledge. This is the traditional position of agnos-
ticism. On the other hand, I can say that those things
which I do not know do not exist, but that too is a
statement of belief, belief that they do not exist
since they are not under my control by knowledge. Such
is the position of atheism.

Or like Jaspers, I can say that a discipline such
as philosophy has its own set of beliefs and that religion has its own beliefs, and that the one is separate
from the other. For a philosopher such as Jaspers
"religion appears as the place of authority, the enemy
of liberty" (280).

> In the face of religious faith, philo-
> sophic faith senses itself to be in
> danger, without direct communication
> with a supreme Thou, without miraculous
> and authoritarian guarantee, without
> sociological statute comparable to the
> Church; the philosopher is, if you
> will, the supreme heretic . . . ." (281).

For Jaspers, philosophic faith is the reading of
the ciphers, the symbols, the transcendent in the limit
and paradoxical experiences of human situations. Philosophic faith and religious faith are in conflict. At
best, one can hope for coexistence (277).

In contrast, Marcel's philosophy is one of
reconciliation for which faith is a central theme. In
fact, his philosophy "is a reflection on the 'I believe' in its relations with the 'I exist.'"

> Faith is not an imperfect knowledge,
> but on the contrary, something like a
> new immediacy, as infallible as sensa-
> tion (267).

The basic question is: does my life have a value?
Can I stake it on something? If not, I am enveloped in
despair: my life appears as mere accident and suicide
becomes a logical consequence. On the contrary, to rid
oneself of such despair is to stake one's life on something. Such a stake in life makes the difference
between suicide and sacrifice. While suicide is essentially refusal, sacrifice, on the other hand, is essentially fidelity. Such fidelity to the stake in life to
which we adhere is the spirit of our life. Our spirit
may be lost or saved, but it is precisely the hope that
it may be saved which provides its on-going creation
(269-270).

Philosophy, then, can be defined "as the tension
between the spirit and the test, between the sacred and
the tragic" because any search into the human condition
is no longer profane. It is involved in the concrete
situation which asks the questions about spirit, about

the sacred, about mystery, even about Christian
revelation, recognizing that another person may find
these words foreign to his or her situation. No matter
how much one may wish to, one cannot abstract from the
historic situation of being a Christian or of being
heir to the Christian tradition or of another tradition
quite different from that of the Christian. One can
ask questions about the totality of human experience,
including the experiences and traditions of which the
Christian tradition is not a part, but the one asking
the question always stands in a particular historic
perspective.

This is not to say that philosophy is Christian,
nor that Christianity is philosophy, but only that
there is "a consonance of concrete philosophy with
Christianity" (274).

> The Christian mystery explodes in the
> ontological mystery, the incarnation of
> Christ in the world where I am incar-
> nate, the redemption in a human condi-
> tion where a thou is able to be evoked.
> It is this consonance which is ex-
> pressed in the homonym of _mystery_ for
> the philosopher and of _mystery_ for the
> believer . . . "the essential con-
> formity between Christianity and human
> nature" . . . where human nature is not
> scandalized by revelation, but is dis-
> posed towards it (274-275).

Such a philosophy is not a castration of experience but
an elevation.

Ricoeur has called Marcel his great teacher, and
it is possible to see a consonance between his commentary on Marcel's philosophy described above and his own
development, including articles on a hermeneutics of
revelation and a hermeneutics of testimony which will
be described later.

Philosophy and Religion

In an article on "The Relation of Jaspers'
Philosophy to Religion," Ricoeur offers a critique
which provides another perspective on the relation
between philosophy and religion. According to Ricoeur,
Jaspers' difficulty was that he stopped with an analysis of the false claims which religion too easily

makes, rather than analyzing the real intention of
religion, which for Ricoeur is the salvation of freedom, the saving of freedom.

> The primary religious intention is to
> save freedom from its "vanity," from a
> specific nothingness which keeps it in
> bondage; hence, to liberate, to save
> freedom. That is its true problem
> (631).

According to Ricoeur, Jaspers confuses guilt and
finitude because he sees guilt as one of the ultimate
situations of human being. It is by reason of existence that human being is guilty. Existence is chosen
for me before I even come to exist. My only choice is
in accepting that choice. Thus my guilt is part of
anything I may call freedom (632).

For Ricoeur this is "in contrast to the whole
Christian tradition which conceives guilt only as <u>fall</u>,
that is to say, as a debasement with respect to . . .,
as a lost primordial innocence" (632). Guilt for the
Christian is not the condition of the creature. On the
contrary, "Finitude was the condition of the creature,
but guilt 'entered the world.' Finitude was a state,
guilt an event" (632). For the believer guilt can
never be separated from forgiveness. It is always
related to restoration and redemption.

How does this relate to the problem of freedom?
For Ricoeur there are levels of freedom. The anguish
of choice so dominant in existentialist thought is only
the lowest degree of freedom.

> And is not the highest degree of
> freedom beyond the freedom of option,
> in a freedom of adhesion, beyond all
> risk, in responsive freedom, in a free-
> dom of recollection, and beyond an-
> guish, in a freedom of assent? . . .
> Then the question is less to be free
> than to be liberated, to be freed by a
> healed freedom. The primary thing is
> no longer freedom as it relates to the
> Self, but the articulation of this gift
> of freedom (636).

Liberation is then an experience in which freedom
becomes recreation or new creation (638).

> The moment in which the self seems to
> treat God as a second person is the
> moment in which the self discovers God
> as the Transcendence before which human
> being is almost nothing. The moment in
> which Transcendence seems to render
> invocation futile is the moment in
> which human being rises to full
> responsibility in the world . . . . For
> the great persons of prayer did not
> flee, but changed their life and trans-
> formed existence around them . . . .
> Who talks to God as Thou can talk of
> God as Transcendence, so far as that is
> fitting for human being (639-640.
> Translation modified).

Witness

But to talk of God is to be a witness. What is a
witness and what is the relationship of a witness to
faith, to religion, or to philosophy? The question
poses a difficult challenge. A witness speaks with
authority: This is what I have seen. This is what I
have heard. Such is the original authority of the
scriptures and of the church, an authority which has
its unique witness in a revelation, in a founding
event.

> The witness constrains no one. He or
> she shows the truth which has author-
> ity, but which is not the authority of
> a group of persons. To be sure, this
> authority conferred on the witness
> necessarily comes into conflict with
> the authority of the truth according to
> science and according to the philoso-
> pher (640-641).

The authority of a witness is that of one who has
experienced an event which is transformative and which
claims response. The authority of the scientist or of
the philosopher, on the other hand, is that of one who
is seeking knowledge of reality through rational discourse and demonstration. The truth of the philosopher
or of the scientist is subject to logical criteria for
judgement.

Such rational discourse and logical criteria are
both the strength and the limitation of philosophy or

science. They are the strength because they make possible rational dialogue and the growth of knowledge. But rational discourse and logical criteria are also limitation because the analysis of certain areas of human experience defies their competence. Within such limitation, how does one account for the witness of a truth which seems not to accord with those limits?

The problem is similar to that posed by Einstein with his theory of relativity which did not accord with Newtonian physics or Euclidian geometry. But the problem is very different because Einstein or others could develop new proofs subject to new scientific verification. The problem is also similar to that posed by the artistic genius whose new insights defy the old ways of thinking and who has no method of proof except his or her art. How does one account for the intuition of Picasso?

Rational discourse and logical criteria are very helpful in discerning the validity of the testimony of a witness, but they are of a different category from that of the testimony. We can speak of scientific truth, of mathematical truth, of existential truth, perhaps even of artistic truth. On the one hand, Jaspers can describe the truth of the reading of the symbols, of transcendence. On the other hand, we can speak of the truth of a witness describing his or her experience. In still another sense, we have in the gospel of John a record of a person described as the truth.

We are faced with the question: in what way do these truths correspond with each other? We do not know the answer. We are only on the road to understanding such correspondences. For the present we can only explore their varieties.

CHAPTER TWO

Faith and the Problem of Language

The language of faith poses a problem for us in
our practical day-to-day lives as well as on a theoretical level. We try to describe a faith experience
and we find that the words are meaningless to the person we are talking to. Or sometimes the words are
familiar but the other person has never internalized
them, and so communication breaks down. At another
time someone from a fundamentalist or charismatic community interprets experience in terms which appear
threatening or unreal, just as the liberal is a threat
to the fundamentalist. In all of these situations, we
usually find we do not know how to respond. The communication system is not working, but we lack a theory
to explain why. We only know that we seem to be worlds
apart. What is distinct about a language of faith?
What part does it play in our search for meaning?

We are in a cultural time when people either feel
alienated by a language of faith, or find it is entirely foreign to them. Many people have no idea of
what it means to be born again, to be lost, or to be
saved. People enter college or come to the end of
their lives never having heard the story of Jesus, much
less the story of the Exodus, or the cry of the
prophets.

> It is in the Gospel itself that we now
> find a cultural framework of cate-
> gories, of notions, to which our cul-
> ture renders us strangers. How can we
> make ours something to which we have
> become strangers? (The Philosophy of
> Paul Ricoeur, 223).

We can begin to overcome this problem of cultural
distance by asking two kinds of question. The first is

the kind of question which analyzes, demythologizes, and ultimately reconstructs the cultural world which the faith language is describing. Biblical exegesis, interpretation, and commentary have always been about this task. In ways similar to many others, Bultmann carried demythologizing to its logical extreme, and at the same time realized that such demythologizing carried with it destruction of large areas of faith. It was necessary, therefore, to counter with existential correlates in order to save the meaning. But for many persons the second task seemed disproportionate to the first.

There are similar problems for those who recognize what has been called the "dead end" of historical criticism. Some persons have become masters of philology, form criticism, redaction criticism, and even structural criticism, but have lost the meaning. The text no longer speaks.

For this reason, Ricoeur calls for a second kind of question, the question of our own assumptions, a critique of the world we take for granted, an analysis of what we assume to be the believable and unbelievable in our contemporary existence. This calls for a continuing struggle with the perceived believable and unbelievable. Such a struggle is a threat, because it calls into question the assumptions of modern men and women. It begins a process of alienation from our own cultural assumptions. It calls for taking seriously the radical questions of other times and places.

Ricoeur sees two traits as fundamental to the process of secularization which constitutes most of the modern world, and of which we are a part. The first is "the extension of rationality to all areas and all levels of reality" (225). We are in a continuing process of objectifying everything. We reduce everything "from the mysterious to the problematic." We can solve everything. Either there is nothing left to stand on its own, merely to be contemplated, or, if there are things which defy objectification, we set them aside as unreal, antiquated, or of no importance.

This tendency to objectify everything is accompanied by a second development, which is the setting up of human being as totally autonomous, completely responsible for and dominant over the whole universe. Human beings can go to the moon, can defoliate Vietnam, can deforest the Amazon, can level Hiroshima and plant the seeds of cancer, and yet

disclaim any responsibility for a total ecological
system, a universe of which human being is only a part.

In the practical order, this brings about the
second fundamental trait: if everything is objective,
everything can be managed. Technology is no longer
merely a tool. On the contrary:

> Technology is a way of viewing the
> world, a means to practice it, as a
> universal manifestation of the avail-
> able. In this sense, technology repre-
> sents a new ontological regime . . . .
> Death is no more than an accidental
> rupture which happens to the available.
> Birth and death are eliminated as sig-
> nificant experiences and as instructive
> destiny (225).

Living with such a way of viewing the world is
living on the surface of life, is skimming over the
surface of the water, without plunging into the depths,
without seeing the sky above which leads to infinity.
It is a forgetting or an ignoring of the origin and the
destiny of life.

Fundamental questions have no place in such a way
of viewing the world. What is the meaning of my life?
Where did I come from? Where am I going?--Such questions are a language foreign to the modern mentality.
The challenge for faith is "to restore a signifying
language, a language of being and of existence" (227),
to call into question the process of secularization.
The challenge is to confront our culture and ourselves
on our own ground, at the heart of our being, to build
a preunderstanding in which faith may become
meaningful.

Ricoeur proposes three directions for the building
of such a preunderstanding. The first direction is
that of consciously building a philosophical anthropology. This is the task described earlier which
Ricoeur has assumed as part of his life work. For him
such a task is in the phenomenological mode:

> Here, it seems to me, the task of
> comprehension is to show that in
> proportion to the progress of our ob-
> jective knowledge, the condition of
> existing hides and conceals itself to
> itself. Comprehension is, then, a

> struggle against the deceit which
> progresses along with our knowledge and
> action, a step toward the primitive,
> the primordial, the original. What is
> there under this layer of objective
> knowledge? (228).

Everything that calls forth a primordial reading of our
birth and death, of our decisions and our relationships, of our joys and sorrows and creativity is part
of the restoration of this preunderstanding.

But the task of understanding what a human being
is belongs not only to the philosopher. It belongs to
every human being who recognizes the call to live a
fully human life. What makes my life and that of
others more human? Where can I find beauty and truth?
Where can I find a language which helps me articulate
my experiences of being on the edge, my experiences of
birth and death, of growing and aging?

A second direction for such preunderstanding is
reestabishing humanity as a whole. This was part of
the attraction of early Christianity, the vision of all
human beings becoming one. It was part of the view of
Augustine when he wrote The City of God. It was part
of the often distorted missionary activity which was
concomitant with the spread of Christendom.

But such a view of the totality is also part of
the attraction of the Marxist dream, of the Soviet
world dream, of Teilhard's vision, and the attraction
of the Eastern view of the all. The great forces of
our economy, of our politics, and of our cultural
images and valuing are always straining in this direction. We want to have more, we want to dominate more,
and we want to see the whole.

To see humanity as a whole, then, makes possible a
preunderstanding in which the questions of relationships, of origin, and of destiny are put in dialectic.
Fundamental questions can be asked. The experience of
an American working in a Cambodian refugee camp raises
questions that can lead to the primordial, and that can
make possible a language of faith. A Marxist analysis
of economic and political institutions has enlarged the
world view for many in Latin America to rethink the
language of faith.

The third direction for preunderstanding is the
level of language itself. We are called to conserve or

save a language of faith which can continue to enable
us to ask the questions about human life which are
essential to us, but we are also called to discover
anew and to create anew a language which enables us to
articulate our own existential needs and longings within the context of "a humanity that seeks to become
whole" (230). We are what we eat, but we are also what
we speak: we are our language. If our language is
only technical, confined to the ordering of demonstrated information, then our humanity is also thus
limited.

> We are in quest of a language which
> would be appropriate to the kind of
> imagination which expresses most char-
> acteristic existential possibilities.
> Yes, it is necessary to say; it is this
> opening of human possibility . . .
> imagination, here, is the organ of a
> veritable ontological exploration
> (231).

The problem is: how to restore meaning, how to
restore a language which is the reverse of demythologization. Ricoeur sees two tasks as basic to addressing
such a problem: the task of validating symbolic language and the task of arbitrating between the polarizing and contradictory tendencies of contemporary language world views (232).

Symbolic Language: Symbolic language pertains
especially to three aspects of our humanity. It belongs first to our power to dream. Homer records the
importance of dream in the ancient Greek world. The
Bible, too, reflects a long tradition of recognizing
the communication power of dream to help us understand
our inmost being as well as our relation with the universe and other human beings. In his studies of the
unconscious, Freud discovered new dimensions of the
power of dream which raised substantive questions about
the objectivity of our accepted perception of reality.
We are faced with the knowledge that we are symbol-
making beings, whether we acknowledge it or not.

That is precisely the problem in a technological,
object-centered view of existence. We leave no place
for the dream and the symbol. It is interesting to see
that a growth in science fiction and science fantasy
has paralleled development of a technological world.

Symbolic language belongs also to the universe of
which I am a part. Water, fire, earth, wind, sky speak

of themselves. But they also speak dimensions of
existence I am not able to comprehend. They speak of a
world larger than I can understand. Although they are
known, they express the unknown. This is the double
meaning of such cosmic representations.

Besides the dream and cosmic aspects of symbol,
there is the poetic aspect of our symbolic language.
The poet or anyone who creates new meaning, whether in
words or in some other medium, is shaping images,
words, experiences in ways which did not exist previously. She or he is creating a new reality.

Symbolic language, then, is not a lesser language.
On the contrary, it is the only language appropriate to
certain aspects of human existence. It releases meaning. It explores. It creates.

> All symbolic language is a language
> which says something other than what it
> seems to say, and by its double mean-
> ing, releases meaning, releases sig-
> nification. And in the same way, it
> plays the role of an exploratory in-
> strument of my existential possibili-
> ties, of my situation in being (233).

Of course, scientific language also explores and
creates. But in another way, scientific language and
symbolic language differ greatly. Scientific language
struggles against double meaning. It strives for a
language which cannot be misinterpreted. But if it
cannot be misinterpreted, it also cannot be interpreted. It is closed. On the other hand,

> Symbolic language . . . says more than
> what it says . . . says something other
> than what it says . . . and grasps me
> because it has in its meaning created a
> new meaning (233).

The key is in understanding that there are two
kinds of equivocation or double-speaking. One is by
default. In other words, I do not make my meaning
clear. I vacillate. Such equivocation is opposed to
the development of science and logic. The other kind
of equivocation, usually not acknowledged in our society, is equivocation by excess. There is more meaning
than can be confined to words. My meaning defies the
limits of logic. This is the language which we have
forgotten and which we need to restore in order to be

fully human. It was not enough to demythologize our
myths. We must now free our myths to the fullness of
symbolic language so we can truly read their meaning.
We must pass from a false rationality to a true rationality. We must save the myths.

Besides the task of validating symbolic language,
however, we also have the task of arbitrating among the
various types of language. Only such arbitration can
free a language for faith. Yes, we can recognize the
great value of scientific language. We can be grateful
for the demythologizing which has freed us from the
illusion of a false factualism. We can continue to use
all the resources of historical criticism and of structuralism to dispel superficial and erroneous language
from our faith. But we cannot stop there. We must
ask: What do we affirm? We are called, not only to
accept reality, but also to ask: what is possible? We
must be judge and witness of the strengths and weaknesses of the various kinds of language. We must make
possible a language of faith.

> Do we know human being better than we
> know God? In the end, I do not know
> what human being is. My confession to
> myself is that human being is insti-
> tuted by the word, that is, by a lan-
> guage which is less spoken by human
> being than spoken to human being . . .
> the faith that human being is founded
> . . . by a creative word. Is not The
> Good News the instigation of the possi-
> bility of human being by a creative
> word? (237-238).

CHAPTER THREE

Faith and Ideology

> How do we experience the fact of
> language? Language is not a wholly
> individualized human reality; no one
> invents language; its sources of dif-
> fusion and evolution are not indi-
> vidualized; and yet, what is more human
> than language? We are human because we
> speak: on the one hand, language
> exists only because each person speaks;
> but language also exists as an institu-
> tion within which we are born and die
> (History and Truth, 113).

Our faith is interrelated not only with our
language, but also with the ideological structures of
which our language is one manifestation. What do we
mean by ideology? And how is ideology related to language and faith?

Ideology and Illusion

Ricoeur has been strongly affected by those he
calls the "three masters of suspicion--Marx, Nietzsche,
and Freud" (The Philosophy of Paul Ricoeur, 213). They
must be taken together, he feels, in order to see their
impact on our culture. Although we can now recognize
that each of these masters was narrow in his own critique of culture, we can see through their combined
critiques various facets of what is a major problem for
the modern mind--the problem of false-consciousness. A
major insight is that illusion is not just a defect of
personal judgement. On the contrary, illusion is a
structure of culture, part of all our social exchange.

Marx pointed to the illusions in our views of
political economics. Nietzsche showed us the underlying currents of the will to power in our cultural
structures. Freud opened up the whole realm of the
unconscious as an integral element in our personal,
cultural, and artistic strivings. Together they make
clear the necessity for a new kind of critique of culture. Together they call for a new kind of self-doubt,
a new kind of suspicion, a new kind of demystification.
We are now called to decipher appearances. Things are
not always what they appear. It is now clear that we
can signify something else than what we believe we are
signifying. A new method of destruction has appeared,
which the contemporary world continues to struggle
with.

How does this affect our understanding of
religion? The two are not unrelated.

> Marxism, let it never be forgotten,
> appeared in Germany in the middle of
> the last century at the heart of the
> departments of Protestant theology. It
> is, therefore, an event of western
> culture, and I would even say, of west-
> ern theology (215).

Marx sees ideology as a symptom of the phenomena
of domination and submission. Religion then becomes a
coded language in which the submissive are consoled
with the ideas of paradise or reward and the powerful
rationalize an ideological justification for their
power and righteousness. Such an interpretation becomes a denunciation of that kind of religion which is
ignorant of its economic and political motivations.

In the same way, Marx offers a critique of
economic systems which are ignorant of their responsibility for the false creation of values. Capital which
rationalizes its power and profit-making as benevolence
and response to the needs of the economically poor is
under as much illusion as a religion unaware of its
motivation.

> We can surely apply this critique to
> ourselves; we must appropriate it to
> ourselves as a task of truth and
> authenticity (216).

In a similar way, Nietzsche added to the critique
of culture by pointing out the illusions of our willing

by attempting to decipher beyond the masks the
intentions and significations of our willing. In his
turn, Freud offered through dream and art analysis a
critique of the ideals and values in our culture.
"This critique concerns religion as far as it is effectively for us a compensation stemming from fear or a
substitute for prohibited pleasures" (217).

But Ricoeur sees the contribution of these three
not only in their negative critique of culture, that
is, in the doubts, suspicions, and demystifications
which they provide in order to unmask illusion, but
also in their positive contributions. Their task
essentially was to affirm human being. "The task of
human being is to reappropriate his or her own substance, to stop this bleeding of substance into the
sacred." The task is to aim for transparency, the end
of false-consciousness, to make what we say equal to
what we do. Then we can overcome ideology as illusion.
To overcome ideology is to smash the gods of our own
creation. It is to fight against idols. But it is
only in smashing the idols that we can truly let symbols speak. Then we can make possible a mature faith
appropriate for contemporary human beings. In other
words, we have to become atheists in regard to human
gods to make true faith possible. That is why the
critique of religion as a mask, whether of fear or
domination, is a necessary path for the development of
any true faith.

Ideology and Founding Event

But is it possible to step outside of the
ideologies of which we are a part? Are we not so en-
closed within our language and cultural systems that we
are unable to see them clearly? Yes, Marx was able,
partially at least, to step outside of the dominant
religious and economic systems of his time, and thereby
to critique them. But was he not, at the same time,
creating a new ideology which he was not in a position
to critique? Many of the first Christians were able to
critique those aspects of Jewish ideologies which they
were rejecting, but were they able to see the new systems which they were constructing?

Ricoeur describes five characteristics of the
phenomenon of ideology which are helpful in our understanding of faith and ideology. First is the necessity
for a social group to give itself an image of itself,
to "represent itself in the theatrical sense of the

word" ("Science et idéology," 331). With Jacques
Ellul, Ricoeur sees as basic the connection between
ideology and the founding event of the group. For
example, is it possible to think of American ideology
as separate from the Declaration of Independence, or of
modern France as separate from the French revolution?
A particular ideology grows in social memory, not only
to spread the original ideas of the founders, but also
to perpetuate the original energies of the founding
event. There grow up images, representations, models
of the founding event which become accepted as fact in
the past and as models to be reactualized. What began
as insight and energy soon become consensus, conven-
tion, and rationalization. It is then an easy step to
justification.

A second characteristic of ideology is its
dynamism. An ideology is always more than a reflection. It both justifies itself and projects itself
into the future. It generates tasks, programs, and
institutions which are believed in as just and necessary because of the context in which they have been
generated.

Such dynamism is able to continue because of the
energies of a third trait which is that an ideology
both simplifies and provides a diagram, a model, or a
code to give a particular point of view, not only to
the group, but also to history, and even to the world
and the universe (332). An ideology transforms the
system of thought itself so that it becomes a system of
belief. First there are the celebrations of the founding events themselves. These soon become ritual and
stereotype. This makes possible the fact that ideology
is received. Not only is it expressed in maxims and in
slogans, but it develops its own rhetoric of the probable and the persuasive. Such schematization,
idealization, and rhetoric are the price to pay for the
social efficacy of the ideas.

Fourthly, an ideology provides an interpretive
code which is a structure in which we live and think.
It is not an idea which we possess. It is operational
rather than thematic. It underlies all that we do, all
that we think. Because it is total, it is easy for us
to be deceived by our ideology, to be non-critical.
This seems to be a necessary base, in fact, for our
working in a particular ideological code.

This pervasive quality of ideology is further
complicated by the fifth trait, which is the particular

temporal characteristic of ideology. Although the
ideology itself grew out of another social situation,
it recognizes that the new is an implicit threat to its
directing scheme. We are faced then with the double
characteristics of a thrust toward orthodoxy and an
intolerance of marginal ideas which threaten the code.

> Every group presents the traits of
> orthodoxy, of intolerance of margi-
> nality. Perhaps any society radically
> pluralistic, radically permissive, is
> not possible (334).

Intolerance begins when a grave threat makes it
possible for a group not to recognize itself. This
characteristic of its being imbedded in time and of a
certain necessity for intolerance is a contradiction of
the primary thrust of an ideology to preserve the
thrust of the founding event. Paradoxically, ideology
is both the effect of the wearing away of that initial
thrust and the resistance to such wearing away (334).
It is an interpretation of reality, but at the same
time an obstruction of the creation of the possible.
We can speak, therefore, of an ideological closure.

Coextensive with the constitution of a group are
problems of integration, domination, and authority.
How can the group preserve its unity? How can it solve
the problems of the one and the many, the problems of
domination and submission? How can it best use and
regulate authority? These are questions not easily
answered, but the solutions are specific to each
ideology.

Ideology, Utopia, and Faith

What is the relationship between faith, ideology,
and utopia? Ricoeur admits that there is no easy
answer, but he hopes to begin an analysis by developing
a theory of cultural imagination. If ideology is a set
of ideas reflecting the social needs and aspirations of
an individual, a group, or a culture, what do we mean
by utopia?

A utopia is implicit in every ideology. It is the
perfection or idealistic goal to which the ideology is
directed. But utopia is literally a "no-place," a
projection into the future of what is not yet. The
utopia implicit in Marxism is an end time of a class-
less society of equals. The complex of relationships

between ideology and utopia, with all their
constitutive and distorting aspects, is, according to
Ricoeur, cultural imagination.

Ideology may be said to have three levels:
symbolization, legitimation, and distortion (<u>Philo-
sophical Hermeneutics and Theological Hermeneutics:
Ideology, Utopia, and Faith</u>, 23). On the first level,
the cultural imagination creates a system of symbols
which constitute action. On the second level, this
system of symbols is given credence, invested with an
aura of truth, and constituted with implicit and explicit authority. The third level is the correlative
distortion, an unavoidable result of singling out one
model of reality over another, but also a distortion
reinforced by the necessity of keeping the model in-
tact, preserved from outside threats, and subject to
the authority controls within the system. The function
of ideology is to pattern, consolidate, and provide
order to the courses of action.

> This function expresses one of the
> dimensions of imagination, which is to
> duplicate reality with portraits, pic-
> tures, <u>replicas</u>. It seems that any
> kind of group needs such images by
> which its identity is reasserted by
> being pictured and staged (23).

Then what is utopia? Utopia is the model of
reality proposed, not only as the end goal of an
ideology, but, on the other side, as an alternative and
opposing way of looking at power and authority. It
shatters the present order. It proposes other modes of
existence, of action, and of thought. It proposes an
unlimited capacity for the possible, for otherness
(23). Whereas ideology provides an integrative function, utopia provides an eccentric function, a moving
out from the center, which includes a non-congruence
with perceived reality. Both ideology and utopia,
then, belong to the depth structure of cultural imagination and of symbolic action.

What is the connection with faith? "There are
senses in which faith is an ideology and/or a utopia.
There are other senses in which it is neither one"
(24).

In what way may faith be called an ideology? The
answer depends on the persons or groups who are making
the analysis. Following Feuerbach, Marx labeled

Christianity an ideology in a pejorative sense.
According to Marx, the believer is induced to a submission to the whole hierarchical structure of society by
models and institutions which legitimate pain, oppression, and obedience as the result of evil and sin and
which postpone liberation to an indefinite future.

Ricoeur says that we must take this critique
seriously, especially in recognizing its effects on the
institutions and models we may take for granted. For
example, in what ways are the biblical models of God as
king, father, or judge instruments of such an ideology?
In what ways are our institutions channels of
oppression?

But Marx's critique is narrow. It does not take
into consideration the following three points:

1) To critique Christianity as ideology or
    distortion is to posit an original framework
    which came to be distorted. What is that
    which has been distorted?

2) It is also to acknowledge implicitly a similar
    critique and distortion of other ideologies
    belonging to the superstructure, such as those
    in the law, government, medicine, education,
    art, economy, philosophy.

3) To critique Christianity only in a negative
    sense is to deny the religious resources of
    ideas and convictions about human dignity,
    freedom, equality, and justice which provide
    seeds for such a critique.

In this third point, we glimpse "the strange
paradox which constitutes the kernel of the problem--
the paradox that a critique of religion as ideology is
never as strong and radical as when it is furthered by
faith as utopia" (25).

In contrast to Marx, Ricoeur thinks that faith may
also be described as ideology in a positive sense. In
a theory of culture, an ideology is a construct which
provides "a blueprint for the organization of social
and psychical processes" (26). With Geertz, Ricoeur
sees that religion may be described as a cultural system with a number of components. First, it is a system
of symbols acting and interacting. Such symbols in
system bring about motives and moods which create a
world of existence which appears to be fact and

uniquely real.   In this way a cosmic world view and an
ethical attitude are integrally linked.   One has, not
only a way of understanding existence, but of enduring
suffering in a meaningful context.

The place of authority in such a cultural system
is crucial.   Insofar as authority uses religious
imagery or system to support its own power as primary,
it is on the edge at least of distortion.   But there is
an implicit paradox because religion is never merely
political.   It always includes dimensions of the cosmic, historical, and ethical, as well as the deeply
personal.   It is a model of a world view, but also a
model for how to change.   The first is more what we
consider ideological, the second more what we see as
utopian.

Depending, then, on our point of view and our
level of analysis, we may think of faith as an ideology
or as a utopia, or as partaking of both, in either a
negative or positive sense relating to the conditions
of faith being analyzed.   Jesus' sayings, actions, and
parables as signs of the kingdom were a threat to the
prevailing ideology insofar as they opened new possibility, a new way of seeing, a new world, and therefore
a utopia.   Christianity thereby may be seen as both
ideology and utopia.

But it is the imagination which constitutes both
ideology and utopia.   It is only in the tension between
the two, in the essential conflict, that we can read
the work of creative imagination.   It is only in recognizing the power of ideology that we can comprehend the
image of who we are.   But it is in the power of utopia
that we recognize the possibility of the image being
other than what it now is.

Christian faith is most often perceived as
ideology or utopia, or as partaking of the tension and
conflict between the two.   But Ricoeur sees faith as
rooted much deeper than this.

> Why? because its ultimate constitution
> is the denial of the dichotomy itself:
> As the Remembrance of some epoch-making
> events--the Exodus and the Resur-
> rection--it shares something with the
> positive concept of ideology.   As the
> Expectation of the Kingdom to come it
> shares something with the positive
> concept of utopia.   Even at the level

> of its literary genres it connects the
> Narrative which makes sense of the past
> and the Prophecy which shatters all
> security grounded in the past. The
> root of faith is somewhere near that
> point where Expectation springs forth
> out of Memory (28).

In this way, faith constantly calls to healing the
broken aspects of both ideology and utopia. It recognizes that ideology gives pattern, consolidation, and
order to action within a society. While ideology con-
serves in both the good and bad senses of the word, it
can also distort. While its symbols provide legitimation, at the same time they can be used to preserve the
power of a group or the dominance of a particular
authority. On the other hand, utopia constantly calls
to the possibility of new worlds and thereby tends to
be subversive of the prevailing social constructs.

CHAPTER FOUR

Faith and Interpretation

What is interpretation? To interpret is to offer
an explanation, to clarify, to translate. We are always involved with interpreting. We interpret our own
actions: why did I do that? We interpret one person's
actions to another: he didn't mean to hurt you. We
interpret the meaning of a textbook, a newspaper, or a
magazine. The meaning is not clear. We try to make it
clearer.

How is faith connected with interpretation? In a
way, everything we have said thus far about faith pertains to interpretation. Religion, philosophy, language, ideology are all related to the problem of how
we interpret things and events. Here we will look
specifically at Ricoeur's developing theory of interpretation, but confining our study to some specific
relationships with faith. A fuller development of his
theory of interpretation will be saved for the last
part of the book.

Faith, Validation, and Verification

Pilate asked, "What is truth?" But long before
that and continuing long after, we still ask the question. Most persons think of truth as that which has
some correspondence with reality, but that raises the
questions: What is reality? How do we know what is
real? How truthfully can we or do we communicate that
reality? These are questions Ricoeur continues to
wrestle with. They are perennial questions for
philosophy and for faith.

It would be desirable to begin a
meditation on truth with a celebration

of unity. The truth does not contradict itself,
falsehood is legion. The truth brings people together,
falsehood scatters them and sets discord among them.
But it is not possible to begin in this way. The One
is too distant a reward; it is an evil temptation
(History and Truth, 165).

Ricoeur begins rather with a study of the levels
or orders of truth. In our culture truth at this point
is not one. We speak of the truth of science, of the
truth of the artistic experience, of the moral truth of
someone who is attempting not to deceive, of the testi-
fying truth of the witness in the courtroom. In other
words, we are pluralistic in our attitude toward truth.

In our society we tend to equate the scientific
with the true. "It has been proven scientifically," we
say, with the assumption that thereby truth has been
established. There is no doubt that seeking the truth
is a foundation of experimental science and of experimental method. But such seeking of the truth in the
scientific mode includes several assumptions which need
to be examined. One assumption is that only that which
can be verified by experimental method is true. This
assumption, in turn, is based on the premise that
everything is objectifiable, that everything can be
measured. In other words, the scientific view of truth
grew out of particular world views which prize the
mathematical, which assume speculative and applied
theories about perception and the nature of reality,
which use instruments developed within those theories,
and which apply categories of logic and of analysis
which attempt to preclude other kinds of truth. Implicit within such assumptions is the separation of the
objects perceived from the scientist perceiving. But
if the truth belongs to the objectivity, then how can
the scientist judge the rising of the sun and the tast-
ing of bread and wine? Are these experiences less true
because they are not subjected to scientific analysis?

Science aims to verify its findings, to establish
the truth of its observations through mathematical
formulas which can substantiate the finds and render
them predictable. On the other hand, except in periods
of dogmatic formalism, art seeks for a different kind
of truth, a truth of respect for the materials and
respect for the vision, which is always being made new.
Another kind of truth, moral truth, is the aim, not
only of someone who is trying not to deceive, but it is
the attempt by human beings to assume responsibility
for their growth in knowledge. This is the kind of

truth brought dramatically to the fore recently, precisely in the areas of experimental science. Yes, we acquired sufficient knowledge to make an atomic bomb. But what responsibility corresponds with such knowledge? Yes, we can maintain bodily organs almost indefinitely. But what is our responsibility for the quality which defines human life? Yes, we can create new life in the laboratory. But do we also have the right to patent the process which creates that new life?

 And what of the truth of the witness in the courtroom? We ask that such a witness be faithful to his or her perceived experience. But how do we corroborate that witnessing? By other witnesses if they are available, by scientific verification if that is possible, by proving the avoidance of deliberate or indeliberate deceit, by showing the continuation of a pattern of action or of tradition, but we are still left with the challenge of making a judgement. And we find, to our amazement, that juries still split, and judges' decisions are still reversed.

All of these are examples of interpretation, of interpreting how adequate the truth is to the reality observed. In the case of experimental science, verification by approved methods is primary. In art, ethics, and in the courtroom, we rely more on other kinds of criteria. Verification in the experimental sense may not be possible or even desirable. But we do look for validation, for the proving of the worth of the truth described.

The object of faith as a set of beliefs, is other than the object of experimental science, of art, of ethics. Faith is more akin to the testimony of the witness in the courtroom. The witness describes his or her experience in relationship to certain events within a particular horizon or world view. So does the faithful witness. In contrast to the witness in the courtroom, however, the faithful witness describes a horizon which goes beyond a particular human experience to embrace the universe, the known-unknown, the continually opening out experiences of the limit-situations of human life and death.

All of these orders of truth have polarizing tendencies. They tend to the dogmatic insofar as they pretend to comprehend a totality of the truth. They tend to the problematic insofar as they are open to other orders of truth and to an on-going process of

knowing and validating. Similarly, they aim at unity
both as goal and as fault. They aim at a oneness and
unity of truth, but such a goal, while perhaps laudable
and necessary, capitulates easily to the fault of
short-sightedness, pretension to a unity of truth which
excludes the valid truths of other spheres of human
experience, and which aims at achieving a unity of
truth before it is possible in time.

Given then that we are only on the road toward
truth, we cannot claim that we have the truth. Nevertheless, we can hope that we are within the realm of
truth in our various enterprises. We can hope that we
walk in the truth as we walk in the light. Ricoeur has
outlined some tasks for walking in a spirit of truth.

First is to recognize a complexity correlative to
the various orders of truth. Second is to respect the
autonomy of scientific research where it is applicable.
Third is to avoid personal, institutional, or ideological defense mechanisms. This will then make possible
aiming, fourthly, not necessarily at quantitative probability, but at qualitative probability in the Aristotelian as well as in the contemporary sense.

> As concerns the procedures of
> validation by which we test our
> guesses, I agree with Hirsch that they
> are closer to a logic of probability
> than to a logic of empirical verifica-
> tion. To show that an interpretation
> is more probable in the light of what
> is known is something other than show-
> ing that a conclusion is true. In this
> sense, validation is not verification.
> Validation is an argumentative disci-
> pline comparable to the juridical pro-
> cedures of legal interpretation. It is
> a logic of uncertainty and of qualita-
> tive probability ("The Model of the
> Text," 549).

Such a logic of validation avoids the extremes both of
dogmatism and of skepticism. Like legal verdicts,
though, interpretations are always open to new challenges and new interpretations. Ultimately, however,
the interpretation is validated in the existential
appropriation, which is the power of disclosing a
world.

The fifth task is to rediscover and make new the
Christian view of the unity of truth of the last day.

Keeping ultimate destinies in mind is an excellent way
of avoiding both dogmatism and skepticism. "Perhaps
Christians could then live among the extremest multiplicity of the orders of truth with the hope of 'one
day' comprehending unity just as they would be comprehended by it" (HT, 191).

Last is the task of making the existential
appropriation which discloses a world, which creates
being, which makes new. This is the final test of a
faith which is a commitment, of a witness.

Symbols, Metaphor, and Analogy

Given that there are multiple orders of truth in
our present cultural situations, and that we are seeking for the truth, that we are we hope "in the realm of
truth," and that we strive to develop criteria for
judging truth, the truth of our faith and the truth of
our other human experiences, we still have only touched
the surface in our discussion of the problems of faith
and interpretation. Our studies of faith and language
and of faith and ideology have made clear how easily we
can deceive ourselves, and how difficult it is to interpret.

Three aspects of language have been focal points
for Ricoeur as he has explored the phenomenon of human
beings speaking and communicating: symbol, metaphor,
and analogy. The three are interrelated and are vi-
tally related to any study of faith.

Symbol: In the tradition of faith of the early
fathers of the church, of Augustine, of Aquinas, and of
most writers until the last several hundred years,
symbol or symbolum referred primarily to the Christian
creed, the gathering together, the summary, and the
sign of Christian faith. At the same time, their world
views were such that what we now think of as symbolic
thinking was an implicit part of their perception of
the human reality. With the rise of experimental science, however, such symbolic thinking often came to be
looked upon as less scientific, as so subjective as to
be completely relative, as so allegorical and imaginative as to preclude reality.

While he carefully follows a rational method of
study and description, Ricoeur is nevertheless continually concerned with the symbol and with symbolic language. The symbol signifies one thing, but at the same

time it also signifies something else. Ricoeur has
studied carefully and continues to draw on, besides his
original study of symbol in Jaspers, three major areas
of symbol analysis. The first is that developed by
Freud in his analysis of dreams; the second is that of
poetics, considered here as the study of the

> privileged images of a poem, or those
> images that dominate an author's works,
> or a school of literature, or the per-
> sistent figures within which a whole
> culture recognizes itself, or even the
> great archetypal images which humanity
> as a whole--ignoring cultural
> differences--celebrates (Interpretation
> Theory, 53).

Such an understanding of symbol is close to the
third area on which Ricoeur draws in his study of symbol, that used by Mircea Eliade in the study of the
history of religions. Eliade shows how universal is
the use of and perception of such realities as trees,
mountains, sky, water, and fire as pointing to something beyond themselves. But the symbol belongs to too
many fields of research today. The multiple studies
make it difficult to sort through the possible analyses
of symbol.

Besides the problem of proliferation in the study
of symbol, there is another difficulty. This is the
realization that symbol is both linguistic and non-
linguistic.

> Thus psychoanalysis links its symbols
> to hidden psychic conflicts; while the
> literary critic refers to something
> like a vision of the world or a desire
> to transform all language into litera-
> ture; and the historian of religion
> sees in symbols the milieu of manifes-
> tations of the Sacred, or what Eliade
> calls hierophanies (54).

Such richness and difficulties point out the
richness and difficulties of symbol and faith. Faith
is integrally bound with symbols. Symbols are the root
system, the present reality, and the future goal of
faith. Striving to clarify symbol, then, is an important task related to faith.

Metaphor: As his studies of symbol developed,
Ricoeur came at the same time to a new appreciation of

the importance of metaphor. It seems that to clarify a
theory of metaphor is a way to work toward the clarification of the complexity of symbols. In the tradition
which stems from Aristotle, metaphor is understood as a
figure of speech which transfers a term from one object
to another in order to make an implicit comparison.
For example, we can say that a cloud is the glory of
God. We transfer the characteristics we perceive in a
cloud to what we perceive as the glory of God. This is
usually referred to as the substitution theory of
metaphor.

Following English and American literature critics,
Ricoeur has developed a theory of metaphor based rather
on the idea of metaphor as a "semantic innovation,"
that is, a verbal making-new, a verbal or meaning
creation.

> [A metaphor] only exists in the moment
> of invention. Lacking any status in
> established language, a metaphor is in
> the strong sense of the word, an event
> of discourse (64).

Metaphor makes use of a tensive or tension use of
language in order to express a tensive or tension concept of reality (68). In other words, our language is
ultimately inadequate to our experience. Much of our
experience, particularly in areas related to faith, is
paradoxical experience. How do we explain the paradox
of our perception of a tree as "a biological reality"
and also as a symbol of the numinous, the Other? Such
paradox is a tension and it pushes our language to a
tension which is expressed in metaphor. "The heavens
tell the glory of God."

> Metaphors are just the linguistic
> surface of symbols, and they owe their
> power to relate the semantic surface to
> the presemantic surface in the depths
> of human experience to the two-
> dimensional structure of the symbol
> (69).

In other words, we experience in the human situation
birth or death, sickness or health, joy or sorrow,
insight or darkness. We are experiencing the structure
of the symbol which points in at least two directions:
to the process of that which we are going through and
at the same time to the meaning which we are giving to
the experience. We experience the tension of the

double thrust: the given of what we are experiencing
and the meaning we are creating out of the experience.
We try to bring this to language, and stumble with the
effort at metaphor.   "It was like going through a tunnel and coming out into the light."   "I was in the
pits."   "I was soaring."

Faith experience is always stumbling with
metaphor.   "I heard him in the still small voice" (1
Kings 19.12).   We take the images of human experience:
images of desert, of journey, of marriage, of love, of
friendship, of banquet, and we predicate them of an
experience which somehow is not desert, journey, marriage, love, friendship, or banquet.   Yet we have no
other language.   We draw on our own experience, vicari-
ous and otherwise.   We draw on the experience of
others, different in time and place.   We draw on the
traditions of which we are part.   And we try to articulate our metaphors, which are inadequate to what we
want to say, but which help clarify and define the
experience, and which give a linguistic life to the
experience.

Analogy: But are there really similarities
between what we experience and what we describe?   This
too is an old question for Western thought, but it is
one being made new in Ricoeur's developing theory.

Aristotle had developed a theory of analogy which
Aquinas used to develop a theory of analogy in relationship to faith.   This theory was too easily misinterpreted in the development of a natural theology and
often became a rationalistic description of the attributes of God and a loss of the idea of the Totally
Other.   We are always tempted to try to bring God down
to our size.

But what is analogy?   It is the statement of a
correspondence of a proportionality between one thing
and another.   There are some similarities between this
object and that one.   In his efforts to speak of God,
Aquinas speaks of two kinds of proportionality: the
one by attribution, the other transcendental.   In the
first we attribute to God qualities we know from our
human experience.   We attribute them symbolically of
God.   So we say that God is a rock or a lion.   We pick
out some aspects of our experience of rock or lion--
solidness or strength, for example--and we say this
symbolically or analogically of God.

The other kind of analogy is transcendental.   In
traditional philosophy the transcendentals include

"being," "good," "truth," "beauty." According to
Aquinas these include no defect and are not dependent
on matter for their existence, and therefore only they
can be properly attributed to God. But such a statement is easily subject to misinterpretation. Although
the transcendentals are phrased as positive attributes,
and although they denote something of which we know--
that is, we have some glimpse of what we mean by goodness or truth--essentially we are saying what we do not
know. Perhaps we have some glimpse of a person who is
good, but we can only imagine what we mean by goodness.
We have some idea of what we mean to say that a statement is true. But we are like "blind lions in the
desert searching for water" when we try to imagine what
we mean by truth. Yet, according to Aquinas, insofar
as we define good as the absence of evil, God must be
good. He cannot be evil. Insofar as we define the
true as that which is not false, God must be true. In
other words, what we know of God is negative knowledge.
Essentially, we only know what he is not because our
imagination and our experience cannot reach far enough.
We are, after all, creatures.

> "All names applied metaphorically to
> God are applied to creatures primarily
> rather than to God, because when said
> of God they mean only similitudes to
> such creatures." Metaphor indeed is
> based upon "similarity of proportion";
> its structure is the same in poetic and
> in biblical discourse. The examples
> given prove this: to call a meadow
> laughing and God a lion is to use the
> same sort of transposition--the meadow
> is pleasing when it is in flower, just
> as a man is when he laughs. By the
> same token, "God manifests strength in
> His works as a lion in his." In both
> cases the meaning of the names issues
> from the domain from which they are
> borrowed. On the other hand, the name
> is said primarily of God, not of the
> creature, when we are dealing with
> names that aim at his essence: thus
> goodness, wisdom. The split, there-
> fore, does not separate poetry from
> biblical language, but these two modes
> of discourse taken together form theo-
> logical discourse (Rule of Metaphor,
> 278-279).

But, given this insight, Aquinas's view of
metaphor is limited by his world view which precludes
the insights from language studies available to us in
this century. Making use of those language studies,
Ricoeur has formulated an enlarged view of metaphor
which provides a framework for asking the questions in
a modern world.

Ricoeur reminds us that our manner of being in the
world is characterized by a symbolism that seems basic
to us as human beings. Such a symbolism "presides over
the most primitive metaphorical order" (IT, 65). In
other words, we are placed in space and time. While we
are on this earth, we speak of above and below. We are
absolutely dependent on the orientation of the sun.
Its rising and falling are for us a rising and falling.
We are subject to basic experiences of wind, fire,
water, house, journey. Such symbolic experience calls
us to the work of creating meaning through the creation
of metaphor which appropriately brings to language at
least some aspects of that symbolic experience. Insofar as that experience relates to the object of what we
call faith, we can speak of symbolic experience and
faith, and the creation of meaning in faith.

Faith and a Developing Theory of Interpretation

Two factors related to faith have assumed a
dominant importance in Ricoeur's developing theory of
interpretation: revelation and testimony. They are
concepts foreign to most philosophers but ones that,
for Ricoeur, are not only proper but necessary for
consideration. Ricoeur recognizes what difficult problems the two concepts pose for philosophers, but he is
willing to work toward an understanding.

Revelation: The term revelation is clouded with a
history of various interpretations. One such interpretation is that of revelation as authoritarian and
opaque. This is opposed to a "concept of reason which
claims to be its own master and transparent to itself"
("Toward a Hermeneutic of the Idea of Revelation," 1),
a concept held by most philosophers. Ricoeur's goal is
to recover an idea of revelation and an idea of reason
that may be, not identical, but in dialectic in such a
way as to bring forth an understanding of faith.

The authoritarian concept of faith includes,
according to Ricoeur, three levels of language, although these are not usually differentiated in the

discussion. The first is the level of the confession
of faith, the avowal or the telling of one's faith as a
believer. The second level is that of church dogma, in
which a particular community "interprets for itself and
for others the understanding of faith specific to its
tradition; and third, the body of doctrines imposed by
the magisterium as the rule of orthodoxy." According
to Ricoeur the discourse of faith of the confessing
community loses its flexibility insofar as it succumbs
to the rigidity of a dogmatic tradition associated only
with one kind of theological discourse, particularly as
that is imposed by a ruling and authoritarian magisterium. While the second and third levels are necessary tasks for a faith community, they are subordinate
to and dependent on the first level, that of the discourse of faith, that of the level where the faith
originates. The philosopher may learn much from an
analysis of this level of discourse, particularly from
"the believer who seeks to understand himself or herself through a better understanding of the texts of his
or her faith" (2). Especially is an analysis of such
discourse helpful because it has such a variety of
expressions as provided in the writings which belong to
the Jewish and Christian scriptures. As Ricoeur analyzes these varieties of discourse, he finds, not a
monolithic view of revelation, but one that is pluralistic, many-leveled in the meanings communicated, and
analogical.

     The primary form of faith discourse for Ricoeur is
the prophetic, that belonging to the prophetic movements of the Hebrew Bible. The prophet claims to
speak, not in his or her own name, but in the name of
Yahweh. In such an example of revelation we may think
of the prophet and Yahweh as authors both of the spoken
and of the written word, or as one voice behind another, usually referred to as inspiration. This is too
narrow a view of revelation: an idea of the scriptures
as dictated. Such a view is also too narrowly linked
to the future, since much of classic prophecy is involved with predicting what is to come.

     Prophetic discourse is in tension with another
kind of discourse which predominates in the scriptures:
that of narrative, the telling of a story, an account
describing the unfolding of events. This genre characterizes much of the Pentateuch as well as the synoptic
Gospels and the Book of Acts. What can we say of revelation in narrative discourse? Yes, someone or some
persons are telling the story, but such narrators disappear before the power of the events being described.

Much more attention is given to the primary actor in
the events, Yahweh, the one who is perceived as leading
and guiding the events. Instead of speaking, then, of
a double author as we might in prophetic discourse, we
are confronted with double actors--Yahweh and those
about whom the story is told--and a double object of
the story: the intentions of Yahweh in salvation history and the intentions, positive or negative, of those
involved in making that history.

    Such narratives communicate an idea of revelation
in that the events are described as marking the beginning of an epoch. Such are the events of the exodus
and of the resurrection. These events are then "transcendent in relation to the ordinary course of history"
(5). They describe Yahweh in the third person: Yahweh
brought us out of Egypt with a mighty hand (Deut.
26.8), but easily move to an invocation of Yahweh as
second person: Here then I bring the first fruits . .
. that you, Yahweh, have given me (Deut. 26.10). The
believers' faith statements, then, take place through
narration. In fact, "God's mark is in history before
being in speech" (6). The events happen and then are
brought into the speech-acts of narration. The events
of history provide a realism for the word events as
well as incorporating prophecy within the narratives.

    But there is a tension between the prophetic
discourse and the narrative discourse. Prophecy an-
nounces the terror of the last day and thereby offers
the possibility of shattering history. Since revelation is involved in both discourses, revelation is
involved in a similar tension: thrust between the
security of the account of the founding events and the
threat by the prophet that all can fall apart, that
reason does not hold, that only hope can hold together
the founding belief and the future. "A gulf of nothingness separates the new creation from the old" (8).
Such a tension allows for no simplistic idea of provi-
dence or the design of God.

    The third kind of faith discourse which Ricoeur
considers is that incorporated within the Hebrew concept of Torah. Although the word is usually translated
as "law," such a translation is often misleading.
Torah first of all is incorporated within the founding
events of the exodus from Egypt, of the liberation of
the people. "The memory of deliverance qualifies the
instruction in an intimate way. The Decalogue is the
Law of a redeemed people" (9). Such a law is characterized by a relationship of covenant, unfolding within

a dynamism that is historical, and which calls for a
transformation into love: You shall love Yahweh with
all your heart (Deut. 6.5). Such a love is continually
being made new. As the prophets before him, Jesus
describes the Law and the Prophets as summed up in the
torah from Deuteronomy: So always treat others as you
would like them to treat you; that is the meaning of
the Law and the Prophets (Matt. 7.12). Such an idea of
prescriptive discourse brings an ethical dimension to
the concept of revelation. Such a revelation is a call
to the human will:

> If we continue to speak of revelation
> as historical, it is not only in the
> sense that the trace of God may be read
> in the founding events of the past or
> in a coming conclusion to history, but
> in the sense that it orients the
> history of our practical actions and
> engenders the dynamics of our institu-
> tions (11).

Wisdom is the fourth kind of discourse which is
vehicle for the idea of revelation. Although we can
speak of a characteristic wisdom literature, that of
which the psalms and proverbs are part, wisdom transcends all forms of discourse. It communicates the art
of living well, the way to happiness. Wisdom confronts
human being in those limit situations of solitude, of
evil, suffering, and death, where human being is faced
with great misery and with great possibility. In
Hebrew wisdom the seeming annihilation of human being
can be at the same time the manifestation of the incomprehensibility of God. Wisdom faces head-on the questions of the injustice of the suffering of human being,
the questions of the sense or senselessness of human
existence. Wisdom does not give the answer, but does
propose models for or ways of journeying through, or
enduring. It shows us how to place suffering and
senselessness into a meaningful context of hope,
whether through the model of the suffering servant of
Isaiah's songs, the model of Job, or the model of Jesus
on the cross giving a new spirit.

> Wisdom was personified into a
> transcendent feminine figure. She is a
> divine reality that has always existed
> and that will always exist. She lives
> with God and she has accompanied crea-
> tion from its very beginning. Intimacy
> with Wisdom is not to be distinguished
> from intimacy with God (13).

Thus wisdom discourse brings multiple qualities to
the concept of revelation which Ricoeur is developing:
qualities of ways of living through human suffering and
senselessness, qualities of a transcending hope, and
qualities of an intimacy with God.

Hymnic discourse is a fifth kind of speech event
found in the texts of the Hebrew and Christian scriptures. Hymns of praise, of petition, and of thanksgiv-
ing belong to the psalms, as well as to other songs
found throughout the Bible. In wisdom discourse we
recognize "a hidden God who takes as his mask the anonymous and non-human course of events" (14). In the
hymns we predicate a second relationship: We praise
you, O Lord. Revelation, then, "is this very formation
of our feelings that transcends their everyday, ordinary modalities" (15).

In summary, Ricoeur says that an interpretation of
revelation must give first place to these forms of
religious discourse that are at the origin of the
Hebrew or Christian experience. Revelation cannot be
limited to such propositions as "God exists." On the
contrary, revelation is precisely in the diverse forms
of discourse or speech-event as those described above.
This means that revelation is on many levels and takes
many forms. In no way is it dominated by a comprehensive knowledge. The opposite is the case: "the idea
of something secret is the limit-idea of revelation.
. . . The God who reveals himself is a hidden God and
hidden things belong to him" (17).

> The confession that God is infinitely
> above human thoughts and speech, that
> he guides us without our comprehending
> his ways, that the fact that human
> beings are an enigma to themselves even
> obscures the clarity that God communi-
> cates to them--this confession belongs
> to the idea of revelation. The one who
> reveals himself is also the one who
> conceals himself (17-18).

How can philosophy respond to such a multi-leveled
concept of revelation as that described above? It can
reject it, of course, as inappropriate for a method
which emphasizes reason. But this is to bracket from
philosophy a large segment of human experience and to
imply in philosophy, not a strength, but a weakness
that has no tools to use in analyzing a large body of
records of human experience and reflection. A more

responsible view, in Ricoeur's thinking is to recognize
such levels of revelation as "an appeal which does not
force one to accept its message" (19).

Ricoeur is not advocating a rational theology in
the old sense of providing proofs for the existence of
God or of reducing biblical insights to rational statements. He seeks rather a truth that can be spoken of
in terms of manifestation rather than verification.
Here the philosopher, or any human being, must free
himself or herself from the arrogance of the pretension
to complete and independent self-consciousness. The
philosopher stands before the experiences of manifestation and dependence, not necessarily in relationship to
a concept of God, but as experiences integral to the
record of human beings.

Unlike Merleau-Ponty or Husserl who analyzed the
experience of being-in-the-world, and unlike Heidegger
who emphasized the human quality of angst, Ricoeur for
his analysis will use the idea of a text such as a
psalm or a parable as a manifestation of a world of
being. A parable reveals a world, a way of existing.
It projects, not only what is, but what can be. Such
writings are examples of poetic discourse. Poetic
discourse is used here, not in a way which is confined
to what we think of as a poem, but in the sense derived
from Aristotle. Ricoeur calls this the revelatory
function of poetic discourse (22).

> My deepest conviction is that poetic
> language alone restores to us that
> participation-in or belonging to an
> order of things which precedes our
> capacity to oppose ourselves to things
> taken as objects opposed to a subject.
> Hence the function of poetic discourse
> is to bring about this emergence of a
> depth-structure of belonging-to amid
> the ruins of descriptive discourse
> (24).

Poetic discourse here, of course, is not confined
to the poem. Because it makes a new world, the world
of the text, it is larger than--it escapes--the limited
horizon of the original author and the original audience. It is also a work, a particularized creation
inherent in the particular genre such as those described earlier. It assumes a referential function.
That is, it refers to a way of being in the world.
This is precisely a kind of revelation, though not

necessarily in a religious sense. It is, however, in
harmony with the concept of religious revelation developed by Ricoeur. In other words, in both cases, truth
is manifestation. One doesn't try to prove a poem,
although one can validate its effectiveness. The dis-
tinctness of the religious discourse of the Bible is
the particular reference or set of references which it
creates. We speak of the text opening a new world, a
new creation, a new convenant, the kingdom of God. How
does one respond to such a creation? Ricoeur explores
this problem through an analysis of testimony.

   Testimony: In the philosophic traditions of which
Husserl is a part, the assumption of Descarte's "I
think, therefore I am" takes for granted the primacy of
human consciousness in meaning. This "pretension of
consciousness to constitute itself is the most formida-
ble obstacle to the idea of revelation" (30). It is
analogous to the absolutizing of the scientific method
to verify reality. Ricoeur's emphasis on interpretation brings about a movement of conversion which is the
exact opposite of such pretension. It calls for consciousness to abandon its "pretension to constitute
every signification in and beginning from itself."

   Such a criticism and such a call rest on ideas
developed at length by Ricoeur in his unfolding interpretation theory: 1) Consciousness is always mediated
by a universe of signs: the ideas, works, actions, and
institutions which objectify our consciousness. 2)
Such a mediation sets up a relationship of participation or belonging-to in which reflection is of a second
order, in the sense that we can never fully step outside of that world of which we are a part. 3) In such
a world the signs are texts: writings and works. We
are called therefore to understand ourselves before the
text.

          To understand oneself before the text
          is not to impose one's own finite capac-
          ity of understanding on it, but to
          expose oneself to receive from it a
          larger self which would be the proposed
          way of existing that most appropriately
          responds to the proposed world of the
          text (30).

   The concept of the world of the text is non-
historical or transhistorical. The idea of testimony
gives an absolute character to a moment of history. It
brings to the world of the text the quality of

historical contingency. What do we mean by <u>absolute</u>?
That which is complete, finished, free, no longer relative or conditioned.

The concept of testimony rests on the idea of the
givenness of reality, an affirmation of that reality at
our originating point, and a stripping of the self, or
a letting go, an abandonment, a surrender of oneself to
the fullness of that reality. Testimony, then, is
understood as an account of the experience of the absolute, of this fullness of reality.

> Only testimony that is singular in each
> instance confers the sanction of
> reality on ideas, ideals, and ways of
> being that the symbol depicts to us and
> which we uncover as our ownmost possi-
> bilities (32-33).

But testimony needs to be tested. It requires
interpretation as well as a discernment between false
testimony and true testimony. It calls for a "dialectic of the witness and the things seen" (33). Such a
dialectic has three moments: 1) the dialectic of event
and meaning:

> We exist because we are seized by those
> events that happen to us in the strong
> sense of this word--such and such en-
> tirely fortuitous encounters, dramas,
> happinesses or misfortunes that . . .
> have completely changed the course of
> our existence. The task of understand-
> ing ourselves through them is the task
> of transforming the accidental into our
> destiny. The event is our master.
> Each of our separate existences here
> are like those communities we belong
> to--we are absolutely dependent on
> certain founding events. They are not
> events that pass away, but events that
> endure. In themselves, they are event-
> signs. To understand ourselves is to
> continue to attest and to testify to
> them (34-35).

2) The second moment is the dialectic of true and
false testimony. Here we look for those most eminent
witnesses of the truth, for the testimony of those
persons whose words, deeds, and lives most predicate
the "divine," the fullness of reality, a glimpse of the
whole.

3) The dialectic of historical testimony is the third moment of the dialectic of the witness and the things seen. Historical testimony provides a presentation of what in reflection remains only an idea. The idea of civil rights was made present by the life of Martin Luther King, Jr., particularly since his witness was a testimony unto death. In such an historical presentation the meaning is never exhausted.

We are called, then, by the testimony of truth as manifestation and by revelation as appeal, not to submit our will in servitude, but to open our imagination to the possible. The poetics of the Exodus and the poetics of the Resurrection are addressed precisely to our imaginations as a call to open ourselves to a fullness of reality of which our finiteness by itself is incapable but which we can make our own by appropriating dimensions of reality larger than ourselves. Such is the power of testimony and of revelation.

PART III. RICOEUR
AND THE CHRISTIAN TRADITION

CHAPTER ONE

The Christian Context

Although Ricoeur is neither exegete nor theologian, his life and his work have always been basically within the Christian tradition. Whether it is the working out of his philosophical anthropology, his reflections on evil, his study of faith, or his involvement in Christianisme social, his context is primarily the western European reform tradition of Christianity. Nevertheless, this context is always in tension with Ricoeur's philosophic tradition rooted in the pre-Christian world of Greece, allied with Christianity for centuries, and then fragmented into the variety of philosophic schools present today, representing both those which are sympathetic to Christianity or other religious expressions as well as those which deny or scorn the validity of religious experience. What are some of the ways in which Ricoeur's writing reflects his interaction with the Christian tradition?

The Christian Context: Early Reflection

The tradition of Christianity and the historical events of France in the twentieth century are two of the "givens" for Ricoeur's life and work. Family religious roots in Brittany, acceptance of church as institution, the trauma of World War I, the transitional seeds for upheaval planted and sprouted during the 1920's, the prison experience of World War II, the pain and excitement of post-war rebuilding of society and of faith, the disillusionment and tensions of the late 50's and 60's--all these are context for Ricoeur's reflections. In his early volume History and Truth, Ricoeur included a number of essays explicitly Christian, knowing that he was making a decision which other

philosophers would reject, but which his own
authenticity required. These essays reflect some of
the concerns which claimed his attention and which
foreshadow later developments.

Christianity and History: Contradiction or Paradox?

> Faith in meaning, but in a meaning
> hidden from history, is . . . both the
> courage to believe in a profound sig-
> nificance of the most tragic history
> (and therefore a feeling of confidence
> and resignation in the very heart of
> conflict) and a certain rejection of
> system and fanaticism, a sense of the
> open (HT, 96).

History, our story as human beings, is interpreted
in many ways. We think of it as one, yet at the same
time, we know it is multiple and exceedingly varied.
Because we are moving on in time, because we are creating events, artifacts, and meaning, we have fashioned
the idea of progress: we are stepping along, we are
moving from one level or place to another.

But on reflection, we know how ambiguous such a
concept is. We have seen the rise and fall of civilizations. We see the apparently senseless suffering and
death of millions of individuals, indeed of whole nations. The Greeks and other ancient peoples were faced
with the same ambiguity. Is the story cyclical or
linear? Does it have meaning or is it absurd?

Out of their journeys and struggles, the Hebrew
people developed a view of their story which holds the
ambiguity in tension. Events of history become sacred
moments of their relationship with their God: In the
beginning God created, but human beings rebelled from
such creation and began their wanderings in search of
wholeness and salvation. Nevertheless, God constantly
followed them, making covenant, leading them from slav-
ery to liberation, calling them through his word. For
Christians the event of Christ's death/resurrection
added new dimensions: new creation, new covenant, new
liberation, new word, new history.

> In light of these exceptional events,
> human beings were made aware of those
> aspects of their own experience which
> they did not know how to interpret.

> Their own lives were also made up of
> events and decisions and marked off by
> important alternatives: to rise up in
> rebellion or to be converted, to lose
> life or to gain it . . . history ac-
> quired meaning, but it was concrete
> history in which something happens, in
> which people themselves have a per-
> sonality which may also be lost or won
> (84-85).

The Christian believes in salvation. "Faith in
the Lordship of God dominates the entire view of history" (93). But this is a faith interwoven with the
ambiguity of the unfolding of events. It is a faith
struggling for and creating meaning, but ultimately
dependent on a hope that meaning will make sense on the
"last day." The meaning is always a hidden meaning.
Life is therefore a task, a task of trying to discern
meaning, of creating meaning, of building the new creation, but of also recognizing the mystery. Mystery and
meaning are the warp and woof of human existence. Hope
which grows out of the mystery remains in tension with
the absurdity of our daily experience.

Image of God/Image of Human Being

How we view our history and how we interweave
.mystery and meaning depend on how we view God, human
being, and relationships with others. Ricoeur's developing view has drawn, not only on the Jewish and Christian scriptures, his own experience, and the philosophic tradition of which he is a part, but also on
classic and contemporary theological reflection. The
statement in Genesis--"Let us make human being in our
image and likeness"--has provided food for thought for
thousands of years. What does it mean to be made in
the image of God? What or who is this God whose image
we reflect?

> What . . . if we should see the image
> of God not as an imposed mark but as
> the striking power of human creativity;
> if we treat it not as the residual
> trace of a craftsman who has abandoned
> his work to the ravages of time, but as
> a continuous act in the creative move-
> ment of history and duration?
> (110-111).

Such a view is not limited to meditation and emphasis on the individual. On the contrary, the individual is human being only in the context of all human beings, only in the context of the epic of human being as image of God. Such a comprehensive view sees creation continuing even in the midst of great evil and by means of continuing grace, gift, and new creation.

For some Jewish people, the experience of the holocaust was so horrendous that one can no longer think of God as possible. For other Jewish people, the experience of holocaust was equally searing and plunged them into depths of evil and mystery previously unimagined; nevertheless, somehow there is hope; somehow there is God.

For many Christians and also for many philosophers the holocaust or other traumatic experiences led to the conclusion that in the face of such evil, God is not possible. But for many others, including Ricoeur, the experience led to a new depth of faith:

> If Irenaeus and Tertullian included evil and grace in a vision of creation, it is because Christ was for them the path, in the creation of human being, from evil to grace, the restarting of creation, the renewal of the image of God . . . . "Because of his immense love he became what we are so that he might make us become what he is himself" . . . . [Such is] an _epical_ sense of our personal existence situated again within the perspective of a vaster epic of humankind and creation (112).

That broader perspective includes human being as one and many, individual and collective. What does such a perspective say about relationships? Is a relationship of neighbor possible in such an epic view?

Who Is My Neighbor?

Jesus was asked the same question: Who is my neighbor? How shall I treat other human beings? As was his custom, he answered this question too with a story: A man when down from Jerusalem to Jericho and

fell among robbers (Luke 10.30+). It seems that I make
myself one's neighbor by compassion, by encounter, by
making myself present to the other, by helping.

But the good news according to Matthew presents a
paradox: Come, blessed of my Father. . . . For I was
hungry and you gave me to eat. . . . The just will
answer him. . . . Lord, when did we see you hungry and
feed you? . . . As long as you did it to one of these
my least brethren, you did it to me (Matt. 25.31+).

> The object of this primordial behavior
> is called one of the "least," the man
> who has no leading role in history. He
> is merely the supernumerary providing
> the amount of suffering necessary to
> the grandeur of the true "historic"
> events. . . . He is the private first
> class without whom the great generals
> would miss their strokes of genius as
> well as their tragic errors. He is the
> laborer doing monotonous and repetitive
> work without which the great powers
> could not construct modern industrial
> equipment. He is the "displaced per-
> son," a pure victim of great conflicts
> and great revolutions (100).

In contrast to the directness of the story of the Good
Samaritan, this saying describes an indirectness of
relationship, a meaning and a history which are hidden.
But both of these are contrary to the accepted behavior
in much of modern society, particularly as that behavior is affected by our institutions. The Christian,
then, seeks to elaborate a "theology of the neighbor"
(103) which will embrace both aspects of relationship
which Jesus referred to, and yet which will not deny
the reality of social institutions.

> It is with the same emotion that I love
> my children and take an active interest
> in juvenile delinquency. The first
> love is intimate and subjective albeit
> exclusive; the second is abstract but
> has a wider scope. I am not discharged
> of all responsibility to other children
> by simply loving my own. I cannot
> escape others, for although I do not
> love them as my own or as individuals,
> still I love them in a certain collec-
> tive and statistical manner. . . . It

        is the same charity which gives meaning
        to the social institution and to the
        event of the encounter (103).

    Why, then, do institutions often become so
dehumanizing? Why is the person they are intended to
serve often their victim? Why does it seem so easy for
institutions to be perverted?

    Ricoeur appreciates the complexity of modern
institutions. There is no point in condemning
machines, technology, government administrations in
themselves. Rather, he points out that institutions
have the potential for inherent fault, inherent evil,
built into the nature of the institution itself. By
reason of their striving to be objective, they tend to
make objects of those they are trying to serve. Tasks
become fragmented, monotonous. There is psychic and
physical frustration. Administration tends to become
separated from those being ministered to. Thus relationships become abstract, removed. By reason of their
complexity, institutions breed power, a power too
easily corrupted, too easily removed from those it
should serve.

    "The theme of the neighbor is . . . an appeal to
the awakening of consciousness" (107). It provides a
continuing critique of social relationships and of the
relationships in institutions. The mystery is that we
seldom if ever really know the effect we have on persons whether in the one-to-one encounter or through the
channels of institutions. We are called to be neighbor; to act with love, and to act with justice. But
this is a call which touches a span of history ultimately incomprehensible. Christianity offers a continuing hope for the possibility of acting with love
and with justice, whether in the one-to-one relationship with neighbor or in the more complex relationships
through the institutions of our cultures.

CHAPTER TWO

Evil--The Unsolvable Problem

Evil is radical--it is at our roots. In the
twentieth century we are somewhat overwhelmed with the
evil around us: continuing wars, famine, oppression,
nuclear armament, breakdown in social relationships,
our own temptations and proclivity toward non-being.
For Ricoeur, not only his roots in the reform tradition, but also his experience of war and of the consequences of war--holocaust, displaced persons, colonial-
ism, disorientation--raised the problem of evil to a
key place as a human, philosophic, and religious question. What is evil? What is the relationship of evil
to a philosophy of the will? What is the Christian
experience of evil? The questions will not be answered, but they can be explored for a better understanding of the human situation.

In the earlier work Fallible Man, Ricoeur explored
the question of the possibility of evil, the fallibility of human being. In the next volume The Symbolism of Evil, he explores the problem of fault. What do
we mean when we say, "It is my fault"? What is the
phenomenon of the experience of feeling guilt?

The book is in two parts, the first concerned with
the elementary symbols of defilement, sin, and guilt,
the second with four types of myth of the beginning and
of the end.

The Primary Symbols: Defilement, Sin, Guilt

These three make up the cycle of the primary
symbols of evil. Since an understanding of the symbolization which begins with defilement can show the
growth of conscience, it is helpful to analyze each of

these three symbols, as well as the relationships of
one with the other.

1) <u>Defilement</u>. What is defilement? Because it is
a symbol, an attempt to reduce its meaning to words
will necessarily limit the richness it contains; nevertheless, the symbol gives rise to thought. At first
sight, defilement is a view of consciousness which
belongs to primitive human being, which we have left
behind, and which is therefore distant from us (SE,
26). The sense of defilement is experienced as ethical
terror, as dread, which comes as a result of a connection perceived between defilement and an anticipated
vengeance. In this view, defilement brings about its
own vengeance, even before it is attributed to a god or
to a "natural order." The perceived sequence of defilement, vengeance, and suffering places the physical
order within the ethical, and therefore, it is assumed
that rites of purification can prevent suffering. Both
the Babylonian and the Hebrew Job testify to the attempts to separate the physical world of suffering from
the ethical order. But such a separation is costly,
because then suffering, that universal human reality,
becomes inexplicable. If one cannot blame the gods, or
a disruption of a "natural order," who shall be blamed?

Another view of defilement is the symbol of stain.
Defilement was never literally a stain, a dirtiness.
Lady Macbeth had washed the blood off her hands, but
still continued to wash them. Stain is a symbol of
evil, the symbolic expression of a human reality experienced. In the same way, ablution is never merely a
washing. Obviously, there are psychological and sociological explanations too of these experiences, but they
should not undermine or rule out the importance of
understanding the symbolic structure involved (39).

2) <u>Sin</u>. How does the second symbol, sin, differ
from the first one, defilement? The difference is
phenomenological, rather than historical. In spatial
terminology, sin moves the experience more within the
consciousness. For a relationship of contact in space,
there is substituted a relationship of orientation in
which is discerned a relationship with a god. If the
god is absent, he or she is replaced by the attack of
demons. The evil is experienced as within the body,
even in the muscles and the tendons.

Ricoeur here distinguishes within the Hebrew
tradition five categories or types of such an experience as that which is symbolized by sin. The first is

in the context of the experience of the presence of
Yahweh, the "before God" of the Covenant, the Berit.
This is the governing type or category. In this view,
sin is breaking the covenant.

A second matrix for understanding the symbolism of
sin is the infinite demand voiced by the prophets. To
the "Seek me and live!" and the demands for justice and
righteousness of Amos, Hosea adds the tenderness involved in the metaphor of the conjugal bond. In this
figure, sin is adultery. A tension already glimpsed in
Amos is brought to the fore in Isaiah, but particularly
in Jeremiah and in Ezekiel, a tension between the infinite demand and the finiteness of the command formulated in a law. The latter is always subject to the
false security of legalism. In this context, there are
two opposing directions which the symbolism of sin may
take: that of always falling short of the infinite
demand sounded by the prophets, and that of measuring
sin by a false righteousness in carrying out the law.

In the third category, or the type of the "Wrath
of God," Yahweh's anger is inserted into the expecta-
tion of the "Day of Yahweh." Tied in with the political evolution of Israel, and the unfolding of a
theology of history, the idea of the "Day of Yahweh"
suggests together and alternately the presence and the
distance of the God of Israel. Even the absence of God
is a relationship. The symbolism of sin is then placed
in the context of historical events and their interpretation.

Within contexts such as the above, sin may be
viewed positively or negatively. Some ways of expressing sin as nothingness are: the loss of a bond (in the
relationship of the covenant); missing the target;
being on a tortuous road; rebelling; being lost. In
the Jewish expression of sin, this nothingness was
assimilated to the nothingness of idols. This experience of nothingness was compensated by the motif of
pardon-return.

The concept of sin as something positive perdured
even in the prophets, in spite of their tendency to
"demythologize" in other respects. There is a binding
force of sin, a spirit of wickedness, which cannot be
reduced to the subjective or individual dimension.
This symbolism is countered by the symbolism of redemption: buying back, freeing, liberating. "All our
ideas of salvation, of redemption . . . proceed from
this initial symbol" (93. Translation-modified). What

is to be said of ceremonial rites of expiation? In a
way, they are the praxis, the attempt to objectify, a
mime of the experienced reality. The same symbolisms
are, one might say, dramatized.

3) Guilt. After defilement and sin, the third
primary symbol which Ricoeur examines is guilt. One
may understand guilt by seeing its relationship to the
previous two symbols. In one sense, it is a break from
the others because of its emphasis on the subjective.
Guilt is only possible to a person who is free. Guilt
results from the misuse of freedom. It moves the
remedy for sin from revenge to amendment. Ricoeur
calls this a "revolution in the experience of evil"
(102). But the radical symbol of guilt is not only a
break from the symbols of defilement and sin, in that
it adds a new dimension; it also gives new meaning,
retroactively as it were, to defilement and sin by
incorporating their values within its own. This effects the paradox implicit in the symbol of fault, that
human being is responsible and yet captive, the concept
of the servile will.

This concept of the servile will receives strong
emphasis in Ricoeur's early work. Although the term is
usually associated with Luther's theology of human
being totally sinful, in a broader sense it reflects a
perception of human being as, paradoxically, having a
will, that is, being able to choose, to be free, but at
the same time, being bound, realizing that often, that
which he wills to do, he does not do. For Ricoeur,
then, servile will suggests the radical duality of
willing which human being experiences within the self.

Two results of the subjective aspect of guilt are
that fault can now be regarded as strongly individual
and that guilt has degrees. Thus not only will a person be punished for a wrong, but the punishment will be
proportioned to the wrong. The interaction with the
social imputation of guilt elaborated within the structures of the sacredness of the Greek city, and through
the exile experience of the Hebrews has continued over
the centuries. Punishment for an offense committed
against an explicit law must be exacted.

Another direction of guilt is toward scrupulous-
ness. Ricoeur uses the stereotype of Phariseeism as an
outstanding example of this direction. After an extensive analysis, the dilemma is posed: the basic problem
is that of justification by the law as opposed to justification by grace. This brings to the discourse

another symbol, both enigmatic and fundamental: grace
or justification.

> It is, then, impossible to reflect
> philosophically on fault while omitting
> the fact, embarrassing for reflection,
> that the ultimate meaning of fault
> could be manifested only by means of
> the great contrasts set up by the first
> passionate thinker of Christianity:
> justification by the practice of the
> law and justification by faith; boast-
> ing and believing; works and grace.
> Whatever weakens those contrasts dissi-
> pates their meaning (148).

In other words, for Ricoeur, a consideration of guilt
leads to the questions: how can one avoid guilt, and
how can one restore the integrity destroyed by guilt?
A philosophy which asks these questions is brought to
the concept which the rational tradition of western
philosophy finds embarrassing: the concept of grace,
gift, or justification.

The three primary symbols of the fault, then, move
toward the concept of the servile will, which remains
an indirect concept, and which acquires all its meaning
from the primary symbols. In summary, Ricoeur outlines
a threefold schematism of the servile will, emphasizing:
1) the "positiveness" of evil: in our language, we
say: the Lamb of God takes away the sins of the world;
2) the externality of evil--evil as the "outside" of
man's freedom, symbolized by the outside
influence of the serpent in the Genesis account of the
fall; and 3) evil as infection: the problem of evil is
also within human beings in their very humanity.

The Myths of the Beginning and of the End

After his analysis of the primary symbols arising
from the fault in Part I of The Symbolism of Evil,
Ricoeur proposes an exploration of the myths of the
beginning and of the end. He defines myths as second-
degree symbols which provide a medium for the primary
symbols already described. Although myths are sometimes embarrassing to modern thinkers, Ricoeur is
encouraged to use them for his reflection for two
reasons: 1) Plato set the precedent in recognizing
implicitly that, as symbol, the myth gives rise to
thought; 2) paradoxically, it is only the modern person

who can truly recognize the myth as myth, because
criticism has made it possible to separate history from
myth.

Ricoeur organizes his exploration of myths in
three parts: 1) an introduction affirming the symbolic
function of myths; 2) an elaboration of four types of
myth, those of the drama of creation, of the wicked
god, the Adamic myth, and the myth of the exiled soul,
all situated within a cycle of myths; 3) a conclusion
reiterating that the symbol gives rise to thought.

What is myth? A myth is a narrative embodying
symbols. It cannot be coordinated in time and space in
the sense in which history and geography use those
terms. It is a second degree symbol because, by means
of the persons and events employed, it adds another
dimension to what the primary symbols reveal. Because
it is a kind of symbol, myth is distinguished from
allegory, just as the symbol in general is. After an
allegory is translated, the true meaning is achieved;
the allegory is no longer necessary. This is no more
true of myth than it is of symbol. The myth too is
opaque: it is not reducible to the "clear" language of
science; its meaning is inexhaustible because it is a
language in symbol. Ricoeur's working hypothesis
regarding myth embraces three terms: a concrete universality, a quasi-historical orientation, and an ontological exploration. In the first, experience is
universalized, as when Adam becomes universal man, and
Eve becomes universal woman. Nevertheless, the narrative receives a seemingly temporal quality by an "At
that time," or the equivalent. But both of these aim
at an ontological statement; for example, human beings
are destined for happiness but in the present they feel
alienated.

One of Ricoeur's aims is to separate myth from
gnosis, the specialized knowledge of an elect, initiated group, for gnosis is the constant danger for
myth. The myth is made to supersede reason, while, on
the other hand gnosis is acquired. Ricoeur wishes to
recover myth as myth, before it slips into gnosis, "in
the nakedness and poverty of a symbol that is not an
explanation but an opening up and a disclosure" (165).
Although exceedingly rich with meaning, a symbol paradoxically is poor in its lack of rational explication.
Nevertheless, without the symbol and the myth, a dimension of human experience remains closed and hidden.

Perhaps even more than symbol, myth aims at the
totality. There is a fullness which it tries at least

to touch, but the very reaching makes it subject to
paradox and contradiction. Just as one symbol often
contradicts another, so does one myth often speak the
opposite of that which another poses. In fact, within
even one symbol there is contradiction. The ocean is
both infinite beauty and overwhelming terror. So too,
within one myth there is the tension of unresolvable
conflict. This same attempt to reach a totality accounts for the multiplicity of symbols and of myths.
No matter how great the number of symbols or myths, the
totality of meaning aimed at is never exhausted. Such
a statement, nevertheless, is not a denial of the efforts of Lévi Strauss and of others to define the
structures underlying myths. The structuring of myths
may be similar, but the content is never subject to
reduction.

     1) The myth of the drama of creation. The first
typical myth which Ricoeur examines is the drama of
creation, a ritual vision of the world. Exemplified in
the Sumero-Akkadian theogonic myths, as well as in
those of Homer and Hesiod, the type recounts the victory of order over chaos. The conflict, the victory,
and the generation of the gods was translated, often in
a yearly celebration, by ritual ceremonies, so that
what had once happened cosmically became historicized
within the celebration of the rite. Among the
Babylonians, as well as among others, the historical
King was easily assimilated into the cosmic-historical
conflict; thus order and chaos were translated into
political terms. Ricoeur calls the Hebrew concept of
the King a recessive form of this myth. Following
Mowinckel and Pedersen, he comments on the enthronement
psalms in this context. This form of the myth is
recessive because the Hebrews both historicized and de-
mythologized the myth. The images or symbols are continuous, but what they signify has modulated into a new
meaning, a new interpretation. A similar kind of
transformation takes place in the movement from King to
Son of Man to the Lord of the Gospels.

     2) The myth of the wicked God. The wicked God and
the tragic vision of existence provide the second of
the types of "Myths of the Beginning and of the End"
which Ricoeur investigates. This is the type best
known from Greek tragedy. After a discussion of some
of the pre-tragic themes, such as the blindness imposed
by a god which Homer incorporates into the Iliad,
Ricoeur lists the elements of the tragic as 1) blindness sent by the gods, 2) daimon, 3) lot or portion,
and 4) jealousy or immoderation which become

ingredients in the conflict, properly called tragic, between an implicit predestination to evil and the greatness of a hero. Whether it is Prometheus or Odysseus--or even one of Shakespeare's tragic heroes-- the paradox presented is the symbol which involves contraries of human experience, a certain fate which compromises human freedom, but which is confronted by the reality of that freedom. Deliverance from the dilemma comes not so much from without as from within. Suffering brings understanding: terror and fear on the part of the spectator become catharsis and pity, a transcendence by means of the poetic.

3) The Adamic myth. The most anthropological of the myths is the type represented by the account of Adam, not because Adam means man or human being, although that is significant, but because this attempt to account for the origin of evil is so strongly situated within the human reality. Ricoeur lists three charac- teristics of this anthropological slant: 1) the origin of evil traced to an ancestor of human beings; 2) the separation of the origin of evil from the origin of good in God; and 3) the important though subordinate role of such figures as Eve and the Serpent. Only in understanding the myth as myth is it possible to elicit the full meaning of the symbols involved; the myth as hermeneutics, as interpretation, provides far more meaning than a misnamed "true history." The power of the myth is that it opens so much to be explored; in fact, the myth gives rise to thought precisely because it is an interpretation of the symbols. In this con- text Ricoeur posits a sequence of the interpretations involved: the primordial symbol of sin may be placed first; next, the Adamic myth may be thought of as a first degree hermeneutics interpreting that primary symbol; lastly, one may look at a second degree hermeneutics, the speculative interpretation formulated in the theology of original sin.

It is perhaps obvious that this analysis in particular is of interest to theologians and to Chris- tians familiar with the idea of original sin. The Hebrew account of Adam and Eve includes not so much the symbol of a fall as that of a deviation; the fundamen- tal symbols in the Jewish experience of sin are devia- tion, revolt, going astray, perdition, captivity. The story of the first man and woman symbolizes both a transhistorical unity, as well as an anthropology of ambiguity. The figure of Eve does not represent a "second sex," because "every woman and every man are Adam; every man and every woman are Eve; every woman sins 'in' Adam, every man is seduced 'in' Eve" (255).

How shall one interpret the Serpent? Ricoeur
examines some of the aspects of externality and quasi-
externality which are symbolized here. As a symbol of
the beginning, the Adamic myth must also be interpreted
with the implicit movement toward the end, that is,
with the eschatological, the end-time, symbols of the
Son of Man and of the second Adam. The bridge is the
symbol of the Suffering Servant who is both victim and
victor, whom the Christians recognized in the historical figure of Jesus. Ricoeur is at the boundary again
of the philosophic and the theological:

> That Jesus could be the point of
> convergence of all the figures without
> himself being a "figure" is an Event
> that exceeds the resources of our phe-
> nomenology of images. All the images
> we have examined are subject to our
> hermeneutic method insofar as they are
> scattered images, but their temporal
> and personal unity is not; the event
> announced in the Gospel, the "fulfill-
> ment," is properly the content of the
> Christian Kerygma. Hence, our exegesis
> of the figures stays on the hither side
> of the Christian Kerygma. . . . On the
> other hand, we can very well give an
> account of the enrichment that those
> fundamental images received from their
> being remolded by Jesus in the Synoptic
> Gospels and from their convergence in
> his own person (269).

It becomes clear, then, in retrospect, that it is the
symbol which animates the mystical life of the Spirit.
The symbol gives what it says; one can only live what
one has imagined. " . . . even life is a symbol, an
image, before being experienced and lived" (278).

   4) The myth of the exiled soul. Besides these
three types of myth of the beginning and of the end,
that of the drama of creation, of the wicked god, and
of the Adamic myth, the fourth and last type is that of
the exiled soul exemplified by Orphism, and elaborated
by Platonism as well as by all the various strands of
Neo-Platonism. It is the only one of the types which
includes the myth of the body and of the soul, the
latter divine, the former earthly. Here the body is
the prison of the soul, and the soul is in constant
struggle to be free, bringing the paradox of life and
death to the fore: what seems to be life in the

present is really a kind of death, and in contrast, it
is death which brings true life. A corollary is the
concept of eternal punishment and eternal reward in a
life that comes after death.

The mythic symbol includes consequences which have
had far reaching effects on the development of theology
and of the Christian tradition: the attribution of
evil to the body and of good to the soul, and the concept of salvation and immortality as specialized ini-
tiation opposed to the desire and passion of the body.

Although Ricoeur gives a privileged place to the
Adamic myth because of its suitability to a Christo-
logical faith for which he has already given his
reasons, he recognizes that new life is given to the
other myths by the preeminence of the Adamic. In spite
of the fact that the Adam story is anti-tragic, for
example, it nevertheless has tragic elements which in
turn illuminate and are illuminated by the tragic myth.
The dialectic of understandings, for example, provided
by the symbols of Adam and Prometheus can throw light
on both. Ricoeur gives special attention to the struggle between the Adamic myth and the myth of the exiled
soul in the history of ideas, particularly in the line
of thought articulated by Paul, and interpreted first
by Augustine, and later by Luther. The assimilation,
even the contamination, of one symbol or set of symbols
by another requires careful and exhaustive study and a
constant critique. This is one task which theology and
the Christian tradition should hold in preeminence: to
provide continuous correction, correction without end
(The Conflict of Interpretations, 349).

Conclusion: The symbol gives rise to thought.
The last chapter in The Symbolism of Evil presents a
conclusion which in a way is also a reiteration of
Ricoeur's guiding theme: The symbol gives rise to
thought. Admitting again that symbols pose a problem
for philosophy, that they do not belong to pure reflection, he nevertheless reemphasizes that such a reflection cannot understand evil or the concept of the
servile will, both of which are parts of human experience. The philosopher therefore first recognizes his
presuppositions, and then gives a reason for them.

Modern culture calls for this philosophy of
symbols because now is a time of forgetting and of
restoration, a time of forgetfulness of human being's
relationship to the sacred and also of the consequent
need of restoring that relationship where it has been

lost. A reflection on symbol makes it possible to
become aware of all that has been forgotten, with the
concomitant impoverishment of the human situation, and
to take steps to bring about the enrichment which will
compensate for that poverty.

But what is suggested here is not a romantic
naiveté, but a union of criticism and belief, a criticism which not only recognizes all the insights un-
covered by modern sciences, but which continues to
remain open and in dialogue with those interpretations
of the human reality. Incorporating that criticism, a
second naiveté is possible to modern human beings
through interpretation of symbols, through a
hermeneutics of symbol.

But this is not to be caught in the circle of
hermeneutics; one must move beyond that circle by
changing it into a wager. Ricoeur wagers that he will
better understand human being and "the bond between the
human being and the being of all beings" (SE, 355) by
following the line drawn by symbolic thought.

The symbols are like a geiger counter by which one
can detect reality; they are manifestations of the link
between human being and the sacred. A philosophy which
starts from symbols is one which starts from the fullness of language, and which therefore opens itself to
the fullness of reality.

It was suggested earlier that Ricoeur is an
explorer searching out an area in order to open it up.
He explored the phenomenon of fault by examining the
primary symbols of the experience of evil: defilement,
sin, and guilt. He then tried to uncover the symbolic
function of the myths of the beginning and of the end.
He discovered that it was through these myths that
human beings tried to unfold in narratives the dynamics
of evil and of human freedom. The exploration led
Ricoeur to reaffirm: The symbol does give rise to
thought. Human beings can better understand themselves
and their relationships to reality by reflection on
symbol.

CHAPTER THREE

Christian Interpretation in Conflict

> Every reading of a text [--no matter
> how objective--] is always made at the
> interior of a community, of a tradi-
> tion, or of a current of living
> thought, all of which develop from
> presuppositions and from particular
> requirements (The Conflict of Interpre-
> tations, [3]. My translation from the
> French CI, 7).

The modern problem of interpretation grew out of
the ancient problem of exegesis. How is one to interpret a text correctly or appropriately? For Aristotle,
meaningful discourse is interpretation. As soon as we
are saying something that is meaningful we are interpreting.

We recognize the differences of particular
traditions of interpretation. The rabbinic tradition
of interpreting Torah has its own set of presuppositions. In the light of their experience of Christ, the
early Christians departed from that tradition to a
degree and reinterpreted the events recorded in the
Jewish scriptures in a new way. The Reform tradition
of interpreting scripture differs from that of Funda-
mentalists. In turn, the latter is different from
Roman Catholic interpretation. Each of those may be
different from or may overlap with an academic interpretation. It is clear that interpretations are often
in conflict.

What emerged as an exegetical problem, however, is
really a much broader problem. Not only do we have
different interpretations of texts which are important
to us, but we have different interpretations of a

particular experience. Two persons witnessing an
automobile accident see and hear differently depending
on their differing interpretations. A husband and wife
try to understand why each sees the checkbook differently. They strive to understand each other, but often
are left with differing interpretations. Two candi-
dates hear about the same political event, but differ
considerably in their interpretation of that event.
The problem of interpretation and the problem of the
conflict of interpretations are part of the general
problem of understanding.

As Ricoeur grafted a hermeneutics, or an
interpretation theory, onto his phenomenology, he
examined in The Symbolism of Evil prime symbols of
defilement, sin, and guilt as they appear in ancient
confessional literature. He felt that only by such an
interpretation could he properly explore the fundamental problem of evil. He then applied his analysis to
four examples of myth which describe in narrative similar symbols of the experience of evil. In The Conflict
of Interpretations, he included several articles which
expand his explorations by using some Christian concepts. On a speculative level these develop further
the interpretation of the experience of evil. They
move from a study of "Original Sin" to a study of
"Freedom in the Light of Hope." Reflecting the complexity of and the conflict of interpretations, they
show one more example of the interaction of Ricoeur's
philosophy and his relationship to Christianity.

"Original Sin"--What Does It Mean?

What Ricoeur studied as images and myths in The
Symbolism of Evil, he now studies as theological concept. Following Augustine and then Luther, the Reform
churches emphasized at the beginning and then in their
development the concept of original sin as hereditary
vice, a vice which is truly sin before God, and which
condemns the entire human race, even children not yet
born. The concept is one which also prevailed in the
medieval and in the later Roman Catholic tradition.
Ricoeur explores the concept, not as dogma, but as a
concept of human discourse. In fact, his intention is
to deconstruct the concept in order to aim at the good
news, the kerygma, the gospel itself.

> I think that the concept must be
> destroyed as a concept in order to
> understand the meaning intention. The

concept of original sin is false
knowledge and it must be broken as
knowledge (CI, 270).

But false knowledge may at the same time be true
symbol. Picasso had much the same insight when he said
that art tells a lie in order to make the truth appear.
It is helpful to understand the setting in which the
concept of "original sin" developed in order better to
understand the intention behind its development.

One of the earliest streams of thought with which
Christian thought interacted was gnosticism. The word
comes from the Greek gnosis, knowledge. Such knowledge
initiated an elect group into an understanding and a
"purity" which enabled them to escape a cosmos essentially evil. They were good as opposed to a world
which is evil. In contrast to the psalmist who looked
at the stars and the sky and saw the glory of God, the
gnostic follower perceived the world and the universe
as evil.

Against such a materialistic concept of evil, the
Fathers of the early church consistently pointed out
that evil has no nature. Evil is not a something. The
world is not sin. On the contrary, sin somehow comes
into the world. It is precisely against the Babylonian
materialistic concept of evil that the story of Adam
and Eve was formulated: creation is good--"And God saw
that it was good"--, but somehow human being is the
point at which sin enters into human experience. Human
being is free and therefore responsible. But it is not
quite that simple. There is also the Satan, the adver-
sary. Somehow there is an outside source of the evil
human being experiences in the world.

It is this tradition which Augustine attempted to
defend. Against a tragic vision that the universe is
evil, Augustine elaborated an ethical vision in which
human being can claim both freedom and responsibility.
Such freedom and responsibility allow for history and
for hope. Augustine said: "If there is repentance,
there is guilt; if there is guilt, there is will; if
there is will in sin, it is not a nature that con-
strains us" (274). As conversion is a turning toward
God, so sin is a turning away from God.

But in his exegesis of Paul's "Through one man sin
entered the world, and through sin death . . . . For if
by the offence of one man, many died, much more the

grace of God . . . which is by one man Jesus Christ"
(Romans 5.12 ff.). Augustine was led by his necessity
to argue against Pelagianism to a description of original sin which becomes, in Ricoeur's view, not anti-
gnostic as Augustine intended, but quasi-gnostic, because it moves from the level of symbol to the level of
dogmatic concept. The concept is too easily interpreted in a way that is pre-Christian and legalistic,
in a way that denies grace and attempts to justify God.

Ricoeur believes that concepts do not have their
own consistency. They are always third level expressions of language which refer back to a more basic
language. Concepts strive to be clear, rational, logical. All that is to the good, but at the same time,
they thereby also exclude the excess of meaning which
characterizes symbol and myth. The concept of original
sin too easily expresses a false clarity. To understand, not only the Adamic myth, but also the intention
of Paul, as well as that of Augustine, we must attempt
to recover the idea of original sin as a rational symbol, that is, as a symbol for reason.

Such a recovery of meaning includes the biblical
characteristics of sin: Sin is real; it is communal;
it is not only a situation in which human being finds
existence, but it is a "power which binds and holds
human being captive . . . a fundamental impotence . . .
the distance between 'I want' and 'I can.' It is sin
as 'misery'" (283).

What Augustine intended, in his interpretation of
the pseudo-concept of original sin was the preservation
of the insight that sin is not nature but will. "Evil
is a kind of involuntariness at the very heart of the
voluntary. . . . If evil is in a symbolic and not in a
real sense at the radical level of 'generation,' conversion itself is 'regeneration,' the new birth" (286).
Original sin is the antitype, but always in reference
to grace. "Where sin abounded, grace did much more
abound" (Romans 5.20). Accusation and punishment are
overcome by hesed, God's faithful love.

What is grace? What is the gift which overcomes
evil? What is the excess which calls to new birth and
which gives life? Ricoeur explores these questions as
"hearer of the Word," as hearer of the good news, the
kerygma of freedom. Such freedom is what makes hope
possible.

Freedom, Hope, and Resurrection

For Ricoeur the hermeneutics of religious freedom
is the interpretation of the meanings of freedom which
flow out of the preaching of the good news. This
aspect of religious freedom is the fulfillment and the
completion of religious freedom understood as a free
act of faith, as well as that religious freedom which
is a political and human right.

To consider religious freedom in the context of
the proclamation of the good news is to pose a problem
for the philosopher. Ricoeur faces the problem by way
of a philosophical approach which he calls approximation.

> I understand by this the incessant work
> of philosophical discourse to put it-
> self into a relation of proximity with
> kerygmatic and theological discourse.
> This work of thought is a work that
> begins with listening, and yet within
> the autonomy of responsible thought
> (403).

Ricoeur stands within the Christian tradition, a
tradition which gives primacy to the Word, the logos of
Christ. Ricoeur understands that word to require of
him "as a philosopher nothing else than a more complete
and more perfect activation of reason; not more than
reason, but whole reason" (403). As hearer, Ricoeur
listens to the good news, the message of freedom.

The Good News of Freedom

> What is freedom in the light of hope?
> I will answer in one word: it is the
> meaning of my existence in the light of
> the Resurrection . . . as reinstated in
> the movement which we have called the
> future of the Resurrection of the
> Christ. In this sense, a hermeneutics
> of religious freedom is an interpreta-
> tion of freedom in conformity with the
> Resurrection interpreted in terms of
> promise and hope (406).

Ricoeur meditates on a long tradition of relating
freedom to future: the Choose life of Deuteronomy
(Deut. 30. 19-20); the call of John the Baptist to new

life; the call of Jesus to the fullness of life; the
either/or of Kierkegaard; the existential decision of
Bultmann; the passion for the possible. Such a tradition opposes a theology of the Name to the worship of
idols. God is "He who is coming." We can thus speak
of two conceptions of time, one emphasizing an eternal
present, the other a present constantly moving into the
future. That there is a history implies that there is
a history to come. These two conceptions of time generate two conceptions of freedom: the freedom of the
stoics who strive to remove themselves from time and
history, and the freedom which is allied with a passion
for the possible, a freedom flowering into hope. Such
freedom and hope are "allied with the imagination insofar as the latter is the power of the possible and the
disposition for being in a radical renewal. Freedom in
the light of hope . . . is nothing else than this creative imagination of the possible" (408).

But freedom is also a listening, a following. One
may choose to follow or not to follow, to respond to
the promise or not. If one responds, one accepts the
call implicit in the promise. Here Ricoeur uses the
language of Moltmann: "promissio involves a missio"
(408); the promise involves a commissioning. Far from
being only personal, this mission or sending has "com-
munitarian, political, and even cosmic implications
. . . . A freedom open to new creation is . . . centered on . . . social and political justice" (409).
What is Christian freedom for us? It is "to belong
existentially to the order of the Resurrection." It is
to embrace hope and freedom in spite of the reality of
death, and to walk in the wisdom Paul never tired of
describing as the superabundance, the "how much more,"
the joyous overabundance of the gift, of grace.

Philosophy, Freedom, and Hope

How can the philosopher speak of freedom in the
light of hope? Ricoeur is a philosopher, not a theologian. As philosopher, how does he respond to the message of hope? Two things challenge him to the task:
the kerygma of hope provides first an innovation of
meaning which challenges him as philosopher. Second,
such a message of hope demands the effort to make it
intelligible. How can one approximate both its innovation and its meaning?

Hope begins as "a-logical." It effects
an irruption into a closed order; it

opens up a career for existence and
history. Passion for the possible,
mission and exodus, denial of the reality of death, response of superabundance of meaning to the abundance of
nonsense--these are so many signs of
the new creation whose novelty catches
. . . unawares . . . . Resurrection
surprises by being in excess in comparison to the reality forsaken by God
(411).

With other philosophers, Ricoeur is heir of the
great traditions of Kant and of Hegel. But we are
radically post-Kantian and post-Hegelian. Though
chronologically Hegel follows Kant, each provides critique for the other, and the followers of each or both
provide additional critique. Nevertheless, "it is this
exchange and this permutation which still structure
philosophical discourse today. This is why the task is
to think them always better by thinking them together--
one against the other, and one by means of the other"
(412).

Such exchange and permutation create constant
tension and call for dialectic, the reading of one
against the other. Human being can think of that which
does not exist, as well as of that which may or which
might exist. Human being can think of the uncondi-
tioned. But human being cannot understand the uncondi-
tioned. The symbol gives rise to thought. But without
critique, such thinking leads to illusion and to false
hope. Nevertheless, the possibility of illusion and of
false hope should not rule out the effort to think of
and to create the truly possible. "Others ask why? I
ask why not?" There are reasons for saying that the
Why not? may point to illusion, but that possibility
should not rule out the true and possible creation of
the new.

With practical reason, the philosopher may
formulate goals and this precisely leads to a philosophy of the will which aims at totality. Such a philosophy must overcome two illusions: the theoretical
illusion of false knowledge or false hope as well as
the practical illusion of a false happiness removed
from the totality. "The connection . . . between
morality and happiness must remain a transcendent synthesis, the union of different things . . . . Happiness
is not our accomplishment: it is achieved by super-
addition, by surplus" (417).

Kant asked, "What can I hope for?" Human being
demands totality both theoretically and practically.
To see how the philosopher may approximate the kerygma
of hope, Ricoeur examines three postulates of Kant as
approximations of hope. The first is that of freedom
of the will. Such freedom, in Ricoeur's view, has a
direct relation with hope. It is a freedom which is
able to will, the freedom of a rational being who can
will, who is constantly stretching for a fullness of
being. Such freedom can will good just as it can will
evil. It is also concrete: it wills concrete, objective good. But this freedom is also a freedom which
does not stand alone, which participates with other
persons, with institutions, with networks, in the realization of the willed good. For Ricoeur, this is freedom according to hope.

The second postulate of Kant is the immortality of
the soul, and the third is the existing supreme being,
God. For Ricoeur, these make explicit the potential of
hope indicated in the first.

> Kantian immortality is therefore an
> aspect of our need to effectuate the
> highest good in reality; now, this
> temporality, this "progress toward the
> infinite," is not in our power; we
> cannot give it to ourselves; we can
> only "encounter" it. It is in this
> sense that the postulate of immortality
> expresses the face of hope of the
> postulate of freedom: a theoretical
> proposition concerning the continuation
> and indefinite persistence of existence
> is the philosophical equivalent of the
> hope for resurrection (420).

What about the third postulate, that of the
existence of God? Basic is the understanding that this
is a theoretical proposition, the postulate of that
which is the entire object of our will, that is the
highest good. "The transcendent synthesis of the highest good is . . . the closest approximation of the
Kingdom of God according to the Gospels" (421).

The philosopher, then, is concerned with the
regeneration of freedom, with the figures of hope, of
understanding and of love, with liberation from "the
idols of the market place" (424). A philosophy of
religion is thus within the limits of reason alone, but
at the same time it approximates the good news of the
resurrection. It is a process which can lead toward
freedom.

CHAPTER FOUR

Fatherhood and Beyond

How can we be liberated from the idols of the marketplace? How can we engage in a process which can lead toward freedom? For Ricoeur as philosopher of faith, the process is through continuing philosophical analysis and an on-going interpretation of the good news which is both faithful to biblical traditions and also significant in the contemporary situation. Yes, the interpretations available are in conflict, but that does not deny the need for reaching through and beyond the conflicts to new and renewed understanding.

One of the key images for idol-making in the human experience is that of the father. In his efforts toward demystification of human illusions, Freud devoted his chief work toward the explication and revelation of the idol of father. Long before, the Hebrews had been wary of the religious traditions around them which made of god a father-progenitor. In contrast, their God was the one who led them through the desert; their God was the unnamable, the I AM WHO AM.

Ricoeur sets for himself a similar task in a study of fatherhood not as a structure, but as a process which is dynamic and on-going. What seems so obvious and so unneedful of explanation is shown to be, under Ricoeur's scrutiny, an image which most needs to be freed from its distortion as idol to its poetic construction as symbol (CI, 469).

Ricoeur uses insights from three differing methodologies to analyze the figure of father: psychoanalysis, phenomenology, and a philosophy of religion. An analysis in the style of each with the accompanying comparisons leads him through a process of demystification to a liberation of the symbol.

Psychoanalysis and the Figure of Father

In his massive study on the interpretation theory implicit and explicit in Freud's writings, Ricoeur rejects the dominance Freud gives to an economy or a system of unconscious and instinctual desires. He nevertheless retains for his analysis of father the three themes incorporated in the formation, destruction, and enduring permanence of the Oedipus complex. Freud named the complex after Oedipus, the mythical Greek king who unknowingly killed his father and married his mother.

From Freud's theory, Ricoeur abstracts images of a father who keeps power in order to deny his son. Such castration leads to the desire to kill. There follows the glorification of the killed father with concomitant efforts toward reconciliation and expiation of guilt. Key in the process is the recognition of the father as mortal. At that point, the image of father is no longer idol but representation of relationship.

In other words, Freud describes a context crucial to human experience. To recognize the foundational quality of the complex is to make possible its destruction. The desires exist, but they can be recognized and unmasked. To recognize an idol as idol is to begin the process of unmasking and of freeing.

Such recognition and unmasking makes the killing unnecessary. A father who is mortal does not need to be killed but only recognized. Although Freud's perspective, then, is limited, his analysis provides a methodology for unmasking the figure of father as idol, and for freeing the figure as symbol.

Phenomenology and the Figure of the Father

As a phenomenologist, Ricoeur is heir to Hegel's philosophy of spirit, from which he takes for his analysis of the figure of the father a key idea: the movement from consciousness to self-consciousness, a movement of infinite desire.

Ricoeur understands the phenomenological method as reflection which reads the concrete signs that express the personal and cultural works of human being. "I am not the kind of person who does that. But I did that. Therefore I must be the kind of person who does that." "We are not the kind of nation which exploits other

peoples. But we are exploiting other peoples around
the world. Therefore we must be the kind of nation
which exploits peoples." Such is the path by which we
become conscious of the self.

Hegel's chief paradigm, however, is not the
father-son relationship which Freud developed, but the
master-slave relationship. For Hegel, and in turn for
Ricoeur, the latter is far more educative. The phrase
is used in the context of Hegel's analysis of self-
consciousness. It has some analogy to the use of the
phrase "independent-dependent relationships" in the
study of personality. A new translation uses the words
"lordship" and "bondage," which for some may be more
helpful.

Why the importance of the master-slave
relationship? It is primary because the roles described are unequal, but nevertheless reciprocal. In
contrast, natural fatherhood and sonship are neither
reciprocal nor open to reciprocity. As children grow,
the death of the parents comes closer. Begetting and
being begotten is a linear pattern. It is caught in
the concreteness of life.

The great challenge is to recognize the
restlessness and the infinity of our desires and to
confront them with the reality of our concrete situation. We are called to accept the father as mortal and
the death of the father as part of nature. But, in
turn, that calls for a movement from fatherhood as
natural phenomenon to fatherhood as a designation.
Only gradually does a child learn to acknowledge relationship in such a way that she can call someone mother
or father. When does a person finally understand the
relationship: when she has a child of her own? when
her child has a child? Never?

The difficulties of understanding such
relationships are what push Ricoeur to use the model
from Hegel. The master-slave relationship breaks out
of the closed aspect of the father-son pattern, and
ultimately throws light on that relationship itself.
For Hegel, the master is the one who has faced death
and nothingness, and who, in spite of and through that
confrontation, has become independent in his or her
self-consciousness.

On the contrary, the slave is characterized by his
or her dependent consciousness of living and being for
another. However, the slave has one advantage over the

master. He is in touch with the realities of everyday
life. He works on things. He labors. He takes raw
material and makes things. He is constantly forming a
thing, and as he forms it, he in turn is formed. The
master, by facing death, the slave by transforming
things, move beyond the limitations of the Oedipus
complex. They show alternate paths for self-
consciousness.

But in a philosophy of culture there are many more
possibilities of relationship. From Hegel's Philosophy
of Right, Ricoeur draws another model, the model of
contract, to throw new light on our understanding of
relationship. Two wills confront each other over their
rights to appropriate or to own. One or both must
compromise. The compromise, the agreement, becomes
contract. This represents a juridical relationship to
things which we then designate as property. The juridical relationship between persons who own the property
or have the rights is the contract.

What do these other models of relationship show us
about the father-son, mother-daughter relationship?
They show a way to move beyond the Oedipus complex, a
way to break out of the begetting-begotten paradigm, a
way to move toward an independence of self-
consciousness, a way to move from phantasm to symbol.
It is then possible to move from an unrecognized
fatherhood which leads to death and the killing of our
unlimited desires to a recognized fatherhood which can
tie together love and life.

Religious Representation and the Dialectic

After working through an analysis of the Freudian
Oedipus complex, and then through an analysis of a
phenomenology of the cultural figure of a father,
Ricoeur looks next at a dialectic with religious representations. How do we use such representations? For
Hegel, religious representations are the forms of the
self-manifestation of the absolute. Ricoeur, of
course, differs from Hegel on the understanding of
absolute knowledge. Such knowledge is aimed at in some
amorphous way by the representation, but the aim, by
definition, is never achieved. For Ricoeur, religion
is concerned less with: What can I believe? than
with: What can I hope for? This is precisely what
representation is about. We know some things, but
there is an excess which we cannot know. There is no
concept for that excess. We can use only representation, symbol.

For the dialectic here, Ricoeur uses the
representation of the "Father" in the Jewish and Christian traditions. He does this, not through theology,
but through exegesis. Theology is a meta-language, one
step removed from representation. On the other hand,
exegesis of the texts of the Jewish and Christian
scriptures goes directly to the designations of God,
including designation of God as "Father." Such exegesis respects the forms of discourse in which the representations are found. These forms of discourse include
narratives or sagas, myths, prophecies, hymns, psalms,
and wisdom literature. In each form of discourse the
designation of God differs.

What does exegesis show about the designation of
God as father? In the Jewish scriptures it is surprising how seldom the term Father is used in connection
with God, fewer than twenty times in the lengthy compi-
lation of books dating over many centuries which we
call the Bible. The scarcity is significant. For
Ricoeur it is indicative of his thesis that the figure
of the father has somehow to be lost before it can be
reinterpreted by other figures and thus move from phantasm to symbol.

How did such a process take place in the Jewish
scriptures? Ricoeur continues his analysis on the
three levels: that of instinct, of cultural figures,
and of religious representations. Comparative history
of religions shows a fairly common use of the designation of father for God. On the other hand, the history
of the Jewish people as recorded in their scriptures
shows a departure from such traditions in their more
dominant way of speaking of God as the one who acts in
their history, as the primary one who acts in the narratives of their being saved and delivered. In such
narratives Yahweh is not father. In fact, father is
precisely not God: Abraham says, "My father was a
wandering Aramaean," and Yahweh is "God of our
fathers."

Besides being designated as the primary one who
acts in their history, Yahweh is designated by other
figures which reflect the development of the understanding of the name of God. God is the one who enters
into covenant with Noah, with Abraham, with his people
at Sinai. He is God of the promise. He is also the
one who gives Torah. But ultimately he is the "I am
that I am." This name puts in perspective all anthro-
pomorphic attempts to name God, including the figure of
the father. Sonship, literal descent, is seen as

blasphemy. The naming of God as "I am who I am" is the destruction of idol, and a pushing of the horizon of meaning beyond the projected to the realm of symbolic meaning.

The designation of God in the creation stories reflects a similar avoidance of the more expected figure of father. God is not the begetter of creation. He is the maker. He makes human beings in his own image and likeness.

All of these figures developed so strongly in the Hebrew scriptures free the designation of God from a begetting, idolatrous figure of God as father, and therefore make possible a recovery of the meaning of father on the symbolic level. For the Israelites, God is not an ancestor; their relationship with him is not that of kinship. Rather, their God is their liberator who led them out of oppression to the land of promise. He is the lawgiver. He is the "I am who am," as well as the creator of all that is good.

When the term father is used in the Hebrew scriptures, it is used to add certain connotations of tenderness, of closeness, of dependence and familiarity to the more dominant relationships indicated above. In a similar way, the term mother is used of God to indicate comparable connotations of trust, nourishment, and tenderness. It is especially in the prophets that the term is developed. A key text is Jeremiah 3. 19: "And I said, Thou shalt call me, My father; and shalt not turn away from me." As the Hebrews are called to a new future through exile and a move toward universalism, the figure of father becomes a universalizing relationship that both expands the vision of the people of God, but at the same time intensifies the relationship of familiarity, love, and tenderness.

It is out of this context of God as father that Jesus develops his use of "Abba, Father," as a term of familiarity. Jesus had read in Isaiah "Thou art our Father" (Isaiah 64.8) and in Psalm 89.26 "Thou art my Father, my God, and the rock of my salvation."

But from the quite isolated usages in the Jewish scriptures, the Christian scriptures record an amazing growth of emphasis. Although Mark uses the term for God only four times, Luke fifteen, and Matthew forty-two, in the gospel of John God is designated as Father more than one hundred times. In every case, calling

God Father seems to reflect authentic tradition from Jesus, but at the same time is always in relationship with the more dominant images of God as author of a covenant relationship, God as lawgiver, God as initiator and goal of the kingdom to come.

"Our Father" is the father of the kingdom to come. If one becomes a little child, one can enter into that kingdom. Jesus is child to his Father. He is son, and he prays, "Our Father, hallowed be thy name, thy kingdom come." Such a prayer is in the prophetic tradition of being directed toward the future. It looks, not backward toward an ancestor, but forward toward a new kingdom, a new creation, a new world, in which all people are children of a common father.

But the fullness of the relationship becomes clear only in the passion narratives, in the paradigm of death-resurrection. The suffering servant, the just one, the child of God, God himself, somehow is killed, somehow dies, and such a death somehow is metamorphosis to new life. Somehow father and son die in a more limited sense and the possibility of father and son on a new level of autonomous adult independent relationship is now opened up. Death is transformed from death as murder to death as offering. The death of the father and the son make possible the creation of the symbol of fatherhood and sonship. Such death and creation generate redemption, the fullness of salvation, and the making of a new world.

CHAPTER FIVE

Listening and Proclamation

Just as Bultmann and those who followed him
pioneered in the demythologization of the biblical
stories, so Mircea Eliade pioneered in this century in
the comparative study of the phenomenology of the
sacred. The two areas have in common a hermeneutic of
religious language, but they differ in their thrusts
and thereby raise questions which Ricoeur, both as
Christian and as philosopher, finds stimulating. For
Ricoeur, a hermeneutic of religious language is the
work of interpreting and reinterpreting. A group or an
individual is thus continually making its own the content of meaning which resides in the speaking and acting which found the existence of the group and the
individual as community and as person ("Manifestation
and Proclamation," 13).

The proclaiming of the Word of God is an important
part of the Jewish, Christian, and Islamic traditions,
with its focus on the acts of speaking and writing,
with a concern for the historic transmission of the
founding tradition, and with interpretation as an essential part of the tradition. In contrast, what is
meant by a phenomenology of the sacred, a manifestation
of the holy? Drawing on the work of Eliade, Ricoeur
outlines five traits: 1) the sacred is experienced as
awesome and overwhelming; 2) it is manifested or shown
in space and time without a dependency on words; 3)
there is a bond between the symbolism of this manifestation and the ritual which expresses it in action; 4)
this symbolism is bound to a sacred universe, to creation; and finally, 5) the manifestation is dependent on
the "capacity of the cosmos to signify something other
than itself," that is, on a set of correspondences
between nature and the sacred.

Somewhat in contrast to Eliade, Ricoeur sees the
Judeo-Christian tradition as disruptive of such a view
of the sacred. The Hebrews constantly fought against
the sacral manifestations of the Canaanite cults. For
them the word is far more important than the numinous;
Torah is more important than image. The Name has
superseded the idol. Nature and ritual are subordinated to the historical, and a new system of meaning is
created.

Particularly in Jesus' parables, proverbs, and
eschatological sayings, a logic of correspondences with
the sacred is uprooted and opposed by a new logic, a
logic of limit-expressions. The parables of Jesus are
not mythological stories. They are apparently stories
of the ordinary, fictional tales which have a symbolic
function not tied to nature as sacred, but which, on
the contrary, serves as an instrument of redescribing
reality. Like other fictions, the parables redescribe
life through their stories. With the proverbs and the
eschatological sayings, they point to the metaphor of
the kingdom of God. But their ordinariness is deceptive; in fact, one soon realizes and is shocked by the
extravagance within the story because something quite
extraordinary is found. Ordinary speech is ruptured
and the universe described by the parables is an ex-
ploded universe: the parables are language in tension
which point to experiences in tension. They make use
of limit-expressions to point to limit-experiences,
metaphorically expressed as the kingdom of God.

Having set up this polarization of the
manifestation of the sacred and the proclamation of the
word, what course may we follow? We may take the route
of iconoclastic discourse, acknowledging the fact that
nature is no longer sacred for most human beings, that
nature does not provide signs. At the same time, we
can recognize the remains of the sacred in our culture,
in cultures which we newly discover, or in the unconscious worlds of dreams and visions. Perhaps, in the
spirit of Bonhoeffer, we can even help develop an
a-religious Christianity.

But Ricoeur is not satisfied with such a course or
courses. Instead, he prefers to look for a mediation
between the manifestation of the sacred and the proclamation. The idealization of science, the absolutizing
of the scientific-technological, and the secularization
of the religious all point to a forgetfulness of our
roots. But humanity is not possible without the
sacred. We need origins, rites of passage, vision,

festivals. We need a proclamation which can set forth
the new being which the sacred proclaims. Thus the
manifestation of the sacred can be reaffirmed, made
new, and made part of the proclamation of the good
news. The dialectic of proclamation and sacrament can
be renewed in a thrust toward a continuing new
creation.

How Do We Listen to the Parables?

It seems a lost cause to preach on the parables
today (The Philosophy of Paul Ricoeur, 239). They
perhaps seem childish, unscientific, rural when our
dominant population is urban. Are not the images worn
out?

Ricoeur thinks not. To preach the parables is a
wager that we can still listen to the parables and be
astonished and renewed. The parables are secular
stories. They are not about angels and saints; they
are about workers and landlords and stewards. Essentially they are about ordinary people doing ordinary
things. They are "narratives of normalcy," but paradoxically the kingdom of God is like this. That is the
paradox: that the extraordinary is like the ordinary.
The apparent contrast of the two calls us to search.
It is as ordinary persons, as secular persons, that we
are called.

The stories are in motion. The kingdom of God is
not compared to the persons in the stories but to what
happens in the stories. It is the unfolding of the
plot to which we are called to listen. This means that
we need to follow the structure of the drama, looking
not only at the characters, time, place, and images,
but more particularly at the critical moments, the
turning points, the climax, and the dénoument.

Ricoeur reflects on one of the shortest parables,
Matt. 13:44, in which he discerns three critical
points, finding, selling, selling, and buying. First,
what is the finding? Ricoeur interprets this as calling our attention to all the findings in our lives:
encounters with people, with tragic or joyful situations, even with death. We find ourselves or we find
others; we find elements of our worlds. Such finding
is an event because it is finding a way of being.

But the finding leads to other critical points,
selling all and buying the field of the new treasure.

In other words, the finding leads to a reversal, a
conversion, or a turning. There is new direction,
vision, imagination, and action. The kingdom of God is
compared to the unfolding of these acts: being open to
the finding, turning to the new direction, and giving
all to the new vision.

Not all the parables are built in this same way,
but each one is concerned with at least one of these
critical points. Some of the growth parables lay emphasis on events similar to the finding. The surprise
here is in the overwhelming growth. The tiny seed
becomes a tree so that we are overwhelmed, surprised,
and overturned. The event is a gift which disorients
in order to make possible a reorienting.

Other parables emphasize the reversal: the
prodigal son changes his mind and returns to his
father. Still others give prominence to the extrava-
gant action: the good Samaritan does much more than is
required.

But we are told only what the kingdom of heaven is
like. That leaves us still asking the question: what
is the kingdom of heaven? or where is it? That is
precisely the rub. We have to follow through the story
to ask what is happening, to ask what does this mean?
And as we do that, we are caught in the tension which
crosses centuries, miles, and worlds to touch our
lives.

The parables as we have them do not stand alone.
Whatever the difficulties posed by historical-critical
or redaction study, it is agreed, nonetheless, that
parables form a set within the gospels. They give us a
bundle of metaphors or a network of images and stories.
Although they make sense together, they also include
contradictions and paradoxes. In them there is more to
think through than any simple theology can comprehend,
more than can be said in rational theology, just as
there is more in life than can be rationalized. Parables are neither moral theology nor dogmatic theology.
They are not even practical theology in a direct sense;
that is, they provide directly neither ethics nor politics. But what they do provide is paradox and exagger-
ation which shake us out of our complacency and heal
our myopeia. That is, we are disoriented so that we
can be called to reorientation.

What Does It Mean to Be a Listener?

"To confess that one is a listener is from the very beginning to break with the project dear to many, and even perhaps all, philosophers: to begin discourse without any presuppositions" ("Naming God," 215). The presupposition of a listener is that the speaking he is listening to is meaningful. As a listener to Christian preaching, Ricoeur stands within a tradition which gives preference to certain texts and in these texts God has already been named. Contrary as it is to the philosophic thrust toward the universal, Ricoeur never- theless recognizes that thinking is linked to specific events and to the accounts which tell about these events.

But what is the relationship between religious experience and texts? It is acknowledged that at the origin and limit of any interpretation is an experi- ence, a faith, an event articulated sometimes as ulti- mate concern, as absolute dependence, or as a "yes." But to take as presupposition the attitude of listening is to presume that such an experience is articulated through language. Some texts, some accounts of an experience of faith, have preceded my life. The name of God has come to me because these texts have been preached, proclaimed and interpreted within a communi- ty. Such texts then become independent of their authors and of their original contexts and audiences. They are not unlike musical scores which depend on musicians to bring them to life. In some way God is the ultimate referent of these texts. They are poetic, not only in the usual sense of being poems, but in the larger sense of "making new." They reveal what has been hidden and they manifest a truth in the sense of letting what is show itself. And what is is a world in which I may live--a new world.

Because the Bible is a polyphony of texts, one must rule out an absolutizing of knowledge about God in a dogmatic theological or philosophical sense. One must also rule out a subjectivism which confines knowl- edge to what I can understand and rationalize. If I listen to Christian preaching, I place myself within a long tradition which is polyphonic, that is, it has many voices. I am not placed at the beginning nor at the center. In fact, I am called to lose my life if I want to find it, to listen to the language by which people in a community of faith have interpreted their experience and have named the God to which that experi- ence pointed.

Is this naming of God the same as the naming of Christ? Unlike the "death of God" theologians who call for a Christian atheism, Ricoeur places the unnameable name of the exodus experience alongside the limit expressions of the New Testament. In his view, the stories of the exodus and of the resurrection arise from the same narrative genre.

What Jesus preaches is the kingdom of God and it was that God to whom he cried out from the cross, "My God, my God, why have you forsaken me?" Jesus names not only his God, but the God of his fathers, of Moses and of the prophets. His cross is the culminating sign of the relinquishment of God, that is, of the weakness of God within all the attempts of naming. "And the resurrection may only be understood through the memory of God's liberating acts and in anticipation of the resurrection of every human being" (224).

Christology is at the crossroads which celebrates at the same time the Old Testament theme of God's total power and the New Testament theme of God's total weakness. We are led then to the paradox of the power of weakness signified by the preaching and the kenosis of Jesus and the power of new creation signified by the resurrection and the coming of the kingdom.

In what way is such a naming of God a poetic language? Poetic language, again, is used here not as limited to what we call a poem, but in the Aristotelian sense of poiesis, language which breaks away from our everyday expectations to use language in a new way. Such language opens up a new world and thereby calls the listener or the reader to understand the self in the face of that new world.

Religious language is poetic language of this type but with a difference, because religious language attempts, not only to open a new world, but to open up precisely that world whose referent is God. Whatever analogies, metaphors, or limit-expressions are used, and whatever the genres of narrative or prophecy, the intention is to open up the world of the unnameable name. Such expressions or genres are like schemas or models which show human beings reaching out for God and which record the experience of God accompanying his people. Such models defy system because they include father, mother, servant, child; by being so diversified they defy the systematization of the naming of God. They function within the tension between the unnameable name and the idol.

What effect does this language have on the
practical, on the world of politics, on the world in
which we live? By politics here is meant the art of
the possible, the art of living in the human community.
Such language has a radical effect, because it opens up
the understanding of a new world, and the other side of
the possibility of a new world is a world of change.
The new world and the change called for is not a particular dogmatic code or ethic nor is it a specific
mode of politics, but it is the surpassing of what is
usually understood as the ethical or the political. It
is the call for new models of what a human world can
be, a call for new horizons of liberation.

Such understanding of listening to the world of
the text and to what it opens up is the task of a hermeneutic or interpreting theology, which, on the one
hand, never loses sight of the transcendence of God
modulated in biblical poetics, but which, on the other
hand, is always mindful of the effect which such a
poetics has on one's self-understanding and therefore
on one's world. In this sense, politics and poetics
serve as corrective and complement for each other.
They call for the continuing standing before and unfolding of the world of the text. Such unfolding is
the coming of the kingdom, but the kingdom of a God who
is the unnameable name and who calls for a new world.

A Listener Is Salt of the Earth

The Christian is called to be salt of the earth.
In such a metaphor we have expressed the continuing
tension between poetics and politics, for the Christian's world is in time and place, in interpersonal
relations, and in relations within the structures of
society. But the position of the church in the world
and of Christians in the world is a difficult one.
Obstacles come from within as well as from without:
inertia, self-preoccupation, failure to see the needs
of people close at hand as well as those of people
round the world. A constant temptation is an escapist
form of pseudo-piety. But even should these obstacles
be overcome, the challenges can be overwhelming. Society has become so technical, bureaucratized, and complex that problems seem impossible of solution.

Politics is a struggle of power in which persons,
groups, and institutions work to achieve through compromise, coalition, or force their own good or what
they perceive as the common good. More often than not,

Christians and the churches stand in ambiguous
relationships with such struggles. What is named a
Christian Party or a Christian stance is in the view of
many Christians exactly the opposite. The name of God
or the name of Jesus often continues to be used for
exploitation rather than liberation. Different traditions and different theologians have wrestled with the
tension and have come up with different solutions dependent on their own situations and interpretations.
For example, Augustine wrote about the city of God;
Aquinas discussed tyranny, oligarchy, and democracy;
Luther separated the kingdom of this world from the
kingdom of God; Bonhoeffer joined a plot for the assas-
sination of Hitler. How can Christians be salt of the
earth without losing the savor?

     Ricoeur, too, wrestles with the tension and draws
certain conclusions (Political and Social Essays, 113
ff.). The Christian acknowledges the earth as it
exists. The view is realistic, even pessimistic in the
light of the history of the twentieth century. But at
the same time, the Christian always hopes, always believes that something can be done. The church's good
news of seeking for truth and love is a message for all
times and places. We must therefore recognize the
structures and the struggles of power which exist; that
is, we must be knowledgeable about the world in which
we live.

     To live out a Christian love which is salt for the
earth is to see through the impersonal structures and
events which often seem to dominate our lives and to
perceive the importance of these events for persons as
persons; it is to refuse to let persons become abstrac-
tions or things. Such an attitude often involves one
in a struggle against bureaucracy or against the misuse
of technology. Both methods and objects of social
action must be humanized.

     A Christian involved in such struggle may well be
drawn into the prophetic mode, because the Christian
who hears the gospel is concerned for the poor, the
exploited, the oppressed, wherever they may be. Who
are the poor today? They may be old people or young,
disabled or abused, hungry or bored, near at hand or on
the other side of the world. The Christian is called
to see such needs both at home and in a world context.
Such a stance leads from egoism to a love that can be
revolutionary.

     As salt of the earth, Christians are always
seeking the truth because the truth makes us free. But

truth is by definition critical of ideologies whether
in the form of capitalism, militarism, socialism, or
communism. A Christian is always in the position of
smashing the idols, of calling for a return to realities, a return to the seeking for truth.

But what about the realities of politics--by
definition the art of the possible, the resolution of
conflicts, and the compromising of positions? The
metaphor of being salt of the earth calls for the constant tension of ideals and actualities, of working
toward a new world within the remaining structures of
the old. Like the wheat and the tares, both ideals and
actualities exist together in the real world of our
daily existence.

Logic, Poetics, and Politics

Although it corresponds to much of our daily
experience, the tension of being salt of the earth is
illogical by our ordinary standards. It raises for us
certain questions. Is there a logic in our daily behavior? Is such a logic consistent with our Christian
beliefs? What do we find in the gospels? Is there a
logic of Jesus, a logic of God?

The understanding and use of logic has varied
through the centuries with time, place, and customs.
What is logical in New York may not be perceived as
logical in Dakar. An ancient logic which we are surprised sometimes to find still prevalent among us is a
logic of vengeance, a basic, primitive desire for
equivalence. You do this to me: I'll do that to you.

Among others, the Babylonians expressed such an
equivalence in the myth of punishment which we call the
Babylonian flood story. In the reinterpretation of
that story, the writer of Genesis interjects the logic
of the exception, narrated as the repentance of God.
In fact, the paradox of the logic of the exception
becomes the logic of superabundance ("The Logic of
Jesus, The Logic of God," 325). It is such a logic
which is carried through the prophetic tradition.

As prophet of the kingdom of God, Jesus
continually expresses a similar logic of superabundance. In Matthew, we have Jesus reinterpreting the
law of equivalent punishment. No longer is "an eye for
an eye" an appropriate guideline. On the contrary, our
standards are overturned. We are disoriented, even

repelled. If someone strikes us on one cheek, we are
to offer the other one. If someone in law wants to
take away your tunic, let your cloak go too. If someone forces you one mile, go another one as well. What
do we have here--a way to subordinate the underprivi-
leged? No--although we must admit that the sayings
have been misused to exploit and oppress peoples
throughout the ages.

What Ricoeur finds here is a call for an attitude
and an action which is the opposite of our natural
tendency, a call for a new way of thinking and acting.
The extreme language of Jesus' sayings, as well as of
his parables, is a language of paradox which disorients
us in order to call us to reorientation. Our imagination is called to look for new ways of thinking, new
possibilities for human behavior. We are called to
look for new ways of responding to situations, new ways
which are not limited to one-to-one correspondence. We
are called to a generosity and to a giving which contradict the equivalence of penal law.

Such generosity on the part of God is encapsulated
in the saying of Paul: "For if, by the fault of one,
many died, how much more the grace of God and the gift
conferred by the grace of one person Jesus Christ have
abounded" (Rom. 5:17). A logic of equivalence emphasizes sin, death, and a limited idea of law, while on
the other side, a logic of super-abundance calls for
justice, grace, and life. In other words, Jesus is the
"how much more" of God.

What are the implications of such a logic of
super-abundance? Ricoeur suggests a few. Called to
search for new and generous ways of imagining and acting, we must seek for prevention of crime and renewal
of society instead of punishment for individuals or
nations. We must examine our personal, national, and
international economies and discern where a policy of
exploitation, punishment, or even equivalent logic is
operating. We must look for and create ways of acting
which flow from generosity and gifting. That is, as
Christians, we must seek for the logic of Jesus, the
logic of God.

PART IV. RICOEUR
AND THE CRISES OF SOCIETY

CHAPTER ONE

Human Action and the Model of the Text

How do we relate the Christian faith with the
continuing changes in society? Do we take the stand
that faith and society are two different entities and
strive to keep them separate in our institutions and in
our personal lives? Or do we take the opposite position that faith permeates all of society and that
Christians should be intimately involved in politics
and social change? In the history of Christian traditions, official and unofficial positions have veered
from one side to the other, depending on the situation
and the on-going interpretations of the Christian faith
and of the gospels. For Ricoeur, not only have his
philosophic and his Christian traditions continued to
raise such questions, but indeed the events of history
which affected the unfolding of his life have made them
paramount. His writings which are explicitly political
belong more to his work during the 1950's and 1960's,
but the questions are not far even from his most abstract and his more recent writings. In them he asks
questions about the foundations of moral philosophy,
about the ideologies which have created the twentieth
century, and about the relationship of utopian models
and the possibilities for our hopes.

At first sight, the interpretation of texts and
the interpretation of human actions seem disparate.
But Ricoeur offers the hypothesis that the idea of a
text serves as a good model for the human action which
is the object of the social sciences ("The Model of the
Text," 529). Moreover, the methodology appropriate to
text-interpretation serves as a good model for interpretation in general in the human sciences.

The event of discourse disappears just as the
event of any human action disappears. In the act of

being said, the event of discourse is gone. To
determine the meaning, we can ask the speaker what she
or he means, and in that sense, the meaning is in the
discourse as well as in the intention of the speaker.
But when the speaker is no longer available to help us
ascertain the meaning, our interpretation is dependent
on someone else's continuing interpretation in discourse, or it is dependent on the interpretation of the
discourse committed to writing; in this case, the meaning of what was said is fixed in writing.

Following the theory of the speech act as
formulated by Austin and Searle, Ricoeur recognizes
three levels of the act of speaking: 1) the act of
speaking itself, the proposition of what we are saying;
2) the force of what we are saying, for example, an
order which we give; and 3) that which we do by our
saying, for example, the fear which we can create by an
order which we give. The large sense of the word meaning covers all of these levels.

What happens when such an event of meaning is
committed to writing? In the first place, the relationship between the intention of the sayer and then of
the writer and the meaning of the text become much more
complicated. Once committed to writing, the meaning of
the text is no longer limited to the horizon or to the
world view of the writer. For this reason, many poets
refuse to interpret their poems. Instead, they will
ask, "What does it mean to you, the reader?" The meaning, as well as the limitations for interpretation, are
lodged within the text itself.

When two persons engage in discourse, they are
referring, not only to themselves, but also to the
situation, or to the "world" of which they are a part.
For a written text, such a situation is very difficult
if not impossible to recover. Archeological, historical, sociological, or philological studies may be exceedingly helpful, but they can never make possible the
recovery of the situation itself. Nevertheless, human
beings stand, not only within situations, but within
worlds, worlds of meaning, which together and sepa-
rately they have constructed. Such worlds are embedded
within the meaning of texts themselves.

> For us, the world is the ensemble of
> references opened up by the texts.
> Thus we speak about the "world" of
> Greece, not to designate any more what
> were the situations for those who lived

> them, but to designate the non-
> situational references which outlive
> the effacement of the first and which
> henceforth are offered as possible
> modes of being, as symbolic dimensions
> of our being-in-the-world (535-536).

Thus when we bring to life the world of the text, we also bring to life our world. The correlates lie at the intersection points of meaning. But, by reason of its being written, a text is opened, not only to the person or persons to whom it is initially written, but to all those who are able to read. That is why the love letters between two persons can be published and read by others not only to give insight about the original writers, but also to give meaning to the readers in their own situations. The written text escapes the narrowness of the writer's situation, and makes possible the opening up of the universality of worlds of meaning as well as the meaning of worlds.

How do we apply such understanding of a text to the idea or model of human action as meaningful? Ricoeur elaborates on the basis of four criteria: fixation, autonomization, importance, openness. We speak of actions leaving their mark. Such an action has become fixed, and continually calls for reading or interpreting. Analogous with the description of the speech-act elaborated above, we can say of particular actions that there are three levels for analysis: the action itself, the force of the action, and its effect.

Not only can an action become fixed, but it can also become autonomous, that is, it is freed from the intention and situation of its original actor and becomes a phenomenon of the course of history, whether of an individual or of a society. It has left its trace in the way people act or in the way society structures its worlds. As such, it continues to call for interpretation.

It is this autonomy which enables an action to escape from the limitations of its particular situation and become a paradigm or a phenomenon of culture which seems to have a life of its own. Such an action, whether it is embodied in a work of art, or of music, or of a political event, constitutes a new system of symbols, a new way of being-in-the-world.

Finally, like a text, the reading of a human action is not limited to the situation of the original

observers or participants. On the contrary, once
completed, it is freed to the world of the future.   It
is material for interpretation by anyone who has the
ability to read its meaning.   Such interpretation,
however, requires from within certain criteria.

Following Hirsch, Ricoeur finds such criteria
within the circular interaction of understanding and
explanation; by understanding is meant an intelligent
guess as to the meaning; by explanation is meant an
attempt at scientific validation or probability of
meaning. Understanding and explanation are always in
interaction with each other, one bringing light to the
other, each raising new questions which the other has
to address.   Their movement is circular, or spiral,
except in the sense of our personal commitment to the
greater validity of one interpretation over another.

The Christian, then, or the social scientist,
interprets human action. She or he guesses at its
meaning, seeks for intelligibility, and attempts to
validate that intelligibility by probable norms.
Whether it be problems of violence or non-violence, of
freedom or oppression, of life or death, one interprets
the crises of persons and the crises of society.

CHAPTER TWO

The Foundation of Moral Philosophy Today

What foundation can we supply for moral philosophy today? How can we ground our process of judging and of making decisions? Many persons simply follow law or customs without reflection or critique. Others reject law or customs according to their personal desires. Ricoeur looks for a foundation more radical than law in any of these senses.

How do we establish or analyze the ethical intention? Ricoeur considers three moments as basic: 1) the concept of freedom as the source of ethics; 2) freedom as lodged not only in myself but also in the other person; and 3) the role which institutions play in mediating this freedom between and among persons.

How can I know that I am free? Or how can I become more free? First, I must create a vision or image of myself as free; I must believe that I am free, but I can only prove this as valid through the works which reflect this freedom. I am a certain kind of person in a certain situation. Therefore I can do certain things. I can do what I am. In other words, there is an integral connection between my beliefs and my actions. But freedom is not established in a single act; on the contrary, it is the continuing life, and, in fact, a whole life, which attests to our being free or not being free. Am I acting or doing, or am I being acted upon?

Ethics, therefore, is a moving toward becoming free, toward actualizing the potential which can only be guessed at. It is the tension between what I am and what I can be. But to say I am is not only to say that I exist; it is also to say that I value or give worth to myself, to others, to certain kinds of actualizations.

But actualizing my own being is only one aspect of ethics. I do not exist alone. In fact, I cannot come to be, I cannot develop, I cannot become free except in relation to the other. So to posit my own freedom is also to posit the freedom of the other. To will my own freedom in honesty is also to will your freedom. I am an "ego," but you are an "alter ego," another I. If I do not believe myself to be free, then neither do I believe you to be free, and the reverse is equally true.

But the freedom of myself and of the other is not easy of attainment. On the contrary, our histories and our contemporary situations are dominated by slaveries, oppressions, inequalities, exploitations, wars. We are brought to Ricoeur's third moment in his analysis of freedom, the part played by institutions in the resolution and in the actualization of this freedom.

Institutions may be family, voluntary associations, political groups, states, churches, or international organizations. These are all penetrated by relations with creation or ecology, by economic considerations, by the struggle for power. In the context of such interactions, valuing becomes objectified in norms, patterns, customs, or laws. Symbolic systems develop, ideologies gain power, and world views become accepted as reality. Neither I, nor the other, nor valuing exists previous to these systems, ideologies, or world views. My freedom and yours are always mediated through these nonpersonal, objectified systems of relationship. We are always in the struggle of I-you, we-they, and them. Whatever importance we may give to the personal, we are nevertheless also involved in the dailiness of providing services, acting out roles, and actualizing works which constitute us, others, relationship, institutions, and the world of which we are a part.

To extend his analysis of freedom, Ricoeur develops insights by looking at the four concepts of value, norm, command, and law. Value starts from myself as subject, but it proceeds to be embodied in a work or an act which then may be viewed as object. But as soon as I look at the other, I am put in the situation of distinguishing between what I desire and what I value. Insofar as I want you to be free and you want me to be free, you and I enter into a system of values which makes community possible and which can allow for reciprocal freedom.

But values do not arrive from nothingness. There are already situations, traditions, institutions,

relationships, symbolic systems. So a value is always
within a situation of compromise. We are always forced
into the situation of asking what is this value worth.
Which value is worth more? "This is worth more than
that if you are to be yourself, if I am to be myself,
and if we are to be" ("The Problem of the Foundation of
Moral Philosophy Today," 183).

The distinction between what I value and what I
desire, coupled with the question of what value is
worth more, leads to the establishment of norms. We
move from what we value to what we should do. And
immediately we see the split. What we value is seen as
arising from within us, as congruent with our freedom,
but to carry out the implications of those values sets
up norms, patterns of expected behavior, things we
should do and things we should avoid. Yet a norm is
what makes possible the duration or the continuation of
a value. By norms we are able to objectify values as
goals, as promises, as standards, and are thereby freed
from the arbitrariness and fickleness of constantly
changing individual, social, or institutional values.

We are then in a position to see the place of the
command or the imperative. I recognize within myself a
scission. I desire this, but I value that. Therefore,
I command myself or tell myself to forgo this desire
for the sake of that value, or if I choose the desire
over the value, I recognize that I have reversed the
valuing or have chosen not to follow it. So we have
the phenomenon of the voice of conscience, and we can
see how there arises within relationships the imperative: do this, do that, don't do that. By extension,
we see the imperative operating within social groups
and institutions as a way of embodying the values and
imperatives. The language of the imperative may be
modified to be more democratic, more shaping, more
group oriented, but these are all merely different ways
of articulating the command.

As soon as we have the imperative in a social
group or an institution, we can perceive an analogous
split revealing those who are more in the position of
giving the commands, of articulating the norms, and
those who are the hearers of the commands. In other
words, an authority is constituted. The model may be
associative, communal, oligarchal, or tyrannical, but
an order is established wherein values are embodied,
norms are accepted, and imperatives are assumed. But
such a model is accepted only if it is perceived as
making possible my pursuit of freedom and my
realization of the values which I treasure.

When values, norms, and imperatives are
universalized, we can speak of a law. We attempt to
put the values in a rational form, to put meaning in a
larger context. We look for rational actions and a
meaningful universe. We strive to discover laws which
are the models by which we can understand the physical
universe, and we look for analogous patterns by which
we can understand human behavior. To both we constantly bring the critique of the values which we consider important. So we look at the perceived order of
the stars; we try to discern the laws or the patterns
which are operating. Then we look for an analogous
regularity in human relationships, both within and
without. One symbolizes the other, and the idea of a
"natural law" in human behavior may well serve as a
limit concept in searching for the meaning of human
freedom, but at the same time, we recognize that, at
least in our present understanding, there is a distinction between the physical laws which we have discovered
and the laws which pertain to human behavior.

In the concept of "natural law" as a limit idea,
Ricoeur finds three functions: 1) It may serve as a
protest notion against the tyranny of the state, as
well as against the arbitrariness of the imposition of
cultural conventions. 2) Correlatively, by seeking for
what is naturally lawful for human beings, we may well
develop powerful critiques of a status quo which is
opposed to freedom. 3) On the other hand, the third
function of "natural law" as a biological concept
whereby we assume norms for human behavior is much more
suspect, because it is impossible to see persons or
institutions operating in a purely biological or
"natural" state. Human beings do not know a time or
place without institutions, the institutions of language, of meaning, of symbols, of relationships. One
cannot hide behind a concept of "natural law" as a way
of avoiding the struggle for meaning and for freedom.

How does this analysis of valuing relate to the
Christian who tries to follow the gospel? What insights do we have in the gospel for understanding the
ethical situation? Ricoeur notes that the biblical
word "save" means "to free" or "to liberate freedom"
(189). The gospel calls, first of all, for a regeneration, a healing of freedom, the restoration of a capacity for freedom. Secondly, through the morality of the
love of neighbor, it calls for a restoration of the
intending of the other person. Your freedom and my
freedom must go forth together. The two are mutual.

What of the level of institutions? Jesus calls
for the coming of the kingdom of God, "a community of
free human beings" (190). On one level, this certainly
leads to a kind of anarchism, an abolishment of the
law. St. Paul wrestled with this problem and concluded
that true law is always in harmony with true freedom,
that we are called to be free. Augustine said, "Love
God and do what you will." On the other hand, Christ,
Paul, and Augustine each lived in a particular time and
place and had to deal with the realities of relationships, institutions, and governing powers. Such realistic interaction is another aspect of the ethical
which we find also recorded in the gospels.

But there is a third possibility. Under the name
of gospel morality we may see the possibility of a new
order of values and a new concept of institutions,
flowing from freedom and leading to freedom. This is
in contrast, of course, to the oppressive use of the
gospel which has characterized much of Christian history. Nevertheless, the call of the gospel is a call
to freedom.

At the same time, we may also look at the ethical
directions of the gospel as paradoxical. The logic of
the parables, the proverbs, and the eschatological
sayings is a logic of extravagance, The models in the
parables never provide norms. Our worlds, our expected
norms, are overturned. The father welcomes his prodigal son with apparently little attention being paid to
the son who has remained with him. The shepherd goes
after the one lost sheep. Such is an ethics which
disorients and thereby makes possible a reorientation.
Existence is dismembered. The whole ethical process is
called into question. There is the continuing surprise
that things are not as we expect. We have to be prepared for that which we cannot master. Here we see
both the use and the abuse of structures. We are
called to be attentive to the limit experiences of our
lives, and to recognize that these open up for us new
spaces for the imagination and for the ethical. What
are the possibilities which we have not yet looked at?
What are the worlds which we have not yet imagined?

We can see, then, that ethical levels must remain
in the realm of the dialectical. We make a mistake to
strive too hard to unify ethics. We remain in two
domains, that of the absolutely desirable and valuable
and that of the relatively possible. Ricoeur calls the
first a morality of conviction and the second a morality of responsibility, that in which we respond to a
given situation in time and place.

Perhaps, therefore, we should not try
to unify ethics, but leave it open in
that open dialectical situation concerning which I will say that it makes
ethics a "wounded" undertaking. We
cannot unify the poetic of the will and
its politics, its utopia and its pro-
gram, its imagination and that limited
exercising of violence that is the use
of power (192).

CHAPTER THREE

The Challenge of Particular Issues

Although we may describe patterns in the crises of society, or generalize the ethical challenges to individuals and groups, such crises or challenges are always in the particular. It is always this concrete violence, or this concrete need, or this concrete seeking for justice. Seeking for justice in the abstract is an illusion. Justice and freedom are of the here and now, of the particular.

As a person interacting with the groups and societies of which he is a part, Ricoeur continues the attitude which has been characteristic of his life. He is one affected by the events of his day. In turn, he is engaged in acting and interacting in such a way as to affect those events. He is a citizen of the polis. Not only is he affected by his daily reading of the newspaper, by his concern for the latest political or cultural crisis, but he does what he can to enter into the struggle for freedom, the seeking for justice. He is concerned about the needs of the people in Algeria, Cambodia, or South Africa. As expression of that concern he is, for example, a member of Amnesty International and writes letters on behalf of political prisoners.

It is helpful to look at some of Ricoeur's responses to particular crises which have arisen in the societies and cultures of his time. The variety of questions and of topics may surprise us. "What is sexuality?" "What is humanism?" "How do we understand the relationship between violence and language?" "How have urbanization and secularization affected each other?" Topics have included those as diverse as the following: Marxism, Communism, Socialism. Education.[1] The place of time, of consciousness, of intersubjectivity, of practical reason, of a theory of action, in

understanding human beings. Psychiatry and Moral
Values. We cannot elaborate here the profundity and
comprehensiveness of some of Ricoeur's analyses, but we
can suggest some of the breadth as well as certain
thrusts of his philosophical thought as he has addressed the challenge of particular issues in the
crises of society.

Sexuality and Wonder

As a participant in a study on Sexuality in the
Modern World sponsored by the French journal _Esprit_,
Ricoeur prepared an article called "Wonder, Eroticism,
and Enigma." In it he searches for "a new understanding of the sacred in the ethic of contemporary marriage" (133). Then he looks at the problem of eroticism and the possibility of sexuality without meaning,
and concludes with a recognition of the underlying
enigma.

Ricoeur is impressed with the universal
acknowledgment in ancient rituals that sexuality be-
longed to a comprehensive understanding of the sacred.
Sexual symbols were intertwined with the agricultural
symbols of life and death, whereas at the present they
are usually limited to the realm of individual desire.
Ricoeur feels, however, that the naive sense of the
sacred had to collapse so that a de-personalizing
"cosmic-eroticism" can give way to the making of a
marriage which is personal and mutually personalizing.
The Jewish tradition of marriage as a transcendent and
immanent sharing in creation and the Christian tradition of the incorporation of eros in agape in the servant figure of Jesus call for ascribing the quality of
tenderness or sensitivity to such an ethic of marriage.

It is an emphasis on person and mutual
personalization which marks the movement from the ancient idea of the cosmic-vegetative sacred to an understanding of the sacred as personal, that human beings
are responsible for giving life. Procreation is not
irresponsible and hazardous, but assumed into a new
concept of the sacred. A new sensitivity strives to
build an integrity of the flesh, a recognition of person, an inter-personal marriage.

The institutionalization of marriage is both a
commitment and a risk:

> Marriage attempts to protect the
> duration and the intimacy of the sexual

bond and thus make it human, but to a
large extent it contributes to the
destruction of this duration and intimacy. The wager implicit in an ethic
of tenderness is that, in spite of
these risks, marriage remains the best
chance for tenderness (136-137).

Nevertheless, our cultures today are pulled in
opposite directions. One is a direction to make love
once again sacred. The other is a direction to remove
all aspects of the sacred. Eroticism is a point of
focus which makes these directions clearer. Eroticism
may be seen as an art of loving which builds upon
sexual pleasure. As such it may belong to the kind of
sensitivity described above, as long as it is personal
and reciprocal and not narcissistic. But eroticism can
also pull in the opposite direction in which it is
fragmented and becomes a technique of the body so that
a false egoism and pleasure destroy the personal.

In contemporary culture Ricoeur sees several new
modalities of such an eroticism. Since sexual experience has lost most of its taboos and is seen as readily
available, it has lost much of its meaning. Sexuality
becomes public and vulgarized. Ironically, it leads to
depersonalization and even anonymity. People find
themselves unable to love or to hate. "People make
love without loving" (139).

Disappointed in the meaninglessness of work,
disappointed in the ineffectiveness of politics, people
seek outlets in leisure and in pursuits seen as anti-
civic. Eroticism becomes both a dimension of leisure
and a rebellion against feelings of powerlessness.
Eroticism becomes a revolt against the experience of
absurdity. If nothing makes sense, eroticism substi-
tutes instantaneous pleasure as meaning. On reflection, however, it cannot compensate for the loss of
more enduring values.

Sexuality remains an enigma. It cannot be reduced
to language, technique, or institution. It is part of
love which remains both restless desire and at the same
time a contradictory longing for permanence. What is
called for is the human challenge of creative fidelity.

Humanism and Modern Life

Is the idea of humanism viable in modern society?
Is there such a thing as modern humanism, or is that a

contradiction? What is humanism? In what way does it
correlate with the concept of the humanities or with
the heritage of western culture?

Ricoeur views humanism first in the narrow sense
associated with reflection rooted in the traditions
which originated in the Greek-Roman cultures of the
past and which have been renewed or rediscovered a
number of times in the history of the west. Such a
humanism is tied to the learning and reflection associated with leisure and the university. It is a remembrance of the self, of the heritage, as opposed to
those aspects of modern culture which seem not to have
a memory, which are always starting over. Such a
humanism is not simply a repetition of past ideas and
attitudes; on the contrary, unless it is a humanism
made new, it betrays its heritage; nevertheless, it
always finds itself in opposition to that thrust of the
modern which is forgetful of its past.

There is a larger way to think of humanism and of
the humanities. This is in the sense of culture as
leisure. Culture in this sense is a resistance to the
dominance of the technological, a resistance to the
oppression of being subordinated to the consuming of
goods. It is an emphasis of the human over objects of
production. It is an attempt to overcome the aliena-
tions described by Marx and experienced by those workers today who feel they are exploited for profits and
thereby robbed of their humanity. Such a humanism is
characterized by a lack of exploitation and oppression.

But there is a third way to look at humanism, as
"the very heart of the civilizing movement" (Political
and Social Essays, 75). In this sense, humanism is the
conviction that human beings determine and choose themselves, and that through reflection their choices can
be better. Such choices transcend a mere self-
interest; they are more in the nature of a wager, a
dedicated belief that can be self-fulfilling. It is a
rational belief, a "postulate" of practical reason.

Linking the various aspects of humanism is to call
for a renewal of humanism. What are the characteristics of such a renewal? Ricoeur comments on two: the
critical aspect and the poetic aspect. The attitude of
humanism, as well as its expressions, whether in philosophy, arts, or literature, is always that of the
critique. Marcel's philosophy of creative fidelity, a
painting by Picasso, and a story by Borghes are implicit critiques of the status quo, of the culture of
which they are a part.

A humanistic work clarifies, lays bare, raises
questions, makes assumptions explicit, and thereby,
even if that is not the explicit intention, attacks and
protests. That is why such a work is often divisive or
threatening if really understood. It is creative of a
new world which may topple or at least modify the prevailing one. The creator of such a humanistic work
opens new horizons of new possibilities. This is the
poetic aspect of humanism. It contributes to a possible revolution, a possible evolution of a new human
being.

A person, then, who is a humanist, a person of
culture, will be a person who thinks, who is intelligent, who is an intellectual, in the sense of someone
who is able to make rational choices or judgements. A
humanist is one who engages in rational thought expressed in speech, art, or meaningful action which is
not measured by quantity or product. For that reason,
a humanist is sometimes considered useless, dispensa-
ble, or unessential. The contrary is true. A culture
is in grave need of its humanists.

Humanism grounds itself in a realism, but whether
negatively or positively, it casts its faith into the
future, into its project and hope for a new future, a
true liberalism, a true area for human freedom. It
refuses to bend before oppression, whether technological, economic, ecclesiastical, or political.

Lastly, Ricoeur sees humanism as a "philosophy of
limits" (85), developed both in Christian and Kantian
thought. Christian thought always includes the idea of
a Last Day which puts the perspective of limits on all
else. Events and ideas within history cannot be absolutized. Ricoeur feels that Kant's concept of limits
must be applied to all history. Human being is only
human being. To be human is to be mortal. Humanism is
a seeking of wisdom, both in affirming the human and in
recognizing its limits.

The Relationship of Violence and Language

The antithesis suggested by the word violence is
violence/non-violence, but what is violence? And what
is the relationship of violence and language? What is
the philosopher's view of violence? Ricoeur sees violence first of all in the widest view possible, as the
exterior forces of nature which human beings must constantly work with or fight against, whether floods or

hurricanes or fire. But there is also to be considered
the nature within that often overwhelms us: desires,
fears, hate, the will to murder.

In what way is language the opposite of such a
violence? As human beings who speak, who enter the
realm of rationality through speech, that violence can
be considered as a problem. In other words, violence
enters the realm of meaning through its opposite, language. "A violence that speaks is already a violence
trying to be right: it is a violence that places itself in the orbit of reason and that already is beginning to negate itself as violence" (89).

One may object that language itself is often
violent. In Ricoeur's view, a language which is violent or fraudulent is a distortion of language. True
language is discourse, is rational, is searching for
meaning, and therefore is opposed to violence. But
there is a gray area, an area of tension, where language and discourse struggle through the tunnel, struggling out of violence into meaning.

Ricoeur looks at this struggle between violence
and discourse in three areas: politics, poetry, and
philosophy. In politics, violence in the extreme is
tyranny, to which philosophy as rational discourse has
always been opposed. The tyrant makes use, not of true
discourse, but of its distortion in seduction, flat-
tery, and sophistry. Whether in the illusion of a
common fate or of a false sense of glory, whether in
the violence of fear or anger, tyranny conquers the
will and distorts the rational. Such tyranny or oppression continually tries to assert itself, not only
in those governments recognized as tyrannies, but also
in the workings of those national and local governments
which aim for democracy through rational exchange.

What of the poet? In one sense the poet is at the
opposite end of violence. "Poetic language emerges
from a certain opening that allows some aspect of Being
to appear" (94). The poet places the power of expression at the service of meaning. The poet lets being
be, lets the reality of the perceived meaning come to
expression. But in another sense, the poet wrestles
with meaning, and, in fact, in order to create, does a
certain kind of violence both to the things being described and to the words used in the description.

There is a similar tension in the quest of the
philosopher. The philosopher's thrust is toward

meaning, toward coherent discourse. But such thrust is
through the particular question, the particular cultural horizon, and it is always tempted to a totalization or a closing which is a form of violence. "The
hard road of the 'loving struggle' is the only road
possible" (97).

What conclusions can we draw? Ricoeur sees that
the call of language is to the expression of all that
is thinkable. That call is a project of openness which
is "on the road" and which cannot see the possible
turns in the road, much less the end of the road.
Reason, then, is not limited to what we understand here
and now, nor to the parameters of a particular world
view, but it struggles with the rational, that is, with
the relational. How is human being related to human
being, to existence and meaning, to nature, to violence, or to language? How can human being make a way
which acknowledges the opposition of violence and discourse? How can language be used to name the violent
and also give expression to the non-violence of discourse? The testimony of the non-violent person leaves
its place in history and calls others to renew the goal
of history as one of non-violence. We are reminded
that the only way to work toward rational discourse is
out of an openness which respects the diversities of
language and which seeks for relationship in meaning.

Particular Issues and the Crises of Society

Although there are recurring and to a degree
universal patterns in the crises of society, the particular issues are always concrete and new. No matter
how similar to the challenges faced before, the new
issues, the new crisis always has to be faced in the
here and now. A philosopher concerned with the here
and now is a paradox, but searching within such a contradiction is the call of the philosopher. In
Ricoeur's most abstract analyses, there is understood
the underlying data of concrete human life. In turn,
concrete analyses are always in the context of the
search for meaning, the thrust toward coherent discourse. It is possible here only to suggest the comprehension and particularity of Ricoeur's studies. The
preceding discussion has given some examples. We will
indicate here even more briefly some of the other
topics which Ricoeur has addressed as a philosopher of
his times.

Ricoeur presumes the tradition of the citizen as a
member of the polis. This comes through in his concern

for the political events of France and of other
nations, with particular emphasis on the western tradition and the European-North American arena. Among his
writings, then, we find "Adventures of the State and
the Task of Christians" (PSE, 201 ff.), in which he
analyzes the national state as it has moved from an
autocratic to a constitutional stage, with the contemporary presumption of long-term and comprehensive planning. The state is a phenomenon of power which affects
the life of individuals and the meaning of their lives.
From his biblical background as well as from his philosophical search, Ricoeur raises questions about the
relationship of the Christian and the state. In
Ricoeur's view, there is not a Christian politics, but
there is a politics of the Christian as a citizen. In
fact, there is a style peculiar to the Christian in
politics. Such a style searches for the appropriate
place of politics in human life. It is important but
not absolute. It is important because it is an initia-
tion into a certain desire on the part of the group for
order and justice. Ideally, it makes possible an outer
freedom, but it is limited because it does not reach to
the roots to liberate human being in an existential
sense. It strives to make possible the pursuit of
happiness, but the existential liberation takes place
on other levels. The Christian takes seriously a
responsibility and commitment to work for justice, as
well as a vigilance founded in that kind of realism
which acknowledges the limitations and shortcomings of
the state, but which nevertheless strives for the possibility of reciprocal love among human beings.

     In a similar way, Ricoeur has analyzed Marxism,
contemporary communism, socialism, and the tasks of a
political educator. But such political-philosophical
analyses are only one aspect of Ricoeur's concerns. As
he looks to the inner dimension of the human experience, he has often conducted his studies in the context
of the psychoanalytic. In the present context, an
article entitled "Psychiatry and Moral Values" (976
ff.) develops insights which pertain to the critical
aspect of societal and individual life. Ricoeur comments on the particular contribution of psychoanalysis
as part of contemporary culture, a contribution of
tearing away illusions. Psychoanalysis demystifies,
but it does not prescribe. It does not moralize. In
fact, it makes moralizing impossible. The ethical
value which is brought into play by psychoanalysis is
truthfulness. In fact, psychoanalysis is a technique
of truthfulness. In the classical statement, Oedipus
says, "Now I know who I am." The work of the technique

of psychoanalysis is precisely that it works to meaning
through speech, through discourse. Such an ethic of
truthfulness changes our conscience. We have less
cause for deceiving ourselves and others. We can therefore more readily acknowledge the complexity of human
decisions and actions, as well as the painfulness of
the struggle of working toward truth and wisdom.

CHAPTER FOUR

Action Theory, Practical Reason, and Time

Human beings not only do, but they say their
actions; therefore, a philosopher of language studies
not only language itself, but also that which the language speaks. It is in discourse that the structures
of human action can be described. It is here that
Ricoeur sees a meeting place for analytic philosophy,
which emphasizes language, and phenomenology, which
emphasizes meaning.

A Theory of Action

What do we mean by a discourse of action? Ricoeur
explores the contribution which language makes to a
philosophy of action (La sémantique de l'action, 3).
He emphasizes, however, that it is a philosophy of
action which he explores, as distinguished from the
human sciences which treat of action in different ways.
For example, psychology observes behavior, and so does
sociology, but each has its own parameters, concepts,
and methodologies. Ricoeur's work is neither psychology nor sociology; it is not even an ethics. In fact,
it precedes ethics because it seeks to know how to
describe the discourse by which human beings say their
actions.

Such a description may be seen on three levels,
the level of concepts, the level of propositions, and
the level of arguments (5). At the level of concepts,
we are concerned with that language which we use to
answer such questions as: What are you doing? Why?
How? The level of propositions is focused on what are
called performative or verifying statements. For example, when I promise something, I both say the promise
and perform the act of promising. Or I verify that

something has, in effect, been accomplished: Peter closed the door. The third level is the discursive level itself which analyzes the network or sequence of events. What brings this about? We generate, then, a logic of action, in which we can study the interrelationships of intention, action, and effect, and in which we can look for meaning which is implicit, derived, or extenuating.

How does a phenomenology of language relate to other disciplines which study human action? For the most part, they complement one another. Ricoeur points out, however, that each has strengths and shortcomings. For example, the older psychological phenomenology through its reflexive approach often took a shortcut based more on intuition than on a study of the objective forms in which experience is organized. On the other hand, the limits of analytic philosophy are both its strength and a parameter which is complemented by a phenomenology of language. A phenomenology of language is concerned with those continuing alterations of signs in language which affect reality, which make meaning relative in that it is meaning for me or meaning for you. The opposition of theories is often not on the level of description, but on the level of strategies (13).

What is the relationship of a philosophy of action to ethics? On the one hand, an analysis of the discourse of action precedes the discourse of ethics (18). What is the intention? What is implicit? On the other hand, there is another area of discourse which is not descriptive, which does not proceed by distinctions and differences, but which, on the contrary, prescribes and establishes. In fact, it engenders meaning (19). It is a discourse which mediates and which opens to a view of the whole.

Through a phenomenology of language-which-acts, Ricoeur recognizes the limits of his analysis, but also the strength of continuing to ask the question of origins, including the question of the origin of meaning.

Reason for Acting and Practical Reason

We are concerned here with three phrases: known action, reason for acting, and practical reason. The first two are more familiar in discussions of action theory, especially in English-speaking countries. The third is more usually connected with Kant's Critique of

<u>Practical Reason</u>, although Ricoeur uses the term in a sense considerably different from that of Kant.

<u>Known action</u> is that action of which the person can give an account. It is intelligible either to the person doing the action or to the person to whom it is being told. The action may be rational or irrational in another sense, but it is intelligible according to the language codes of the community. The statement gives answers to the questions: What are you doing? Why are you doing it?

<u>Reason for acting</u> is an extension of answers to the question above: Why are you doing this action? Here Ricoeur ("Practical Reason," 4) follows Anscombe who outlines three categories of motivation: "desirability-characterization, description of the motive as a style of interpreting, and teleological structure of all explanation in dispositional terms" (7). Desirability-characterization refers to the fact that in language my motives can be arranged in order of preference. This is more desirable than that. As we generalize these desires, we use the language available to interpret our desires. "I did that because I love her." The teleological structure refers to the end or the goal at which I am aiming. It is within a global context in the sense that a goal or an end implies a world view with its constituent parts so that I can do this action in order to aim at this goal. I put my money in particular kinds of bond with the presumption that the world view which makes them valuable will endure.

To these three categories developed by Anscombe, Ricoeur adds a fourth, <u>practical reasoning</u>, which moves out of the area of action theory. Practical reason adds the concept of the intention with which we do something, the intention which accompanies the action. Practical reasoning makes use of all the various reasons for acting, but it orders them and arranges them into a strategy (9).

At this point Ricoeur introduces the concept of a "rule of action," that is, rule-governed or norm-governed action. There develops in culture a system of signals which gives meaning to every action and which circumscribes the context as well. For example, a speech given in a parliament is recognized in its context, whereas a similar speech given in another context might communicate something quite different. Actions have a public character. They are encoded within the

social system of which they are a part. These systems
are symbol systems or systems of exchange, and are
already interpreters of our behavior even before we
begin a more conscious interpretation. Within a society, these systems are legitimatized and form ideologies through which a community remembers and hands on
its traditions.

It was Kant who put the concept of practical
reason in the context of the question of freedom, the
question of personal autonomy. It is here that Ricoeur
perceives an "epistemological break between practical
reasoning and practical reason" (19). As Kant develops
his Critique of Practical Reason, he links freedom and
law, and the discussion since then has been in that
context. The tendency, continuing through Hegel and
beyond, is to objectify or even reify institutions and
states and their relationships with individuals.

> For if a person, group of people or
> party claims to have the monopoly on
> practical knowledge, it will also claim
> the right to do what is best for every-
> one no matter what they think. In this
> manner, then, knowledge of objective
> Mind engenders tyranny (34).

In contrast is the work of Husserl, Max Weber, or
Alfred Schutz. The state rises out of inter-subjective
relationships or the network of interactions among
individuals. Practical reason, then, lies in a middle
area between science as a knowledge of the necessary
and arbitrary opinions, whether of individuals or of
groups. In this sense, practical reason is not a body
of knowledge but a set of strategies working to bring
about and maintain the delicate balance of freedom and
institutions. Practical reason provides a critique of
ideologies, and thereby makes possible a continuing
watch against the distortion and oppression to which
ideologies, whether mediated through individuals,
groups, or states, are subject.

Time and Culture

In the introduction to a volume of cross-cultural
studies on the concept of time, Ricoeur points out some
of the relationships of time and culture, relationships
which are potentially foundational to crises which
arise in societies. Analytic philosophy strives to
reduce our speaking about time to a minimum concept,
while a reflective philosophy seeks to lift our

experience of time to its spiritual maximum
("Introduction," Le temps et les philosophies, 11).
The one wishes to speak about time, the other wishes to
describe the profound experience of time. Such experience is always communicated through symbolic systems
which are immanent to various cultures.

To say that something is happening now is to say
that the event being described is simultaneous with the
statement about the event. But such a statement implies the existence of a consciousness which makes the
statement. Analytic philosophy deals with the first,
but stops short of the second. The experience of time
is the experience of the extension of consciousness.
Such experience is not easily, if ever, really understood. Far from being clear, the experience is opaque,
"thick." The variety and multiplicity of culturally
divergent symbolic systems to express the experience of
time witness to the contradictions within the experience. Such contradictions often precipitate or modify
crises within our various societies.

A materialistic view of time, of which the marxist
view is one, emphasizes time as an "objective reality,"
matter in movement. The chronology of geological time,
the rhythms of biological clocks, the movement of physiological reflexes (13-14) are taken as models for the
reality of time. Evolution or development is one-
directional and irreversible in its movement into the
future. In such a view, it is not human consciousness
which orients toward the future, but physical forces of
which human beings as matter are part. The formation
of projects, scientific predictions, rational planning
for society are aspects of such a view. Eternity then
is a continuation of such a view, with the inherent
concepts of duration and succession. Such movement
into the future implies a belief in the future, the
creativity of the process of time.

What are the symbolic structures of our experience
of time? Using the model of genetic codes as organiz-
ing systems by which beings organize and create their
experience, Clifford Geertz (15) develops the idea of
cultural codes by which human beings organize their
experience. Such codes both reflect actions which have
preceded and prescribe actions which are to be carried
out. Such systems provide the justifying ideology for
action and change. They thereby engender prophecy,
both as critique and as call for change, eschatology as
a view of the end envisioned, and utopia as the ideal
aimed at but never reached. Such systems are "models

of" and "models for." They are incorporated within
everyday language, they are an integral part of a society's stories and myths. Grouped together in narratives, they become the histories which people tell
about themselves. We thus make intelligible for ourselves the inconstancy of human happenings.

To recognize the symbolic structure of our
experience of time is to recognize the diversity of
such symbolic systems, and their bonds with particular
languages or cultures. Among the cultural studies used
as examples are those which reflect animism, industrial
society, a mixed society such as we have in Latin
America, an arab-moslem view, a prophetic view, and the
view of futurology.

To walk into the world of animism is to understand
that the "realities" of the western world do not apply.
In fact, the question is raised: is it possible to
interpret the culture of animism in western language
without a destructive distortion? To look at the view
of time incorporated within industrial societies is to
uncover what one writer calls a pathological view (18):
a view of time which requires rapid change, acquisition
in the now over transmission, programming and reasoned
predictions. The clock, the work week and the weekend,
retirement as obsolescence, and futures as money now
are some of its symbols.

Latin America reveals dramatically the variety of
time cultures existing side by side: tribal groups,
Indian descendents of the Peruvian empires, Blacks,
Creoles, Portuguese, Spanish, industrialists, each to a
degree the contradiction of the other.

The arab-moslem view emphasizes the concept of
dahr: the unchangeable succession of night and day,
the passing of one generation and the coming of another.

The idea of prophecy presupposes the possibility
of breaking into time, of disrupting the dailiness, the
inevitability. The prophet is a person who can read the
signs of the times and speak the word of God. Quite
different is the Zen master who is a master of wisdom,
a master of eternity, who transmits that wisdom to his
disciples. Similar is the guru who is a seer. The
power of a seer is the power of truth, of the eternal.

And what of futurology? Futurology is the western
study of the possible future, based on projections of

what is happening in the present. Given this present
development in technology, what may be the present one
hundred years from now?

    Understanding the cultural symbol systems of the
experience of time is critical to the understanding of
the crises of society. Different views of time reflect
radically different value systems, in conflict with one
another and disruptive of one another. Whether it is
the "generation succeeds generation" view of the arab-
moslem, the forgetfulness of the subject-person of
science or of technology, or the traditional western
emphasis on consciousness as time, with an implicit
consciousness of youth, age, past, present, and future,
or whether it is a concept of creativity, love, or
imagination as creative of future and eternity--these
all are intimately involved with the crises which our
societies face.

PART V. RICOEUR

AND A THEORY OF SYMBOL

CHAPTER ONE

Symbol and the Hermeneutic Task

Though crystallized in certain parts of his writings, and referred to relatively seldom in his later work, the theory of symbol which Ricoeur has developed penetrates almost all of his work, sometimes without the explicit use of the word. Moreover, his study of symbol was crucial in the development of his theory of hermeneutics. In 1971 Ricoeur wrote:

> I readily grant today that the interpretation of symbols is not the whole of hermeneutics, but I continue to hold that it is the condensation point and, if I may say so, the place of greatest density, because it is in the symbol that language is revealed in its strongest force and with its greatest fullness. It says something independently of me, and it says more than I can understand. The symbol is surely the privileged place of the experience of the surplus of meaning ("Foreword," in Hermeneutic Phenomenology, by Don Ihde, xvi-xvii).

It will be helpful then to ask the questions: how did Ricoeur's theory of symbol develop? where are the intersection points? in what way did the hermeneutic task assume dominance? Here symbol can be used as a focus for showing the development of Ricoeur's work especially as expressed in Freud and Philosophy and in The Conflict of Interpretations.

In his early work, Ricoeur drew on the theory of "cipher" elaborated by Jaspers. He said that he basically agreed with Jaspers in his description of three

levels of cipher: 1) a primitive language of symbol;
2) the language of myths by which the primary symbols
are mediated; and 3) speculative symbols ("The Symbol . . . Food for Thought," 201).

Ricoeur's major study of the voluntary and the
involuntary was an effort to reconcile the ontologies
of the two philosophers he admired so much: the reconciled ontology of Marcel and the paradoxical ontology
of Jaspers. There is a unity in the mystery of an
existence which is incarnate, which is reconciled, but
within that unity there is the experience of a dualism,
an experience of the paradox. The voluntary and the
involuntary are related both by reconciliation or
union, and by rupture, and, in turn, this paradox is
reflected in the paradox of freedom and nature. Perhaps the key to this paradox is the fault, defined as
accident, interruption, fall (VI, 24). But fault must
maintain its primordial character; it must not be secu-
larized. It is not merely a superficial mistake, for
example, in the sense used by some naturalistic philosophers or psychologists. For this reason, Ricoeur will
not place it within the limit situations as Jaspers
did, nor in the schema of care as Heidegger did in
Being and Time. The fault cannot be divorced from
Transcendence because "the integral experience of the
fault is the fault experienced as before God, that is,
as sin" (29). This difference from Jaspers and from
Heidegger is one indication of how radically Ricoeur's
philosophy is oriented within Christianity.

In Fallible Man the task of understanding symbol
and its relationship with hermeneutics or interpretation becomes clearer. Fallible Man and The Symbolism
of Evil were originally published in French as Volumes
I and II of Finitude and Guilt. It was in Fallible Man
that Ricoeur studied the phenomenon of fault; his study
led him directly to the hermeneutic problem which he
addresses explicitly in The Symbolism of Evil.

In the first of the two volumes, Ricoeur states
that fault cannot be included in an eidetics or pure
description of human being since fault is by nature
opaque and absurd; it cannot be described in the ordinary way of phenomenology. How then can it be brought
within the realm of philosophic discourse? Through its
constitution in language which appears on three levels:
1) the language of avowal or confession of fault; this
is the level of the primary symbols, for example,
stain, sin, guilt; 2) the language of myths which formulates mythical symbols into narratives, such as those

describing a battle between the forces of order and
those of chaos; and 3) a language using speculative
symbols such as matter, body, and original sin. The
primary symbols of level one cannot be understood except through an exegesis or critical explanation of
symbol, and this, in turn, requires rules for deciphering, that is, a hermeneutics, an interpretation.
Through such an exegesis, these primary symbols are
brought one step closer to philosophic discourse.

The earliest exposition of symbol as such, and as
it was evolving in his understanding, was published by
Ricoeur in 1959 in Esprit, the journal which Mounier
had founded. Ricoeur used as title the maxim he had
taken from Kant: "Le symbole donne à penser" (published in English as: "The Symbol . . . Food for
Thought"). Here Ricoeur explicitly takes a stand
orienting all symbol in language. He speaks of a philosophy of the symbol as most appropriate at this time
in history, because such a philosophy is both "the
moment of forgetting and the moment of restoring."

What does he mean by the moment of forgetting?
The word moment suggests an important interval of time,
one with a certain dynamism of its own, such as is
associated with the word momentum. At this point, what
has human being forgotten, or what is human being now
forgetting? Human being has forgotten relationship
with the sacred. Human being has forgotten hiero-
phanies, those manifestations of the holy which inspire
awe, wonder, terror. Moreover, we have forgotten how
to read the signs of the sacred, and as a result of
this forgetting, we no longer know ourselves. We no
longer know how to situate ourselves in the world.
Ricoeur decided he will not succumb to the frustration
of seeking a philosophy without presuppositions. His
will be a thought that starts with symbols, that confronts language and the meaning that is already there.

While this present point in time is a moment of
forgetting, it is also a moment of restoration, of
remembering. What is to be remembered? The symbol
will lead the way, will give the stimulus, will provide
food for thought. In a way, everything has already
been said; such is the enigma. But thought always
starts over. From symbol, Ricoeur hopes to give new
life to language, to start out again from its fullness.

A criteriology of symbols. As a criteriology of
the symbol, Ricoeur lists and describes the realms of
the symbol and then analyzes its structures. He

concludes by elaborating what he calls three stages in
the movement of symbol toward thought, and thus toward
a possible philosophy.   The three realms or domains of
the symbol are those areas where symbols appear: 1)
the language of the sacred bound to myths and rituals;
2) oneiric, nocturnal, or dream symbolism, such as that
explored by Freud or Jung; and 3) the area of the
poetic imagination.   This latter refers not just to the
image of a reality, in the sense that the retina produces a replica of what it sees, but to what perhaps
may be called an ontological dimension of language.

> "The poetic image," M. Bachelard says
> in his Introduction à la póetique de
> l'espace, "brings us to the origin of
> the being who speaks."   And later on:
> "It becomes a new being in our lan-
> guage; it expresses ourselves by making
> us into what it expresses."   This word-
> image which is no longer representa-
> tion-image is what I am here calling
> symbol . . . . The basic point is that
> what is born and reborn in the poetic
> image is the same symbolic structure
> that runs through the most prophetic
> dreams of our inner development and
> that sustains sacred language in its
> most archaic and stable forms (198).

Next Ricoeur analyzes the structure of the symbol
by distinguishing it from sign, allegory, symbol used
in symbolic logic, and myth.   First, symbol is a sign
in that it indicates something else, but it differs
from other signs in that it is opaque: it has a depth
which is inexhaustible.   Although it has a double intentionality which suggests an analogical relationship,
it differs from an analogy because the relationship
cannot be objectified.   The symbol is a movement by
which I participate in a hidden meaning and am assimilated to that which is symbolized, although I cannot
grasp this intellectually.

Secondly, the structure of symbol may be discerned
as different from that of allegory which provides a
relation of translation.   The allegory is unnecessary
once the translation has been made, once the real meaning is clear.   On the contrary, a symbol cannot be
translated.   It evokes or suggests; it yields its meaning in enigma, but its meaning is never exhausted.

As his third distinction, Ricoeur points out that
symbol as he is using the term, is precisely opposed to

the meaning of symbol in symbolic logic. Symbols in
the latter case are characters, numbers or ciphers,
which do not need to retain a connection with the
spoken word, which may be used in calculations, which
are, insofar as possible, stripped of extraneous or
surplus meaning. The symbol with which Ricoeur ·is
intrigued is exactly the opposite: it is bound to
thought which is not formal; it points to the fullness
of language.

Finally, Ricoeur differentiates symbol from myth.
The symbol is formed spontaneously, for example, if
water is experienced as a flood which destroys. Myth
is a kind of symbol, one articulated into a narrative,
but the time of the myth is not that of critical history, and the place of the myth is not that of demon-
strable geography.

The stages through which symbols move. Having
analyzed the structure of symbol by contrasting it with
sign, allegory, symbol as formal character, and myth,
Ricoeur is then ready to describe the three stages
through which symbol moves toward thought: 1) phenomenology, 2) hermeneutics, and 3) philosophizing which
starts from symbols. In the first stage, the phenomenological, one symbol throws light on another, or one
is comprehended by the bonds which link a world of
symbols. For example, in a given system, the values
associated with the symbol sky may illuminate the
values joined to the symbol mountain. Following the
suggestion of Eliade, Ricoeur distinguishes four forms
of comprehension within the phenomenological stage: 1)
comprehending a symbol by comparing one of its values
against another; 2) comprehending one symbol by another
as described above; 3) comprehending a symbol by a rite
or a myth; 4) comprehending by perceiving how a symbol
unites different levels of experience, even those in
apparent contradiction such as death and rebirth.

But such a phenomenology is not enough. Where do
I take my stand? What do I believe? Symbols are in
conflict, one with another: they are "mutually iconoclastic" (203). On the other hand, they also have a
seemingly opposite tendency--they tend to petrify into
idols. This makes necessary the next stage, that of
interpretation, of hermeneutics.

Much of modern criticism, including scriptural
studies as well as psychoanalysis, has torn away illusions. Ricoeur thinks it is now time to interpret anew
so that we may hear. One must believe in order to

understand, and understand in order to believe, in the
sense that hermeneutics calls for an affinity between
thought and that which is being interpreted, not a
psychological correspondence, but a union of criticism
and belief.

Following the stages of phenomenology and of
hermeneutics is the third stage of the movement of
symbol, that which is properly philosophical, thought
starting from symbols. The philosopher will use symbol
to detect reality. This is not only in the spirit of
Kant who used myth in the Essay on Radical Evil, but
even of Heidegger who equated the interpreting of symbols with the formulating of existentials. By thus
starting from symbol, the philosopher can strive to
resituate human being within the whole.

There is a line, then, from Ricoeur's early
meditations on the philosophies of Marcel and Jaspers
in the 1940s to the explicit affirmation in the article
published in Esprit in 1959. Marcel's orientation to
the mystery of incarnate being, and Jaspers' concern
with paradox, especially in his ideas of transcendence,
of the reading of symbols (ciphers), and of the description of the fault provided part of the matrix in
which Ricoeur could develop the theory he elaborated
initially in 1959. The concept of symbol seems to have
been and to be for Ricoeur like a pebble thrown into
the water which triggers a series of concentric cir-
cles, one rippling out from the other, and in turn
affecting those which have preceded.

It will be recalled that The Symbolism of Evil is
Volume II of a two part publication entitled Finitude
and Guilt, originally published in 1960. From the
first volume, Fallible Man, which examined the possibility of evil in human being, it was a logical transi-
tion to move to a study of fault, which has an unlimited potentiality for symbolic richness (SE, 26).

The bridge from fallibility to fault Ricoeur finds
in what he calls the language of confession; his description is therefore a phenomenology of confession.
The type of avowal used for illustration is, "O God,
blot out my sins," the texts taken from such sources as
Pritchard's The Ancient Near East and the Hebrew scriptures. Ricoeur proposes a reenactment as midway between the religious experience of the confession and a
philosophy of fault. This reenactment is propaedeutic,
a phenomenology that simply describes. Even before it
is mythic, the language of confession is symbolic.

Thus the philosopher who considers the language of
avowal as the expression of human experience is already
confronted with symbol. Like an innate idea, it is
already there. The philosopher confronts it, and asks,
"Why?"

     In recognizing the privileged position of fault in
an attempt to understand human being, choice, and freedom, Ricoeur acknowledges his debt to Jean Nabert, and
especially to his work Éléments pour une éthique.
Fault is a particular focus on the ancient questions,
"Where does suffering come from? Why is there suffering?" The problem of fault is so radical, it will
serve as an ideal example for Ricoeur's attempt to
understand human being's relationship with symbol, and
with that extended symbol called myth.

     With the focus, then, on the language of
confession, Ricoeur offers in the Introduction to Part
I of The Symbolism of Evil a criteriology of symbols,
which is an elaboration with many examples of the categories, structures, and movements of symbol outlined in
rudimentary form in the article "The Symbol . . . Food
for Thought." The three categories, or domains, are
now called the three dimensions of symbolism (SE, 10-
11); the word dimension seems to suggest a greater
integration. The type of symbol described by Eliade is
now labeled "cosmic" while the two other categories
retain the names "oneiric" (dream), and "poetic" (creative). These three characteristics, then,--cosmic,
oneiric, and poetic--are dimensions of every symbol.

     Although there is no philosophy without
presuppositions, it is well to realize that introducing
symbol into discourse introduces a contingency which
cuts at the roots of the traditional philosophical
position limiting itself to what reason can logically
describe. Because this dependency on the symbol provides a certain orientation, it is thereby limited, but
such limitation is only a recognition of the real possibilities of knowledge. The philosophic questions are
Greek in origin and in orientation. When the meeting
with the Jewish world view provided the first encounter
with the otherness of a world view, the encounter posed
problems and compelled an ambiguity which two thousand
years of Western history and of Christianity have not
solved. (In a way, the encounter has not yet taken
place with regard to the civilizations of the Far East,
with their world views.) A philosophy of contingency,
therefore, includes the remembrance of and the awareness of one's history, as well as the realization that

there exists no objectivity which lacks a situation.
In other words, objectivity always arises out of a
particular viewpoint and out of a particular set of
pre-suppositions.   In The Symbolism of Evil Ricoeur
examines first the primary symbols defilement, sin, and
guilt, and then four myths of the beginning and of the
end (See above 168-181).

CHAPTER TWO

Exploration of Symbol Through a
Dialectic with Freud in *Freud and Philosophy*

A superficial reading of Ricoeur may give the impression that his work is eclectic or so diffused as to lack unity. A careful reading shows the exact opposite to be the case. The question arises here: what connection does a reading of Freud have with the investigation of defilement, sin, guilt, and the symbolic function of myths which was presented in The Symbolism of Evil? As an explorer, Ricoeur does not choose terrain haphazardly. In the article, "The Symbol . . . Food for Thought," he had spoken of the three domains of symbol: cosmic, oneiric, and poetic. The Symbolism of Evil was, among other things, a lengthy meditation on the symbol as cosmic; the inquiries gathered in Freud and Philosophy provide a reflection on the symbol as oneiric; a poetics is in process.

Ricoeur's interest in Freud is not new, since it was stimulated by his first professor of philosophy Roland Dalbiez, who published La méthode psychanalytique et la doctrine freudienne in 1936.[1] There are references to Freud or Freudianism in the early works on Marcel and Jaspers and on Husserl. Freud's pioneering investigation of dream interpretation, as well as the fact that a dream is an interpretation, even in Freud's vocabulary, made his texts an obvious choice for the dialectic which Ricoeur posed for himself. One may ask why he did not select Jung for the dialectic, since Jungian commentary on symbols specifically aims at the sacred and at archetypes. It is the very limitation of Freud's enterprise which Ricoeur finds useful.

> Psychoanalysis is limited by what justifies it, namely, its decision to recognize in the phenomena of culture

> only what falls under an economics of
> desire and resistances. I must admit
> that this firmness and rigor make me
> prefer Freud to Jung. With Freud I
> know where I am and where I am going;
> with Jung everything risks being con-
> fused: the psychism, the soul, the
> archetypes, the sacred (FP, 176).

Still another reason why a study of Freud is harmonious
with Ricoeur's task is that both emphasize desire,
Freud in the terminology of an economics of instinct
and affect, Ricoeur in the concepts of a philosophy or
poetics of the will, of the desire to be.

Freud and Philosophy is divided into three books
within one volume. The first involves situating Freud
within the problem of hermeneutics and of language; the
second is a reading of Freud, an analysis further ap-
portioned into three subdivisions: 1) the relationship
of desire and interpretation, that is, of energetics
and hermeneutics; 2) the interpretation of culture; 3)
Eros, Thanatos, Ananke; the third book is actually the
dialectic, a philosophical interpretation of Freud,
concluding with hermeneutics as an approach to symbol.

Freud's Place in Hermeneutics

The key question which runs throughout Freud and
Philosophy is a confrontation with Freud's reduction to
illusion of the representations in dreams. Given that
these representations are a showing-hiding, both a
presentation of meaning and a concealing of desire, is
such a showing-hiding which is characteristic of all
symbols always a dissimulation, or may it not also be a
revelation of the sacred? The problem of double meaning, of equivocal language, is not limited to Freudianism, but belongs to many other areas, among which may
be mentioned the phenomenology of religion. Double
meaning expressions are the privileged theme of all
hermeneutics, the constitutive element, in fact, for
hermeneutics is that theory of interpretation which is
broader than psychoanalysis but not as comprehensive as
the theory of language.[2] As soon as one recognizes the
difference between univocal and plurivocal language, he
or she is faced with the problem of hermeneutics, how
to interpret an expression which may have more than one
meaning.

In the first book, Ricoeur again provides a
criteriology of symbol, repeating many of the points he

had formulated in the article "Symbol . . . Food for
Thought" and in The Symbolism of Evil, at the same time
adding to or modifying some concepts in a way that
reflects his thinking about Freudian interpretation.
Freud had discovered that human being's repressed or
unconscious desires cause a person to translate·meaning
in such a fashion that it is no longer apparent what
the person really means, and the ascertaining of that
meaning requires an interpretation which is often difficult. Ricoeur now says that the symbolic function is
"to mean something other than what is said" (12).
There is a double duality in the symbol. The first
level involves a sensory sign and its signification;
for example, the sun signifies light and warmth.
Superimposed on this duality is the symbol and what it
symbolizes: sun as symbol has been interpreted to
symbolize Ra, Yahweh, or Christ, as well as life, love,
and so on indefinitely. Ricoeur reemphasizes the dependence of symbolism on the person who speaks, besides
reiterating the three modes of symbolism, the cosmic,
the oneiric, and the poetic. He now defines the
oneiric as embracing the dreams of our days, not only
those of our nights. Again, the symbol is not a mere
analogy because the intellect is not really able to
dominate the similarity of the symbol and what it symbolizes.

     To illustrate the conflict of interpretations,
Ricoeur uses the examples of Aristotelian and biblical
hermeneutics which represent two different views of
what the interpreter is about. The first is a very
broad view, not unlike that of Cassirer in the twentieth century. In this tradition, anything said about
something is an interpretation. On the other hand,
biblical hermeneutics has limited itself to a theory of
rules for the exegesis of a text. Three characteristics are important here: the development of the four
senses of scripture,[3] the relationship to an authority,
and the limitation of the interpretation to a written
text. Since there are so many interpretations of human
reality, and since many are contradictory of one another, and at this point in knowledge and time,
irreconcilable with one another, Ricoeur speaks of a
war of hermeneutics. To make the concept clearer, he
contrasts two extreme positions for hermeneutics, a
hermeneutics of suspicion which tears away illusion and
a hermeneutics of restoration which believes in order
to understand. The former is represented by Marx,
Nietzsche, and Freud, the latter by Eliade, Van der
Leeuw, Leenhardt, and Ricoeur. A hermeneutics of suspicion tries to take away unnecessary mystery, to

dispel illusions, to tear off the masks. At the
opposite end of the continuum is faith, the seeking of
a second naiveté, of a desire to be addressed; faith is
a willingness to listen, to hear a proclamation.

> Is not the expectation of being spoken
> to what motivates the concern for the
> object? Implied in this expectation is
> a confidence in language: the belief
> that language, which bears symbols, is
> not so much spoken by human beings as
> spoken to human beings, that human
> beings are born into language, into the
> light of the logos "who enlightens
> every person who comes into the world."
> It is this expectation, this confi-
> dence, this belief, that confers on the
> study of symbols its particular serious-
> ness. To be truthful, I must say it is
> what animates all my research (29-30.
> Translation modified).

Ricoeur recognizes that the philosopher's using
symbols is somewhat scandalous, superficially, at
least, out of keeping with a science which strives for
univocal statements. What happens to a philosophy
which cultivates the equivocal? It is forced not only
to admit but also to justify: 1) the fact that by
reason of culture, a contingency pervades all aspects
of life; 2) the fact that much language remains and
will remain equivocal; and 3) that there will continue
to be conflicting interpretations. How does this affect reflection? Reflection becomes concrete; it becomes a "reappropriation of our effort to exist (45).
It is a reappropriation because something has been lost
which must be recovered; once again I have to make it
proper to me.

The English "proper," "appropriation," and other
cognates lack the force of the Latin root proprium,
which means "one's own," "that which particularly,
individually, personally belongs." Reflection, then,
means looking into the efforts I make to exist, to be,
to live fully, to see what those efforts are, and
consciously and willingly to make them my own. I can
read these efforts in the signs of human being, those
which belong to me individually, and those which make
up the culture of my milieu and of the world. In this
sense I cannot ignore any science or interpretation
which attempts to decipher the signs of human being.
There are then three crises, those of language, of

interpretation, and of reflection, but these will only
be solved together.

A Reading of Freud

Book II within Freud and Philosophy is a reading
of Freud, a phenomenological description from a philosophical point of view. Each of three parts grows out
of the preceding. In the first Ricoeur tries to determine what interpretation is in the Freudian scheme; the
second widens the frame to an interpretation of culture; the third incorporates the findings connected
with the death wish and the conflict between Eros and
Thanatos, as well as the interpretation of the reality
principle.

To decide what Freud's concept of interpretation
is, Ricoeur first tries to ascertain the characteristics of the Freudian energetics, the economy of desires. With his usual thoroughness, Ricoeur had
studied the original texts and the major authorities;
he provides a new translation of the texts he quotes.
Moreover, he again presumes that the reader has a background comparable to his. Ideally, the reader of
Ricoeur would place the Freudian texts by his side.
His first important comment is that, although Freud had
received his professional training in an environment
which emphasized the scientific method of the time and
a mechanistic view of the brain, Freud's clinical discovery of the neurosis, its symptoms, and the hypothesis of the sexual causes led him away from the anatomi-
cal to a deciphering of symptoms which is already a
kind of hermeneutics. The core of the system of energies, the driving force, is the libido. Ideas essentially sexual become charged with energy, bringing into
force a psychic state of tension with the concomitant
impulse to relieve that tension. The energy concepts
of repression, inhibition, defense, resistance, and
transference arise from that impulse. But each of
these energy concepts implies a concept of interpretation, so that meaning is integrally bound to the
interaction of the forces of energy. Freud himself
said that he hoped to reach philosophy by way of medical and clinical work. Ricoeur believes that a
hermeneutics was operating even as early as Freud's
"Project" of 1895.

This implicit hermeneutics becomes explicit in
Freud's The Interpretation of Dreams. For Freud, to
interpret a dream is to assign it a meaning. Ricoeur

points out that such an interpretation involves the
economic concepts described earlier. To interpret a
dream is to follow the memories to the unconscious,
which is the realm of the earliest childhood desires.
As the repressed impulses of an individual's childhood
come to consciousness, so does the childhood of human-
kind, "recapitulated in that of the individual" (91).
In this basic concept of regression, one moves from
meaning to forces of energy and discovers the intimate
relation between the archaic and the oneiric. There
are two vectors of dreams, as it were, one which is
propelled toward meaning through narrative, the other
linked with desire, energy, will to power, libido. The
dream is at the point where meaning and desire intersect. But a dream is also a disguise; it manifests
something, but it also distorts under the control of
the "censor." "In the idea of censorship the two systems of language are very closely interwoven: censorship alters a text only when it represses a force, and
it represses a forbidden force only by disturbing the
expression of that force (93).

     Given that Freud sees his work as an interpreta-
tion, what place does he give to symbol in his rules
for interpretation? Ricoeur provides comment as well
as a lengthy footnote on Freud's concept of symbol, for
which there is not as yet a systematic study. Freud
tends to limit the word symbol to the stereotyped over-
determinations which appear in dreams, but Ricoeur
feels that he gave more and more attention to the symbolic function as Ricoeur himself understands it.
Freud had warned that translating dreams involved much
more than translating the symbols within them. Ricoeur
thinks that Freud's understanding of symbolization was
too narrow, that a distinction should be made among
levels of symbolizing, a task which he reserves until
later when he will have exposed more of the Freudian
theory.

     Ricoeur next analyzes some major concepts in
Freud's "Papers on Metapsychology," which he thinks
represent a mature elaboration of the ideas Freud was
developing over a period of time. The first typography
of the unconscious-preconscious-conscious is coherently
described, as well as a new relationship between instinct and idea. From this interaction is derived what
is perhaps the most basic theory of psychoanalysis:
that it is through instincts that the body is represented to the mind. After completing this part of the
study, Ricoeur formulated two conclusions: 1) the
language of meaning can never overcome the language of

desire; and 2) affects need ideas to resolve the energetic tensions, and use the channel of ideas for this purpose.

Having analyzed Freud's fundamental interpretation with its typography of the conscious and the unconscious, the importance of the network of desires, and the key element of dream interpretation, Ricoeur broadens the study, following Freud, to embrace the interpretation of culture.   Three ideas should be kept in mind: 1) Freud's interpretation of culture is an analogy making use of the psychoanalytic interpretation of dreams and neuroses; 2) the application of the model to culture has affected the model itself; 3) the final interpretation is only attained in presenting the conflict between Eros and death.

For Freud the interpretation of culture depends primarily on the analogy of dreams.   Dreams supply a model for all the strategies of desire; they have a meaning which must be interpreted; because of regression, they reveal the archaic; dreams open up the typical and universal aspects of the symbolic function. Applying dream interpretation to art, as Freud did in his study of Michelangelo's Moses and of Leonardo, shows both the great possibilities of psychoanalysis as well as its limitations.   Ricoeur's comment on the Moses study illustrates the relationship to his theory of symbol:

> This overdetermination of the symbol
> embodied in the statuary indicates that
> analysis does not close explanation
> off, but rather opens it to a whole
> density of meaning. The Moses of
> Michelangelo says more than meets the
> eye; its overdetermination concerns
> Moses, the dead Pope, Michelangelo--and
> perhaps Freud himself in his ambiguous
> relationship to Moses. An endless
> commentary opens up, which, far from
> reducing the enigma, multiples it (169-
> 170).

In dreams human being looks back to the past; in art he or she looks forward, so that art is a "prospective symbol" focusing a personal present toward the future, opening up the possibility of new understandings regarding symbols themselves, as well as the process of sublimation.

The latter problem of sublimation Ricoeur takes up
in a discussion entitled "From the Oneiric to the
Sublime," although, as he notes, Freud does not use the
word sublime, but sublimation. The movement is from
the dominance of the Oedipus complex to the establishment of the ego ideal, or the superego, from the sexual
drives of the first to the desexualized sublimation of
the second. The importance of this process for conscience, ethics, the understanding of religious symbolism, and education, cannot be overestimated.

What of Freud's analysis of religion as illusion,
the wish-fulfillment worked out of a primeval and communal Oedipus complex? Ricoeur willingly admits that
psychoanalysis is by nature iconoclastic, but affirms
the importance of this step. Such destruction of
idols, of symbols which are idols, opens to the possibility, not only of a lack of faith, but also to the
possibility of the fullness of faith, of a purified
faith. Freud's interpretation of religion also serves
the purpose of showing once again how meaning and desire are related. In the Freudian scheme there is a
constant interaction between the two, illustrated by
the displacement of the father figure onto the totem,
the gods, the God of Abraham, the God of Jesus.
Ricoeur reserves his critique until the end of Freud
and Philosophy.

After analyzing, one step at a time, the
interrelationship of meaning and desire, and the interpretation of culture, Ricoeur, following Freud, moves
to the broad view, a global perspective, a world view.
As the names Eros, Thanatos, and Ananke suggest, this
is not so much a psychology, or even a philosophy, as
it is a mythology in the positive sense of that word
which Ricoeur had clarified in The Symbolism of Evil, a
mythology which is a second degree interpretation of
symbols, an attempt to put into a meaningful narration
the human experience of reality.

The nucleus of this global view is found in
Freud's Beyond the Pleasure Principle. Ricoeur thinks
that the polarity and the tension between the pleasure
principle and the reality principle, and Freud's attempt at interpretation, move not only beyond the
pleasure principle, but also beyond the reality principle, to the larger view of life wish and death wish.
The tension is held in balance by what Ricoeur labels
the prudence principle, understood in the Aristotelian
sense of the word with its focus on the "real world" of
practical life.

In what is admittedly speculation, Freud tries to
understand the dualism of instincts represented by Eros
and Thanatos.   There is an instinct toward the conser-
vation of life illustrated by the migrations of fish
and birds to their place of origin, the genetic recapi-
tulation of the embryo, with the concomitant instinct
to see death as necessary for life.   Although life
marches inexorably toward death, sexuality is the constant witness that death does not dominate.   The struggle against death is by means of Eros, which always
implies the reaching out to the other.   But Eros and
Thanatos are in one sense not separable; their roles
overlap, their realms are coextensive.   Moreover, their
conflict is not limited to the biological, but extends
itself to the psychological, and to the cultural.
Ricoeur had analyzed guilt as one of the primary symbols of the fault; now he sees it in the context of
Freud's interpretation of culture:

> The sense of guilt is not seen as the
> instrument which culture uses, no
> longer against the libido, but against
> aggressiveness.   The switch of fronts
> is important.   Culture now represents
> the interests of Eros against myself,
> . . . and it uses my own self-violence
> to bring to naught my violence against
> others (306).

Negativity, Satisfaction, and Necessity

As conclusion to his reading of Freud, Ricoeur
explores three topics which he thinks Freud did not
resolve completely: negativity, satisfaction, and
necessity.   Negation may be thought of as the practical
application of the death wish, working itself out in a
growing consciousness of what is repressed, as well as
in a constant testing of reality.   This negativity is
assumed in every use of symbols as an attempt to master
that which is absent or that which is lost.   Ricoeur
uses an example here that intrigued both Freud and
Ricoeur: A little child had been taught not to cry
when his mother went out of sight, but he symbolically
represented the disappearance and the return of the
mother by making a wooden reel first appear and then
disappear, at the same time saying "fort" and then "da"
("gone"--"there").   Negation itself is a symbol of that
which is repressed or denied; in fact, the disappearance and the reappearance of play have counterparts in
artistic creation and in perceptual judgment; for

example, the artist producing a painting or the poet
creating a lyric symbolizes the presence of that which
is really absent; in the same way, the driver of a car
learns to symbolize the possible presence of an oncom-
ing car at an intersection. Thus, paradoxically, a
function of the death wish, negation, is at the same
time the testing of reality.

So too the problem of satisfaction remains a
paradox. The struggle between life and death means
endless dissatisfaction:

> Eros wishes union, but must disturb the
> peace of inertia; the death instinct
> wishes the return to the inorganic, but
> must destroy the living organism. This
> paradox continues on into the higher
> stages of civilized life: a strange
> struggle indeed, for civilization kills
> us in order to make us live, by using,
> for itself and against us, the sense of
> guilt, while at the same time we must
> loosen its embrace in order to live and
> find enjoyment (323).

The last of the three topics of negativity,
satisfaction, and necessity is symbolized by the Greek
Ananke, which stands for a world view that will not
shirk the difficulties and sufferings of life. To
recognize that death terminates life is to have a new
appreciation of what life is. The tension between a
desire for pleasure or satisfaction and the necessity
of facing reality is maintained in equilibrium by the
artist. Although he wants to run away from reality,
through his fantasy, his symbols, he finds a way back
to reality: he creates a work of art--a drama, a piece
of sculpture, a symphony--which becomes a new reality
and which can lead to wisdom. "The symbolic resolution
of conflicts through art, the transfer of desires and
hatreds to the plane of play, daydreams, and poetry,
borders on resignation; prior to wisdom, while waiting
for wisdom, the symbolic mode proper to the work of art
enables us to endure the harshness of life, and, suspended between illusion and reality, helps us to love
fate" (335). Art is one aspect of an education to
reality. Lying midway between illusion, which is
represented by religion, and reality, which is
represented by science, art is able to be the recon-
ciler.

With this exploration of the unresolved aspects of
Eros, Thanatos, and Ananke, Ricoeur concludes the

second of his three books within Freud and Philosophy.
In the first book he had situated Freud within the
hermeneutic problem; in the second he had attempted a
descriptive reading of Freud; in the third he will
provide a philosophical interpretation of Freudianism,
concluding with a theory of interpretation which is an
approach to symbol.

A Philosophical Interpretation of Freud

At the completion of his reading of Freud, Ricoeur
realizes how large is the task he had set himself, and
how unrealistic his hope for an early answer. To say
that symbols may be interpreted in different ways is
not the obvious statement it seems to be; on the contrary, the mere statement poses the problems of why
symbols can be interpreted in different ways, and more
particularly, of the correspondence or the lack of
correspondence between different interpretations. In
the last of the three books in Freud and Philosophy,
Ricoeur provides, not a solution, but some philosophic
comments which he hopes will contribute to a theory of
hermeneutics and to a better understanding of symbol.
The comments are arranged under three topics: 1) the
relation of Freudian theory and epistemology; 2) an
archeology of the subject, that is, a theory of the
structure of the subject who is knowing and choosing;
3) a teleology which, in the Hegelian style, clarifies
earlier concepts by later ones, so that there is a
progression of understanding; and 4) an attempt to
formulate the problem which is at the heart of Freud
and Philosophy, the conflict within Ricoeur and within
contemporary culture between an interpretation which
demystifies religion and an interpretation which tries
to recognize a call, a kerygma, a proclamation in the
symbols of faith.

First we may ask, what contribution does Freudian
theory make to an epistemology? Although the theory
does not meet the requirements of a strictly scientific
psychology, it does provide a model which has certain
similarities to points of view held by many psychologists today; however, it differs radically in those
aspects which cannot be measured or observed, such as
infantile repression and the Oedipus complex. Does
Freudianism then define consciousness in a way that
approximates that of phenomenology? The answer here is
negative too, but a comparison does sharpen the
Freudian concepts. The phenomenological reduction
tries to avoid the pitfall of appearances as self-

evident, just as Freudianism refuses to accept the
superficially "true." Both are concerned with intentionality, recognized as ordinary but unfathomable.
Both attribute importance to language and to intersubjectivity; nevertheless, psychoanalysis is not phenomenology because it is not reflexive, but dependent on
the technique of analysis, a special kind of interpretation. If Freudianism is not psychology, and it is
not phenomenology, what is its specific contribution to
a theory of knowledge, to an epistemology? Freud
showed the relationship of the knowing subject to his
origins, to his childhood desires, to his unconscious;
this is a relationship that neither psychologist, nor
philosopher, nor theologian should ignore.

In his philosophical interpretation of Freud,
Ricoeur next asks whether such structures as the
unconscious-preconscious-conscious model can be incorporated within a philosophy of reflection. Admitting
that such an interpretation cannot be part of the
eidetic method Ricoeur had maintained in his early
philosophic work, he reaffirms the necessity and the
justification of a hermeneutic method which recognizes
that knowledge is not autonomous, that it is rooted in
existence; that is, it is rooted in desire and effort.
Desire as such refers back to a substrate that cannot
be symbolized, but it is oriented toward language: "it
is in potency to speech" (457).

Ricoeur then moves to a chapter which he feels is
the radical dialectic, in which he juxtaposes archeology and teleology, an understanding of the beginnings
which Freud has so elaborately developed, and an understanding of direction toward an end worked out by Hegel
in The Phenomenology of Spirit. It would be easy to
make the superficial conclusion that the one comple-
ments the other. On the contrary, Ricoeur feels that
the dialectic reveals the implicit teleology of Freud--
a fate absolutely dependent on the desires of the
child, a culture dependent on the primitive working out
of unconscious desires. But, in contradictory fashion,
Freudianism also affirms a progress, a coming-to-be of
consciousness. This is summed up in his concept of
sublimation which Ricoeur calls empty, as far as it is
elaborated by Freud. Sublimation is a final symbol of
the factor which Freud has not really faced, the factor
of becoming conscious, of becoming the ego. Analytic
practice puts the progression of sublimation into practice, but it is not adequately thematized in Freud.
Sublimation includes regression, the work of understanding primitive beginnings, and the work of

progression, which moves forward to a new
consciousness. Both of these processes take place
through the same symbols. "Symbolism is the area of
identity between progression and regression. To understand this would be to enter into concrete reflection"
(493). But this is not a conclusion, but a task, the
task which Ricoeur holds out for himself in the future,
especially in his projected poetics of the will. Nevertheless, he feels he has advanced in the understanding
of himself, of Freud, of the hermeneutic enterprise,
and of symbols.

Hermeneutics: The Approaches to Symbol

        After exploring myth in The Symbolism of Evil,
Ricoeur summed up in the last chapter the new application or insights he had perceived about symbols. So
too, at the end of Freud and Philosophy, there is a
lengthy essay, the fruit of his investigation of Freud,
which concretizes the results in regard to symbol. In
spite of the long analyses in the two books, he realizes that he still has achieved only an approach to
symbol, which is a propaedeutic to the extensive work
not yet within reach--a general theory of hermeneutics.
Nevertheless, there are many new insights.

        The regression and progression of the archeology,
that is, of the structure of the knowing subject, and
of the teleology described above, can only be seen in
the concrete mixed texture which is symbol. The concrete symbol is the fullness or peak of understanding,
but for the philosopher, this must be preceded by the
discipline of thought in order not to lose the abundance of meaning which the symbol can supply. The poet
does not necessarily take this route; his or her understanding may be more intuitive. Parallel with the
process Ricoeur pursued in Freud and Philosophy, the
philosopher's discipline embraces three stages: 1) a
dispossession of consciousness such as the Freudian
theory can supply; 2) an antithetic, in which there is
a juxtaposition of apparent or real contradictions; and
3) the dialectic itself in which the opposites no
longer clash but pass one into the other. Then the
philosopher is able to reappropriate the symbol, to
listen to language; his or her reflection becomes the
fullness of speech, becomes hermeneutic, interpretation, a concrete reflection; the person has moved from
a precritical naiveté to a postcritical, informed
naiveté.

It is the two vectors of symbols, one impelled
toward the past, the other toward the future, which
carry the paradoxical qualities of concealing and revealing, the two sides of one symbolic function. Although analysis separates the two, they are really one,
as the process of sublimation makes clear. In fact, it
may be said that sublimation is the symbolic function,
in that it subsumes the primitive drives and wishes of
childhood, for example, the Oedipal wish to be the
mother's lover, and channels such a desire to a creative symbolism which becomes a work of art or a religious attitude. It is this creative orientation toward
the future which Freud denied, or occasionally left
open as he did in his positive placement of art, and to
which Ricoeur wishes to give a renewed and proper emphasis.

Freud's definition of symbol was too narrow,
confined to the stereotypes which tend universally to
appear in dreams; yet, his interpretation widened to a
broader scope. To bring order to the contradictory
definitions, Ricoeur hypothesizes three levels of creativity of symbols: 1) a lowest level, a sedimented
symbolism, which includes broken and stereotyped remains of symbols; these are the symbols of dreams,
fairytales, legends, so commonplace they have only a
past; 2) an intermediate level, which includes the
symbols of everyday life, those which are useful in the
carrying out of social life; these have both a present
and a past, and make up the subject matter of structural anthropology; 3) at the highest level are
prospective symbols which reach down to the living
substrate of symbols to create new meaning.

As a framework in which to explore the movement of
symbols, Ricoeur makes use of a hierarchy of fundamental feelings, which he had taken from Kant and developed in his own Fallible Man. The section is even
labeled: The Hierarchical Order of Symbol. The three
are: avoir, pouvoir, valoir--having, power, valuing,
the first being incorporated into the second, and both
having and power being incorporated into valuing.
Although in the Freudian scheme, these three are derived from the unconscious, from childhood sexual desires, they are in Ricoeur's opinion quests which are
properly human, which create new relationships to
things and to persons. Part of human being's becoming
conscious of self is the experience of a new mode of
existence: having things and using them as extensions
of self, or experiencing their lack as a form of alienation in the way described by Marx. All aspects of

having are, of course, permeated with symbolism, from
the symbolism of the welfare check to the symbolism of
the Cadillac.

Beyond and including the level of having is the
level of power, described by Hegel as comprising the
relation of obeying and commanding which is essential
to political structure. "Hence one can say that human
being becomes human insofar as a person can enter into
the political problematic of power, adopt the feelings
that center around power, and deliver the self up to
the evils accompanying that power (509). This area,
too, is obviously pervaded by symbols, whether it be
the larger desk and the name on the door, or the position of keeper of the keys.

Valuing is the uniquely human sphere of meaning
which includes the levels of having and of power. In
contrast to the fields of economics and of politics,
Ricoeur calls the area of valuing the region of culture, in which the symbols of human being are to be
found in law, art, and literature. Van Gogh's painting
of a yellow chair is also a symbol of a human being and
his world of meaning. It is through the symbols on
this level that human being has the possibility of
achieving dignity or of destroying the self. Through
an analysis of Sophocles' Oedipus Rex, a privileged and
prototypic symbol, Ricoeur demonstrates the profound,
though paradoxical identity of both the regressive and
progressive hermeneutics, that is, the identity of the
archeology and of the teleology. In his analysis,
Freud seemed aware only of the first, interpreting the
narrative as a fulfillment of the childhood wish to
kill the father and marry the mother. Ricoeur acknowledges the profound insight of such an interpretation,
but also emphasizes the progressive symbolism which
creates a new meaning: Oedipus Rex as a tragedy of
truth. In his pride, Oedipus has a passion for not-
knowing; he does not wish to see the truth. Through
his suffering, he comes to see; paradoxically, he
achieves light through blindness. Thus the symbol
created by Sophocles maintains its unity through its
double power of disguising and revealing.

The following lines of continuity may help clarify
some of the relationships described above. Each continuum is dynamic, with constant backward and forward
movements; each belongs in the interacting spheres of
having, power, and valuing. Each part also has a cosmic aspect which is not shown here.

night- dreams	day- dreams	play, humor	folklore, legends	works of art

```
<─────────────────────────────────────────────────>
 dreams/                              works of art/
 oneiric                                     poetic

 disguise                             disclosure
<────────────────────────────────────────────────>
 distortion                           revelation


 sedimentary          everyday          creative
<────────────────────────────────────────────────>
 symbols              symbols           symbols
```

This double value of disguise and disclosure
opens the meaning of certain words which seem to have
within themselves contradictory connotations. One
example is the word education.

> Thus the term "education" designates
> the movement by which human being is
> led out of childhood; this movement is,
> in the proper sense, an "erudition"
> whereby human being is lifted out of
> the archaic past; but it is also a
> Bildung, in the two-fold sense of an
> edification and an emergence of the
> Bilder or "images of human being" which
> mark off the development of self-
> consciousness and open human being to
> what they disclose. And this educa-
> tion, this erudition, this Bildung
> function as a second nature, for they
> remodel human being's first nature
> (523-524).

Thus, education is both a leading out and a going
forward. Both are going on simultaneously, each influenced by the other.

Symbols maintain a unity, in spite of their
disparate uses and aims in realms as various as dreams
and works of art, through what Ricoeur calls "hyletic
matter" (521). He uses hylê in the way Husserl uses it
to connote "matter" which includes sensations, as well
as affectations or feelings. In other words, the symbol remains substantially the same, whether it appears
in a dream, a folk tale, or a drama, but it is transformed, or sublimated, or directed differently in vary-
ing uses and situations, so that at a given time there
may be more emphasis on the disguising function of the

symbol, and another time more emphasis on the revealing
function. For this reason, it seems likely that any of
the great symbols used in literature or art have their
roots in the conflicting desires of the individual
childhood, or in the "childhood" of human being.

This same unity-and-ambiguity of the symbol is
also true of religious symbols. Nevertheless, Ricoeur
warns against a facile analogy; in the context of the
kerygma, a word proclaimed to him, Ricoeur agrees with
Karl Barth about the radical Otherness of the One addressing the word. Genesis is not reducible to archeology, nor is eschatology reducible to teleology.
Nevertheless, the Wholly Other is revealed in the
kerygma, which paradoxically is an annihilation of the
radical otherness. The meditative thought which draws
on a phenomenology of the sacred and a kerygmatic exegesis offer new symbolic expressions which are at the
edge of the break and the rebonding, the rupture and
the suture, between language and the Wholly Other. In
this context, the symbols of evil are not just one set
among many, but privileged because they save a decisive
aspect of human being; they are, as it were, the water-
shed of human history.

Human being is constantly tempted to objectify the
Wholly Other, to objectify the symbols. If persons do
this in the area of metaphysics, they objectify God as
supreme being; they reduce the sacred to a realm of
objects and institutions. In Ricoeur's view, this is a
diabolic transformation, the illusion described by
Freud, the idolatry which the prophets denounced. To
avoid that illusion and that idolatry human being must
constantly engage in the dynamics of the archeology and
the teleology, looking back to demythologize desires,
to remove the distortions of meaning, and looking ahead
to create new meanings. The same dynamics apply to
becoming conscious, to being educated, and to becoming
religious in the nonidolatrous sense of that word.
Just as a person is subject to alienation in the progressive spheres of having, power, and valuing, so is
the religious attitude tempted to idolatry in each of
those areas. The kerygma offers the possibility of
liberation, of salvation, in those same realms.

In the three books, then, of Freud and Philosophy,
Ricoeur attempted to place Freud within the problematic
of hermeneutics; he provided a philosophical reading of
Freud and concluded with a philosophical interpretation
oriented toward hermeneutics as an approach to symbol.
At the end of the study, he had attained new insights,

not only about Freud and about himself, but about
symbols, and especially about religious symbols.

CHAPTER THREE

Symbol in *The Conflict of Interpretations*

Some important concepts regarding symbol are contained in the collection of articles published originally in 1969 as The Conflict of Interpretations. The earliest date for an individual paper is 1960, the latest, 1969. The articles are grouped under five topics: 1) Hermeneutics and Structuralism, 2) Hermeneutics and Psychoanalysis, 3) Hermeneutics and Phenomenology, 4) The Symbolism of Evil Interpreted, and 5) Religion and Faith. Some of the papers seem to have been revised to be included as chapters in The Symbolism of Evil or in Freud and Philosophy, since some sentences are identical and much material is similar. Sometimes there is a fuller treatment in the article in The Conflict of Interpretations. In other cases, Ricoeur seems to have picked up an idea first presented in The Symbolism of Evil or in Freud and Philosophy and to have developed it more fully in an address published in The Conflict of Interpretations. An example of this kind of development is "Fatherhood: from Phantasm to Symbol," an address given at Rome in 1969. Some of the basic ideas appear in the last chapter of Freud and Philosophy, published in the French edition in 1965.

For the purpose of this study, although the dates of some of the articles are earlier than the publication dates of The Symbolism of Evil and of Freud and Philosophy, the comments on symbol will be considered supplementary to those already presented, and viable since Ricoeur gathered them for publication in 1969. Rather than repeat observations which have been sufficiently developed already, this section will elaborate only those concepts which significantly add to the theory or extend its implications. Sometimes also, the different wording in The Conflict of Interpretations may provide an insight to Ricoeur's meaning.

The insights from these articles will be grouped
under four headings: 1) symbolism and interpretation,
2) the symbol of original sin, 3) medieval symbolism,
and 4) liberty and the act of faith.

Symbolism and interpretation. These two are
correlative concepts, that is, wherever there is a
multiple sense, there is also interpretation; similarly, when one interprets, one reveals the multiple meanings. The cogito is only able to know itself through
the documents of its life, its objects, its works, and
its acts. Where it finds equivocal language, it must
separate equivocation which is only confusion from that
which is the result of an excess of meaning, such as
that which properly belongs to the symbol. In that
excess of meaning, there is not a formal logic, but a
transcendental logic, subject to its own norms of validation.

Although the symbolic is dependent on language,
paradoxically it is the matrix of expression for a
reality which is outside of, or beyond language, so
that one may say that there is no mystery in
language--the phonemes, morphemes, etc., can be properly classified; one should rather speak of the mystery
of language. In an analogous way, one may say that
analysis and synthesis do not coincide; although analysis of a symbol can sound its depths to produce certain
resonances, at the same time, that very analysis
destroys its integrity which is only maintained in the
synthetic view, summarized in the expression of Gustave
Guillaume: the signs are the reverse of the universe
(CI, 260).

The time of symbols has a double relation to
history. On the one hand, as the symbol is transmitted
in interpretation, it is subject to the process of
sedimentation, so that what was once a living symbol
becomes a dead symbol; at the same time, paradoxically,
the same symbol bears the tradition which can constantly converse with, criticize, and renew the symbol.
This metamorphosis of meaning Ricoeur compares to a
palimpsest, a parchment written upon several times, one
text being erased before the next is written. The
erasure, however, is not complete, so that one layer
can be detected beneath another, often with the concomitant problem of determining whether material belongs to one layer or another.

The symbol of original sin. Such a process can be
seen operating in the symbol of original sin. From

their Hebrew tradition, the early Christians inherited
a penitential literature, which included elements of
human responsibility and the attribution of evil in the
world to human being--to Adam. As Paul meditated on
that tradition in the light of his understanding of
Christ, he provided an interpretation which wedded the
two: a parallelism of Adam and Christ: through Christ
grace entered the world, just as sin had entered
through Adam. The interpretation has both enlarged and
restricted the original symbol: it enlarged it to
include righteousness, the gift of Christ with all the
theological possibilities which that implies, but the
interpretation also restricted the original symbol by
channeling the myth into a parallelism which implied a
sort of one-to-one correspondence, and thus opened the
way to some of the misleading and overly simplified
allegorizing of the first Christian centuries. In
order to express the symbol, Paul necessarily interpreted it.

     For the rational person, especially in the western
tradition, symbol moves easily from the level of image
and myth to the level of speculation, and as it does,
it hovers at the edge of an abyss on either side, the
abyss of allegory or the abyss of gnosis. The interpreter more inclined to reflective thought, to the
rational, to the logical, tends toward allegorizing;
the interpreter with more aptitude for the intuitive is
disposed to gnosis. Although he spent his Christian
life interpreting the symbols, Augustine recognized in
his own interpretations the very difficulties described
above. In his earlier writings, he had conceptualized
"original sin" along the lines initiated by Paul; he
opposed an "evil will" to an "evil nature." But in his
later writings he tended to confine himself to the
basic symbol of an "inherited sin." In spite of the
fact that it seems to contradict intelligence, false
knowledge may be at the same time true symbol. That is
why a twentieth century theologian may criticize the
exegesis of a Paul or the speculation of an Augustine
without denying the symbol of "original sin," just as a
theologian five centuries from now will criticize the
limited knowledge of twentieth century theologians,
while affirming the validity of the same symbols.

     Medieval symbolism. One aspect of medieval
symbolism saw nature as a "book" mirroring the book of
the scriptures, the first to be interpreted in the
light of the second. This was a perception that one
symbol is understood in the context of a set of symbols. In this medieval world view, each element of the

visible creation was a reflection of an invisible
creation. Again, the interpretation both reveals by
its creative exploration, and hides by the limitations
it introduces. The heights of medieval mysticism and
the fullness of the "life of faith" testify to the
creative and creating aspect, while the abuses of the
bestiary and the excesses of superstition in regard to
relics, for example, witness to the distorting quality
of this interpretation.

In the medieval exegesis of scripture, Ricoeur
recognizes and recommends the work of de Lubac on the
four senses. Ricoeur finds especially harmonious with
his own work the emphasis on the unity of the interpretation, that hermeneutics extends to the whole economy
of Christian existence, and that the explication of
texts must coincide with the exploration of mysteries,
with the event of Christ as the controlling symbol,
giving life to the others.

Liberty and the act of faith. For Ricoeur, the
freedom of the act of faith is a particular case of the
general power of choosing, or of forming an opinion.
On a second level, he defines religious liberty as a
particular case of the general right to form opinions
without interference from the public power. And on
still a third level, he sees religious liberty as a
quality of freedom which belongs to the religious phenomenon as such. "A hermeneutics of religious freedom
is an interpretation of freedom in conformity with the
Resurrection, interpreted in terms of promise and hope"
(CI, 406). Ricoeur sees freedom as arising from the
possibility proclaimed in the kerygma, especially as
interpreted by Moltmann in his theology of hope which
places the kerygma in the context of the promise, of
the kingdom which is to come, with an implicit mission
to take part in bringing that kingdom to reality. In
practice, such a mission cannot be separated from a
deciphering of the signs of the new creation, that is,
from a reappropriation of the desire to be through the
works which bear witness to that desire. Such a sending, with the corresponding reading of the signs and
the concretizing of the desire to be, generates an
ethics with social, political, and even cosmic implications. The kerygma thus understood shifts the center
of ethics from the subjective of personal authenticity
to the reconciling power of social and political justice. Thus, Christian liberty belongs to the order of
the resurrection. Following Luther, Ricoeur sees this
as a freedom from death, a freedom for life, the folly
of the cross, and the wisdom of the resurrection. But

to affirm liberty is to attribute to human being the
origin of evil. And what does this signify for ethics?
Again the paradox: human being is entirely a sinner,
but more or less blameable. The very capacity for evil
limits freedom. The apparent contradiction is saved by
the hope for deliverance, a hope which works itself out
in a deliverance through grace or a deliverance through
law, such as was analyzed under the topic of Phariseeism in The Symbolism of Evil.

The three levels, then, of religious liberty are
permeated by the power of the symbol. Even the initial
forming of an opinion is dependent on the symbols
operating in the one forming the opinion, whether they
are the symbols belonging to the archeology described
by Freud, or the symbols belonging to the possibility
of resurrection. On the second level, the State has no
right to impose symbols or to impinge on symbols in
such a way as to restrict religious liberty in the
political sense. Lastly, symbols are integral to
ethics, whether it is a question of choosing the "God
of the promise" or the choosing of God as idol, whether
it is a question of salvation through the law or salvation through grace. In other words, symbols are integral to the reappropriation of the desire for life
through the acts which witness to that life.

After Freud and Philosophy and the articles in The
Conflict of Interpretations, there is relatively little
mention of the word symbol. There are two reasons.
One is that Ricoeur came to understand, as he had noted
at the beginning of Freud and Philosophy that the use
of symbol in diverse ways in so many disciplines tends
to diffuse its meaning and lead to confusion instead of
clarity. The other reason is that his work moved to
more of an emphasis on language, including metaphor and
interpretation, as the focus for pursuing his studies.
He had both broadened his understanding of the concept
of symbol--closer to that of Cassirer--and yet narrowed
the foci of his studies for greater clarity.

Nevertheless, symbol is never lost sight of. It
appears in "Metaphor and Symbol" in Interpretation
Theory and is alluded to frequently in the context of
"symbolic function." The concept of a "double meaning"
expression underlies much if not all of the structure
of the work on metaphor and narrative.

CHAPTER FOUR

Symbol and the Task of a Philosophy of Language

In the last chapters Ricoeur's theory of symbol
was elaborated with insufficient reference to the
totality of his work. The theory will now be placed in
the overall context of his philosophic task. This
enlargement of perspective will make use of four horizons, each, as it were, more extensive than the previous one. The first is Ricoeur's early orientation,
guided by his study of Husserl, Jaspers, and Marcel;
the second is the project Ricoeur originally set for
himself of elaborating a philosophy of the will; the
third horizon is that of a growing hermeneutics; and
the fourth is a concern for the fullness of language.
In Ricoeur's work, each of these horizons has grown out
of those which preceded; the unanswered questions
raised in one investigation have dictated the direction
for the next inquiry. Such openness makes a systematic
synthesis difficult; it also leaves one exposed to
criticism, but at the same time, it approaches reality
with more truth than that supplied by a myopic view of
pseudo-synthesis.

Early Orientation

In May, 1971, Ricoeur summarized the modifications
of direction his work had undergone up to that point,
and the directions he saw emerging. He set this early
period in the context of an existential phenomenology:

> In my first work I had relied heavily
> on a reflective method which came from
> both Husserl and the existentialist
> pair, Jaspers and Marcel, to whom I had
> devoted two books. I may now call this
> kind of first description an existen-
> tial phenomenology (PPR, 86).

The central problem was "embodiment" in the sense
explored by Husserl emphasizing body as a physisch-
aesthesiologische unity (Husserl, 63), and in the sense
which Marcel described as "incarnational existence."
At this time, in company with other phenomenologists,
Ricoeur assumed that a direct language was available,
that is, the ordinary language which includes words
such as purpose and motive. Although the problem of
symbol had not arisen yet, the phenomenological emphasis on perceived experience opened the way to the emphasis in The Symbolism of Evil on the primitive experience of the primary symbols of defilement, sin, and
guilt. In regard to language, Ricoeur would discover
through his investigations of myth and of Freudian
psychoanalysis the inadequacy of the direct language of
phenomenology. On the other hand, he would try to
maintain the basic phenomenological methodology, even
when describing the experience of symbol.

Another emphasis derived at least partly from his
work on Husserl was the concern for consciousness.
Although Husserl defines consciousness as a power to go
beyond itself, this creativity is always led by the
object as transcendental guide. As Ricoeur examined
"fault" in Fallible Man, as he came to understand the
necessity of indirect language to describe the experience of defilement in The Symbolism of Evil, and as he
acknowledged the Freudian insights in regard to the
unconscious and the symbolic function of dreams, his
concept of consciousness and its relationship to object
were enlarged so much that he found it necessary to
speak of grafting a hermeneutics onto his phenomenology.

In spite of the fact that the phenomenological
understanding of consciousness was found to be inadequate, the concern for the growth of consciousness, the
coming to awareness of oneself, the explication of
experience as a means of discovering oneself, is the
very orientation which helped lead Ricoeur to the importance of incorporating the symbol within his phenomenology.

In his study of Husserl, there is also revealed an
early concern with sign, "the phenomenology of signification" (Husserl, 4).

> The question is whether the facts of
> the understanding, concepts, and judg-
> ments should be studied as psychologi-
> cal facts, consequently with all the

> subjective conditions which accompany
> them in their formation, or whether
> they should be considered as general
> elements of representation, elements
> independent of the consciousness we can
> have of them (4-5).

There seems to be an anticipation here of the
representational aspects of symbol, as well as an awareness of the importance of the reality which is not
entirely subject to consciousness. There is also an
awareness of cultural objects, such as monuments,
works, and institutions, as reflections of consciousness, although they are not yet designated as symbols
(81).

The Project of a Philosophy of the Will

Because Ricoeur had limited his first volume The
Voluntary and the Involuntary to an eidetics, a "pure
description," of the voluntary and the involuntary, he
found it necessary to set aside or bracket both "fault"
and "transcendence." Such a step forced him to ask the
question: had he thereby set aside the most important
elements in human experience? In spite of the probability of an affirmative answer, Ricoeur pursued his
task by examining decision making, human capabilities,
and the relationship of consent and necessity. At the
conclusion of his work, Ricoeur felt that he had expelled the false dualism of "mind" and "will"--"To will
is to think"--but that at the same time, he had exposed
a more "radical duality at the very core of the subject, the duality of aspects or moments of willing"
(VI, 482). Through coming to understand the limits of
willing, he had arrived at an understanding of the
limited character of freedom. Freedom arises out of
indecision and always involves risk.

Although symbol is not often mentioned explicitly
in The Voluntary and the Involuntary, and although the
theory would not be expressed precisely until nine
years later in the article "The Symbol . . . Food for
Thought," this eidetics of the will is imbued with the
"cipher" or "symbol" theory which Ricoeur had absorbed
from Jaspers. One example may serve to illustrate.

> The only objective symbol of willing is
> a certain oriented manner of behavior,
> a specific "form" of action; we shall
> see in what manner the remarkable

> studies of the "gestaltist" school are
> able to help us to disengage this func-
> tion of "diagnosis" of the body-as-
> object with regard to the body-as-one's-own (221. Translation modified).

Here the total act of willing is objectified in the
symbol or the figure of a body-in-action. It might be
the "practiced ease of a dancer," or the "tension of
the athlete straining to the limits of his power." As
symbol, it reveals that which is not reducible to
words, an "extra-linguistic reality" which requires an
interpretation. This kind of interpretation is so
taken for granted in ordinary communication that the
power of the symbol is usually ignored, unless a dancer
or an artist creates it for us anew.

As Volume I, then, of a Philosophy of the Will,
The Voluntary and the Involuntary presented an eidetics
of the will which, while removing the false dualism of
a mind-body dichotomy, revealed a perhaps more radical
duality in the moments of willing, that same duality
described by Paul in Romans 7.19: the good which I
want to do, I fail to do.

Volume II, the empirics of the will entitled
Finitude and Guilt, appeared ten years later, in 1960,
in two books Fallible Man and The Symbolism of Evil.
To call human being fallible is to say that the possibility of moral evil is inherent in human being's constitution, that the human reality has the specific
limitation of not coinciding with itself. "Feeling is
conflict and reveals human being as primordial conflict
(FM, 216). Although Ricoeur had anticipated that fault
does not belong to an eidetics of human being, his
working out of what he had projected as an empirics led
him to realize that fault is not accessible to any
description, even one based on experience. This is
where he was led to the concreteness of myth and the
language of avowal analyzed earlier in the context of
The Symbolism of Evil.

The concept of fallibility makes it understandable
that evil has come into the world, so that one may
speak of "an anthropology of fallibility" and "a philosophy of disproportion." The servile will is a rid-
dle: somehow, a will that is free is also bound, and
always finds itself bound. This is "the ultimate theme
that the symbol gives to thought" (FM, xxiii). Ricoeur
states that he could have used as a subtitle for the
book Fallible Man the phrase "Grandeur and Limitation

of an Ethical Vision of the World," because the
recovery of a symbolics of evil tends toward an ethical
vision of the world, that is, toward a continual effort
to understand freedom and evil by each other. As the
Adamic myth indicates, human being is responsible, and
therefore guilty, but at the same time, human being is
somehow victim. A person brings evil, but paradoxically, evil was already there. It was the consideration of evil as it developed through the absurd of the
fault in Fallible Man and the necessity of an indirect
symbolic language in The Symbolism of Evil that compelled Ricoeur to confront the linguistic perplexities
which refocused his endeavors. He found himself thrust
into the heart of the hermeneutic problem, the problem
of interpretation. From the first horizon, then, of a
phenomenological method in the style of Husserl, and a
meditation on mystery and paradox stimulated by Marcel
and Jaspers, had grown the second horizon of a philosophy of the will; now the stimulus of symbolic language
as necessary to express the fault enlarges the horizon
still farther to what we may call a growing hermeneutics.

A Growing Hermeneutics

This horizon is called a growing hermeneutics
because its beginnings were anticipated long before the
myth exploration of The Symbolism of Evil, and because
the fourth horizon of the fullness of language is an
extension, as it were, of hermeneutics, that is, of
interpretation theory.

In both of the volumes of Finitude and Guilt,
Ricoeur had perceived explicitly the importance of
hermeneutics. In the preface to Fallible Man, he had
realized that a symbolics of evil, although it would
enrich his philosophic discourse, would also necessi-
tate "a revolution in method, represented by the re-
course to a hermeneutics, that is, to rules of deciphering applied to a world of symbols" (xxi). Having
used this revolution in method throughout The Symbolism
of Evil, Ricoeur summarized the process and the insights in the last chapter, which he called the key to
the two volume work: The Symbol Gives Rise to Thought.

> What we need is an interpretation that
> respects the original enigma of the
> symbols, that lets itself be taught by
> them, but that, beginning from there,
> promotes the meaning, forms the meaning

in the full responsibility of
autonomous thought (SE, 349-350).

Since symbols have always been and are now a part of
human experience, interpretation is always necessary.
Now, however, modern hermeneutics is able to take advantage of critical thought; this should not increase
alienation, but should enable us to appropriate the
meaning, to make it our own, in a way heretofore not
possible. As children of criticism, we should be able,
by means of criticism, to go beyond it, not to have
less meaning, but to have more, in other words, to work
for a hermeneutics which restores meaning. Ricoeur
feels that this purpose animated Schelling, Schleiermacher, and Dilthey, as well as thinkers like Eliade,
Jung, and Bultmann. In fact, a second naiveté, a
second immediacy is only available through hermeneutics: "we can believe only by interpreting" (352). By
interpreting we can hear again. Stimulated by criticism and by the philosophic task itself, Ricoeur seeks
to transform the hermeneutic circle by turning it into
a wager, a wager that he will have a better understanding of human being by following the direction of symbolic thought; moreover, he will also understand better
the bond between human being and the being of all beings.

Such a recognition of the essential part played by
hermeneutics in the understanding of human experience
dictated the direction of the next work pursued by
Ricoeur, which culminated in the publication in 1965 of
Freud and Philosophy. Though less appealing to a buying public perhaps, the French title more clearly indicates the place of the book in Ricoeur's total enterprise: De l'interprétation. Although the focus is the
work of Freud as the subtitle "Essays on Freud" indicates, Ricoeur's purpose is far larger than an understanding of Freud. It was in Freud and Philosophy that
the problem of symbol became explicitly for Ricoeur the
problem of hermeneutics, of interpretation. In his
summarizing address in 1971, he reflected on his developing discernment of the hermeneutic field.

But I must now say that at the time I
was not aware of the real dimension of
the hermeneutical problem. Perhaps
because I did not want to be drawn into
the immensity of this problem, I tried
to limit the definition of hermeneutics
to the specific problem of the interpretation of symbolic language. I

        still held this position in my book on
        Freud (PPR, 88).

It was here that he discovered that there are two
hermeneutics, one reductive like those of Freud, Marx,
and Nietzsche, the other restorative, moving toward a
recollection of the original meaning of the symbol.
Hermeneutics was henceforth a battlefield. Ricoeur saw
his problem as that of seeking, not only to understand
these two approaches, but to link their dynamics in
moving from a first pre-critical naiveté to a post-
critical second naiveté, that is, in moving to self-
knowledge which "is a striving for truth by means of
this inner contest between reductive and recollective
interpretation" (89).   Earlier, Ricoeur had perceived
that a hermeneutic of symbols also opened the way between "the naive historicism of fundamentalism and the
bloodless moralism of rationalism" (CI, 285).

        Although in Freud and Philosophy, Ricoeur felt he
was limiting the hermeneutic problem, the breadth of
the problem seems nevertheless to have been implicitly
apprehended:

                Reflection calls for an interpretation
                and tends to move into hermeneutics.
                The ultimate root of our problem lies
                in this primitive connection between
                the act of existing and the signs we
                deploy in our works; reflection must
                become interpretation because I cannot
                grasp the act of existing except in
                signs scattered in the world. That is
                why a reflective philosophy must in-
                clude the results, methods, and presup-
                positions of all the sciences that try
                to decipher and interpret the signs of
                human being (FP, 46).

Once again, Ricoeur here notes his debt to Jean Nabert
who had linked act and sign. Human being can only
understand his or her own existence, can only understand the self, through the signs--personal and
cultural--scattered in the world, and a person only
understands as he or she interprets these signs. By
1967 Ricoeur defines interpretation as "the discernment
of a hidden meaning in an apparent sense," and he describes as hermeneutic any discipline "which proceeds
by interpretation" (CI, 264). The integral connection
between hermeneutics and self-understanding is always
kept sight of as well: "in reflective hermeneutics the

constitution of <u>self</u> and that of meaning are
contemporaneous" (WT, 145). The constitution of self
is a strong phrase; it should be taken for its full
value. A person only becomes a self as he or she
builds meaning, and a person builds meaning only
through the interpretation of the signs in the world.
    As Ricoeur extended his understanding of her-
meneutics, he was gradually led to realize that the
"language of avowal," "mythic language," and the
desire-meaning language of Freudian interpretation were
only parts of the larger problem of language itself.

The Fullness of Language

    A gradual enlargement of perspective has described
three horizons in the development of Ricoeur's work: a
first horizon of his early orientation formed by his
study of Husserl, Marcel, and Jaspers; a second horizon
of the projected philosophy of the will; and a third of
a growing hermeneutics. This brings us to the fourth
horizon of the fullness of language, a phrase used by
Ricoeur, and apparently the subject matter of "a philosophy of language" and of "a phenomenology of language."

Anticipation of the Importance of Language

    As a Christian and as a teacher, Ricoeur had long
been interested in the Word. Two articles in History
and Truth make this clear: "Work and the Word" and "La
parole est mon royaume." In the first there is an
emphasis on the relationship of doing and saying and on
the power of the spoken word. Through the word human
being becomes a signifying being, one who pronounces
upon the self at the same time making a judgment on the
self and bringing the self's own being to light. The
word renders service to work by acting as a corrective
of the division of work, by giving meaning to leisure,
for example, in politics, in the novel, in the theater,
in conversation; the word provides the foundation or
theory for the pragmatic activities of human being--
here education, and especially the university, finds
its task. Lastly, as creation, the word is at the
roots of the building of civilization: "through literature and the arts is pursued the invention and the
discovery of a sense of human being which no state can
systematically plan or arrange, which is the supreme
risk for the artist and for the society which produces
the artist" (218).

Two years later in a special issue of Esprit on
"The Reform of Teaching," Ricoeur proclaimed, "The Word
is my Kingdom."

> What is that which I do when I teach?
> I speak. I have no other livelihood
> and I have no other dignity; I have no
> other manner of transforming the world
> and I have no other influence on men.
> The word is my work; the word is my
> kingdom. . . . My reality and my life
> is the empire of words, of phrases, and
> of discourse (PEMR, 192).

But this importance of words is not only personal; it
is essential to the enterprise of education, and thereby to the work of civilization itself:

> The university is the universe of the
> multiple powers of language in the
> moment of the communication of speak-
> ing. From then on there is only one
> thing that a reform of teaching is not
> able to propose to change: the end of
> the rule of the word in teaching. All
> reform is reform at the interior of the
> language that one generation speaks to
> the other in order to transmit the
> fruits and the movement of its culture
> (193).

Besides his concern for the word as a Christian
and as a teacher, Ricoeur's philosophic work constantly
kept the problem of language before his mind. Reflecting on the philosophies of Jaspers and Marcel made
Ricoeur affirm that consciousness seeks an intimate
relationship with the object so that it may become
sign, language, and witness of being, such as it is for
poets and mystics (KJ, 100). At this point, Ricoeur
spoke of three levels of language: first, a primitive
base of ciphers or symbols which, like the experience
of an awe-inspiring sunset, precede language, but express the immediate language of being; secondly,
figures or symbols which have need of a mediation, the
language of human beings, a mythics of being; and
thirdly, the speculative language of philosophy (GMKJ,
281).

In Fallible Man, Ricoeur noted the root concepts
of a theory of language in Plato and in Aristotle: the
logos of Plato which has the two-fold function of

communicating to others (indicating) and of designating
something (signifying), and the interpretation of the
pathe in Aristotle, which is the statement. Language
is not the perception of what is seen, but it transmits
the intention. To achieve meaning, the word becomes a
sign. "What is said, the lekton of my legein, . . .
transcends, as an ideal meaning-unity, the simple experience of the statement" (FM, 43).

As has been indicated already, The Symbolism of
Evil was a turning point in Ricoeur's philosophic development: he came to realize that it was necessary
"to renounce the chimera of a philosophy without presuppositions and begin from a full language" (SE, 19).
He hopes for a re-creation of language because "we wish
to be called again" (349).

The centrality of language becomes explicit in
Freud and Philosophy; indeed, human being is language
(FP, 383).

> It seems to me there is an area today
> where all philosophical investigations
> cut across one another--the area of
> language. Language is the common meet-
> ing ground of Wittgenstein's investiga-
> tions, the English linguistic phi-
> losophy, the phenomenology that stems
> from Husserl, Heidegger's investiga-
> tions, the works of the Bultmannian
> school and of the other schools of New
> Testament exegesis, the works of com-
> parative history of religion and of
> anthropology concerning myth, ritual,
> and belief--and finally psychoanalysis.
> Today we are in search of a comprehen-
> sive philosophy of language to account
> for the multiple functions of the human
> act of signifying and for their inter-
> relationships (FP, 3).

But at the same time, language is "from the outset and
for the most part distorted: it means something other
than what it says, it has a double meaning, it is equivocal" (FP, 7). Because persons are born into language, language is not so much spoken by them as spoken
to them. Ordinary language has an incurable ambiguity,
amphibolous constructions, and a confusion inherent in
idiomatic expressions and in metaphor. Just as symbolization (in Freudian interpretation) is the counter-
part of dissatisfaction, so speech is the result of

unsatisfied desire, for the symbolic relation is formed within language. But for Ricoeur, the restoration of meaning always moves toward kerygma:

> I speak of the Wholly Other only
> insofar as it addresses itself to me;
> and the kerygma, the glad tidings, is
> precisely that it addresses itself to
> me and ceases to be the Wholly Other
> . . . for what annihilates itself in
> our flesh is the Wholly Other as logos.
> Thereby it becomes an event of human
> speech and can be recognized only in
> the movement of interpretation of this
> human speech (FP, 525).

Paradoxically, there is also another power of language, a call in which I leave off all desire and demand, a call to which I listen.

Toward a Philosophy of Language

Since the publication in 1965 of Freud and Philosophy, Ricoeur's work seems to consist largely in explorations which will comprise a philosophy of language. He lists four reasons for this shift from a philosophy of the will to a central concern for language: 1) the reflection on psychoanalytic theory; 2) the change in the philosophic scene in France, where structuralism threatened to replace existentialism as well as phenomenology; 3) the continuing interest in religious language and specifically theologies of the Word; and 4) an increasing interest in the British and American school of ordinary language philosophy (PPR, 88). The emphasis here will be to indicate Ricoeur's investigations which reflect his interaction with the ideas presented by structuralism and by ordinary language philosophy.

In "New Developments in Phenomenology in France: The Phenomenology of Language," Ricoeur shows how a concern for language grew out of phenomenology since "all being comes to description as phenomenology, as appearing, consequently as meaning to be explained" (NDPF, 10). Although this concern was in a form which excluded any connection with modern linguistics or the semiological model, Ricoeur hopes to continue the development, but at the same time, to satisfy the demands posed by the semiotic disciplines. Defining semiology

as the science of signs, Ricoeur calls Ferdinand de
Saussure its founder and Louis Hjelmslev its theoreti-
cian. For them, language is a closed system of signs,
each sign defined by its difference from others; for
example, "up" may be defined as the opposite of "down,"
but there are no meanings, only values, that is, relative, negative, or opposing characteristics. Such a
system has neither subject nor reference; it may be
compared to the rules of chess, without the moves, the
players, or the game. Phenomenology must respond to
the challenge "of semiology, of structural linguistics,
of all the 'structuralisms' which have proliferated in
the neighboring sciences, in the critical literature
and even in the substantive works that become their own
object in a kind of mirror relationship" (19). Phenomenology must renew the meaning of transcendence in
sign, the importance of the speaking subject, and the
symbolic function itself by which human being creates
meaning.

Opposed to the semiotics of a closed system of
language is the semantic function, of which the basic
unit is the sentence. Although one can and should
describe the semiotics involved, the fullness of meaning emerges only in the semantics which implies an
interpretation. An example may make this clear. If
one examines the phrase "Our Father who art in heaven"
semiotically or structurally, one can define father as
that relationship opposed to son, heaven as a relationship opposed to hell and relative to earth. A phenomenology making use of the interpreting function of a
communication episode will be more aware of the multiple possibilities such as those outlined in the article
"Fatherhood: From Phantasm to Symbol."

> The problem of multiple meaning, which
> is perhaps the pivot of all semantic
> problems . . . is only properly ap-
> proached if one has grasped the rela-
> tionship between form and meaning and
> if one has correctly connected semi-
> ology and semantics, first in the sen-
> tence, then in the word, and finally in
> all the elements of speech (NDPF, 23).

One of the persons in France influenced by the
semiotic model of linguistics, and in turn, influencing
its development was Claude Lévi-Strauss. For two
decades, through debate and writing, Ricoeur has tried
to point out both the strengths and weaknesses of Lévi-
Strauss' structural anthropology. The weaknesses are

similar to those Ricoeur finds in the semiotic model
itself, the absoluteness of a closed system, the lack
of concern for subject, for the transcendence of sign,
and for the function of interpretation. The strengths
are those of scientific method, and of the insights
regarding the underlying symbolic structures both of
language and of social relationships. Writing in 1967,
Ricoeur felt that "no one was nearer than Lévi-Strauss
in recognizing this transcendental character of the
symbolic function with respect to the various systems
of signs known to sociologists, psychologists and linguists" (28-29) because he recognized that the signifying in language was a radical change in evolutionary
development. Moreover, Lévi-Strauss had realized that
there is a similar architecture between formalized
expressions of the linguistic structure and the structure of society; "structural correspondences, for example, as between kinship systems, social organization,
folklore and myths, go back to this first condition of
signification, this symbolic function, which is not one
function among others but the condition of each and
every one of them" (29). If the semiological order is
an order of signs without a subject, the order of symbolism compels a return to the speaking subject and to
the transcendent relationships of interacting speaking
subjects.

      Some links, both with Ricoeur's previous
investigations of symbol and with his new interest in
the Anglo-American inquiries into the philosophy of
ordinary language, are provided in "The Problem of
Double-Meaning as a Hermeneutic Problem and as a Semantic Problem."

      This problem I have called the problem
      of multiple meaning. By that I desig-
      nate a certain effect of meaning, ac-
      cording to which an expression, from
      variable dimensions, while signifying
      one thing, signifies at the same time
      another thing, without ceasing to sig-
      nify the first (CI, 63. Translation
      modified).

For hermeneutics, it is the text which has a multiple
sense: a problem posed today for exegesis, whether
biblical or not, for the phenomenology of religion, for
Freudian and Jungian psychoanalysis, and for literary
criticism. Although these fields of interpretation
differ in technique, in rules for interpretation, and
in their epistemological viewpoints, they all share the

problem of the hinge between the linguistic and the
non-linguistic, between language and lived experience,
based on the fundamental condition according to Ricoeur
that the "symbolic is a milieu of expression for an
extra-linguistic reality" (66.   Translation modified).

This same problem of the multiple sense is faced
by those analyzing ordinary language. Language is an
instrument of knowledge precisely because a sign can
designate one thing without ceasing to designate another. Ricoeur quotes Ullmann and agrees that the
"cumulative intention of words is a fecund source of
ambiguities, but it is also the source of analogical
predication, thanks to which the symbolic power of
language is put to work (69-70. Translation modified).

For both the multiple sense of the words posed by
ordinary language, and the multiple sense of the text
faced by the hermeneut, the context acts as a filter.
So, as with the explication of a poem, the best interpretation is that which most fully accounts for all the
possibilities within the poem and their interrelationships. Such investigation leads Ricoeur to a more
exact understanding of symbolism:

> It [symbolism] appears to us now as an
> effect of meaning, observable on the
> plane of discourse, but built on the
> more elementary functioning of signs.
> . . . multiple sense and symbolism
> belong to the constitution and to the
> functioning of all language (71-72.
> Translation modified).

But the multiple meaning is saved from absolute
equivocation or absolute diffusion of meaning by that
which the context provides: the isotopes of a discourse; that is, certain interpretations are harmonious
with the total context, others are discordant. There
is then possible scientific rigor as well as progress
in interpreting, but the interpretation is always open
to new interpretation. This is the source of the continual openness of literary works, including the Judaic-
Christian scriptures, to new interpretation, to new
discovery of meaning.

The multiple sense also makes possible the
infinite creation and re-creation of the word, and
leads to an ontological dimension of language. "Words
have a mode of presence other than the mode of existence of the structures" (74).

In spite of the relatively dry and abstract
terminology of multiple sense, isotopes, and hermeneutics, one should not lose sight of the personal importance of the theory. Yes, it is the responsibility of
the philosopher to save the unity of language, but the
theory of interpretation is always ultimately concerned
with the individual, the knowledge of self or growth in
consciousness, and appropriation of being, becoming
more fully alive. Interpretation is not a process
which reads a self-understanding into the text. On the
contrary:

> Interpretation is the process by which
> disclosure of new modes of being--or if
> you prefer Wittgenstein to Heidegger,
> of new forms of life--gives to the
> subject a new capacity for knowing the
> self. If the reference of the text is
> the project of a world, then it is not
> the reader who primarily projects self.
> The reader rather is enlarged in the
> capacity of self-projection by receiv-
> ing a new mode of being from the text
> itself (IT, 94).

The interpretative process which occurs in ordinary
language foreshadows the more complex interpretative
process of text-interpretation and of the whole hermeneutic problem. The latter has its roots in the way
ordinary language functions.

PART VI. RICOEUR
            AND BIBLICAL RESEARCH

CHAPTER ONE

Hermeneutics, Theology, and Biblical Research

The post-Bultmannian schools of theology,
especially those of Ebeling and Fuchs, provide help to
Ricoeur in coordinating phenomenology and the philosophy of language because, in a way, they have followed a
development parallel to his own work. Because the work
of Bultmann had led to the polarization of myth and
kerygma, demythologization became the central problem.

In "Contribution d'une réflexion sur le langage à
une théologie de la parole," Ricoeur recalls that,
although some elaborate a specific theology of the
Word, the term belongs uniquely to Christianity, which
consists of faith in the Word which became flesh, which
grew through the witness of the first Christian community proclaiming the Word, and which must constantly be
actualized in a renewal of the Word for our times. In
these contexts, every theology is a theology of the
Word; nevertheless, a theology which specifically tries
to understand this process of the Word as a central
focus merits the specific title of a theology of the
Word.

For such a theology, hermeneutics assumes a
central place, and the sciences which derive from the
linguistic model pose a particular challenge. The
challenge calls for a two-fold task: the systematic
task of unifying all the realms of theology under the
concept of the "coming-to-be" of the Word, of a process
of the Word; and the critical task of engaging in serious confrontation with the linguistic disciplines and
with the other sciences which stem from them. Ricoeur
treats of the contribution of language to a theology of
the Word on three levels, those of structuralism, of a
phenomenology of language, and of an ontology of language.

Two basic distinctions provided by structuralism
can contribute much to theology: a first distinction
between language and speech, and a second distinction
within language between the synchronic and the diachronic. As indicated earlier, it was de Saussure who
made the structural distinction between language and
speech and who presented the analogy of the chess game:
language is like the state of play at a given moment
while speech is like the act by which we produce a new
configuration. In other words, language is the closed
system of signs, one unit defined by its relationship
with one or more other units. In this sense, a dictionary is the listing of this closed system of signs,
since each word is defined by means of others within
the same dictionary. On the other hand, speech
(parole) involves not only "the individual performance,
the psycho-physiological execution of language, but
also the combinations freely constituted by starting
from the limited inventory of signs" (336). Examples
would include the preaching which brings new life to
those who are listening and the poem which opens worlds
previously unknown.

The second distinction is that between the
synchronic and the diachronic in language. These indicate two different points of view: "the synchronic
point of view corresponds to the way in which language
is organized at a certain moment, let us say, in a
state of system; in the second point of view, called
diachronic, one considers the changes, the transformations" (337). Ricoeur mentions Pere Chenu's Nature,
Man, and Society in the Twelfth Century[1] as revealing
this diachronic aspect of language. Chenu shows how
the great symbols of western culture, originating in
the semitic, Greek, or proto-hellenic worlds, because
they rest on a universal base were transformed by the
thinkers of the twelfth century to be part of their own
dominant structures. Ricoeur also mentions Kittel's
Theological Dictionary as mixing the two points of
view, the synchronic and the diachronic, and insists
with James Barr in his Biblical Semantics that theology
must meet the challenge brought by structuralism in
this area.

On the other hand, while incorporating the
insights of structuralism, theology will always go on
to the interpretative process which involves the speaking subject, the transcendent, and the creation of new
being. Here especially, it can make use of the insights provided by a phenomenology of language, particularly in terms of multiple sense, transcendent, and

speaking subject.   A work like The Symbolism of Evil
shows the possibilities which are opened up here.

The contribution of an ontology of language to
theology stems from investigations such as those of
Heidegger in Being and Time. Ricoeur thinks important
the insight which Heidegger presents: that one does
not start from language, but that one comes to language. (However, in another context, Ricoeur says that
Heidegger's "on the way to language" should be modified
to "Language is the way.") Heidegger's thought supplies a remedy especially for French philosophy which
Ricoeur feels is immersed in the closed world of signs.
In Being and Time the German philosopher asks us to
find again in the act of speaking itself a modality of
being. Language then, particularly through interpretation, is able to appear as one of the fundamental determinations of human being. Silence is restored to a
philosophy of the word because it signifies that our
first relation to language is being silent before meaning, is hearing rather than speaking.

Another text of Heidegger Ricoeur calls
magnificent:

> Heidegger says that the word--the act
> and the work of the word--is at the
> same time the submission of human being
> to the openness of being and the re-
> sponsibility of the speaking being who
> "preserves" being in its openness.
> . . . In preserving that which has
> been once opened, the word gives to
> things to become that which they are;
> by language, they penetrate within the
> space of openness, within the space of
> revelation over which human being exer-
> cises responsibility as a speaking
> subject (CRLTP, 346).

Specifically for biblical theology, such an ontology of
the word suggests the following: Christian preaching
implies that being is carried by the word. For Ricoeur
this does not mean a watering down of Christ as the
Word of God to a species of universal revelation; he
thinks exactly the opposite--and this is where he differs radically from Heidegger:

> The uniqueness of the word of God in
> Christ not only is not opposed to the
> universal unveiling of being as logos

> from the word of the poet or of the
> thinker; but this uniqueness is compre-
> hended rather as the central actualiza-
> tion around which are grouped all the
> figures of the manifestation. The
> uniqueness of the revelation and the
> universality of the manifestation are
> mutually reinforced (347).

Words outside of the gospel, whether they are the words
of the prophet or the thinker, or the words of the
classical or modern poet, are multiple manifestations
of being by which "I am disposed to receive the unique
word of Christ as the central and decisive manifestation."

In a preface to a French edition of some of the
writings of Rudolf Bultmann, Ricoeur provides not only
an appreciation but a critique in the context of his
developing understanding of the task of interpretation,
of the problem of text, and of the complexity of language. The task is not that of demythologizing, of
understanding the author better than he understands
himself, but the task "to submit oneself to what the
text says, to what it intends, and to what it means"
(CI, 397). It is the task of trying to understand the
relationship of the two testaments because "Jesus
Christ himself, exegesis and exegete of Scripture, is
manifested as logos while opening the understanding of
the scriptures" (384. Translation modified). Moreover, "to decipher Scripture is to decipher the witness
of the apostolic community" (388). More than any other
discipline which treats of signs, exegesis requires an
existential appropriation; without such an appropriation, that which it says is no longer the living word.

Ricoeur thinks both with and against Bultmann.
With him, he believes that a "text accomplishes its
meaning only in personal appropriation. . . . The
moment of exegesis is not that of existential decision
but that of 'meaning'" (397). Nevertheless, this moment of meaning must be distinguished from that of
signification, the "moment when the reader grasps the
meaning," when the meaning is actualized for the
reader. According to Ricoeur, Bultmann's theory of
interpretation moves too quickly to decision, neglect-
ing the objectivity of the moment of meaning. The
semantic must precede the existential. In Ricoeur's
view, Bultmannians move from exegesis to the existential or to the theological without asking what happens
in between. Bultmann lacks a sufficiently developed
language theory.

Development and Directions
for the Seventies and the Eighties

In 1971 Ricoeur defined his position as an
evolving one:

> I had to depart from my previous
> definition of hermeneutics as the in-
> terpretation of symbolic language. Now
> I should tend to relate hermeneutics to
> the specific problems raised by the
> translation of the objective meaning of
> written language into the personal act
> of speaking which a moment ago I called
> appropriation. In that way, the
> broader question, What is it to inter-
> pret a text? tends to replace the ini-
> tial question, What is it to interpret
> symbolic language? The connection be-
> tween my first definition and the new
> emerging definition remains an unsolved
> problem for me, which will be the topic
> of my forthcoming work (PPR, 91).

The appropriation referred to is that which happens
"when the world of the reader and the world of the text
merge into one another." Ricoeur recognizes that this
phenomenon is the same as that described by Hans-Georg
Gadamer as a "fusion of horizons." In order to pursue
this problem of the linguisticality of human experience, Ricoeur compares the insights of John MacQuarrie
and Langdon Gilkey in religious discourse, of Gerhard
von Rad, Joachim Jeremias, Daniel Via, and Norman
Perrin in narrative form or in the form of the parable,
and Wittgenstein and Austin in the philosophy of ordinary language.

But this shift should not be seen as a movement
away from symbol; in one sense, it is a broadening of
symbol to an appreciation of the multi-valent characteristic of all language:

> I have already alluded to the
> connection between the functioning of
> symbolic discourse and the polysemic
> structure of our ordinary words. We
> may extend the parallelism further:
> understanding, in the most ordinary
> sense of the word--let us say, in
> conversation--is already an

intersubjective process. Inasmuch as
ordinary language differs from an ideal
language in that it has no fixed expressions independent of their contextual
uses, to understand discourse is to
interpret the actualizations of its
polysemic values according to the per-
missions and suggestions proposed by
the context. What happens in the far
more intricate cases of text-
interpretation, and what constitutes
the key problem of hermeneutics, is
already foreshadowed in the interpretive process as it occurs in ordinary
language. Thus, the whole problem of
text-interpretation could be renewed by
the recognition of its roots in the
functioning of ordinary language itself
(PPR, 93).

There are important points here. Every time there
is discourse, communication between two persons, the
words, the situation, the worlds being shared have
multiple values, are subject to multiple interpretations, although the context suggests and allows only
certain possibilities. In other words, every human
expression is a symbol in that its meaning is poly-
valent involving an apparent meaning which conceals a
hidden meaning. By extension, anything said about
something is an interpretation. Although these statements are simple, and may even seem obvious, the implications for ordinary communication, for education, for
the interpreting of scripture, of dogma, and of preaching, are radical. In spite of the fact that studies in
each of these areas are moving in this direction, such
studies are often handicapped by being confined to
their own disciplines--they lack the breadth of a
general theory of interpretation: Ricoeur's present
task.

CHAPTER TWO

Interpretation Theory and the Bible: Genesis

Although he is neither biblical exegete nor theologian in the formal sense, Ricoeur continues to be interested in the Bible and to have an impact on biblical research through his efforts to develop a general theory of interpretation. For him, biblical interpretation or hermeneutics is one aspect of a general theory of interpretation which has its origins in an effort to understand ordinary language as the foundation of the various developed specialized languages and methods which we recognize in scientific as well as in narrative and poetic discourse.

Raised in the liberal Protestant tradition of France in the 1920's, Ricoeur was reoriented, as many others were, by the "Barthian shock," which he experienced in 1936 when he read the French translation of Karl Barth's commentary on Paul's letter to the Romans. The faith called for by Barth, as well as that described by Soren Kierkegaard at an earlier time, continues to provide a centering point for Ricoeur.

Nevertheless, this faith is never in isolation, but is always in the context of a total humanity, which includes the institutions which human beings create. Ricoeur wrote in 1965, "Planetary consciousness, structural obstacles, and conjunctural obstacles form a unitary constellation, which first calls for an analysis and then an acceptance of responsibility" (PSE,134).

Analysis and responsibility--these are the two prongs of the task. The biblical texts give nourishment, reflection, and meditation for such analysis and responsibility. Such texts communicate a message, a call to me, a kerygma; thus the text is never a dead

letter. It is always a call for personal response, but
within the context of history, culture, and human institutions, including politics and the state. For
Ricoeur, then, the Bible is never read merely as an
interesting middle Eastern literature. If the text is
interpreted, it calls for a response. In fact, interpreting is a response.

> Christianity presents itself as a
> kerygma, that is to say a proclamation,
> a discourse addressed to. The Greek
> word "kerygma" has an exact meaning:
> announcement, proclamation, message--
> demystification deals precisely with
> this address, with this discourse ad-
> dressed to . . . . (PPR, 213).

This demystification is that called for by all
those modern disciplines which aim to uncover illusion
or false consciousness, and especially that called for
by those three masters of suspicion, Marx, Nietzsche,
and Freud. In Ricoeur's view, the questions and critique they raise cannot be ignored. Their contributions are not primarily the narrow specific contributions sometimes associated with their names. For
Ricoeur, their contribution is beyond that, a critique
of culture, a sharing in a "general exegesis of false
consciousness" (214); they belong, therefore, to a
theory of interpretation, that is, to a hermeneutics.

Our texts are not transparent; neither is our
consciousness. Texts and consciousness at the same
time both reveal and conceal, and therefore call for a
specific reading, that is, for an interpretation.

> The task of hermeneutics . . . has
> always been to read a text and to dis-
> tinguish the true sense from the appar-
> ent sense, to search for the sense
> under the sense, to search for the
> intelligible text under the unintelli-
> gible text (215).

Bultmann's questions are similar. He reads the
texts and asks about the cultural distance between our
world and our discourse and the cultural world and the
discourse of the Gospel. For Ricoeur, the primitive
proclamation of the Gospel forms a break in the cultural discourse of the time. The preaching of the
Cross is folly for the cultural world of which it is a
part. It cannot prove itself; it is a rupture from the

totally other. But it is only known by becoming part
of culture. It always poses a "relationship of discontinuity."

> This means that the Gospel will always
> be carried by an extraordinarily
> fragile testimony, that of the preach-
> er, that of personal life, that of
> community. There is no proof which can
> support either the experience or the
> rationale. In this sense, the Cross
> remains a folly for the intelligent, a
> scandal for the wise (220).

Nevertheless, we have something which is believable and
which is at our disposal. With Bultmann, Ricoeur would
seek to recognize and then dissolve the false scandal
of the cultural differences and the differences of
discourse between the first century and our century,
precisely in order to reveal the true scandal of the
Cross and Resurrection. Such deciphering of illusions
is necessary in order to affirm the faith of modern
persons. "We have to discover what is more than text,
what is the Preaching of the Person and of the event of
Christ" (221).

> [The hermeneutic circle] can only be
> broken by the believer in the her-
> meneutics when he or she is faithful to
> the community, and by the "hermeneut"
> in the believer when he or she does the
> scientific work of exegesis. This is
> today the dual condition of modern
> human being in whom struggles both a
> believer and an atheist; in the be-
> liever there confront one another an
> adult critic and a naive child who
> listen to the Word (222).

In addressing the problem of evil in The Symbolism
of Evil, Ricoeur became seriously involved in analyzing
ancient mid-Eastern confessional literature, of which
the Hebrew scriptures are a part. Following von Rad
and others, Ricoeur draws on major parts of the Bible
to meditate on the primary and privileged symbols of
defilement, sin, and guilt, under such categories as
"Before God": The Covenant, the "Wrath of God," and sin
as "nothingness." Of major importance in the second
part, his study of four myths of the Beginning and End,
is his study of the "Adamic" myth, with its traditional
topics of fall, temptation, justification, and end time
as implicit in the beginning of history.

Genesis and Structuralism.   In 1969, Ricoeur was
invited by the French Catholic Association for the
Study of the Bible to make several presentations at
their second annual congress.   Other participants included Roland Barthes, a leader in French literary
criticism, and Louis Marin, who has applied the methods
of structuralism to biblical texts.   Robert M. Polzin
considers Ricoeur's introductory paper "a splendid
introduction to methodology in biblical exegesis."[1]

This introductory paper is titled "Du conflit a la
convergence des méthodes en exégèse biblique."   In
Ricoeur's view, one advantage of biblical criticism in
the development of interpretation theory is that the
biblical field is defined by its formal object, the
biblical literature.   On the other hand, it is a field
polarized by different methods.   Ricoeur shows that
these different methods need not remain in unresolved
conflict.   On the contrary, properly understood, they
may be seen as converging.

Ricoeur proposes three moments for his analysis:
1) the historical-critical method as practiced by von
Rad; 2) the semiological model derived from Barthes;
and 3) interpretation as Ricoeur is developing his
theory.   After carefully unfolding the implicit or
explicit structures of the first two approaches,
Ricoeur points out how an author such as von Rad uses
an implicit structural analysis of the accounts of the
faith of Israel.   A rereading of von Rad, using the
distinctions of three levels elaborated by Barthes: 1)
the level of functions; 2) the level of actions; and 3)
the level of the narrative (44), then reveals an implicit structural analysis which von Rad had developed out
of the materials.   Of course, many scholars today would
criticize the method of von Rad, but Ricoeur's theory
is not thereby radically affected.   The point is that
there are implicit or explicit structures, which any
biblical scholar will find and use without the necessity of referring to structuralism.   For this reason,
many biblical analysts will not see that a formally
structuralist analysis adds anything.   On the other
hand, structuralists, and those biblical scholars who
take structuralism seriously, see that the method adds
a particular scientific preciseness and often adds new
insights to the traditional text.

One is then able to ask the question of the
relationship of methods.   It is such a question which
focuses the hermeneutic problem.   What is an exegete
such as von Rad doing when he uses an historical-

critical or genetic method? What is a structuralist
such as Barthes doing in his semiotic analysis?

A key is found in writing, or discourse committed
to a text. Four characteristics of a written text are
important to note. 1) It is the intentional meaning
which is inscribed. 2) At the same time, writing de-
taches the meaning of the discourse from dependence on
the writer. The text is then freed for other times and
places (48). 3) Such writing profoundly alters the
referential function. The reference is freed from the
ostensive limitations of the time and place of origin
because the time and place of the original discourse no
longer exist. This is not to absolutize the text; nor
is it to overlook the historical, literary, philological, sociological, and cultural studies which help us
better to understand a text. On the contrary, such
studies are crucial. Nevertheless, the writing of a
poem frees its author's meaning so that the meaning can
survive, that is, live beyond the author. "A text
carries its own referents" (49), so that its "world"--
the Greek "world," the Johannine "world," or the
"world" of Job--unfolds in front of the text, much as a
"world" unfolds in front of a screen on which we have
projected a slide. We can see there a "world" which
has been "caught" in action, and thereby rendered available to us in the future (4). Finally, for a written
text, the intended audience is anyone who is given the
ability to read the text. The text is addressed to all
those readers who are able to bring out its meaning.

Such reading is not subjective in a narrow sense,
because it requires validation, a logic of probability,
parallel to a logic of empirical verification. Each
method of interpreting a text has its own presuppositions, procedures, and methods of validation. Insofar
as the validations of diverse methodologies move toward
concurrence, there is a convergence rather than a conflict of interpretations.

In a subsequent presentation at the same
conference, Ricoeur applies his theory to an exegesis
of Genesis 1.1-2.4 in the hope of showing the possibility of a convergence of methods. He uses first the
genetic technique of von Rad complemented by that of
Werner H. Schmidt (SEG, 73). Then he recognizes the
structuralist's desire to analyze the text as a synchronic whole, rather than in its genetic parts, in
order better to see the relationship of the parts to
the whole. Repeated phrases, e.g., "and God said
. . . "; series of parallel objects: light, sky,

earth; sequences, e.g., "On the first day"; turning
points, e.g., "the fourth day"; are all structures the
analyst looks for, notes, or questions in relation to
the whole.

Having applied each of the two methods, Ricoeur
then asks a key question for interpretation: "Who
interprets? the theologian or the philosopher? the
preacher or the exegete before him? . . . There does
not exist an innocent interpretation" (80). It is the
structure, whether analyzed genetically or semiotically, which carries the interpretation, so that, when
we interpret out of a tradition, we appropriate the
meaning of the text, that is, we make it our own in
some way. Ricoeur interprets both from within the
historical-critical tradition and from within a semiotic tradition. As he sees it, the two methods do not
necessarily contradict each other, but, on the contrary, they complement and affirm each other at many
points. In fact, for Ricoeur the convergence of the
two methods brings together the two streams of Hebrew
reflection, the historical tradition and the wisdom
tradition, precisely by using a reflective enumeration
of the cosmic elements of Genesis 1, rather than by
using a violent separation of the cosmic elements such
as we may have expected from other examples of the
Near-Eastern creation genre (83).

In a third representation at that same conference,
Ricoeur insists that we are always interpreting out of
a tradition.

> We belong to the same tradition as the
> text: interpretation and tradition are
> the inside and the outside of the same
> historicity. Interpretation is applied
> to a tradition and makes tradition
> itself. The text is the reconstruction
> of a tradition and the interpretation
> is the reconstruction of the text (EC,
> 291).

For Ricoeur, the historical-critical method is
irreplacable; nevertheless, it ought to be corrected by
the overcoming of three illusions: the illusion of the
source, the illusion of the author, and the illusion of
the audience (292). The origin of the text is itself a
function of the text, not a solution to the text. The
diachronic dimension--its history--remains a part of
the text. There is no text without an author, a person
or persons who wrote the text. Nevertheless, we do not

have access to the psychology, the experience, or the
intention of the author or authors except through the
text and the world it signifies. In the same way, we
do not have access to an "original audience or addres-
see" except through the text which we have here and
now.   ·

> This is the signification of the text:
> to know the "work" of meaning in the
> dialectic of tradition-interpretation,
> of which the actual text is the result
> (293).

Interpretation of a text is neither one nor multiple.
There are always many possibilities of reading a text,
but the ways are not infinite. Moreover, the field of
possible interpretations is always limited by the com-
munitarian character of interpretation of which an
individual exegesis is a part (295).

CHAPTER THREE

Interpretation Theory and the Bible: Job

Ricoeur and the Book of Job. Although Ricoeur has
not written extensively on Job in any one place, there
are substantive interpretations in The Symbolism of
Evil, as well as references in a number of other books
and articles.[1]

Since Ricoeur in The Symbolism of Evil treats of
the phenomenology of evil in selected mid-Eastern
texts, it is not surprising to find there many explicit
and implicit references to the book of Job. Ricoeur
analyzes the symbolism of sin as a positive force under
three aspects: 1) the consciousness of sin as criterion of fault (81); 2) sin as "at once and primor-
dially personal and communal" (83); and 3) the hyper-
subjectivity of the reality of sin (84). This latter
is the polarity of the absolute seeing or sight of God
as wisdom and the abjectness of human being as seen by
God.

> The book of Job is the witness of this
> crisis: Job feels the absolute seeing
> as an inimical seeing that causes him
> to suffer and finally may kill him . .
> . the destruction of the old theory of
> retribution raised a doubt about this
> seeing, which suddenly reveals itself
> as the seeing of the hidden God who
> delivers persons to unjust suffering
> (SE, 85-86. Translation modified).

Although one could profitably discuss other
references to Job in the book (e.g., 107, 255, 324), I
will emphasize here the remarks within the section,
"The Reaffirmation of the Tragic" (310-326). Ricoeur
uses tragic in the context of Aristotelian classical

description. The tragic hero awakens in us once again
the great tragic emotions: " . . . terror and compassion, beyond all judgment and all condemnation; a
merciful vision of human being comes to limit the accusation and save from the wrath of the Judge" (313.
Translation modified). In this sense there is a tragic
element in biblical theology, which makes the God of
the Covenant an ethical God, tending toward a "moral
vision of the world" which includes the three elements
of tribunal, retribution, and Judge. ("Ethical" and
"moral" are used in the limiting sense associated with
words such as penal.) However, the suffering of the
innocent is a contradiction of this "moral vision":

> The book of Job is the upsetting
> document that records this shattering
> of the moral vision of the world. The
> figure of Job bears witness to the
> irreducibility of the evil of scandal
> to the evil of fault. . . . Hence, it
> may be asked whether the Hebrew and,
> more generally, the Near-Eastern theme
> of the "suffering Just One" does not
> lead back from the prophetic accusation
> to tragic pity (314).

Through the dramatic movement of the dialogue,
Job, "faced with the torturing absence of God, dreams
of his own absence" (319); there is no answer to Job's
problem: there is no solution to the problem of suffering. The questioner becomes the one questioned. It
is the innocent Job who repents. Here we have a contradiction of terms, a paradox, a symbol. But it is
the symbol which gives rise to thought. Or in later
Ricoeurian terms, we have the metaphorical twist, the
semantic impertinence which redescribes reality.

In the biblical corpus, Ricoeur sees this tragic
contradiction transcended only in the figure of the
Suffering Servant of Second Isaiah, where suffering
becomes an "action capable of redeeming the evil"
(324). Nevertheless, the question may be asked of
Ricoeur if the thrust of the complete narrative of Job,
including the restoration of his goods and family, does
not have an implicit suggestion of the redemption
motif.

In Freud and Philosophy, Ricoeur's analysis
extends the critique of narcissism or false consciousness, and also enables him to see the symbolic
"giving up of the father" as being at the heart of the

problematic of faith (550). It is a similar struggle
in which Job is engaged. Job not only refuses to submit to the false consciousness of his friends, but he
also refuses to delude himself, even though such a
delusion would simplify his problem.

> Job receives no explanation of his
> suffering; he is merely shown something
> of the grandeur and order of the whole,
> without any meaning being directly
> given to the finite point of view of
> his desire. . . . A path is thus
> opened, a path of non-narcissistic
> reconciliation (548-549).

In this interpretation, there is "a certain coincidence
of the tragic God of Job and the lyric God of John"
(536).

   Such contradiction is raised in regard to Job in
similar fashion in two studies in The Conflict of
Interpretations, "'Original Sin': A Study in Meaning,"
and "Religion, Atheism, and Faith." It is against the
false righteousness of accusing and justifying that God
speaks to Job out of the whirlwind (309). True faith
is violently contrasted with the law of retribution; it
is essentially a "tragic faith, beyond all assurance
and protection" (455).

> It would be a faith that moves through
> the shadows, in a new "night of the
> soul" . . . before a God who would not
> protect me but would surrender me to
> the dangers of a life worthy of being
> called human (460).

The order spoken of in Job 38 is beyond human knowing.
Nor is there any intelligible connection between the
physical order and the ethical order. Revelation is in
the voice that speaks to Job, so that "dialogue is in
itself a mode of consolation" (461). Although the
consolation of the word is not resolution, it is nevertheless revelation. The power of saying gathers the
discordances of the world and gives them shape (465).
Word creates and brings about the beginning of the
re-newed.

   In commenting on the exegesis of Genesis 1.1-2.4a
(SEG), Ricoeur makes several references to Job 38.
Following von Rad, Ricoeur recognizes the wisdom tra-
dition of the creation motif originating in Egypt.

"This reasoned, reflective theology ought to be distinguished from the faith concerning election and salvation. Measured by the grandeur of the cosmos, human being discovers the self full of fear and admiration" (70). Job 38 presents a view of the world in which the place of human being is practically nil (78). This view of creation represents a meditation on the ordering operations in creation rather than on the violent struggle characteristic of other creation motifs of the Near East. It is a movement to the radical origin of things, not unlike the movement of modern thinkers (82-83).

"Toward a Hermeneutic of the Idea of Revelation" is the title of a study of Ricoeur's on the paradox which is also at the heart of the book of Job. Those situations "where the misery and the grandeur of human beings confront each other, Hebraic wisdom interprets . . . as the annihilation of humans and the incomprehensibility of God--as the silence and absence of God" (THIR, 11).

> Wisdom does not teach us how to avoid suffering, or how magically to deny it, or how to dissimulate it under an illusion. It teaches us how to endure, how to suffer suffering. It places suffering into a meaningful context by producing the active quality of suffering.
>
> This is perhaps the most profound meaning of the book of Job, the best example of wisdom (12).

The conclusion of the book of Job provides a superb example of religious discourse which moves from the poetic dialogue of complaint and argumentation, to the rhetorical voice of God out of the whirlwind, to supplication and praise. "The knowledge of how to suffer is surpassed by the lyricism of supplication in the same way that narration is surpassed by the lyricism of praise" (14).

> What did Job "see"? . . . The orders of creation? No. His questions about justice are undoubtedly left without an answer. But . . . by repenting for his supposition that existence does not make sense, Job presupposes an unsuspected meaning which cannot be transcribed by speech or logos a human

> being may have at his disposal. . . .
> What is revealed is the possibility of
> hope in spite of. . . .   This possi-
> bility may still be expressed in the
> terms of a design, but of an unassign-
> able design, a design which is God's
> secret (THIR, 12-13).

The idea of revelation differs as it appears in
narrative, prophetic, or wisdom discourse. In the
latter, the sage knows that somehow wisdom has preceded
and that it is through participation that a person is
said to be wise. "Nothing is further from the spirit
of the sages than the idea of an autonomy of thinking,
a humanism of the good life. . . .   This is why wisdom
is held to be a gift of God" (13). Job moves through a
false sense of his autonomy of thinking to a broader
horizon, where he recognizes that for him to comprehend
the universe and the totality of human experience,
which is to understand suffering, is to make his god
too small. To gird his loins and to stand up like a
man is, on the contrary, to see as God sees, a much
larger enterprise, and one that is much more humbling.
Here truth is not something which can be verified
scientifically. Rather, it is a "manifestation, i.e.,
letting what shows itself be. What shows itself is in
each instance a proposed world, a world I may inhabit
and wherein I can project my ownmost possibilities"
(25). Such is the revelation and manifestation in Job.
A world shows itself: a new way of being presents
itself as possibility.

     Wisdom is that aspect of revelation and of the
human condition which "is directly addressed to the
sense and nonsense of existence. It is a struggle for
sense in spite of nonsense" (NG, 221). In contrast
with the narrative, prophetic, and prescriptive forms
of discourse, wisdom is often more cautious about the
naming of God. This is the struggle in which Job is
engaged. His friends too easily name the God of his
suffering. With all his being, Job resists this blasphemy. From his experience, he knows it not to be
true. Such naming of God is idol rather than manifestation. The voice out of the whirlwind manifests a
hidden God. This is the paradox. In his suffering,
Job acknowledges the paradox. He feels addressed. He
responds to the one who has addressed him. He is
called to give testimony to this manifestation, to the
truth of his experience.

CHAPTER FOUR

Interpretation Theory and the Bible: Parables

Understanding the parables is essential to
understanding the New Testament. In the American
biblical scene, 1972 saw the beginning of a new era in
efforts to understand the parables with the formation
of a study seminar within the Society of Biblical
Literature to channel and coordinate the thrust of
emerging scholarship. In Semeia 1 Amos Wilder[1] outlined the development of that seminar. In a complementary way, Norman Perrin in Jesus and the Language of
the Kingdom[2] provided an outline and a commentary on
the progress made in that scholarship. He included all
along his own insights and new thrusts in scholarship,
many of which include references to the work of Paul
Ricoeur.

At the time Perrin and Ricoeur were colleagues at
the University of Chicago, so it is not surprising that
a seminar on the parables offered at the University
would have as faculty not only Perrin, a New Testament
specialist and former pupil of Jeremias who wrote one
of the twentieth century classics on the parables, but
also Ricoeur, a specialist in the philosophy of language, as well as David Tracy, a theologian. The subsequent works of Perrin and Ricoeur testify to the
influence each had on the other. During the seminar
Ricoeur presented lectures which were later published
as Biblical Hermeneutics in Semeia 4.[3] Although a
subsequent article extends his thought, his principal
explicit contribution is contained in these lectures.
At the same time, and more important for his continuing
work, they provide a major forward thrust and outline
for aspects of his more developed work on narrative,
metaphor, and the special qualities of religious
language.

The Narrative Form and Structuralism

As an integral part of his method of the dialectic, Ricoeur takes seriously the presentation of positions other than his own. For a study of the parables at this time in the history of their interpretation, Ricoeur takes as examples of various types of approach the historical approach such as that of Jeremias; an up-dated version with a link to literary criticism, represented by Via; an existential approach as initiated by Bultmann and up-dated by Via as a literary-existential analysis; and a structural approach as practiced by Marin. After pointing out the strengths of each, he then demonstrates the internal or external contradictions.

In Ricoeur's view, structuralism raises questions which point out the inadequacies of other types of analysis; moreover, the various approaches are not essentially reconcilable with one another. On the other hand, structuralism is a dead end and a distortion if it merely finds the code or structure and construes that as the message. Ricoeur wishes to try a more difficult way. After disconnecting structural analysis from structuralist ideology, with which he disagrees, he then hopes to show that a structuralist analysis may enrich an existential interpretation. This is not to deny the contributions which the other methods provide, but only to show the inconsistencies of one with the other, as well as to show the value of linking a structural analysis with the existential hermeneutic.

Structuralism as ideology sees the code as essential and the "message" as unessential. In other words, the code is the message. As such, for Ricoeur, the gospel then is only "a communication about communication." Language is a closed system. It can never transcend that closure.

> Only the way back from code to message may both do justice to the message as such and pave the way to the move from structure to process, such as the one which the understanding of the parables requires. I call dead end not all structural analysis, but only the one which makes it irrelevant, or useless, or even impossible to return from the deep-structures to the surface-structures (BH, 65).

Ricoeur then argues that structural analysis may
not only be disconnected from its ideology, but that it
also may be connected to existential interpretation.
This will show the way back from code to message for
the appropriate understanding of the text as text.

First, the source of the text is discourse, the
bringing to actualization of a speech-act which is not
reducible merely to a language code. The basic unit of
discourse is not the word, but the sentence, except
insofar as a word is short-hand for a sentence. It is
discourse which raises the questions of reference:
reference forward to a reality outside of language,
reference backward to a speaker, and the communication
with an audience. In other words, "discourse has a
speaker, a world, and a vis-à-vis" (66). Discourse
therefore is an event: "the speaker is brought to
language; a dimension of the world is brought to language; and a dialogue between human beings is brought
to language" (66). The object of interpretation, then,
is the text as discourse, and the work is "to bring
back to discourse the written text, if not as spoken
discourse, at least as speech-act actualized in the act
of reading" (67).

The second part of the argument relates to the
place of literary genres of which narrative is an example. For the most part, genres have been used as a
method of classification, such as the grouping of parables, or miracle stories, what form criticism calls the
forms. But Ricoeur takes a new approach. Just as
Chomsky had pointed out the generative aspects of grammar, so in Germany Güttgemanns has described a generative poetics. In a similar way, Ricoeur sees genre,
not as a means of classification, but as a means of
production. Just as a grammatical or literary code
rules the production of discourse as a sentence or a
work, so too does a literary genre provide rules for
encoding or decoding a message which is produced as a
poem, a narrative, or an essay. It is therefore the
work of interpretation to identify the message or the
individual discourse through the modes of discourse,
that is, the codes, which generate the message as a
work of discourse.

What do literary genres such as narratives do?
First, they provide a common ground for understanding
and interpretation. Readers recognize the genre, and
therefore the individual message. The genre also pre-
serves the message from distortion. A particular genre
links a possible speaker and hearer. By means of the

form, the message survives although its original
situation disappears as soon as the original situation
itself disappears. Nevertheless, the genre makes possible the process by which the original discourse can be
recreated in new contexts of discourse and life. Thus
the surface-structure, properly understood, is the
message itself. The last level for structural analysis, then, is the beginning of hermeneutics. Understanding the functions, the genre, the codes, opens the
interpretation toward a world, a situation, a human
experience.

The Process and the Power of Metaphor

Ricoeur's second lecture on understanding the
parables is called "The Metaphorical Process," which he
considers the link between the structure of the narrative and the existential interpretation. After outlin-
ing some of the understanding of metaphor in traditional rhetoric, he then begins to formulate his own
theory by calling into question those traditional
understandings. Rather than being merely a displacement of meaning, metaphor, on the contrary, involves a
semantics of the sentence. It is a process of saying
something about something, that is, of predication, of
forming a predicate. Therefore, we speak, not of words
as metaphors, but of metaphorical statements.

In addition, the tension is not just between two
terms of a sentence, but between two interpretations of
the sentence. Ironically, the meaning of the statement
is communicated through the absurdity of the two interpretations, that is, as far as a literal interpretation
goes. "Metaphorical interpretation presupposes a
literal interpretation which is destroyed" (78) in
order to free the metaphorical meaning. An absurd
contradiction becomes a meaningful contradiction. The
literal interpretation is set aside in the metaphorical
twist or the semantic impertinence.

What is the role of resemblance in this
metaphorical shift? Good metaphors are not those which
merely note a resemblance, but those which are the
result of a new vision, those which create a resemblance. Metaphor is "an instantaneous creation, a
semantic innovation which has no status in established
language" (79). It follows, then, that one cannot in
the ordinary sense translate metaphors. Since metaphors create meaning, they can only be paraphrased, but
their possibility for paraphrase is inexhaustible.

Metaphors, then, are not merely ornaments; they create
new information: they say new things about reality.

        The next part of Ricoeur's analysis depends on
some of his hypotheses about language. In the first
place, following Frege, he distinguishes between sense
and reference. The sense is the inherent meaning; the
reference is that about which it is being said. The
first is linguistic; the second is extra-linguistic.
With Cassirer, Ricoeur sees language as that by which
we bring to articulation our experience of the world.
In this sense he makes a complete break with structuralism, which sees language only as a closed system
with no extra-linguistic reference. While language as
such is closed in on itself, discourse is open to the
world of experience which it wishes to express. It
doesn't stop at a structural analysis, but works to
unfold in front of the text the world which the text
projects. In other words, the movement is toward the
reference, the world to which the text is referring.

        How does this theory apply to our understanding of
the parables? Ricoeur first recognizes that A.
Jülicher, as the founder of modern interpretation of
parables, in his publication in 1888, rejected the
application of traditional metaphor or allegory to the
interpretation of parables. Nevertheless, Perrin in
1967, raises the question in a new way in his article,
"The Parables of Jesus as Parables, as Metaphors, and
as Aesthetic Objects: A Review Article" (Journal of
Religion 47:340-347). For Jülicher, metaphor is a
reading into the parables, and therefore unacceptable.
Ricoeur agrees with Jülicher that the traditional meaning of metaphor is inappropriate as a tool for understanding the parables.

        The parables of Jesus are not so much in the
tradition of the parabolē of Greek rhetoric, in which
the story was used to prove an ethical statement. They
are rather in the tradition of the Hebrew maschal,
which links meaning and attitude, insight and world
view, understanding and commitment or judgement. The
traditional substitution theory of metaphor is obviously inadequate in an analysis of the parables of
Jesus. For this reason, Ricoeur calls for a drastic
revision of the theory of metaphor.

        Parabolic discourse does not function at the level
of the sentence, so one cannot just apply a tension
theory of metaphor to the sentences of the parables.
It is not just a question of a regeneration of the

words as words. A parable is a narrative or a story
about ordinary events in life, but it calls for a new
view of life. So where does the tension lie?

This is not to deny the clustering of metaphors,
nor their importance to one another. On the contrary,
it is to acknowledge certain metaphors as root metaphors, which are foundational to making possible unlimited interpretations of the metaphors in a cluster.
Major themes of covenant, light and darkness, or the
names of God as King, Father, or Householder, make
clear the possibilities and necessities of interrelationships.

Nevertheless, a fictional narrative represents a
particular example of metaphorical process. The tension is not between particular words, but between the
world of the narrative and everyday life. The parable
is a narrative which in its unfolding produces a metaphorical tension between the world of the narrative and
the world of the hearer.

It is here that Ricoeur especially notes a
resemblance between the parable/reality relationship
and the use of model in the theory of science. A model
in science is an open-ended device, a heuristic device,
which breaks up previously inadequate descriptions and
proposes new, more adequate ways of thinking about the
universe, which is not adequately described by either
the old or the new model. Both the parable and the
scientific model link fiction and redescription to
describe a world essentially undescribable.

Are there clues to this metaphor process within
the narrative itself? Yes. We ask: why tell the
story? what is the meaning of the story? In other
words, "How does the symbolic reference work through
the narrative structure? . . . What clues does the
narrative provide for the understanding of its referent
in a metaphorical way?" (BH, 97). The signs are primarily in the group of narratives or parables, but,
nevertheless, we can see certain signs in a single
narrative precisely within the structure of the plot.
The plot moves through crisis to dénouement, downward
or upward according to the tragic or comic modes.
Following Jeremias, Ricoeur sees that the comparison
rides on the referent of the plot. In the parables,
the Kingdom of God is not like the man, or the woman,
or the pearl, but the Kingdom is like what happens in
the unfolding of the story. The plot or crisis, in
other words, is referring to what happens in human

experience outside the story. "The mode of discourse of parable becomes a case of understatement--to mean the most by saying the least--or better, of irony. The parable should be interpreted metaphorically <u>because</u> it pretends to be plain and trivial" (98). There is a paradox here between the closure of the narrative and the openness to what it points to. There is an extravagance here between the "presence of the extraordinary within the ordinary" which "makes the structure itself unstable and even inconsistent." One is forced to move from an internal sense to an outer referent. Ricoeur calls this process a transgression, a step across, which is integral to the language process.

Ricoeur guesses that the parables make sense only if they are taken together. "An isolated parable is an artifact of the historico-critical method" (100). In other words, parables provide a metaphorical network. The tension, then, is not only within an individual parable, between the story and the metaphorical process, but there is tension between and among the various parables. Their intersignifications, their intertextuality, is crucial. In this way, there is not suitable interpretation of a parable, but only of the parables. Within them, there are different patterns of crisis and response.

Not only do the parables have to be taken together, but in turn, they have to be taken together with the sayings of Jesus, as well as, perhaps, the miracles, or other narratives, and, of course, this extends to the genre of the gospel itself. While Ricoeur affirms the validity of historical pursuits, he nevertheless wishes to emphasize that his concern is not historical, but hermeneutical, that is, the question of meaning. The gospel provides the place for the intertextuality.

> The speaker who "tells" the parable is also the "hero" of the inclusive narrative . . . . This identification of the speaker--which allows us to speak of the parables as the parables "of" Jesus--is therefore the crossing point of two processes. On the one hand, the singularity of the speaker is designated by the singularity of his vision of reality. A unique world view implies a twofold reference, a backward and a forward reference, a forward reference to the mode of being which it

opens up in front of the text, and a
backward reference to the speaker who
expresses himself by way of an indirect
confession (104).

But because of the dominant place of the passion
narrative in the gospel, the "parables are not only the
'parables of Jesus,' but of the 'Crucified'" (105).

This paradox must be considered
seriously: the insertion of the parable into the Gospel-form is both a part
of its meaning for us who have received
the text from the church, and the beginning of its misunderstanding. This
is why we have to interpret the parables both with the help of and against
the distortions provided by this ultimate context. But we do not get rid of
the paradox by merely bracketing the
context provided by the Gospel-form
(105-106).

Religious Language and Poetic Language

What is the relationship between religious
language and poetic language? For Ricoeur, the poetic
function is "the power of making the redescription of
reality correspond with the power of bringing the fictions of the imagination to speech" (107). In other
words, our imagination creates the figures or the patterns and expresses them in speech. Such is the redescription of reality, and the power of the one
corresponds with the power of the other. This is the
poetics, or the creation of meaning.

Religious language modifies this function by
intensifying it, that is, by taking it to its limits.
The expressions of such limits Ricoeur calls limit-
expressions. Religious language, then, works to describe human experience in a way analogous to that of a
scientific model. But what do such expressions refer
to? They refer to those limit experiences which human
beings have, those times of being on-the-edge, pushed
to the extreme.

How do such limit-expressions work in religious
discourse? Just as there is an intensification of the
metaphorical process in the parable, so, too, is there

a similar intensification in those other types of
discourse found in the gospel which are not metaphorical. Particular examples are the proclamations of
Jesus and the proverbial sayings, especially those in
the eschatological or apocalyptic mode. These step
across, or transgress, the bounds of expected discourse. As such, they point beyond the edge of human
experiences. For Ricoeur, they point to the "Wholly
Other" (108).

These other forms of discourse, then, the
proclamatory and proverbial sayings, like the parables,
point to the "Kingdom of God," which becomes then an
ultimate referent. Such a referent makes clear the
inadequacy and even the inaccuracy of an existential or
moral application in the traditional sense. The "Kingdom of God" as referent becomes a limit-expression
which takes the hearer beyond the limits of discourse
to an extreme point which thereby becomes an encounter
with the infinite, much as a speculative voyage into
the galaxies points us to the edges of space and thereby to the possibility or even the probability of the
infinite.

Each symbol--"The Kingdom of God is at hand"--,
while it can operate only within the myth, at the same
time transgresses the myth, or goes against it. By
saying "The Kingdom of God is at hand," or "within
you," the traditional expectations of a literal future
apocalypse are upset or broken, and the way is opened
to a new interpretation. While described in time, the
time of the coming of the kingdom escapes time, cannot
be bound by time.

In a similar way, the proverbial sayings of Jesus
make use of the form and the content of sayings in the
Wisdom tradition, but at the same time, they intensify
the language in the manner of paradox or hyperbole.
"Whoever seeks to gain his life will lose it, but whoever loses his life will save it" (Lk. 27.33). The
imagination is thus overturned. Life cannot be a project to be worked out in order.

The proverb points to the referent "the Kingdom of
God" by describing an impossible possibility. To reach
a similar objective, the parable uses the circuitous
genre of story, of narrative. In the creating of the
fiction, the parable disorients and thereby, at the
same time, reorients the hearer. An old world is
broken up at the same time that a new world is being
created. A parable then becomes a poem or a poetics of
faith.

Parallel to the intensification by paradox or
hyperbole in the sayings is the element of extravagance
within the narratives of the parables. The characters,
situations, and plots are apparently realistic, but the
modes of behavior are eccentric. We have extraordinary
behavior in apparently ordinary stories. The stories
are provocative. They scandalize. They shock and call
forth a response. To put it another way: parables
break the limits. They illustrate compassion without
limit or forgiveness without limit. What is symbolic
is not a particular character in the story, but the
extravagance within the narrative. We have the extraordinary within the ordinary.

This language of limits, then, is not a question
of truth or falseness of statement. We are not concerned here with verifiability or falsifiability, but
rather with involvement and a call to commitment, a
commitment, in fact, that is total if one listens and
enters into the language. The language is revelatory.
It provides a disclosure model that opens one to reorientation and commitment. It has universal significance. Such disclosure is opposed to self-
glorification. "It dislocates our project of making a
whole of our lives" (125).

The parables, then, are symbolic narratives which
pose an enigma, call for interaction, and therefore
lead to interpretation.

> But we must add, at the same time, that
> no interpretation can exhaust their
> meaning, not even the "historical"
> interpretation. Our interpretations
> have only to be related to our particu-
> lar situation as the original one was
> to the initial situation. It is in
> this analogical way (A is to B what C
> is to D) that the original import,
> i.e., the historical interpretation, is
> controlling with respect to reinterpre-
> tation (134).

The Power of the Imagination and the Reading
of the Parables

The three lectures on parables described above
were followed six years later by a study presented in
1979 as part of The William Rainey Harper Conference on
Biblical Studies at the University of Chicago. Dean

Joseph Kitagawa invited Ricoeur to address the topic
"The Bible and the Imagination." Ricoeur used the
opportunity to extend his insights on the parables by
reflecting on the power of the imagination and the act
of reading.

Following Kant, Ricoeur conceives of imagination
as a "rule-governed form of invention" or as a "norm-
governed productivity." In other words, the human
imagination creates new forms and new patterns out of
the data, norms, and patterns which are assumed as rule
within a given language or within the tradition of a
particular genre. Imagination is also "the power of
redescribing reality" ("The Bible and the Imagination,"
50).

How does this link to the Bible? Drawing on
recent developments in reading theory, especially in
Germany, Ricoeur sees the act of reading as dynamic.
When we read a text, we are not just repeating sounds,
but we are continuing a process of interpretation of
which the text is a part. The text we are reading puts
into writing certain experiences and reflections. As
we read the text, we are necessarily interpreting the
meaning of those experiences and reflections. We are
guided by the norms which we can uncover within the
text, but as we search for meaning, we are necessarily
involved in freeing the text to live again. Insofar as
we do that, paradoxically we have placed it in context,
but then we have freed the meaning, which implies that
we have also decontextualized it: we have freed it for
other contexts. And since we can actually live and
think and interpret only within the present, of necessity we are placing the text anew in the present. In
other words, we are recontextualizing, whether we use
the language of the past or the present. The act of
reading, especially in narratives, is the intersection
point of the describing and the redescribing of
reality. As such, it is also movement from narrative
to paradigm, from narrative to life experience, opened
to future possibilities. One event enables us to
understand another. Ricoeur quotes H. Richard Niebuhr:
"By revelation in our history, then, we mean that
special occasion which provides us with an image of
which all the occasions of personal and common life
become intelligible" (52. Quoting Niebuhr in The Meaning of Revelation). The process of making a parable in
the text creates in the reader a similar process of
involvement and response.

Ricoeur finds a key to the process in the
concept of intertextuality as developed by French

structuralists. Intertextuality is "the work of
meaning through which one text in referring to another
text both displaces this other text and receives from
it an extension of meaning" (53). He illustrates this
by a semiotic analysis of the two parables common to
the synoptic gospels. Acknowledging that historical-
critical analysis has its own method of exegesis, and
that structural analysis usually emphasizes certain
combinatory devices, Ricoeur nevertheless puts forth
another type of analysis which he thinks particularly
helpful in the process of parabolization, which for him
is at the same time the process of metaphorization.

     For his analysis, Ricoeur draws on some of the
insights both of Ivan Almeida, a professor at the
Catholic University of Lyon, and of A.-J. Greimas, who
developed a structuralist model used by Almeida and
others. Ricoeur sees the two parables of the Wicked
Husbandmen (Mk. 12.1-11) and of the Sower (Mk. 4.1-20)
as complementary embedded narratives within the narrative of the gospel. He discusses their common semantic
themes or isotopes. The first is the vegetation-
economic isotope involving a vineyard, a harvest, an
inheritance, and the sowing of seed. The second is the
spatial isotope involving the relationships among
places, movements inside and outside. The third set
includes apparently disparate semantic themes, that of
sending, fighting, and killing in the Husbandmen as
contrasted with the sowing of seed understood as word.
In the context of intertextuality, it seems that the
dead body of the only Son has been replaced by the
Living word, which brings forth the fruit denied in the
parable of the Husbandmen. And, of course, the parables communicate meaning only against the background of
the Song of the Vineyard in Chapter 5 of Isaiah, and as
embedded within the narrative of the gospel. The parabolization and the metaphorization make sense only in
the tension of the interrelationships, and only in the
context of a gospel process which calls the reader to
respond to the narrator's question: "What do you suppose the owner of the vineyard will do?" The reader is
called to the present and the future, to involvement,
transformation, and decision making.

          In effect, what progressively happens
          in the Gospel is the recognition of
          Jesus as being the Christ. We can say
          in this regard that the Gospel is not a
          simple account of the life, teaching,
          work, death, and resurrection of Jesus,
          but the communicating of an act of

confession, a communication by
means of which the reader in turn
is rendered capable of performing
the same recognition which occurs
inside the text (68).

PART VII. RICOEUR,
LANGUAGE, AND
INTERPRETATION THEORY

CHAPTER ONE

Metaphor as a Key to Interpretation

Ricoeur's study of symbolism in The Symbolism of Evil had led him to pursue a philosophy of language, in which he discovered metaphor as a key element. His studies followed a number of directions and took place in different times and places. They were published in French in 1975 as La métaphor vive and in English in 1977 as The Rule of Metaphor. Their importance was recognized to the point that they were soon published simultaneously in eight additional languages.

At first sight, they seem to have little bearing on religious or biblical studies, whether those of the parables or of other forms. In fact, the work is most aptly placed within a philosophy of language or in a philosophy of aesthetics. However, the careful student will recognize that apparently dissimilar studies are cognate. A study of parables is not just a study of a religious genre, but is also part of the continuing search for meaning within a philosophy of language. In the same way, a detailed study of metaphor as part of a philosophy of language throws light on those examples of language contained in the Bible.

In his introduction to the published volume, Ricoeur acknowledges that the studies were initiated in a seminar in 1971 at the University of Toronto, where he had been invited to the Comparative Literature Department by Professor Cyrus Hamlin. But the studies continued to grow as Ricoeur lectured or taught at the University of Paris-X, at the University of Louvain, or at the University of Chicago.

Each of the eight studies develops a particular point of view, beginning with classical rhetoric, passing through semiotics and semantics, and finally

developing a hermeneutics. This reflects development
from word, through the sentence, to discourse.

The first two studies correspond to the level of
the word. In the first, "Between Rhetoric and
Poetics," Ricoeur explores Aristotle's classic study of
metaphor which so affected the development of western
aesthetics. For Aristotle, metaphor is an element
within the larger study of rhetoric, which covers three
areas: argumentation, style, and composition. The
study of rhetoric was a response to the undisciplined
power of speech in the Greek republics, where a persuasive orator could turn the tide of political events.
Rhetoric creates a technique which counters that raw
power by the power of an organized discipline which can
recognize the techniques of persuasive oratory as ma-
nipulative and which at least raises the possibility of
using them in a more responsible way. Even here we see
the importance of the questions raised, not only about
political, but also about religious rhetoric, whether
of the demagogue, of the sincere sectarian, or of the
liberal preacher.

Plato had condemned rhetoric as one of the arts of
illusion and deception. Aristotle draws the line between the use and abuse of the power of speaking. He
asks how can the art of speaking well be used to
correspond with speaking the truth. How can we distinguish the ability to persuade, or that which is persuasive,--the proofs--from deceit, seduction, or flat-
tery. Mathematics can demonstrate about the necessary,
but rhetoric is in the area of the probable.

The difficulty with metaphor comes in that
metaphor is not only a part of rhetoric, but also a
part of poetics, the art of composing poems, princi-
pally tragic poems, what we usually refer to as Greek
drama. Metaphor, then, has a particular structure, but
it functions both rhetorically and poetically. The
difference of these two functions is what could make
possible the development in western aesthetics of metaphor in the first area as more decorative, as part of
persuasion, and at the same time, through a loss of the
poetics and of the philosophy of which it was a part, a
loss of or at least the lack of the development of the
concept of metaphor as the creation of the new.

The thrust given by Aristotle and followed by his
interpreters for more than two thousand years emphasized the naming aspects of metaphor in the more
limited sense we associate with nouns. From this

follows an idea of metaphor as a borrowed meaning which fills a semantic void.

Ricoeur prefers to take a different direction, which is a legitimate development out of Aristotle's relating of metaphor to poetics, but which is nevertheless a new thrust. He offers three theses: 1) Metaphor occurs not just in the naming, but in the relationship of the two terms involved. As such it disturbs a whole network of relationships. 2) It may therefore be seen as a categorical transgression which deviates from the assumed logical order. In other words, metaphor destroys an old order in order to invent a new one. It reflects, then, a logic of discovery. "Thus, the category-mistake is the deconstructive intermediary phase between description and redescription" (RM, 22). 3) If metaphor opens thought in such a way, then may we not ask if all thought from its very beginnings is perhaps metaphoric in its efforts at naming and classification.

If the above theses hold, then metaphor becomes a verb. It is at the level of discovery, finding, inventing, the level of openness to the future, the level of the heuristic. An old order is violated in order to create another.

In the second study, "The Decline of Rhetoric: Tropology," Ricoeur describes the development of rhetoric especially in France during the nineteenth century, which because it continued in the traditional mode ended in a theory dominated by classification and taxonomy. While these are appropriate for a static account of tropes, they do not allow for an understanding of how meaning is produced.

Studies 3, 4, and 5 pursue an understanding of metaphor within the framework of the sentence as an example of impertinent predication, an apparently irrelevant affirmation which nevertheless communicates meaning. In fact, it creates new meaning.

Ricoeur considers Study 3 "Metaphor and the Semantics of Discourse" as key. Following Émile Benveniste, a French linguist, Ricoeur emphasizes the importance of discourse, which allows him to distinguish between the level of the word and the level of the sentence. A sentence is not just an accumulation of words; it is more than the sum of its parts. In other words, a sentence cannot be reduced to the sum of its parts. In translation, one may know a meaning of each of the words, yet not perceive the meaning, not understand the sentence. These two aspects of linguistics, Benveniste called "semiotics" and "semantics," the first referring to the word-sign-units, the second to the units of meaning which transcend the individual signs.

In his traditional dialectical methodology, Ricoeur develops his theory of metaphor within the semantics of discourse by a reading of each of three writers: I. A. Richards, The Philosophy of Rhetoric; Max Black, Models and Metaphor; and Monroe Beardsley, Aesthetics.

Ricoeur admires Richards for restoring rhetoric to the matrix of philosophy by choosing a definition of rhetoric as "a philosophic discipline aiming at a mastery of the fundamental laws of the use of language" (76). Rhetoric thus is seen as a theory of discourse, a theory of thought expressed as discourse. In this theory, words properly speaking have no meaning of their own. They must always be seen in context. To understand metaphor, then, to metaphorize well, is to enter into the constitutive form of language. It is to acknowledge that one thinks only through making connections.

Black's contribution in his article on metaphor is in the area of logical grammar. Black's analysis raises questions which are important for the discussion. If the entire statement constitutes the metaphor, then how does one explain the focus on a particular word. In a sentence, "The committee plowed through the material," there is a particular metaphorical emphasis on the word "plowed." It seems, then, that some words are accepted more in their literalist sense and others are more clearly focused within their metaphorical context. We are faced with the question about how the multiple contexts are related to the particular word or words. The associations or connotations come out of the language community and, in turn, organize a particular world view, or set of world views. Metaphor communicates a particular insight by suppressing certain aspects of the subject and emphasizing others.

What does Beardsley's Aesthetics with its emphasis on literary criticism add to the discussion of semantics? Beardsley recognizes the sentence as the smallest complete unit of discourse. He acknowledges in meaning a distinction between primary and secondary signification, the first being what actually seems to

be stated, the second the multiple associations which
seem to be suggested. In other words, some meanings
are explicit, others are implicit. To extend the
theory to a work of literature, a poem, an essay, a
piece of prose fiction, we ask the questions: What is
the world which is evoked by the piece of literature?
If this is the sense of the work, what is the reference? The main traditions of literary criticism occupy
themselves with the first question and see the second
as irrelevant or as a matter for explication. On the
contrary, with Frege, Ricoeur sees the second question
as integral to the nature of the discourse.

    In the matter of explication, two principles are
important, that of selection and that of plenitude. In
other words, there is an art of selecting those aspects
of explication which are most appropriate, without
eliminating the fullness of the connotations which are
implicit in the work. The explication, the reading of
a poem, for example, must be accurate, but it is also
unique. The living metaphor, or the metaphor made to
live again, is an event of discourse. A new metaphor,
then, as opposed to a dead metaphor, is a creation of
language, a semantic innovation, a semantic event,
which takes place where a number of semantic fields
come together. The metaphorical twist is then an event
and a meaning, an event that communicates, a meaning
communicated by language.

    In his fourth study, "Metaphor and Semantics of
the Word," Ricoeur examines the work of Stephen Ullmann
in the tradition of Saussurean linguistics. After
demonstrating the inadequacies of a linguistics that is
dominated by a "monism" of the sign, Ricoeur goes on to
show that metaphor should be located in a theory of
discourse as lodged "between" the sentence and the
word, between predication and naming" (125). He expli-
cates this point by what he calls three clues.

    The first clue is given by a recognition of the
paradox that within our so-called lexical system there
are many aspects which are not systematic. While obviously there are patterns and systems which are
operating, nevertheless it is true to say that language
in its entirety is both systematic and non-systematic.
Perceived prevailing systems are always being affected
by social forces, by new experiences, by changes in a
cultural situation.

    The second indicator of his thesis is the
necessary contextuality of any word. A word is

determined by its grammatical possibilities, by its
potential functions in discourse, by the way it is
brought to speech and enters into language.

The third indicator is found in the fact that
words are only actualized in a particular sentence, in
an instance of discourse. The word has an identity,
but it is a plural identity. It is in the context of a
word or words actualized in discourse that we can sort
out the aspects of its multiple meanings, of its
polysemy. The context is at the same time the index of
which meanings are intended.

The fifth study, "Metaphor and the New Rhetoric,"
extends the discussion to the development of French
structuralism which has created a "new rhetoric" emphasizing rules of reduction to basic units or segments,
and rules for combination. In a mode similar to his
stance in regard to Lévi-Strauss' structuralism and all
the off-shoots and extensions of the basic insights
involved, Ricoeur both respects the insights from within and the subtlety of the developmental structures,
but recognizes the inadequacies in terms of a treatment
of referents and in the structure of an essentially
closed system, that is, a system closed in on itself.
Moreover, he points out that even from within, the new
rhetoric suggests from within its limits a theory of
statement-metaphor, although its own methodology is
inadequate to develop the theory.

In his analysis, Ricoeur comments on aspects of
several works which express the new rhetoric. Among
them are: Rhétorique générale, by a group associated
with Université de Liège; Sémantique structurale by
A.-J. Greimas; Figures I by Gérard Genette; and Structure du langage poétique by Jean Cohen. Ricoeur deals
at length with a number of theses raised in these works
which pertain to metaphor. The first is what is called
"Deviation and Rhetoric Degree Zero." The problem
arises when one recognizes that to speak of a figurative language is to posit a language that is non-
figurative. In other words, if one says that a particular trope deviates from "normal" usage, in what way
are the criteria of those norms developed? Was all
"non-figurative" language at one time "figurative"? Is
there a process whereby new language is created at the
level of the figurative, and then, through use, becomes
"non-figurative"? Although one can posit a "rhetoric
degree zero," is that an unreal abstraction?

Pursuing the notion of metaphor as deviation, and
therefore the concomitant problem of the reduction of

deviation as a means of addressing the norm, Ricoeur
finds a certain kinship in the work of Cohen, who from
a structuralist point of view analyzes the poetic function. Cohen sees poetry as a new language founded on
the destruction of the old. Ricoeur differs with him
in his founding this newness in the affective and subjective without his recognizing the objective quality
of the new information created in the poetic act.
Nevertheless, both agree that the reader has to lose as
well as recover the signification intended; in other
words, both the semantic theory of metaphor and the
semiotic as described by Cohen recognize the double
character of the word. On the other hand, none of the
structuralists sufficiently addresses the problem of
the referential function, since, in Ricoeur's view,
that is outside the purview of the structuralist
methodology.

The next three studies, 6, 7, 8, pertain to the
level of hermeneutics, of interpretation as such.
Ricoeur has moved from detailed analyses of word and
sentence in the previous studies to attack the problem
of semantic innovation. In his sixth study, he analyzes what he calls the work of resemblance.

What does resemblance mean? The word traces its
roots through the Old French back to the attempts by
the Greeks and the Romans to describe those things in
which is perceived a likeness, a similarity. Ricoeur
loves to quote Aristotle: "To metaphorize well implies
an intuitive perception of the similarity in dissimi-
lars" (6). The problem of trying to describe what
happens in the perception of a likeness in two apparently dissimilar things is a very old problem. Because
of its importance to him, Ricoeur draws on commentators
new and ancient to come to grips with the process.
Differing with those who depend on merely a theory of
substitution, Ricoeur develops a complex foundation of
the processes involved in aspects of resemblance predicated on semantic analogy, a relationship between that
which belongs and that which does not belong and which
thereby creates an image.

This new image is found in the iconic moment of
the metaphor. The word icon comes from the Greek word
eikon, which means "likeness" or "image." From the
insights of the philosopher Charles Sanders Peirce and
of a more recent interpreter, Paul Henle, Ricoeur perceives the icon as containing an internal duality that
at the same time is transcended in the oneness of the
analogy. In other words, a metaphor functions on a

literal level, but concomitantly also on an iconic
level. Since the iconic representation is not an image
in the simpler pictorial sense, it may point to resemblances which transcend the pictorial image.

After pointing out strengths and weaknesses in
various positions for and against a theory of resemblance, including studies in the "psycholinguistics" of
metaphor, Ricoeur develops more extensively his own
theory of the relationship of icon and image. With the
icon of the Byzantine cult as an example, we may understand the verbal icon as a fusion of meaning and that
which is perceived by the senses. The iconic image is
not just the free image which arises from the association of ideas. The iconic presupposes a "tied"
imagery, a situation in which meaning is controlling
the imagery. In a similar context, Kant talked about
the productive imagination or the schema as a method
for constructing images.

Ricoeur finds helpful here an idea of "seeing as"
which was developed by Marcus Hester following Wittgenstein. The "seeing as" is not a "seeing" in the
ordinary sense of the word but the act of selecting
from the mass of possible images the appropriate aspects of imagery which fit the context. "Seeing as"
gives order to the flow of images. The imagery happens
but it also communicates meaning. By creating meaning,
"seeing as" is part of our on-going language games. As
such, it may succeed or fail. The failure may come in
those metaphors which are forced or which are cliché,
but on the other hand "seeing as" may succeed in those
metaphors which create new meaning, which provide surprise and discovery.

> Bachelard has taught us that the image
> is not a residue of impression, but an
> aura surrounding speech: "The poetic
> image places us at the origin of the
> speaking being." The poem gives birth
> to the image; the poetic image "becomes
> a new being in our language, expressing
> us by making us what it expresses; in
> other words, it is at once a becoming
> òf expression, and a becoming of our
> being" (214-215).

The question of resemblance raises the crucial
problem: that of reference. What is the reference of
the discourse? In his seventh study, Ricoeur addresses
the problem by offering some postulates of reference,
answering some of the objections raised, and examining

theories of denotation and model in order to move
toward a concept of metaphorical truth.

Within a very tightly reasoned demonstration,
Ricoeur points out again the difference between
semiotics and semantics, with the implication that what
is intended in discourse cannot be reduced to what is
called the signified in semiotics. On the contrary,
the intention of discourse is thrust toward an extra-
linguistic reality, toward a world. From the sign we
move to the sense and thence to the reference, whether
the reference is to an object as named, to a state of
affairs, or to a totality of facts called a world.
Sense presupposes a reference.

The discussion of texts, especially literary
texts, brings up a separate discussion in terms of
reference. Literary texts are the production of discourse as a work. A poem or a novel cannot be reduced
to its sentences. There are codes or genres which are
operating and which provide the key to the understanding of the work of discourse. The particularity of a
work, its unique style, is what makes the work recog-
nizable as an individual production. "The structure of
the work is in fact its sense, and the world of the
work its reference" (220).

> Hermeneutics then is simply the theory
> that regulates the transition from
> structure of the work to world of the
> work. To interpret a work is to dis-
> play the world to which it refers by
> virtue of its "arrangement," its
> "genre," and its "style" (220).

In a work of literature, the first-level
denotation is suspended in order to display a second-
level denotation. A literal reference is set aside to
set free the metaphorical reference.

Ricoeur recognizes that not only the
structuralists, but also others provide many arguments
against reference as described above. Ricoeur takes
them seriously, assesses the strength of the arguments
of Jakobson, Wimsatt, Peirce, Frye, and Cohen, but at
the same time finds within each a gap which he locates
in the theory regarding denotation and connotation.

To develop a generalized theory of denotation,
Ricoeur recognizes that he must ask the serious questions about reality and truth. Given that a poem is
neither true nor false, nevertheless,

> "the poetic hypothesis" . . . is
> the suggestion or proposal, in
> imaginative, fictive mode, of a
> world. Hence, suspension of real
> reference is the condition of ac-
> cess to the virtual mode of refer-
> ence. But what is a virtual life?
> Can there be a virtual life without
> a virtual world capable of being
> inhabited? Is it not the function
> of poetry to establish another
> world--another world that corre-
> sponds to other possibilities of
> existence, to possibilities that
> would be most deeply our own?
> (229).

The deliberate category mistake of metaphor makes
possible a new vision. It is "reality remade." It is
the recognition that symbol systems make and remake the
world.

At one point, denotation and reference are
synonymous. What is denoted in a poem is what is referred to. But there are two ways of referring, that
of denotation and that of exemplification. From the
eclipse of the one, the second one is freed. By or-
ganizing language in a different way, a poem unveils a
way of existence. The metaphorical invents in the
sense of creating as well as discovering.

Ricoeur moves next to the relationship of model
and metaphor. The work of Max Black is helpful here.
Whether it is scale models, analogue models, or theoretical models, it is important to know the rules for
interpretation, the hermeneutical premises. It is in
the concept of theoretical models that Ricoeur finds
material for fruitful dialogue regarding an understanding of metaphor. A theoretical model is both a
discovery and a creation to make possible the thinking
through of relationships. Old meanings are displaced
by new. Ricoeur quotes Mary Hesse: "Rationality consists just in the continuous adaptation of our language
to our continually expanding world, and metaphor is one
of the chief means by which this is accomplished"
(243). The model projects a world; so does the poem.
"Poetic feeling itself also develops an experience of
reality in which invention and discovery cease being
opposed and where creation and revelation coincide"
(246). But this raises the question of metaphorical
truth, the next topic Ricoeur approaches.

Truth, the meaning of the verb "to be," may be predicated relationally and/or existentially. The positivist movements in this century have rejected the second possibility, and it is the questions raised by that rejection which Ricoeur wrestles with. He points out the limitations both of an ontological naiveté and of a one dimensional demythologization. He is concerned rather with the tensions 1) between principal subject and secondary subject; 2) between literal interpretation and metaphorical interpretation; and 3) between identity and difference in the statement of the "to be," in the varieties and the interplay of resemblance.

In his last study in the volume, "Metaphor and Philosophical Discourse," Ricoeur develops the ideas for which the previous seven have been preparation. He has moved from rhetoric to semantics and from sense to reference. He is now ready to deal explicitly with the implied philosophical assumptions and challenges. Is a philosophy implied by the theory of metaphor developed? If so, what philosophy is implied? What are the implications for an ontology, an understanding of being?

Wittgenstein had developed a theory positing the radical heterogeneity of language games. While recognizing the discreteness of various language systems, Ricoeur nevertheless makes a case for a relative pluralism of forms of discourse. Although on the one side there is discontinuity between various forms of discourse, for example, that between poetic and speculative discourse, there is still a necessity to account for the interanimation between two such levels as the philosophical and the metaphorical. A theory of metaphor calls for a new way of looking at truth, reality, and being.

In his theory of analogy, Aristotle had formulated one of the earliest attempts to explore the bridge or the separation between levels of discourse. He had found an intersection point in the concept of ousia, being which is shared somehow by all that exists. He developed the idea of attributive discourse, in the sense that we can name or talk about things that we know, and by extension, attribute the elements of that discourse to things we do not know. The concept of ousia or being is therefore at least the crossroads where the questions and the searching meet.

From a modern perspective, Ricoeur recognizes the failure of Aristotle, as well as the failure of the

medieval theologians and/or philosophers who followed
him. Nevertheless, he finds that although the theories
of ontology, the theories of being, which were developed, are inadequate, the questions which they raised
are not addressed adequately either by the closed systems of the structuralists, nor by the radical heterogeneity of language game philosophers.[1]

As Aristotle had posed the problem under the
heading of analogy as the positing of proportional
relationships, so Ricoeur poses the problem of analogy
in terms of the intersection of discourses. Against
those who see analogy as nothing but a pseudo-science,
Ricoeur points out its usefulness in addressing the
identity recognized when we cut through the diversity
of genera. In other words, we can posit "life" even
though we know it concretely only in a series of discrete manifestations. In this sense, analogy is transcendental. In what way is this different from poetic
resemblance?

Before answering that question, Ricoeur moves to a
study of "Metaphor and analogia entis: onto-theology."
As developed by Aquinas, the concept of analogia entis,
the "analogy of being," was directed to the possibility
of speaking rationally of the God of the Judeo-
Christian tradition.

Ricoeur reviews the ways Aquinas develops the
concept, including the distinction between proportion
and proportionality, the first being the relationship
between two quantities of the same kind, the second
being analogy proper wherein there is posited a resemblance of relationship. Many critiques culminating in
the physics following from Galileo and the postulates
formulated by Hume made it clear that Aquinas's concept
of analogy and consequent participation would no longer
hold.

Nevertheless, the questions raised by Aquinas
following Aristotle remain. Rejection of classical
metaphysics or of classical ontology either ignores the
questions or tries to deal with them in new ways.

Ricoeur next takes issue with Heidegger who
subsumes metaphor within the metaphysical, but where
the metaphysical is in the context of a Platonic model
of a visible and an invisible world. From Heidegger's
own writings, Ricoeur demonstrates an implicit metaphor
different from that which Heidegger condemns. Ricoeur
then points out the very different way in which he is

developing his theory of metaphor, as well as the
questions which that development raises for the questions of being.

The next critic whom Ricoeur confronts is Jacques
Derrida who formulates in "White Mythology" a decon-
struction which posits in language a wearing away of
metaphor and a drift toward idealization. In one
sense, this whole process merely begs the question.
All theory of metaphor is itself embedded in metaphor.

Ricoeur concludes his analysis by noting that the
theoretical core common to Heidegger and Derrida is the
positing of a necessary connection between "the metaphorical pair of the proper and figurative and the
metaphysical pair of the visible and invisible" (294).
Ricoeur does not think this connection is necessary.

In contrast, Ricoeur puts forth two related tasks:

> I shall therefore be undertaking two
> tasks at once: to erect a general
> theory of the intersections between
> spheres of discourse upon the differ-
> ence we have recognized between modali-
> ties of discourse, and to propose an
> interpretation of the ontology implicit
> in the postulates of metaphorical ref-
> erence that will fit this dialectic of
> modalities of discourse (295).

Ricoeur then applies a tension theory of metaphor
on three different levels: "the tension between the
terms of the statement, the tension between literal
interpretation and metaphorical interpretation, and the
tension in the reference between is and is not" (298-
299). In metaphor, in other words, there are two
fields of reference, the one referring to a known field
of reference, the other to a field which opens up new
meaning. Ricoeur sees the universe of discourse as one
kept in movement by the interplays and intersections of
these various fields. Interpretation functions at the
place of intersection between the metaphorical and the
speculative. It is pulled on the one hand toward striving for clarity, but on the other hand strives to keep
the dynamism of the tension.

Returning then to the concept denoted by the
French title of the book La métaphore vive, Ricoeur
sees metaphor as living insofar as it gives life to the
language. It brings imagination and the possibility of
thinking anew or thinking more.

This makes possible then a new ontological clarification, a new way of looking at ontology. It is through language that we take the experience of reality and express that experience in discourse. Human being speaks in the knowledge of being in relationship to reality. The word <u>invent</u> means both to discover and to create. The poet in metaphorical discourse and the philosopher in speculative discourse, using a philosophical, speculative set of metaphors, are striving to invent in that double sense of the word. On another level so is the scientist.

The tension of the split reference involved is finally carried to the predication of <u>is</u>. The copula implies being-as, which means at the same time being and not being, is and is not. This leads Ricoeur to recover from Aristotle the more radical distinction between being as potentiality and being as actuality. It is at the point of the split reference where the tension of being as actuality and being as potentiality intersect. It is at the point where living expression somehow expresses living existence, where the poet on one level and the philosopher on another level, are challenged anew both to find and to create.

CHAPTER TWO

Interpretation Theory

The essays in Ricoeur's little book Interpretation Theory grew out of a series of lectures which he gave as part of the centennial celebration of Texas Christian University at Fort Worth. In the preface, Ted Klein calls the four expanded essays "a systematic and comprehensive theory that attempts to account for the unity of human language in view of the diverse uses to which it is put" (vii). In his own introduction, Ricoeur offers the essays "as step by step approximations of a solution to a single problem, that of understanding language at the level of such productions as poems, narratives, and essays, whether literary or philosophical" (xi).

The first essay is called "Language as Discourse." The questions now being asked about language could not have been asked without the progress made in modern linguistics. But the progress has not been made without consequent problematics. The problem with which Ricoeur is concerned is the setting aside of development of a theory of discourse. Under several viewpoints, he sets out to restore discourse to its rightful and necessary place.

Ricoeur begins with a summary and a brief analysis of the structural model as based on Saussure's distinction between the two concepts of langue and parole. The first is the code or the set of codes operating within a language; the second is the message in which a particular speaker makes use of the implicit code(s). The message and the code are related to time in different ways, the first being temporal and relating to the movement of time; that is, it is diachronic. On the other hand, code is synchronic. The code is anonymous, even unconscious, in the sense that it is used and

developed as a given with its own laws of development.
Langue is associated with linguistics, parole with the
speech-act studied within many disciplines.

In the growth of structural methodology, it was
much easier to systematize the structures and systems
of langue, so that study of the speech-act itself was
either set aside, dismissed as bracketed, or diffused
under the methodologies of discrete disciplines. Structuralism became an all-encompassing way of thought,
with the study of language no longer thought of as
relating minds and things.

A similar dichotomy developed between semantics
and semiotics in the analysis of the sentence. Semiotics is the science of signs, including the individual
words, phonemes, and phonological signs which are the
basic units of a code. On the other hand, semantics as
the science of the sentence is concerned with meaning
or sense, which presumes the integration of the parts
of a sentence. While semantics is neglected by structuralists, for Ricoeur "the distinction between semantics and semiotics is the key to the whole problem of
language" (8).

Ricoeur next looks at the dialectic of event and
meaning. For him, "discourse is the event of language"
(9). In spite of difference of translation or of time,
there is an identity in an event of discourse. It can
be said again and again and recognized. This being-
said is its propositional content.

The power of the sentence is that it predicates
something. The author names a subject as a singular
and then predicates or designates a relationship or
action. Discourse, then, has a structure, but it is
not the structure which the structuralist studies. Its
structure involves synthesis and the interplay of identification and predication. In this way, then, discourse is not only event, but also proposition.
Discourse as proposition or meaning is always actualized as event; it is always understood as meaning.
Moreover, it is the meaning which endures. It is the
intention of language, in fact, that the meaning should
endure, so that even if the event is cancelled, the
meaning endures.

What are the references of discourse? First is
the self-reference. The meaning is related to the
speaker, what the speaker intends to say, but it is
also related to what the sentence says in terms of its
actualization of the codes.

What the speaker says points back to his or her
intention under several aspects. According to J. L.
Austin's categories, the first is saying something, the
locutionary act; the second is, in addition, doing
something in saying, the illocutionary act, for example, saying "I promise," which is at the same time a
commitment; the third is, besides saying something,
also producing effects, the perlocutionary act.

In other words, there is a dialectic between the
propositional content and the event. In communication
language, there is a speaker, a message, and a hearer.
Roman Jakobson adds to these code, contact, and context. On these a six function system can be set up:

speaker	-	emotive function
hearer	-	conative function
message	-	poetic function
code	-	metalinguistic function
contact	-	phatic function
context	-	referential function

For most people, whatever difficulty they may have
with it, communication is a given. It is a fact; it is
accepted. But the philosopher has to wonder. And the
more he wonders, the more he considers communication a
miracle, a means of transcendence. One is impressed by
experience, and brings that to expression in language,
and the mystery is that somehow through language the
experience which takes place in the solitude of the
self is able to transcend the barriers of isolation and
find resonance in another. Our words are polysemic--
they can have many meanings, but in the context of
discourse, the selection of meaning can be clear, and
communication can take place. It is even taken as
common-place that through language private experience
can be made public, can enter the community or the
public domain.

These insights bring Ricoeur to a theme which is
crucial for his interpretation theory, the distinction
between sense and reference, meaning and what the meaning refers to. In Ricoeur's terminology, language in
itself is not a world. Language only exists as an
expression of what someone has experienced, of what
someone has experienced within a world. It is because

persons are in a world, are relating to the realities
of that world, that they have experiences which they
then can bring to language. To identify singular
things is to presuppose that they exist, and therefore
to presuppose an ontology, the ontological condition of
the reference. "If language were not fundamentally
referential, would or could it be meaningful?" (21).
Discourse then refers backwards and forwards; it refers
backwards toward the speaker and forward toward a
world.

What are some of the implications for
hermeneutics, or interpretation theory? Ricoeur believes that the above theses put in jeopardy the older
hermeneutical tendencies toward psychologizing or
toward a narrow existentialism. Ricoeur wishes to
follow through by showing that a written text is a form
of discourse, and as such, is also governed by the
notions of event and meaning as well as sense and reference.

In his next chapter on "Speaking and Writing,"
Ricoeur examines three main points: the movement from
speaking to writing, the unique importance of writing,
and the distanciation which takes place in writing. He
examines the message first in the medium in which writing takes place, and then in connection with each of
the elements: speaker, hearer, code, and reference.

Much as we take it for granted, writing is a
fascinating phenomenon. In the event of speech there
is the implicit possibility of detaching the meaning
from the event and thereby freeing it from its original
context. This is not to deny the importance of the
original context insofar as it is recoverable, but to
recognize that the original context is in the text of
the writing which exists here and now. For Ricoeur, as
contrasted with Derrida, "writing is the full manifestation of discourse" (25-26). Ricoeur then uses Jakobson's schema of the six functions to examine what takes
place when discourse is inscribed in writing.

We underestimate, if we even refer to it, the
amazing cultural phenomenon which human being created
of making marks on stone, papyrus, skins, or paper to
indicate meaning separate from the speech event. Discourse ends when speech ends, although its effects may
remain. In contrast, when discourse is fixed in writing, it endures. What writing fixes, however, is not
the event of speaking, but what was said in the event,
the meaning. Moreover, writing can thereby become a

kind of short-hand for discourse, with both positive
and negative effects.

What happens in the relationship of the message
and the speaker? It is no longer a question of speaking and hearing, but of writing and reading. In discourse, the speaker is self-evident. The self-
references are existential and may be reinforced by
gestures, facial expressions, and tone. In contrast,
in a written text, the author's subjective intention is
no longer identical with the text. In Ricoeur's language the text has achieved "semantic autonomy." The
world of the text is no longer confined to the limited
world of the author.

Having said this Ricoeur takes pains to point out
that just as he wants to avoid the intentional fallacy
which holds the author's intention as the only valid
criterion for interpreting a text, so does he want to
avoid the absolutizing of a text, which denies any
relationship of the text to its original author. In
other words, exegesis, as well as historical-critical
and sociological or other studies, are fundamental in
an analysis of a text.

Are there similar differences in terms of the
message and the hearer? In the event of discourse, the
meaning is addressed to "you." On the other hand, "a
written text is addressed to an unknown reader and
potentially to whoever knows how to read" (31). Nevertheless, writing and reading have their own cultural or
social parameters, but there is a dynamism of the cultural and social transformations whereby the meaning of
a text can transcend ordinary barriers. The autonomy
of the text opens up the possible domain of readers and
creates new audiences. The response of the audience
becomes crucial. Multiple readings are possible, and
the interpretation and significance of a text now rest
with the readers and the interpreters.

What is the relationship in writing between the
message and the code? The code is predominantly for
Ricoeur the genre, with all the complexities of elements which make a genre a work, a pro-duction. The
genre inscribes a certain development, a certain movement from beginning to end. This is foundational to
the theory Ricoeur developed for understanding narratives, including parables. Meaning is carried on the
process which takes place, consciously or unconsciously, both from the writer's point of view, and
from the reader's point of view.

The relationship in discourse between event and
meaning becomes in writing the relationship between
sense and reference. In spoken discourse, the reference or the referential world is shared by the speaker
and the hearer. In writing, although ostensive signi-
fiers continue to point to singular elements, the here
and now of the original discourse is severed from the
here and now of the interpreted text. The text is
opened up to places and times not bound by the original
event. Human being is freed from the limitation of the
localized situation and freed to a world.

> For us, the world is the ensemble of
> references opened up by the texts, or,
> at least for the moment, by descriptive
> texts. It is in this way that we may
> speak of the Greek "world," which is
> not to imagine anymore what were the
> situations for those who lived there,
> but to designate the nonsituational
> references displayed by the descriptive
> accounts of reality (36).

But a work of fiction raises new questions which
are essential for developing the idea of the world
created by writing and reading. In a travelogue, it is
relatively easy to construe the world which is
elicited. But in fiction, or works which are "ficted"
or constructed, there is a need for what Jakobson calls
a "split reference." The simpler or more obvious reference is not abolished, but it becomes the medium
whereby another world is created and referred to. This
is the fullness of the poetic function, the poiesis of
Aristotle's theory. It is also the concept which
Ricoeur has referred to over a long period of time
under the name of the poetics, the third part of his
life work. Here, Ricoeur agrees with Heidegger "that
what we understand first in a discourse is not another
person, but a 'pro-ject,' that is, the outline of a new
way of being in the world" (37).

Does not such a theory of the autonomy of the text
not result in alienation? The question is radical and
important. It was a problem faced by Plato, who condemned the alienating and oppressive power of writing
which in the Egyptian culture of the kings displaced
the wisdom of persons to the "wisdom" of written characters, which in Plato's view was a severe distortion
as well as an instrument of ignorance and oppression.
We are reminded in our own time how often written
texts, including sacred or biblical ones, are misused

to the same ends. For similar reasons, Socrates
criticized writing for its misuse. Thinkers through
the centuries, including persons such as Rousseau and
Bergson, have often recognized the distorting power
which writing can be in a civilization.

Ricoeur poses a response to these questions which
is equally radical. He finds in a theory of iconic
augmentation a channel for rethinking the creativity of
a work. In a painting, an artist selects a few elements of a vision and recreates an aspect of the world
by creating it anew. The artist makes us see anew,
that is, makes a new creation. The icon, or the image,
of whatever medium or culture, captures in miniature,
or creates a microcosm, which paradoxically, reveals a
new universe. "Iconicity, then, means the revelation
of a real more real than ordinary reality" (42), that
is, the icon or the image augments reality. The same
is true of writing which trans-scribes reality.

The trans-scription raises a new dialectic, that
of distanciation and appropriation. Distanciation is
the process by which both the author of the original
writing event as well as the reader are put at a distance from the text. Appropriation is to take as one's
own. Even an author has continually to appropriate his
or her own writing. We have the phenomenon of the
writer who says with surprise, "Did I write that?" The
reader's work of exegesis, interpretation, and re-
creation is the work of appropriation.

In his next essay Ricoeur sets "Metaphor and
Symbol" into the context of his interpretation theory.
After reviewing theories in the classical development
of ideas of metaphor, Ricoeur summarizes the implicit
suppositions, and then shows in a way similar to his
development in The Rule of Metaphor the inadequacies of
these descriptions today in the light of the new semantics. He moves from a theory of substitution to a
tension theory of the creation of new meaning.

To show the relation of metaphor to symbol,
Ricoeur then takes a new position in his on-going
theory of symbol. Whereas in his earlier major studies
of symbol in The Symbolism of Evil and Freud and Philosophy, he had defined hermeneutics in terms of the symbol
as semantic structure with a double meaning, he recognizes in this essay that in symbol there is also something non-semantic as well as semantic. This is in
distinction from metaphor which is entirely within the
semantic domain. Ricoeur realizes that the study of

symbols is even more complex than he had previously
thought first because it is part of so many and such
diverse disciplines. A second problem is that symbol
belongs to both linguistic and non-linguistic realms.
The linguistic aspects of symbol are always referring
to something else in the non-linguistic sphere.

Ricoeur then proceeds to clarify symbol in the
light of the theory of metaphor through taking three
steps. The first is to describe the semantic aspect of
every symbol within the structure similar to that of
describing metaphor. Something like the metaphorical
twist happens in the creation of meaning in the symbol.
More meaning is generated than can be reduced to words.
There is a surplus of signification. The inadequacy of
the literal interpretation points to the second level
of meaning, but the two levels are one and are so intertwined that they are in constant rhythm with each
other. The person experiencing the symbol is pulled to
the second meaning through the first. But the second
level is never exhausted. The symbol gives rise to
thought, and thought conceptualizes, but the symbol
remains the unlimited pool or resource for new experiencing and new thought.

By contrast with metaphor, Ricoeur then studies
the non-semantic aspect of symbols. "For something in
a symbol does not correspond to a metaphor and, because
of this fact, resists any linguistic, semantic, or
logical transcription" (57). Whether it is the symbol
of Freud's psychoanalysis, the creative symbol of the
poet, or the sacred symbol described by Eliade, the
symbol is bound to the cosmos, whereas the metaphor is
a free creation of discourse. Human being walks in a
universe where language only touches the surface.

On the other hand, symbols have characteristics
similar to those of metaphor, particularly by reason of
the networks of metaphor, their intersignifications,
and their rootedness, so that certain powerful metaphors can be called root metaphors. Moreover, some
metaphors are so radical that Wheelwright calls them
archtypes, which are similar to the symbolic models
which Eliade has studied.

What are some examples of symbols which are at the
origins of our being in the universe? They belong to
the basic ways in which human being inhabits his or her
world: basic directions, coming and going, the sky,
fire, paths, dwelling places. As human, we are compelled to bring our experience of these basic symbols

to language through the ways we try to articulate that experience.

Ricoeur next compares metaphor with models as defined by Max Black in Models and Metaphors. Metaphor is kin to model, not in the sense of a scale model or an analogical model, but in the sense of a theoretical model which offers a paradigm for interpreting certain experiences and data. In the tension which metaphor sets up between differences and resemblances, a new vision of reality is projected. This is the poetics, the creation of the new.

The fourth essay, "Explanation and Understanding," addresses a problem which is at the heart of hermeneutics. What is the relationship of explanation and understanding? The two words are an elemental part of the German hermeneutical tradition.

In ordinary conversation, it is difficult if not impossible to distinguish the action of each of these words. When are we involved in understanding? When are we involved in explanation? We explain in order that someone may understand. We recognize the stages of procedure. At a certain point someone will say, "Now I understand." It is possible, however, to define explanation as the analysis by which we show the range of possibilities and at the same time narrow appropriate explications. On the other hand, understanding is a thrust toward the whole, grasping the interrelationships.

How does interpretation relate to explanation and understanding? For Ricoeur "interpretation is a particular case of understanding . . . understanding applied to the written expressions of life" (73). It is a dialectic of explanation and understanding which is at work in the progress of understanding. One may think of an original understanding as a minimum grasp of the whole, which is followed by the more analytic process of explanation, which in turn, calls for a view of the whole or a different stage of understanding.

The first act of understanding is a guess. Since the text does not speak of itself, it is necessary for the reader to guess at the context or the meaning. Certain clues dependent on our expertise enable our guesses to be more or less on target. Then begins the dialectic of explanation and understanding.

There are methods for validating both the guesses as well as the quality of our explanations and

understandings. Such validation must address the text
as a whole, but not neglect its individual qualities.
It will ascertain the literary genre, the class of
texts of which this is one, and the types of structures
and codes which are operating in the text.

The texts have a variety of "potential horizons of
meaning" (78) which can be actualized in many different
ways. Theories of genre, structure, metaphor, and
symbol provide essential paradigms for such actualization, but the multiple meaning possibilities are not
exhausted by these disciplines. With E. D. Hirsch,
Ricoeur recognizes a logic of probability rather than a
logic of empirical verification. Although validation
is not verification, it nevertheless puts forth an
argument analogous to a juridical opinion. Where there
are "converging indices" (79) of meaning, there may
also be converging validations of interpretation. Not
just any interpretation will do. An interpretation
must be more probable than other interpretations.

What is the movement from explanation to
comprehension? Ricoeur reviews the contributions of
linguists and structuralists who separate the text from
an outside context and strive for explanation through
an analysis of phonemes, morphemes, lexemes, and
mythemes from within, as well as identification of
narrator(s) and audience(s). While seeing this as
valid and in fact necessary Ricoeur nevertheless disagrees with the structuralists in their denial of a
reference. Their hypothesis of myth, for example,
presupposes a narrative of origins. Moreover, their
analysis of surface and depth structures does indeed
open up a world and therefore a reference. Ricoeur
prefers to see structural analysis as one stage in the
development of a critical interpretation.

> The sense of a text is not behind the
> text, but in front of it. It is not
> something hidden, but something dis-
> closed. What has to be understood is
> not the initial situation of discourse,
> but what points toward a possible
> world, thanks to the non-ostensive
> reference of the text. Understanding
> has less than ever to do with the
> author and his situation. It seeks to
> grasp the world-propositions opened up
> by the reference of the text. To
> understand a text is to follow its
> movement from sense to reference: from

what it says, to what it talks about
(87-88).

Interpreting thereby creates a new mode of being.

CHAPTER THREE

Narrative and Interpretation

In the early 1970's, structuralism within French and American literary criticism began to raise the questions of narrative as genre. This overflowed into the emerging studies of parables from a structuralist point of view. Ricoeur had studied in The Symbolism of Evil selected myths as narratives of symbolic experience. In Freud and Philosophy he had recognized the importance of narrative as related to the process of interpreting dreams and other aspects of the unconscious. Even in his study of Genesis, he had recognized the implicit structural analysis of narrative which von Rad the exegete had developed in his Theology of the Old Testament. But it was in his studies of parables that the problem of narrative as genre emerged as a major category to be addressed in his developing general theory of interpretation.

Defining the literary genre of the parable led Ricoeur to find its narrativity in the conjunction of narrative form, metaphorical process, and reference to a qualifier, that is, the "kingdom of God." His research led him to review and critique the pioneering work of V. Propp, the Russian formalist, who analyzed Russian folk tales. This was the seminal work developed by the French structuralists in terms of functions, characters, actants, surface structures, and deep structures. The American Dan Via drew on categories which he appropriated from American literary criticism to analyze narrative as a plot with two basic kinds of direction, the comic and the tragic. Ricoeur points out the strengths and weaknesses of the various viewpoints, but takes up the more difficult questions raised initially by the French structuralists about the whatness of narrativity. In Germany Erhardt Güttgemanns formulated a theory of narrative production

which he calls a Generative Poetics. As Chomsky had
asked the questions and posed some possible models for
understanding how the grammar of a language is generated, so Güttgemanns proposes the questions and models
for trying to understand how basic the narrative form
is to the human enterprise. In contrast to the structuralists, including Greimas and Marin, while appreciating their work, Ricoeur makes a strong case for
affirming the temporally conditioned or diachronic
aspects of story whatever the import of the achronic or
non-temporal aspects of the analysis. In other words,
there are not only laws of structure but also laws of
narrative transformation which are taking place in the
unfolding of a story. There is a codification, not
only within the structural components of a story, but
also within the narrative production itself. Narrative
is a generative device which produces a singular message, and thereby mediates the message. By telling
stories, human beings exercise a certain ordering of
the chaotic data of their experience. In this sense,
the symbolic level of the parable belongs to the narrative itself. It is in the unfolding of the narrative
of the parable itself that its meaning is communicated.

In a number of seminars and lectures, Ricoeur
began to address the interrelationships of narrative,
time, and history. A key concept for studying the
topics is the notion of event. The word comes from the
idea of coming out or happening. First, event is a
limited and limiting concept in that something happened
which causes us to limit or organize our reconstruc-
tions. What then is an historical event? It is that
happening which we incorporate within the whole of our
story, which validates, or causes us to reconstrue the
story ("Seminar: Narrative," 1).[1]

Events are known through their traces, the signs
available to our senses of the passage or former presence of a happening. Such traces "are gathered,
selected, and preserved for the purpose of doing a
certain kind of history" (13). If there are no
archives or accumulated traces, it is then necessary to
gather the traces which will make a new archives.
Whatever story we intend to tell will shape the kind of
traces which we gather and preserve.

After its successful conference on Metaphor
organized with Ricoeur's consultation, some of the
papers of which were published in Critical Inquiry, the
University of Chicago Extension under the leadership of
C. Ranlet Lincoln and Joan Cowan organized with

Ricoeur's consultation a second conference on
Narrative. Subsequently, many of these papers, including the one by Ricoeur were published in a 1980 issue
of <u>Critical Inquiry</u>.

Under the title "Narrative Time" Ricoeur states
his task and presupposition and then proceeds to develop his thesis. To investigate narrative time,
Ricoeur first acknowledges some aspects of contemporary
views. There are those who speak of the illusion of
sequence. The phrase raises questions about the assumption of a chronology of time in human experience.
In what way can such an assumption be defended? Another response is to reject the illusion and develop
a-chronological views, or the conventions of traditional history, or even the paradigm codes of literary
criticism.

Ricoeur sees narrativity and temporality as
integrally related. In Wittgenstein's terminology,
they are language game and a form of life. For Ricoeur
they are reciprocal. "I take temporality to be that
structure of existence that reaches language in narrativity and narrativity to be the language structure
that has temporality as its ultimate referent" (Narrative Time," 169). Ricoeur works in the tradition of
the analysis of time developed by philosophers from
Aristotle and Augustine to Heidegger and Gadamer. With
Heidegger, Ricoeur divides time into at least three
levels. Reversing Heidegger's order, he first describes how the "within-time" experience differs from
linear time. Despite the fact that we privately and
publicly date and measure time, we nevertheless experience time from within.

The linear, however, coincides with the
development of a sense of the story, a sense of history. We are involved in the attempts to see the relationships among birth, growth, death, generation. We
recognize a plurality, what we call a past, present,
and future, but we strive to group those into a unity,
a history. Faced with the experience of what Heidegger
calls anxiety, care, concern, as well as our mortality,
we strive to give continuity and meaning.

Ricoeur next asks: what is the role of
narrativity? The function of narrative is to create a
plot which provides an intelligible whole that rules
and relates a group of events put in succession. It is
the plot which relates events as a story. As such, it
is at the crossroads of narrativity and temporality.

Although the sun's rising and setting are
foundational ordinarily to our experiencing of time, we
nevertheless experience the now in the making present
of the moment. We "lose a sense of time," we "waste
time," we "forget the time." In other words, we live
within and vacillate between two references, that of
the now and that of the linear.

Telling a story subverts linear time in that it
sets experiences and actions within a different time
frame. A selection and an interpretation have been
made. We are put into a process which has a beginning,
a middle, and an end. The actors within the story are
caught "in the interplay between being able to act and
being bound to the world order" (177). Every narrative, then, has two aspects: the chronological and the
nonchronological, the first episodic, the second configurational. Narrative itself, then, moves back and
forth between within-time-ness and historicality. The
episodic is addressed by our words: first, then, next,
finally; the configurative is grasped in the theme, the
plot, the myth, or in the forms of parable or maschal,
or in terms such as the Renaissance or the Industrial
Revolution.

Once a story is told, it can then be retold. We
can read the time of a story backwards and forwards.
We can establish action in time, but also in memory.
It is memory which repeats or recollects, that is, it
gathers together.

> Yet the concept of repetition implies
> still more: it means the "retrieval"
> of our most fundamental potentialities,
> as they are inherited from our own
> past, in terms of a personal fate and a
> common destiny (183).

This concept of repetition differs sharply from
the tendency of many other methods, including that of
Propp and of the structuralists, in that it does not
require a loss of time. In other words, repetition
offers an alternative to dechronologization. Whereas
dechronologization abolishes time, repetition makes
possible an "existential deepening" (184).

How does it make this possible? Ricoeur explores
several avenues. In repetition, in this sense, memory
is not just a narrative of external adventures or of
episodes. Rather, memory "is itself the spiral movement that, through anecdotes and episodes, brings us

back to the almost motionless constellation of
potentialities that the narrative retrieves. The end
of the story is what equates the present with the past,
the actual with the potential" (186).

At this point, Ricoeur takes a position different
from that of Heidegger by emphasizing the importance of
narrative. It is narrative which gives more importance
to the communal "destiny" of a people over the destiny
of an individual's "fate." Narrative belongs to public
time, to the time of interaction. It is a time of
being-with-others. This thesis departs from
Heidegger's stress on Dasein's being-toward-death.
Ricoeur's emphasis on narrative shifts the horizon from
the individual and death to the challenge of communication between those living in the present, but also
between "contemporaries, predecessors, and successors"
(188). It is a community which takes up the telling of
its narrative, and in telling of its origins, it creates a new founding act, it makes history, and makes
possible the writing of history. Nevertheless,

> Some consideration of death is inherent
> in any meditation on the constitution
> of history. Must not something or some-
> one die if we are to have a memory of
> it or him or her? Is not the otherness
> of the past fundamentally to be seen in
> death? And is not repetition itself a
> kind of resurrection of the dead . . . ?
> (190).

As part of the study of the theme of a Philosophy
of History and Action, Ricoeur was one of the scholars
invited to the First Jerusalem Philosophical Encounter
in December, 1974. In his paper "History and
Hermeneutics," he addressed a dialectic between the
arguments of philosophical hermeneutics and the method
of historical inquiry. In his hermeneutical reflection, Ricoeur outlines similarities and differences
between natural science and social science. Although
the sciences initiated by the explorations of Galileo
and Newton separated definitively the physical object
and the field of perception, there nevertheless remains
a "belonging-to" in any human knowledge or meaning.
Absolutely primordial is the recognition of being affected, that I think on the basis of what I receive.
This belonging-to is even more important to an understanding of the work of an historian. By using the
transcendental principle of analogy, the human being
can "ascribe to himself his own experience like others"
("History and Hermeneutics," 9).

In contrast, the transcendental principle of
communication is set in tension within the desire for
the meaning which unifies human experience. This makes
possible the paradox that "a consciousness open to
history is at once the consciousness of being affected,
the project of allowing oneself to be affected, and the
competence to remain affected" (11).

Just as the natural sciences require a
methodological distanciation, so does historical objectification, in spite of its "belonging-to," require a
recognition of its temporal difference as well as its
methodological distancing. Within its tradition, it
reads the signs, the marks, the traces, strives to
incorporate its skeptical doubt within its methodological doubt, and in its anguish, seeks objective answers
to the questions raised. History will make use of the
data and even the methodology of the critical sciences,
but will also recognize its own task of dealing with
the motive, evaluation, and the intention of those
acting in history.

In 1977 Ricoeur directed a seminar on Narrativity,
the papers of which were published under that title in
1980 by the National Center for Scientific Research in
its series Phenomenology and Hermeneutics. Previously
published were La sémantique de l'action and Fiction et
référence. Ricoeur provided the first three chapters
and the conclusion.[2] The topics are: History as Narrative, The Narrative of Fiction, The Narrative Function,
and Fictional Narrative--Historical Narrative.

In dialogue with the works of Hempel, Danto, and
Gallie, among others, Ricoeur draws on the concept of
the "narrative phrase" and the phenomenology of the act
of following a history, but adds his own critique in
the concept of event or happening and a concept of
history as narrative. The making of history is also an
event. Representation and sequence are incorporated in
a configurational act.

In the second essay on The Narrative of Fiction,
Ricoeur critiques works of structuralists such as
Propp, Lévi-Strauss, Barthes, and Greimas in order to
formulate his own position. The narrative of history
is presumed to be related to facts, experience, or the
truth. What about the narrative of fiction? Ricoeur's
inquiry is to find out whether, in spite of their differences, the narrative of history and the narrative of
fiction nevertheless share a common structure and a
unique mode of discourse.

Narrative embraces a wide variety of expressions:
stories, writings, tales, myths, fables, tragedies,
films. What is the underlying structure which we denote when we call these expressions narratives? Propp
developed a morphology of story or tale in which he
classified basic functions or actions of the characters
defined from the point of view of the character's relationship to the plot. Such functions are limited in
number in spite of the amazing variety of their actualizations.

Following Propp and utilizing aspects of French
structuralism, Greimas developed a syntax of actantial
models. The theory posits three relationships: desire, communication, and action, each based on a binary
operation: subject-object; sender-receiver; helper-
opponent. Greimas then develops the a-chronical or
non-temporal character of these functions. Ricoeur
shows, however, that the temporality of narrative is
irreducible. Temporality belongs to the narrativity
itself. It presumes the basic questions, "And then
. . . ?" "What happened next?" Whether it is conjunction or disjunction, joining or separating, in a narrative it is not a logic which is operating, but a
transformation, which is what story, history, or narrative is about. "The deployment of action implies
alternatives . . . , contingent connections, which
create the feeling of surprise, essential to keep the
interest of the hearer or the reader of the narrative"
(41). The quest is what makes the plot possible.

For Ricoeur, then, there is a universal quality of
all narrative, whether it is fiction or not, which
joins two dimensions, that of sequence and that of
configuration. Such narrative is basic to the structure of action.

Time and Narrative I

Early in his study of metaphor, Ricoeur recognized
that he also needed to address what he had soon perceived to be the related problem of narrative. His
various lectures described above culminated in his
three volume book on Time and Narrative (Temps et
récit, I, II, III. Paris: Editions du Seuil. 1983,
1984, 1986.) In the introduction, he acknowledges the
nuclear studies prepared for the Brick Lectures given
in 1978 at the University of Missouri-Columbia and the
continuing seminars in Paris, Toronto, and Chicago, as
well as the Zaharoff Lectures given at Oxford. The

book, however, is not just a collection of those
materials. Although ideas have been incorporated, they
have been reworked and developed.

On the first page of the Foreword, Ricoeur points
out that the book on Metaphor and the book on Narrative
have been conceived together, the one addressing the
theory of tropes, the other the theory of genres, both
related to the same phenomenon of semantic innovation.
In metaphor, the innovation is in the creation of a new
semantic impertinence by way of an impertinent attribution; in narrative, on the other hand, the semantic
innovation is in the creation of a plot which assembles
actions, sufferings, goals, causes, and coincidences
under a temporal unity of a complete action. Both are
related to the productive imagination. The knowledge
comes from its schematization. Explication is linked
to comprehension. Through the suspension of a direct
referential function, a new reference is created which
makes it possible to redescribe a reality inaccessible
to direct description. Whereas metaphor creates in the
field of sensory and aesthetic values, narrative creates in the field of action and of its temporal values.
This is the focus of the book Time and Narrative I.

The first half addresses the problem of "The
Circle between Narrative and Temporality." This is
divided into three parts: 1) "Difficulties of the
experience of time in the context of Book XI of Augustine's Confessions"; 2) "The Creation of plot--a reading of the Poetics of Aristotle"; and 3) "Time and
Narrative: the triple mimesis."

The dialectic with Augustine considers the
difficulties of the being and non-being of time, the
measure of time, intention and distention, and the
contrast of eternity. Ricoeur underlines the temporal
character of human experience. It is his presupposition that "time becomes human time in the measure in
which it is articulated in a narrative manner" (TN, I,
3. My translation: TR, I, 17).[3] From different
points of view, the analyses of Augustine on the one
hand and of Aristotle on the other, raise the same
question .of the dominance of discordance or concordance
in the configuration of a plot. What is "the power of
the poet and the poem to make order triumph over disorder?" (TN, I, 4).

In his study of Augustine's analysis of time,
Ricoeur considers first the contrast between being and
non-being. The problem is: What is time? For

Augustine the question rises out of the statement in
the Book of Genesis: In the beginning God created.
. . .   What does it mean to say "In the beginning"?

From ancient times the question had been placed in
the context of being and non-being, but the skeptics
pointed out the contradiction that while time exists,
nevertheless time does not have being. Augustine
reaches what Ricoeur calls an elegant solution: the
idea of the present of the past, the present of the
present, the present of the future.

But the elegant solution has a difficulty: how
then can one account for either the anticipating or the
vestigial images? And has one perhaps merely changed
the metaphor from a linear one to a spatial one? At
any rate, the remaining problem is that of the idea of
the "distention of the soul." Such distention implies
the necessity of the narrative of human actions,
whether of an individual or of a group or of a nation.

The second study is a reading of the Poetics of
Aristotle, which Ricoeur titles: "The Making of a
Plot." Whereas for Augustine the problem of the distention of the soul dominated, and therefore also the
problem of discordance, for Aristotle, on the other
hand, the emphasis is apparently the opposite. The
narrative, that is, the making of a plot, a myth, is
not concerned with time. It is a model of concordance
which encloses the discordance. Poetics is the art of
composing a plot.

The pair of words mimesis and myth are crucial
here. Just as myth refers to the art of composing a
plot, so mimesis refers to "the active process of imi-
tating or representing something" (33). Equally
mimesis should be taken in its dynamic sense of putting
into representation.

Although for Aristotle, all the parts of a tragedy
should cohere, nevertheless, "it is the plot which is
the representation of the action" (34, 59. Ricoeur is
here quoting Aristotle). The discordance makes possible different actions, so that the telling of the story
orders the possibilities and thereby provides the concordance. The time is not the time of the world of
events, but the time of the work itself. "To think a
line of sequence or of causality between singular
events is already to universalize" (41, 69).

Catharsis itself is a result of the working out of
the plot. The pathos makes possible the emotions

associated with the perceived discordances, but which
are then woven into the process, the creation of the
network which makes up the plot and therefore creates a
representation of concordance. Catharsis then is the
"integrating part of the process of metaphorization
which joins cognition, imagination, and feeling" (50,
83).

In his new study of Aristotle's concept of
mimesis, Ricoeur develops a theory of a triple mimesis,
the object of his next essay. The first mimesis--
mimesis I[4]--is a reference to the source of the poetic
composition. The second mimesis--mimesis II--is the
creation itself, the representation of the actions
which compose the myth. The third mimesis--mimesis
III--is the dynamic activity of the spectator or reader
whose mimetic activity matches that of the created
plot.

A transposition takes place which moves from an
"ethics" to a "poetics," from mimesis I to mimesis II.
Moreover, in the Poetics, Aristotle speaks of a struc-
turation, that is, an activity to be achieved in the
spector. In other words, there is an implied spectator, in a way similar to the implied reader concept
developed by Wolfgang Iser in his theory of reading.

Ricoeur then places his study of the three aspects
of mimesis under the topic of time and narrative. In
this way he links the insights of his previous essays
and seeks to measure the soundness of his basic hypothesis that the correlation between the activity of re-
counting a history and the temporal character of human
experience "presents a form of transcultural necessity" (52, 85). As Chomsky posits a basic structure of
generative grammar integral to the human, so Ricoeur
posits a basic structure of the narrative.

> Time becomes human time in the measure
> in which it is articulated in a narra-
> tive mode, and . . . narrative attains
> its full signification when it becomes
> a condition of temporal existence (52,
> 85).

Ricoeur's third study in the book is a more
elaborated treatment of the theory of the triple
mimesis. First we have the field of our temporal
experience which we employ in a pre-comprehension of
the world of action. We operate not from deduction but
through description. We recognize structural

characteristics and thereby we are enabled to identify
a series of actions. The structural characteristics
which we can recognize are the symbolic mediations of
the action, in the sense of the word symbolic as used
by Cassirer as well as by many cultural anthropolo-
gists. These symbolic actions are precisely temporal:
they call for the telling of the story. It is the
symbolism, whether implicit or explicit, whether privately interpreted or public, which gives to action a
readability. Such actions can be judged: they have
values. They are placed in the context of rule-
governed behavior.

     Ricoeur finds that his dialectical reading of
Augustine and Heidegger on time enables him to develop
a creative critique. Augustine focused on time as
contrasted with eternity partly through the concept of
the distention of the soul. On the other hand,
Heidegger discusses the withinness of Dasein and the
being-toward-death, a displacement from the future
emphasis of Augustine to an emphasis on history, on
repetition, with a concomitant emphasis on making present, on the now.

     Mimesis II is in the realm of the as if, the realm
of fiction in the classic sense of creating, not in the
narrower sense of the distinction between history and
fiction, the first presumably about that which is true,
the second about that which lacks a reference to reality. For Ricoeur this latter is a false distinction
which he critiques at a later point. Mimesis II as a
function of mediation provides the dynamic character of
configuration. It mediates between the pre-comprehension of mimesis I and the post-comprehension of mimesis III. To the episodic events of experience mimesis II supplies a synthetic dimension. It links them
one to another, making a selection, and providing empha-
ses and relationships. To understand a history is to
understand how the various episodes relate one to another. Their order of time is irreversible, and in
this part of the argument we can understand better the
context of Ricoeur's thrust in the relationship of time
and narrative. It is the productive imagination which
creates the synthesis, a schematization, and a tradition. From innovations and sedimentations are built
the paradigms, the forms, the genres.

     This process leads then to mimesis III, the
appropriation, or what Gadamer refers to as the application. Aristotle referred to this process as mimesis
praxeos, the praxis of mimesis, the way in which the

hearer or the reader follows through in the mimesis.
"Mimesis III marks the intersection of the world of the
text and the world of the hearer or the reader" (71,
109). This concept of intersection is similar to what
Gadamer calls the fusion of horizons. Language is not
constituted as a world unto itself. Nor is it the
whole of the world. The ability to communicate and the
capacity for reference go hand in hand. All reference
is co-reference and dialogic. Here Ricoeur argues
strongly against those critics who posit the idea of
the referential illusion. On the contrary, for him
"the world is the ensemble of the references opened by
all the sorts of texts descriptive or poetic which I
have read, interpreted, and loved" (80, 121). It is
thus that Ricoeur is led from his reading and juxtaposition of Augustine and Heidegger to ask within his
reflective philosophy on narrative the questions about
eternity and death.

History and Narrative

        In the second part of his work on narrative
Ricoeur focuses on history. He addresses the problem
in three parts: the eclipse of narrative as illustrated in the development of French historiography and
in analytic philosophy; renewed arguments for narrative
from a critique of a nomological model and of new
studies of narrative; and the intentionality of doing
history.

        At Oxford in The Zaharoff Lectures Ricoeur had
reviewed some of the developments of French historiography. Here he expands his critique and draws implications in regard to narrative. Narrative is eclipsed
primarily because the object of history is displaced:
the individual is no longer acting, but the total society is studied. The event, the happening itself is
lost sight of. In place of the event is the total
social achievement, including among others economic,
political, and cultural aspects. Important as these
studies may be, the individual event, story, history,
narrative is overlooked. At the same time, the mediation of the witness and the interpretation, the configuration and the refiguration, is forfeited.

        In contrast, Ricoeur poses several assertions. In
the first place, events whether physical or historical
were effectively produced in the past, Secondly, among
those events which happened in the past, some were the
work of agents like ourselves. But, thirdly, those

agents were other in such an absolute sense that our
ability for communication is severely affected.

To these three ontological premises correspond
three epistemological presuppositions. The event
whether physical or human is singular and therefore not
repeatable. On the other hand, because it is, it is
then possible to make "another," and thereby, by extension, to sketch a model.

Whereas it is impossible to reactualize the past,
nevertheless, history rests on the witness of the
"other," and therefore, history requires a double
truth, the truth of faith in the witness of the past
event and the truth of the witness of the historian.

As French historiography provides an example of
the eclipse of the event, and therefore of the eclipse
of narrative in the sense in which Ricoeur is using it,
so analytic philosophy provides an example of a nomological model which, in effect, according to Ricoeur,
so atomizes description that it eclipses comprehension
or the larger view. By extension, then, narrative is
also eclipsed.

Drawing on the work of Carl G. Hempel, Ricoeur
then reaffirms the singularity of the event, whether
physical or human, but also the possibility of the
perception of general laws not only in the physical
sciences, but also in the study of history. This makes
possible the recovery of the concepts of law, of cause,
and of explication, certainly not outside the continuing necessity of critique and of new models, but in the
on-going interpretation of human experience. What is
surprising is that, in spite of the difficulties of
verifying what happened in the past, scientists and
historians each in their own fields continue the attempts to sketch out details, to construct certain
generalizations, to explain and to interpret. In spite
of the inadequacies, the sketch of patterns often rings
true.

Arguments for Narrative

Ricoeur next pursues a critique of two different
writers and finds therein arguments for a recognition
of narrative. The first is the work of William Dray,
Laws and Explanation in History. [5] In the distinctions
which Dray makes between explication and law, in his
extensive critique of the use of the word "cause," and

in his recognition of the polysemic qualities of the
word which therefore call for an analysis of the
context, Ricoeur finds an implicit if not explicit
critique of the nomological model which then calls for
the necessity of a model of narrative not unlike his
own.

In a similar way, Ricoeur analyzes Georg Henrik
von Wright's Explanation and Understanding as well as
earlier works Norm and Action and An Essay in Deontic
Logic and the General Theory of Action. He finds there
a recognition of the two traditions of the formation of
theories in the human and social disciplines, the one
causal and mechanistic, the other teleological. "The
first needs the unity of scientific method, the second
defends a methodological pluralism" (TN, I, 132.   TR,
I, 187).

Von Wright posits conditional relationships
between anterior and ulterior states which are independent, but which, when taken in ensemble, constitute a
possible world.   Such states therefore may be called
"ontological building bricks" (133, 189).   Ricoeur is
quoting from von Wright's Explanation and Understanding, 44. After a detailed analysis of von Wright's
arguments, Ricoeur asks if there is not lacking the
thread which precisely is comprehension, that is, what
Ricoeur calls plot, a synthesis of heterogeneity, a
comprehensive narrative.

Besides the explosion of the nomological model,
Ricoeur finds another argument for narrative in what he
calls "narrativist" arguments (143, 203).   These include the following: the narrative phrase according to
Arthur Danto; what it means to follow a history; the
configuring act; explication by putting into plot; and
how one writes history.

Previously for those who followed a nomological
model, narrative was at best an elementary and poor
mode for explanation.   The break down of the model
raises again the questions of narrative.   One of the
persons pursuing this question is Arthur C. Danto,
especially in his work Analytical Philosophy of History. Ricoeur finds Danto's analysis helpful in its
recognition of the narrative phrase as one of the possible descriptions of human action (144, 205).   According to Danto, such phrases refer to at least two events
separated in time, in which the first event is described in terms of the second. What Ricoeur finds
lacking is the recognition of a third event, that of

the narrator, and it is this third event which both points out the weakness of Danto's argument, and at the same time calls for a theory of comprehensive narrative such as Ricoeur is formulating.

In each of the remaining "narrativist" arguments, Ricoeur renews and focuses a dialectic he had previously pursued. He finds W. B. Gallie's Philosophy and the Historical Understanding interesting especially for the concept of "following a history," which he finds harmonious with his own understanding of narrative. The "configuring act" language of Louis O. Mink adds a dimension of reflective judgement on the total context.

Writers in a number of disciplines are called on under the heading "Explication by putting into plot." Principal among them is Hayden White in Metahistory: The Historical Imagination in Nineteenth-Century Europe. Ricoeur makes special note that White titles his introduction "The Poetics of History." White places plot between story and argument. Story is taken in the limited sense of "telling stories," limited more to a sequential account. Argument refers to what it's all about, the point of it all. The historical narrative is the emplotment, involving the selection and the relationships, with all that implies of judgement. He acknowledges the insight of Stephen Pepper in World Hypotheses in distinguishing four great paradigms: the formal, organic, mechanistic, and contextual, as well as the contribution of Karl Mannheim in Ideology and Utopia in listing four basic ideologies: anarchism, conservatism, radicalism, and liberalism. Putting into plot is thus explication, recognizing or furnishing a genre, composing a narrative.

In the last analysis of an argument for narrative, Ricoeur engages in dialogue with Paul Veyne through his book Comment on écrit l'histoire. History is a truthful narrative. According to Veyne, history has a critique and a direction, but not a method. Not a method? asks Ricoeur (171, 242). Aristotle himself talks about the logic of the probable in the putting into plot. To explain for the historian is to make the flow of events comprehensible. Ricoeur shows that Paul Veyne's book leads to a critical point the idea that history is only construction and comprehension of plots (174, 246).

Ricoeur's last essay on the relationship of history and narrative is on the intentionality of history. He discusses first the imputation of a singular cause, then first order entities of historiography, and lastly the time of history and the destiny of the event.

For the historian to impute a singular cause
between events is at least to ignore the difference in
levels between the narrative level and the level of
epistemology, and to ignore as well the interplay of
continuity and discontinuity. Nevertheless, Ricoeur
thinks it appropriate to speak analogically of a singular cause, and by extension then, to speak of historical explication as a quasi-plot.

What about the entities of the first order of
historiography? That depends on the presuppositions
and the questions which the historian asks. If the
entities are personages such as kings, or quasi-
personages such as nations, you have one kind of intentionality. If you attempt to place these within a
global context, you add certain dimensions. If, on the
other hand, you write a special history of a particular
nation, or a particular society, the characteristics of
the entities are modified. If you take the perspective
of certain aspects of culture, then you may have a
history called economic or political. Indeed, some of
the so-called new history is without personages. Without personages, there is not a narrative (177, 249).
The entities of the first order of the historian are
already the entities of mimesis I, which Ricoeur described earlier.

What is the relationship of the time of history
and the destiny of the event or the quasi-event?
Ricoeur returns at the end of this part of his study of
the epistemology of historiography to the question of
historic time. What is the relationship of historic
time to the time of the narrative? Existence continues. There is temporal continuity. But historians
speak of the short time of the event, the half-long
time of the conjuncture, the long duration of civilizations, the very long durations of the symbolic foundations of social structures. But such statements raise
the questions again of the relationships between the
past, the present, and the future, in fact, between
life and death, beginning and end. Historic intentionality cannot ignore these questions.

Fiction and Narrative

There is a fundamental parting of the ways between
historical narrative and the narrative of fiction. (TN,
I, 52. TR, I, 85); nevertheless, they have much in
common. Ricoeur quotes Hayden White: "History is no
less a form of fiction than the novel is a form of

historical representation" (Tropics of Discourse, 122).
Both participate in the kinds of mimesis which Ricoeur
analyzed earlier. The effort of the historian is to
create a reconstruction of the past. She or he owes a
debt to those who have gone before, whatever the perspective the particular historian is taking. Whatever
the historical reconstruction, the work still belongs
to the great class of the Analogue. It is not the
Same; neither is it the Other. It is in the realm of
the such as or the such as it was (The Reality of the
Historical Past, 25). The historian strives to ascertain the facts such as they really occurred (35).

> Recourse to analogy acquires its full
> sense only against the backdrop of the
> dialectic of Same and Other: the past
> is indeed what is to be re-enacted in
> the mode of the identical. But it is
> so only to the extent that it is also
> what is absent from all of our con-
> structions. The analogue, precisely,
> holds within it the force of re-enact-
> ment and of distancing, to the extent
> that being as is both being and not
> being (35-36).

In a similar way, Ricoeur asks: What is the
function of fiction in shaping reality? ("The Function
of Fiction in Shaping Reality," 123ff). Fiction belongs to a general theory of imagination. In fact, it
is the work of the productive imagination. New meanings emerge in language and these new meanings generate
new images. In one way in fiction, there is a reference to nothingness, but, on the other hand, that is
only to free the narrative to the possibility of a
productive reference. Whether it be "writing a poem,
telling a story, construing an hypothesis, a plan, or a
strategy . . . imagination is 'productive' not only of
unreal objects, but also of an expanded vision of reality. Imagination at work--in a work--produces itself
as a world" (128). There is no dichotomy between
poetic imagination and epistemologic imagination (140).

Time and Narrative II

The first published volume of Ricoeur's study of
Time and Narrative included two parts: I. The Circle
of Narrative and Temporality and II. History and Narrative. So the second published volume, Time and Narrative II includes the third part of the study: III.
The Configuration of Time in Fictional Narrative.

Besides a Foreword and a Conclusion, the study is
in four parts: 1. The Metamorphosis of Plot; 2. The
Semiotic Constraints of Narrativity; 3. Games with
Time; and 4. Fictional Temporal Experience.

In the Foreword, Ricoeur links the study with the
preceding ones by indicating that he is still working
in the area of mimesis II, but now will be dealing, not
with historical narrative, but with fictional narrative. By fictional narrative he means that genre
generally recognized as including the epic, tragedy and
comedy, and the novel. He understands the difficulties
of categorization and will include some references and
discussion as the study unfolds. His interest primarily is the temporal structure involved in the narrative configuration. He hopes to enlarge, deepen, and
enrich the idea of plot as developed in the Aristotelian tradition, and to diversify the concept of
time received from the Augustinian tradition.

The Metamorphosis of Plot

Particularly in this century new fiction has made
clear the inadequacies of the traditional view of plot.
Ricoeur reviews some of the stages in this development.
He is impressed by the extraordinary creativity of
modern novelists, especially in their experimentation
in and expression of time. The traditional view of the
integrity of plot, as described by Aristotle in his
study of the tragic myth, no longer holds as appropriate for novels such as those by Virginia Woolf. The
unity of time found by Aristotle in Homer's Odyssey is
broken in the stream of consciousness techniques of the
modern writer. The traditional development of character is similarly affected. From the medieval romance,
through the development of the picaresque novel with
its emphasis on the social context of its characters,
through adventure novels such as those of Robinson
Crusoe or Don Juan, the narrative form continued to
develop. But the stream of consciousness technique
opened up a complexity on the levels of consciousness,
the subconscious, and the unconscious which was previously unknown.

Aristotle had defined myth as the "imitation of
action." Novels of action, character, or thought,
while often demonstrating an awareness of the contrast
between illusion and reality, nevertheless seemed to
presume an acknowledgement of an accepted reality of
action, character, or thought development. In

contrast, there is presumed today an incoherence of
reality which shatters previous paradigms.

Is there an order of paradigms? Ricoeur enters
into a dialectic with important works of literary
criticism which in the last several decades have addressed related questions. He acknowledges the traditional contributions of critics and philosophers, including phenomenologists, who raise questions regarding
the acceptance of genre, type, or work as appropriate
categories, but he gives particular attention to the
work of critics such as Northrup Frye and Frank
Kermode.

Frye develops extensively his theory of modes
through which he emphasizes the importance of the productive imagination, but nevertheless hypothesizes the
presumption of an order of words, a correlate of a
narrative intelligence which precedes.

Ricoeur asks, on the contrary, in the light of
modern fiction, have we come to the end of the art of
story-telling? The difficulties posed in the question
are challenging. One area of criticism in which the
questions are addressed is in the problem of an ending
or the lack of an ending, the problem of closure or a
lack of closure. Although a number of critics have
explored the difficulties involved, Ricoeur is especially impressed by the work of Frank Kermode in his
work The Sense of an Ending. Kermode addresses the
myth of apocalypse which breaks a number of categories.
Theologically it transcends Jewish-Christian eschatology. In terms of political history, it transcends
the ideology of empire. Epistemologically it extends
outside the theory of models. In the history of literature, it escapes the theory of plot (TR, II, 39).

Following Kermode, Ricoeur recognizes the importance in apocalypse of crisis, and the relationship of
crisis to the reader or the audience. The presumption
of paradigm no longer holds. Particularly important is
the treatment of time. Chronology is rejected, but
more important, even the configuration of a presumed
time is inadequate. Apocalypse wrestles with the need
to bring order from chaos, sense from non-sense, and
concordance from discordance (45).

Ricoeur concludes that, in spite of the challenges
and the amazing varieties of new forms or anti-forms,
the art of narrative has not died. He prefers to think
of the metaphorphosis of narrative. What we describe

as the telling of a story perdures, even though the
forms may change.

The Semiotic Constraints of Narrativity

In this section Ricoeur engages once again in the
dialogue with structuralism. He recognizes the revolutionary insights of someone such as Roland Barthes in
his study of the structural analysis of narratives.
Out of his tradition Barthes aims at a dechronoliza-
tion, and then at a reconstruction of the sense. While
acknowledging the insights from this approach, Ricoeur
nevertheless points out the shortcomings of a closed
system of language.

In greater detail than previously, and with the
particular focus of narrative and time, Ricoeur then
reviews the contributions of Propp in his morphology of
story-telling, of Bremond in his logic of narrative, of
Todorov in his grammar of narrative, and of Greimas in
his theory of semiotic narrative. In typical fashion,
he welcomes the contributions, but also points out the
areas where he feels he can make a contribution.

The terminology of language games has penetrated
not only the discussion of language at the university
level during this century, but within the last several
decades, has also entered into the level of popular
discussion. The use of language to express aspects of
the experience of time is an important topic which
Ricoeur considers next in his study of "Playing with
Time." Again, he enters into the dialectic with those
whose work makes a contribution to exploring the topic.
These include writers such as Émile Benveniste, Käte
Hamburger, and Harald Weinrich.

Benveniste raises the questions of real time and
quasi-time in the context of history and fiction.
Hamburger gives an importance to the grammatical form
of the time of the verb in such genre as epic, drama,
and lyric. In his study of opening and closure in
communication, Weinrich points out three axes of communication (101): the situation of locution, the perspective of locution, and the putting in relief. What
correspondences do these concepts have for Ricoeur in
his theory of mimesis II? Ricoeur points out their
importance, and concludes to a reaffirmation of the
foundational understanding of fiction as in the "as if"
mode, for which verbal time is at the service of the
production of meaning (113).

What is the distinction between the time of the
telling and the time of what is told? Günther Müller
and Gérard Genette are two who have examined some of
the relationships. A working through leads Ricoeur to
a consideration of three times: the time of the act of
the story-teller, the time of that which is told, and
"the time of life" (120). In spite of the complexities
of the questions and the development of ideas related
to this "discourse of narrative," Ricoeur wishes to
push farther in his own analysis.

The last aspect of "playing with time" which
Ricoeur considers is that of point of view and narrative voice. The literature here is extensive. Ricoeur
enters into dialogue not only with Genette, but also
with Wayne Booth, Dorrit Cohn, Jean Pouillon, and
others. What are the relationships of author, narrator, and the narrating personages? What is the relationship of a mimesis of action and a mimesis of
configuration? What is the relationship of the discourse of the narrator and the discourse of the
characters? Dorrit Cohn writes about the "interior
transparence" or "transparent minds" (133). Do we have
a "mimesis of consciousness" and a "mimesis of other
minds"? Kafka and Proust have been the pioneers in
experimenting with some of these forms. Other terms
for the phenomenon include "self-narration," "psycho-
narration," "self-quoted monologue," and "quoted monologue." In addition, what is the relation of the
spatial plane with the temporal plane? (141) Ricoeur
concludes that "the notion of point of view marks the
culminating point of a study centered on the connection
between the telling of a story and a story told" (143).
In turn, the voice is related to the prospective
reader. It is a bi-polar relationship.

The fourth section of the book, "Fictional
Temporal Experience," includes an analysis of time in
three books: Virginia Woolf's Mrs. Dalloway, The Magic
Mountain of Thomas Mann, and Marcel Proust's In Search
of Time Lost. Ricoeur considers these "three fables on
time" (152).

In approximately ten to twenty pages for each,
Ricoeur reviews the main thrust of the story in the
context of a study of time and narrative. In the first
study, Mrs. Dalloway, which he places between "mortal
time" and "monumental time" (152), Ricoeur shows the
complexities of point of view, of spatial shifts, and
of symbolic implications both for the characters and
for the societies which they represent.

Ricoeur sees the second book which he analyzes, The Magic Mountain, as, not only a fable of time but a novel of a mortal sickness. How are these two related, and how are they a comment on the destiny of European culture, so that at the same time, it is "a novel of time, a novel of a sickness, and a novel of culture" (173)? "The detemporalization and the corruption become, by the art of the narrative, the indivisible object of the fascination and of the speculation of heroes" (174).

For his study on In Search of Time Lost, Ricoeur adds a sub-title: "Time traversed" (194). What is at stake in the theme of this book is not so much time as truth (195). It is not so much a problem of memory as the challenge of reading the signs: signs of love, sensible signs, signs of art. Truth has an essential connection with time. The reading of signs becomes a hermeneutic key to unlock the whole work including the "final revelation" (196). The struggle is with time lost and time found, "the extra-temporal which transcends," "the vicissitudes of becoming," and "the resurrection in the work of time lost" (215). "Time found . . . is time lost eternalized by the metaphor" (219). "It is a question," according to Proust, "not of technique, but of vision" (219).

In his conclusion, Ricoeur feels that he has sufficiently demonstrated that historiography and critical literature are two parts of a larger narratology, in which historic narrative and fictional narrative should have equal parts (230). They both belong to mimesis II, the area of narrative configuration. It remains for his next book to explore mimesis III, refiguration, and to show the close relationship between configuration and refiguration, and the potential for actualization of the immanent transcendance of the text (233).

Time and Narrative III

With the publication in 1985 of the third volume of Temps et récit Ricoeur concludes not only his study of time and narrative, but also the longer study begun with his essays on metaphor published under the title The Rule of Metaphor. The first volume addresses the circle of narrative and temporality and history and narrative, two parts of the study published in one volume. The second published volume therefore included the third part of the study: on the configuration of

time in fictional narrative. In turn, the third
published volume is the fourth part of the study, that
which examines the refiguration of time. The three
volumes correspond essentially to the triple mimesis
which Ricoeur describes extensively in volume II.

In turn, Ricoeur sees volume III as a complete
explication of his thesis that narrative configuration
is achieved in the refiguration of temporal experience.
This book is in two sections, the first on the aporetics of temporality, the second on the poetics of narrative, including history, fiction, and time.

What does the word aporetics mean? The Greek
denotes being without resources, being at a loss, not
knowing what to do, being in doubt. In his study of
Augustine on time, Ricoeur described this aspect of our
experience, the uncertainty, the perplexity of our
presence in the flow of time.

On this topic Ricoeur provides three studies, the
first on the time of the soul and the time of the
world, in which he reviews and extends the debate between the insights of Augustine and the insights of
Aristotle. In the second, he contrasts the position of
Husserl with that of Kant in a comparison of intuitive
time and invisible time. In the third he studies
Heidegger, centering on topics such as care and temporality, rendering present, and intra-temporality.

As Augustine has emphasized the intention and
distention of the soul in an effort to understand the
experience of time, so Aristotle takes as focus the
cosmological aspect of time which passes and can be
numbered. Time is relative to movement. It is part of
the Physics. Ricoeur sees his poetics of narrative as
a way to join what speculation separates, as a mediation between the "discordant concordance of phenomenological time and the simple succession of physical
time" (TR, III, 36).

The next essay contrasts Husserl's phenomenology
of the consciousness of time with Kant's description of
the invisibility of time. Drawing on a new reading of
Husserl's Lectures, on the phenomenology of the intimate consciousness of time, Ricoeur explores the relationship of immanent time with the repeated expression
of objective time. In ordinary language we find expressions such as "to begin," "to continue," "to
finish," "to endure." Although Husserl did not note
the metaphorical aspect of such phrases as "a point in

time," "holding on to the moment," or "living and
dying" as applied to a present, Ricoeur finds it important to recognize the semantic innovation with which we
learn to appropriate our experience of time. What is
the "now" of our experience? And how is that translated into the narrative expression of our experience?

Ricoeur next looks at Kant's idea of the
invisibility of time, not as a solution, but as a principle for the dialectic. In contrast to what we find
in Husserl, we find in Kant a description of the indirect character of our assertions about time. Time
itself does not appear; it is a characteristic of that
which appears. Thus the polarity of the phenomenology
of Husserl and the critique of Kant makes clear the
polarity also between the subjective and the objective
in time, and eventually the problematic of the being
and the non-being of time. Succession, simultaneity,
and permanence raise questions and conflicts resolved
neither by Husserl nor by Kant.

In the succeeding study, Ricoeur pursues the
dialectic with Heidegger and the "vulgar" or common
concept of time, centering the discussion around the
three concepts of temporality, historicality, and
intra-temporality. After a careful examination of each
of the topics, Ricoeur concludes that a phenomenology
of time has a privileged place in the ongoing conversation because it is able to uncover the problems, the
polarities, and the incongruities. By analyzing the
problems, by pointing out the relationships or contradictions, a phenomenology of time is able to contribute
to a better understanding of the various aspects of the
human experience and understanding. Neither cosmological time nor phenomenological time is to be subsumed
the one under the other. Neither is to be eclipsed.
On the one hand, the cosmological view surpasses the
phenomenological; but on the other, the phenomenological is not sufficiently accounted for within the cosmological. It is a question, then, not just of the
problems of the phenomenology of time, but the problematics of temporality itself.

The second and last section is the poetics of
narrative itself: a consideration of the relationships
among history, fiction, and time, that is, a study of
the strands of historiography, narratology, and phenomenology. This section includes an introduction and
seven chapters followed by a conclusion.

The first poses the paradox of lived time and
universal time, that is, historic time, placed under

the problematic of refiguration as part of the
phenomenology of a poetics of narrative. Ricoeur's
thesis is that the unique manner in which history responds to the problematics of a phenomenology of time
is precisely in the elaboration of a third kind of time
which acts as mediator between lived time and cosmic
time. History thus is written by means of calendars,
the succession of generations one after the other,
archives, documents, traces (147).

Ricoeur then analyzes the imaginative variations
which fiction brings to time. A striking first insight
is the freedom which the author of fiction has in contrast to the obligation of the historian in regard to
the relationships between lived time and cosmic time.
The author of fiction can provide a wide number of
variations such as those examined by Ricoeur in his
previous volume.

In parallel ways there are a number of variations
of the problems of time as analyzed within phenomenology. Ricoeur discusses such topics as eternity, the
intimate consciousness of time, the key place of mortality as a universal trait of the human condition,
remembrance, and the remythisation of time.

Such discussion raises once again the problem of
the reality of the historic past. Ricoeur organizes
his reflections here under the sign of the Same, the
Other, and the Analogue. In dialogue with Collingwood
among others he pursues the concepts of distanciation
and identification, the relationship of evidence and
thought, reenactment and imagination. In other words,
what takes place in the reeffectuation of the past in
the present?

In the fourth essay Ricoeur examines the world of
the text and the world of the reader and lays out the
essentials of his theory of reading under three headings: from the poetic to the rhetoric, the rhetoric
between the text and its reader, and phenomenology and
the esthetics of reading.

For the dialectic Ricoeur draws on the writings of
Gadamer, Booth, Michel Charles, Wolfgang Iser, and
Roman Ingarden among others. Three moments are important: the direction the author makes toward the
reader, the writing of this direction in the literary
configuration, and the response of the reader as a
public receiver. Among the many important insights are
ideas of the necessity of the reader to complete the

text, of the inscription including a reading within the text, but also anticipating readings to come (TR III, 242). The text as a work comes from the interaction between the text and the reader (245). Reading then becomes a lived experience, a transforming experience. Ricoeur is thus led to posit the concept of a literary hermeneutics.

In the next study Ricoeur returns to the subject of the intersection of history and fiction and examines further and more precisely the fictionalization of history and the historicization of fiction. What is the effective refiguration of time become human time by the intersection of these two concepts? It is in his enlarged theory of reading that Ricoeur finds a movement from divergence to convergence between historic narrative and the narrative of fiction. Ricoeur recognizes how one tradition of language overlaps and transforms another, at the same time laying one theory of knowledge on another by reason of the world views involved. To read the implied theory of knowledge is to read the signs.

We read the signs of geology, biology, or the succession of the generations. Through the intermediary of our imagination, we impose a calendar, a clock, or a history as a way to figure or refigure the experience, as a way of reading the signs. We have the illusion of presence, but the illusion is controlled by our critical distance (274). Ricoeur cites the literature of the holocaust as an example of this double effect of presence and distance. Fiction is thus put at the service of memory: Never again!

In his comments on the historization of fiction, Ricoeur notes how in a certain way fiction imitates the historic narrative. The story predicates an as-if of the past, whatever the complexity of the time relationships within the narration. The predication nevertheless is free from the constraints of history.

In the sixth study Ricoeur returns to the problem of the Hegelian temptation, a view of the totality of the unfolding of history, the positing of a singular collective in the unfolding of history. This is phrased in the concept of the history of the world or the concept of a universal history. If one posits a singular Spirit in the world, and then equates this Spirit with the spirit of a people, one has determined a certain attitude toward history. Ricoeur recognizes that indeed this concept is a result of the artifice of

reason. The same applies to the concept of the stages
of development which is assumed in many views of the
history of a people. The configurations become perennial and assume a quality of permanence. The concept of
representation no longer prevails.

Ricoeur then demonstrates the impossibility of a
total mediation. To renounce the Hegelian position of
a unity in history is to acknowledge the wounded nature
of our perspectives and world views.

Chapter seven works toward a hermeneutic of
historic consciousness. Having moved away from a concept of total mediation, one is left with an imperfect
or hidden mediation, a network of intersecting perspectives. But what are the pieces of these perspectives?
Ricoeur analyzes the concept of time as new, the concept of the acceleration of history, and the concept of
the mastery of history. But one of the first problems
is the illusion of the origin, the beginning (307).
Perhaps even more of a problem is the illusion of the
mastery of history, and the effect such a view has on
our ethical and political orientations. We find ourselves attributing the aspect of truth to our traditions and tradition. Our perspectives assume an
epistemology and an ontology and are thereby legiti-
mized. We are ignorant of the limitations posed by the
distancing.

What then shall be said of the historic present?
Ricoeur gathers his thoughts around some of the topics
he has addressed in other places: the event of
rendering-present, the "body proper" as mediator between lived time and the time of the world, the field
of a theory of action, as well as a theory of systems
(334). Certain views of history then are broken in
order to make possible traditions which are truly
living.

In his conclusion Ricoeur reflects on his entire
enterprise of Time and Narrative. He asked the question whether temporality can be addressed immediately
by a phenomenology of time. He was led to the concomitant question of whether temporality requires the
mediation of the indirect discourse of narrative (349).
The question moved from the epistemological plane of
the configuration of time by narrative, first in the
category of historiography and then in the category of
fiction. Ricoeur determines that the two categories
are integrally related.

The related question is then addressed of the
ontic quality of the refiguration of time by narrative.
Three problematics remain: 1) the dominant problem of
the opaqueness which the phenomenological and the cosmological perspectives bring to each other; 2) what
meaning can be given to the process of the totalization
of the projections of time; and 3) the ultimate impossibility to represent time.

The first problematic is addressed under the
phenomenon of the identity of narrative. Here Ricoeur
summarizes the insights of his study of Augustine,
Aristotle, Husserl, and Heidegger. It is the concept
of the "third time" which makes possible the mimetic
activity of the narrative (354).

For his summary of the second problematic, Ricoeur
polarizes the concepts of totality and totalization.
The complexity of systems requires the constant reading
and re-reading of signs and symbols, and the fusions
and repositionings of horizons.

The last problematic of the inscrutability of time
points out the limits of narrative itself. To think
time is an ongoing human activity. The philosopher is
confronted with the challenge of trying to understand
both the limits and the potentialities of narrative
activity.

Finally, to acknowledge the limits of narrative is
to recognize the challenge for a phenomenology of language. The problems of time call for a poetics of
narrative.

CHAPTER FOUR

Possibilities for a Critique

To critique is to analyze and evaluate. The
extent of Paul Ricoeur's work, even as outlined here,
makes it clear that a critique would be a difficult
task. The intent here is merely to suggest directions
for or elements of a critique. The survey will include
a description of the context, examples of critiques
presently available, Ricoeur's own on-going critique,
the possibilities of a critique from within using the
focus of symbol, and a suggestion of some of the possibilities of critique within the Poetics.

A principal challenge in responding to Ricoeur is
the complexity and interdisciplinary quality of both
content and the concomitant methodology of the material
he is working with. Because Ricoeur incorporates insights from so many thinkers in diverse fields, his
writings have been labeled eclectic, both in the positive and in the negative connotations of that word.
The problem is one that Ricoeur has "consistently tried
to eradicate" (FP, 529). He feels he has taken great
pains to elaborate the dialectic, for example, in distinguishing areas of agreement or disagreement with
Kant, or Freud, or whoever may be involved in the
dialectic of the moment. Perhaps it may be true to say
that Ricoeur is too careful in giving credit by name,
or at least more careful than many writers seem to be.

The tradition of one philosopher or theologian
building on the work of his predecessors has its roots
in Plato and Aristotle, and has been a recognized part
of western thought. But, although it makes progress
possible, it is also accompanied by the hazards of
interpretation. A critique of Ricoeur comprehensively
pursued would also require an implicit critique of
Kant, Hegel, and Spinoza, as well as, perhaps, Luther

and Moltmann. The needs and the possibilities will be
elaborated later in this chapter. The problem looms
large in Freud and Philosophy where the works of Freud
are so basic a part of the text. Although in that work
especially, Ricoeur carefully footnotes the critics,
such a study crosses traditional boundaries and thereby
invites criticism--as well as new, creative, interdisciplinary insights. Perhaps it is Ricoeur's breadth
of vision and creativity which enable him to link concepts others find dissimilar; for example:

> But he [Freud] never suspected that
> this mythology of Eros might concern an
> epigenesis of religious feeling, nor
> that Eros might be another name for the
> Johannine God, and further back, for
> the Deuteronomic God, and further
> still, for the God of Osee (536).

This interdisciplinary characteristic of Ricoeur's work
poses problems even for one sympathetic to, and indeed
appreciative of, his efforts. A colleague philosopher
can admit his incompetency "in regard to the immense
theological material, exegetical or relative to the
history of myths and of religion.[1] So is the theologian likely to be overwhelmed, if not by the philosophic underpinnings, then by the psychoanalytic,
structural, or linguistic insights.

    Ricoeur himself, of course, is aware that he has
proposed a revolution in method, that his methodology
has changed, and continues to change. After an extensive study, Vansina concludes that Ricoeur is well
aware of the limits of the methodology he may be using
at a particular time. In fact, he suggests that the
very concreteness of Ricoeur's methodology is that
which can renew philosophy in a rationality which
avoids an unreal pseudo-abstraction.[2] Even a severe
critic of Ricoeur's methodology, Hackett, who takes him
to task for shortcomings of contingency, of relativism,
of the use of the transcendental method, and of his
understanding of the fullness of language, nevertheless
concludes with an appreciation of "Ricoeur's epoch-
making Philosophy of the Will."

> We can indeed see in his philosophical
> methodology both a complex reminder of
> our human finitude and a provocative
> summons to the self-recovery in which
> reflective philosophy aims at trans-
> gressing that finitude by incorporating

> it into itself in the achievement of
> the only sort of theoretical and prac-
> tical freedom which can reasonably be
> predicated of human existence. We are
> not gods, but we <u>are</u> human: and per-
> haps Ricoeur has enabled us to glimpse ·
> more fully the task of becoming in
> actual fact what we are in fundamental
> essence. [3]

What are the contexts of the principal critiques
brought to Ricoeur's work? It is important to recall
the formative period during the 1930's when Ricoeur was
a student of Gabriel Marcel, when a group of students
met every Friday night at their teacher's home to do
philosophy without the benefit of books or notes in
hand, but when they learned to critique themselves,
each other, and the ideas and writers of their tradition. This period was also the time in Paris when
Husserl and Heidegger, Sartre and Merleau-Ponty,
socialism and communism, with their implied critiques,
were topics of the day. It was in 1936 that Ricoeur
read Barth, and like so many others, found himself
reoriented by the "Barthian shock." The "absolute
paradox" of Kierkegaard and the Word theologies of
Fuchs and Ebeling were also part of the same horizon.

It was as a prisoner in a war camp that Ricoeur
and Mikel Dufrenne studied and critiqued Husserl and
Jaspers, absorbing both method and critique as they did
so. After World War II existentialism and phenomenology and later structuralism came to dominate the critical scene. Under the umbrella of existential phenomenology, Ricoeur wrote the first part of his Philosophy
of the Will.

The hermeneutic turn came in 1960 with the
publication of the second part, and especially with <u>The
Symbolism of Evil</u>. It was the necessity for the hermeneutic that brought about the enlarged diversity and
the interdisciplinary characteristics which both opened
up Ricoeur's work to persons in so many other areas,
but which, at the same time, often took him outside the
narrower arenas of accepted philosophy.

Ricoeur's books and articles reflect the diversity
of these new directions in the 1960's: psychoanalysis,
structuralism not only in anthropology, but also in
literary criticism, religious language both in theologies of the Word and in the analyses of "God talk," and
ordinary language philosophy.

It was in ordinary language philosophy that
Ricoeur during the 1970's was locating his work in
philosophical and theological hermeneutics, metaphor,
and narrative, which by the 1980's had become the doing
of the Poetics.

Examples of Critiques

Early critiques from within philosophy were
mentioned above in examples from DeWaelhens, Vansina,
and Hackett. In a bibliographical essay ("Ricoeur and
His Critics: A Bibliographic Essay," in Studies in the
Philosophy of Paul Ricoeur. Ed. by Charles E. Reagan.
Athens, Ohio: Ohio University Press, 1979. 164-177)
Francois H. Lapointe provides an exhaustive list of
critical material. Among the earliest dissertations
were those of Vansina (Louvain, 1962), Ihde (Boston,
1964), Stewart (Rice, 1965), Reagan (Kansas, 1968), and
Rasmussen (Chicago, 1969). A much larger group of
dissertations[4] appeared in the 1970's from a number of
universities.

In his volume Hermeneutic Phenomenology. The
Philosophy of Paul Ricoeur (Evanston, IL: Northwestern
University Press, 1971), Don Ihde recognizes Ricoeur's
work as a "distinctive hermeneutic phenomenology which
gives and promises to give new perspectives to the
philosophy of language" (xix). Other books of critique
have been published in several languages. Articles are
far more extensive. Lapointe arranges them in separate
language groups, and, including Reviews and Critical
Notices, but without references from the 1980's, the
articles require eleven pages to list.

What do these critics say? For the most part,
their work is descriptive and appreciative, with a
particular emphasis or theme. Two French studies focus
on freedom. Nijhoff in The Hague published two books
by Americans: David Rasmussen's Mythic-Symbolic Language and Philosophical Anthropology (The Hague:
Martinus Nijhoff, 1971) and Patrick Bourgeois's Extension of Ricoeur's Hermeneutic (The Hague: Martinus
Nijhoff, 1975).

Other books and articles analyze Ricoeur's work as
part of a study of a topic to which their authors feel
Ricoeur has much to contribute. Examples of these are
Michel Van Esbroeck's Herméneutique, structuralisme et
exégèse (Paris: Desclée, 1968) and Sandra Perpich's A
Hermeneutic Critique of Structuralist Exegesis, with

Specific Reference to Lk 10.29-37 (Lanham-New York-
London: University Press of America, 1984).

     Charles E. Reagan organized and edited a book of
critical essays entitled Studies in the Philosophy of
Paul Ricoeur (Athens, Ohio: Ohio University Press,
1979), which brings together articles written for this
volume by diverse international scholars who write on
various topics related to Ricoeur's work. Among these
scholars is David Pellauer, whose article Ricoeur in
the Preface calls a "remarkable essay." From a comprehensive viewpoint, Pellauer is able to link together a
number of problems which Ricoeur addressed as he was
led from one question to another.

     Ricoeur also appreciates the essay by Mary
Schaldenbrand "Metaphoric Imagination: Kinship through
Conflict." He recognizes that his contributions to the
problem of imagination have been fragmentary and appreciates Schaldenbrand's linking imagination to the problem of fragile mediation. "I learned a great deal from
this study," writes Ricoeur.

     Of a different type are two essays, one by
Robert C. Solomon on "Paul Ricoeur on Passion and Emotion," and the other by Richard Zaner, "The Adventure
of Interpretation: The Reflective Wager and the
Hazards of the Self." Especially in the light of the
fact that Solomon has explored the philosophy of the
passions extensively in his own work, he finds both a
dichotomy and an inadequacy in Ricoeur's treatment of
the passions in Freedom and Nature. The dichotomy
includes the fact that for the most part, according to
Solomon, Ricoeur denigrates the passions, but on the
other hand, evidently is a person whose passionate
writings contradict some of his explicit statements as
well as his neglect of an extensive treatment of the
passions.

     In the Preface, Ricoeur responds in the manner
which has become for him not only a way of life, but
also a methodology. Michel Philibert comments on this
extensively in his essay on Ricoeur's philosophic
method:

> The trait that makes Paul Ricoeur
> unique in our time, and no less unique
> in the history of philosophy lies in
> the way he combines an eager and humble
> attention to practically all previous
> philosophers with a feeling for our

present situation and a modest but
strong determination to speak his own
mind on any problem he deals with
(134).

Ricoeur recognizes the critique which Solomon
brings but then points out the reasons for his own
development and makes distinctions about points with
which he disagrees with Solomon.

Ricoeur responds in a similar way to the essay by
Zaner. Whereas he appreciates the questions which
Zaner raises about equivocal and univocal aspects of
philosophical discourse especially in the context of
symbols, nevertheless, "It is not possible to respond
to this objection without taking up again the whole
question of the relations between phenomenology and
hermeneutics, as I began to do in an essay which bears
this title. I do not believe that hermeneutics re-
places phenomenology. It is only opposed to the ideal-
ist interpretation of phenomenology" (9).

Reagan's book concludes with a "Bibliography of
Paul Ricoeur" by Frans D. Vansina, which is selective,
beginning with Ricoeur's major publications in 1947 and
continuing through 1976. The extent of Ricoeur's
bibliography is one of the problems and challenges for
his critics. Often a problem that a critic has with
one of Ricoeur's essays is addressed elsewhere in
Ricoeur's writings. But few critics have the leisure,
or even, in some cases, the comprehensive competence,
as DeWaelhens acknowledged, to follow the development
of thought over a life time of prolific writings.

Over the last thirty-five years Ricoeur has often
been part of scholarly symposia or seminars, both in
Europe and in North America, in which the presenting of
papers and conversation provide on-going critique. A
few will be described as examples.

One is referred to by Norman Perrin in his book
Jesus and the Language of the Kingdom (Philadelphia:
Fortress Press, 1976). The subtitle is "Symbol and
Metaphor in New Testament Interpretation," and the
dedication is "To Amos Wilder and Paul Ricoeur who
taught me to look at the problem of hermeneutics in new
ways." In the Preface, Perrin refers to the seminar
conducted at Chicago by David Tracy, Perrin, and
Ricoeur on the hermeneutics of religious language
(xii). This came to be referred to by others as the
seminar on the parables, because Jesus's parables

were the major texts discussed. Ricoeur's three
articles on "Biblical Hermeneutics" which were published in Semeia 4 were the lectures Ricoeur presented
in the last part of this seminar. Over the years,
seminars like this one, at Chicago, at Paris, at
Louvain, provide an on-going critique from outstanding
scholars.

     Another example is the study group on "The
Interpretation Theory of Paul Ricoeur" which was formed
with the leadership of Loretta Dornisch and under the
aegis of the American Academy of Religion and which met
at the yearly national meetings between 1976 and 1982.
Ricoeur had participated in the 1975 symposium from
which the study group was formed. In that symposium
fifteen scholars critiqued Ricoeur's articles on
"Biblical Hermeneutics" and Ricoeur responded. Many of
the papers presented over the years were subsequently
published in various journals. Those presented in 1978
on The Book of Job and Ricoeur's Hermeneutics were
published in Semeia 19.

     Similar critiques have been published in
sequential issues of Philosophy Today, edited by Robert
Lechner. Lechner writes about Ricoeur:

> There is probably no philosopher who
> has been more concerned to share with
> his readers and hearers just where he
> is, what he is about and what he has in
> mind. He is a philosopher in dialogue
> with every issue of our contemporary
> culture. A statement of one specific
> task Ricoeur has set for himself--"to
> graft the hermeneutical problem onto
> the phenomenological method"--is exact
> enough to indicate for us why his dia-
> logical thought has gone beyond a phi-
> losophy of reconciliation to an
> authentic philosophy of hope, the hope
> for something really new. We are very
> pleased to add Philosophy Today to the
> long list of places where Paul Ricoeur
> can be found today--among philosophers,
> theologians, biblical scholars, scien-
> tists, psychologists, anthropologists,
> linguists. He seems to be present
> wherever we find persons seeking the
> truth together with honesty and
> humility (Philosophy Today. XVII,
> Number 2/4, Summer 1973, 87).

The published protocols from the 17th and 27th colloquies from the Center for Hermeneutical Studies, edited by Wilhelm Wuellner, include not only presentations by Ricoeur but the discussion afterwards with various scholars.

Two volumes were published to honor Ricoeur on the occasion of his sixtieth and sixty-fifth birthdays respectively: Sens et existence, en hommage à Paul Ricoeur (Ed. by G. B. Madison. Paris: Éditions du Seuil, 1975) and seven articles in Man and World (Vol. 13, No. 3-4, 1979). Authors include Gadamer, Eliade, Levinas, Wilder, Edie, Greimas, and Panikkar. Although the articles are not critiques of Ricoeur, they imply a recognition of Ricoeur's importance.

Ricoeur's Own Critique

Ricoeur is certainly one of the more important if not his best critic. This has been true from the beginning because it is implicit in his methodology. Ricoeur's primary task is to think, to address a problem and to follow it through, and the presumption is that within his tradition, he does that through interaction with others in the past and in the present who have addressed or who are addressing the problem. As Philibert indicates (in Reagan, 136), Ricoeur not only acknowledges writers whom he selects as important for the dialectic, but he expresses admiration and typically notes what he is learning from the other. His disagreement is never a belittlement. He appreciates the challenge of another viewpoint.

> Patiently, attentively, respectfully, Ricoeur will draw from the author's principles new consequences, from his method new applications, either to cope with new problems he sets up for himself, or to reopen the very problems the author was dealing with, so as to amend his solution; and Ricoeur again will in any case give due credit to the authors, even for those things he finds in them that they could not see themselves (137).

The same applies to Ricoeur's own on-going critique of himself. From the time that early in his professional life he outlined his lifework of a Philosophy of the Will, he has pursued the questions he

addresses against, not only the horizon of western
philosophy, but also against all the books and articles
he has already written and the writers he has included
as part of the dialectic. There is an amusing comment[5]
in his Preface to the Reagan volume when he is responding to the critiques of Schaldenbrand and ·
Pellauer. He critiques the critics when he recognizes
that the first sees mediating imagination as a pivotal
theme, and the second sees the paradigm of the text for
all hermeneutics as central. Ricoeur asks:

> I wonder if my two critics can both be
> right at once? To be honest, I am not
> well prepared to answer. First, be-
> cause it is difficult for me to see my
> books and my articles as steps or
> stages in a single development. Each
> seems to be rather a response to a
> particular question determined by the
> questions left unanswered in the pre-
> ceding work (6).

Nevertheless, Ricoeur recognizes the lines of
development, and indeed acknowledges that whereas
mediating imagination raises the problem of ontology
and the text as paradigmatic raises the problem of the
epistemology of such an ontology, these are indeed the
intersections and exchanges which a Poetics of the Will
must address.

Possibilities of a Critique from Within

For such a prolific set of writings over a period
of more than thirty-five years, there is an unusual
internal consistency. In spite of Ricoeur's comment
above, acknowledging a sense of discontinity, it is
nevertheless clear to the careful reader that there is
an astonishing coherence in the development of
Ricoeur's thought. As a number of critics have discovered, what seems a new direction in one of Ricoeur's
writings has often been foreshadowed long before. At
the same time, Ricoeur will correct himself when his
insights lead him in a different direction. For example, in regard to symbol Ricoeur has shifted his position a number of times. The concept became important
for him from his early study of Karl Jaspers. In
Ricoeur's earlier commentaries on Marcel and Jaspers,
there was an indication of an aspect of symbol not tied
to language.

A distinction of Jaspers may throw some light
here. He describes two kinds of symbol: "those which
can be interpreted (deutbare Symbole), and those that
can only be intuited (schaubare Symbole)" (Kurt
Hoffman, "The Basic Concepts of Jaspers' Philosophy,"
in The Philosophy of Karl Jaspers. Ed. by Paul Arthur
Schilpp. New York: Tudor Publishing Company, 1957,
106).

Although in "The Symbol . . . Food for Thought"
Ricoeur identifies his concept of symbol with Jaspers'
concept of cipher, Ricoeur's development led him in the
direction of interpretation rather than in the direction of intuition. Moreover, he seems at that time not
to have distinguished these two kinds of symbol, with
the necessary result that his theory is tied to language. Jaspers' understanding of language, too, is
helpful here. He uses language in the sense of communication, a term more encompassing than language,
which usually is limited to the verbal.

> The concept of the cipher presupposes
> that reason cannot know the nature of
> the world directly, but that reality
> must be "read" in the secret language
> of the appearances. In this sense Kant
> already spoke of "the ciphers by means
> of which Nature speaks to us." . . .
> For Jaspers the ciphers are not identi-
> cal with the appearances, but are the
> language spoken through them by Tran-
> scendence, not to consciousness-as-
> such, but to Existenz. The direct
> language of Transcendence is not a
> language that is universally intelligi-
> ble. The incompleteness of the empiri-
> cal world points above and beyond every
> rational certitude; this pointing has
> the immediacy of the metaphysical ex-
> perience. It does not follow a method;
> it is adventitious, as it were, a gift
> (Ibid., 107).

Perhaps Ricoeur's efforts to give reasons for his
presuppositions, his efforts, at least initially, to
remain within the tradition of an eidetics, and his
concern with the verbal led him at this point to what
seems to be a narrower definition of language. Language as he develops it in the poetics, however, is
widened considerably.

In <u>The Symbolism of Evil</u>, Ricoeur assumes a second position. Here the primary symbols are stain, sin, and guilt, expressed in the language of avowal or confession. The symbol exists, however, only insofar as it is expressed or articulated in the language of avowal.

In <u>Freud and Philosophy</u> Ricoeur studies Ernst Cassirer's <u>Philosophy of Symbolic Forms</u> (Tr. R. Manheim, 3 vols. New Haven: Yale University Press, 1957), and finds Cassirer's definition of symbol too broad. In the unfolding of the study of Freud, Ricoeur defines or describes symbol in a variety of ways, although the descriptions are consistent. One example is: "A symbol is the very movement of the primary meaning intentionally assimilating us to the symbolized, without our being able to intellectually dominate the likeness" (FP, 17).

In <u>Interpretation Theory</u> Ricoeur summarizes his own critique:

> In my earlier writings, especially <u>The Symbolism of Evil</u> and <u>Freud and Philosophy</u>, I directly defined hermeneutics by an object which seemed to be both as broad and as precise as possible, I mean the symbol . . . . I defined it in turn by its semantic structure of having a double-meaning (IT, 45).

It was for this reason that he shifted his studies to the narrower problem of metaphor, in which the concept of double-meaning can be studied with less diffusion. Nevertheless, the problem of symbolic function and the polysemy of expression remains, and, in fact, is never too distant from the challenge of the poetics. Indeed, Ricoeur came to recognize that his growing understanding of symbol broadened to such a point that his view is consistent with that of Cassirer. Symbol is integral to language. As Ricoeur develops his poetics, both in its ontological and epistemological aspects, Ricoeur continues to ask the questions which he began to ask when he wrote his earlier studies on symbol.

CHAPTER FIVE

The Poetics

What is the poetics? From early in his adult
life, Ricoeur was intrigued by this concept which he
had discovered in Aristotle. He writes:

> Poetizing is the fundamental trait of
> human existence . . . Poetry is that
> which roots the act of dwelling . . .
> in the power of the Word. Poetry so
> defined is poiesis, the act of creation
> in the broadest sense (The Religious
> Significance of Atheism, 96-97).

In his first part of the Philosophy of the Will,
the volume entitled The Voluntary and the Involuntary,
which the English editor called Freedom and Nature,
Ricoeur commented in a footnote on the poetics which he
was projecting:

> In our language, life has an ambiguous
> meaning: it designates at the same
> time the order of limits, and the order
> of sources or creation. In this new
> sense life brings up a new method,
> namely a "poetics" of the will which we
> are here abstracting. One of the cru-
> cial, difficult problems posed by such
> "poetics" of the will will be to know
> why the spontaneity of life below
> serves in turn as a metaphor for higher
> life, and what secret affinity unites
> those two meanings of the word "life"
> (VI, 415, n. 75).

As he finished The Voluntary and the Involuntary
in 1948, he wrote that Transcendence is not only a

limit concept, but "it is a <u>presence</u> which brings about a true revolution in the theory of subjectivity. It introduces into it a radically new dimension, the <u>poetic</u> dimension" (486).

The methods and tasks of the "Phenomenology of the Will" were outlined in a paper Ricoeur presented before the International Colloquium on Phenomenology in 1951. Republished in the volume on Husserl, the paper describes the three parts: the level of descriptive analysis; the level of transcendental constitution; and on the threshold of ontology. As these would develop, they became the eidetics, the empirics, and the poetics.

It is interesting to see at this point what Ricoeur projected for the poetics. He proposed "an ontology of consciousness."

> We shall attempt to circumscribe a privileged experience which, on the level of the voluntary and the involuntary, is constituted as revelatory of my ontological situation. As we shall see, this experience can be an experience of deficiency. of non-being. This experience at least will allow us to denounce as naive the pretensions of the subject to set himself up as the primitive or primordial being under the pretext that he has, in a limited but authentic sense, the transcendental function of "constituting" the involuntary aspect of his life and world (Hu, 214).

It is in the discovery of fault and guilt that human being discovers an ontology of non-being. Paradoxically, then, by reversal, the way is opened to the possibility of an ontology of being. It was in <u>The Symbolism of Evil</u> and in <u>Freud and Philosophy</u> that Ricoeur explored this dark side of ontology in the problems of fault, guilt, and the reciprocity of the voluntary and the involuntary.

Even at this early point, Ricoeur saw the movement from transcendental phenomenology to ontological phenomenology as a conversion which shifts the ego from the center. The poetics of the will would be the "adventure of a <u>poiesis</u>" (233).

Since the adventure of the poetics was and is never far from Ricoeur's current project, references are sprinkled throughout most of his writings from the beginning. With the hermeneutic turn of The Symbolism of Evil, Ricoeur became more and more involved in the philosophy of ordinary language. To the outside reader, and perhaps sometimes to himself, the succession of books often seemed to be a digression from the task of the poetics. Each was a task, however, which needed to be pursued. The questions had to be wrestled with. And so the succession of books followed one another: Freud and Philosophy, The Conflict of Interpretations, The Rule of Metaphor, (with an explicit treatment of ontology), Interpretation Theory. Careful readers began to suspect that indeed the poetics was in progress.

As he was frequently asked, "What about the poetics?" he would sometimes reply, "Perhaps never . . ." or "In the eschaton!" But with Time and Narrative there was a difference: the circle between narrative and temporality, the connections between history and narrative and between fiction and narrative led to epistemology and ontology. When he was asked in March, 1984, "What about the poetics?" he replied with a nod, "O, I'm doing it."

It is impossible to summarize references to the poetics throughout Ricoeur's writings. It is helpful, however, to look at a few examples, as indications of the directions of his thought.

In an essay on existential phenomenology, he wrote: ontology is that "which restores the question of the sense of being for all that is said to 'exist'" (Hu, 212). Being-there and being-symbol are two dimensions of the same world (KJ, 291). It is symbol which speaks independently of me, and which says more than I can understand (F-HP, xvi-vii). It is where I experience a surplus of meaning. By interpreting symbols Ricoeur hopes better to understand "the bond between human being and the being of all beings" (SE, 355). A philosophy which opens itself to the fullness of language opens itself to the fullness of reality. Human being not only speaks, but human being is born into language, into the light which enlightens everyone who comes into the world. Human being expects to be called, to be spoken to (FP, 31). Prospective symbols reach down to the living substrate of symbols to create new meaning. The images which human being appropriates and creates build meaning, build the self, and continually remodel the nature of human being (FP, 523-524).

In speaking of freedom and faith, Ricoeur moves
easily from philosophical to theological language, but
the language is appropriate in the context of a
poetics. The freedom of the act of faith is part of
the general power of choosing, basic to the religious
phenomenon, and independent of public power. "A hermeneutics of religious freedom is an interpretation of
freedom in conformity with the Resurrection interpreted
in terms of promise and hope" (CI, 406).

Ricoeur sees freedom as arising from the
possibility proclaimed in the kerygma, especially as
articulated in a theology of hope which places the
kerygma in the context of the promise, of the kingdom
which is to come, with an implicit mission to take part
in bringing that kingdom to reality.

In practice, such a mission cannot be separated
from a deciphering of the signs of the new creation,
that is, from a reappropriation of the desire to be
through the works which bear witness to that desire.
Such a sending, with the corresponding reading of the
signs and the concretizing of the desire to be, generates an ethics with social, political, and even cosmic
implications. The kerygma thus understood shifts the
center of ethics from the subjective of personal authenticity to the reconciling power of social and political
justice. Thus, Christian liberty belongs to the order
of the resurrection. Ricoeur sees this as a freedom
from death, a freedom for life, the folly of the cross,
and the wisdom of the resurrection.

But to affirm liberty is to attribute to human
being the origin of evil. The paradox then is that
human being is entirely a sinner, but more or less
blameable. The very capacity for evil limits the freedom. The apparent contradiction is saved by the hope
for deliverance, a hope which works itself out in a
deliverance through grace.

The work on metaphor provides a major break
through for Ricoeur in coming to grips with the problems both of epistemology and of ontology. When asked
in 1973 about his position in relationship to metaphysics, he replied that in his next book he would have
to take a stand. Especially the last essay in The Rule
of Metaphor is a working out of the problem of analogy
with all that implies for epistemology and ontology.
Symbol, metaphor, text open to the possible. The meaning is not something hidden, but something disclosed,
not something behind the text, but something in front

of the symbol, the metaphor, or the text. "Texts speak of possible worlds and of possible ways of orienting oneself in those worlds" (PPR, 144).

> What we need is an interpretation that respects the original enigma of the symbols, that lets itself be taught by them, but that, beginning from there, promotes the meaning, forms the meaning in the full responsibility of autonomous thought (SE, 349-350).

It is astonishing, perhaps, to see how much the thrust of the poetics is present at the beginning of Ricoeur's work. In his commentary on Ideas II of Husserl, for example, Ricoeur noted that out of the world of touching is born an art of signs, "a vast grammar of expressions of which the most notable illustration is language. To understand these signs is to constitute human being, to apprehend the Other as 'analogue of myself'" (Hu, 66). Consciousness is at the same time speech and perception, while phenomenology is "the logos of the phenomena" (Hu, 216). Since it is part of my choice as a linguistic being, silence remains within the categories of speech because my silence is willed. The opposite, an absence of willing, is an absence of human being.

In theological terms, in the tradition of a theology of the Word, Ricoeur notes that the term Word belongs uniquely to Christianity, which consists of faith in the Word which became flesh, which grew through the witness of the first Christian community proclaiming the Word, and which must constantly be actualized in a renewal of the Word for our times (CRLTP, 301, ff.). In these contexts, every theology is a theology of the Word; nevertheless, a theology which specifically tries to understand this process of the Word as a central focus merits the specific title of a theology of the Word.

For such a theology, hermeneutics assumes a central place, and the sciences which derive from the linguistic model pose a particular challenge. The challenge calls for a two-fold task: the systematic task of unifying all the realms of theology under the concept of the "coming-to-be" of the Word; and the critical task of engaging in serious confrontation with the linguistic disciplines and with the other sciences which stem from them.

Ricoeur treats of the contribution of language to
a theology of the Word on three levels, those of structuralism, of a phenomenology of language, and of an
ontology of language. While incorporating the insights
of structuralism, theology will always go on to the
interpretative process which involves the speaking
subject, the transcendent, and the creation of new
being.

In his summary article "My Relation to the History
of Philosophy" in the fall of 1978, Ricoeur refers to
some of the background as well as the development of
his formulating of the plan of the poetics. He had
been impressed early by the "majestic composition" of
Jaspers' three volume <u>Philosophy</u>: "Orientation in the
World," "Illumination of Existence," and "Metaphysics."
He admired and hoped to emulate Merleau-Ponty's posi-
tioning between concrete ontology and phenomenology.
Although he continues to be impressed by Heidegger's
philosophy, he recognizes its inadequacies in a number
of respects, including its contribution to the "collapse of the question of the subject," through which
"Heideggerian ontology, in spite of itself, played into
the hands of the new scientism represented by structuralism, even though the latter was worlds away from
Heidegger" (MRHP, 7).

> I might note here in passing that my
> experience as an historian of philoso-
> phy kept me from adhering to the Heideg-
> gerian idea of the unity of "Meta-
> physics"; instead I was struck--and
> bothered--by the singular nature of
> philosophical works, and this raised
> the thorny problem of the unity of
> truth. In addition, this has made me
> resist all the more strongly the Heideg-
> gerian project of "destroying classical
> ontology." In this respect I share
> with Gadamer the heightened sense of
> the continuity of the philosophical
> tradition, at least on the level of the
> great problems, despite the obvious
> discontinuity between the individual
> replies given to these problems by the
> great philosophers.
>
> Classical philosophy has left its
> indelible mark on me. In this way, my
> recent work on metaphor witnesses the
> return in force of Aristotle, and it is

> his notion of being as <u>energeia</u> which
> founds my quest for a Poetics of the
> Will (7-8).

Thus Ricoeur's work in exploring semantic innovation in
language as well as in action theory, or the investigation of human praxis, may well be mediated by the concept of "the creative imagination, the generative
source of a Poetics of the Will" (12).

In his developing past the theory of metaphor the
theory of narrative, including the concept of intertextuality, Ricoeur finds himself at the heart of the
concept of the productive imagination. He is intrigued
by "the transformation of the narrative-parable by the
encompassing text.

> In what way? In a way that already
> notes the dynamism at work in the nar-
> rative in order to understand how this
> dynamism is transgressed by the embed-
> ding. To understand a narrative
> dynamically is to understand it as the
> operation of transforming an initial
> situation into a terminal situation.
> The most elementary function of a nar-
> rative, in this regard, is to account
> for this transformation. To read a
> narrative is to redo with the text a
> certain "line" or "course" of meaning
> (BI, 56).

This is the basic form of imagination, and it is
that which authentically produces meaning. In the
context of the parables in the Gospels, for example,
metaphorization happens precisely through the intertextuality.

> This is how I understand the transition
> between semiotic explication and inter-
> pretation that has its fulfillment in
> the thought, action, and life of inter-
> preting individuals and communities.
> We are leaving the structure (or
> sense), but we are not yet at the appli-
> cation or appropriation (the refer-
> ence). We are accompanying the <u>inter-</u>
> <u>pretive dynamism of the text itself.</u>
> The text interprets before having been
> interpreted. This is how it is itself
> a work of productive imagination before

> giving rise to an interpretive dynamism
> in the reader which is analogous to its
> own (67).

> In this sense, the Kingdom of God is
> not what the parables tell about, but
> what happens in parables (70).

From the beginning, Ricoeur's philosophy has been a wager, a recognition that philosophy is not without presuppositions.

> A philosophy that starts from the
> fullness of language is a philosophy
> with presuppositions. To be honest, it
> must make its presuppositions explicit,
> state them as beliefs, wager on the
> beliefs, and try to make the wager pay
> off in understanding (SE, 357).

In his "The Hermeneutics of Testimony," Ricoeur writes that testimony "gives to interpretation a content to be interpreted" and at the same time, "calls for an interpretation" (EBI, 143). In some sense, not only a hermeneutics of testimony but indeed all of Ricoeur's philosophy is directed toward a poetics. His philosophy gives us a content to be interpreted and thereby calls for an interpretation that well may be our own poetics.

END NOTES

PART I   ( ) = page in text

Chapter One

1. Ricoeur is one of the few persons writing seriously about the problem of evil in our times. His book *The Symbolism of Evil* established his position as one confronting the issues. This excerpt is from an essay for which the reporter called Ricoeur and asked him to comment on the Jonestown massacre. *Time*. Dec. 18, 1978, 51. (8).

2. Ricoeur is here quoting Mounier. During the 1980's the question was raised about the possibility of a relationship of Mounier with the Vichy government in southern France during World War II. Ricoeur was surprised and seemed to find it inconsistent with what he knew of Mounier. (10).

3. Thomas Kuhn, *The Structure of Scientific Revolutions*. Chicago: The University of Chicago Press, 1962, 1970. (16).

Chapter Three

1. Richard McKeon, ed. *Introduction to Aristotle*. New York: The Modern Library, 1947. (35).

2. *Philosophy Today* published Ricoeur's "A Critique of B. F. Skinner's *Beyond Freedom and Dignity*," translated by David Pellauer in Volume XVII, Number 2/4, Summer, 1973, pp. 166-175. "The general mood of my approach to Professor Skinner's book is a mixture of

disagreement at the level of theory and agreement at a practical level" (166). Ricoeur's essay is a critique of diverse views of freedom and dignity (36).

3. In 1973 Ricoeur authored the article "Volonté" in *Encyclopaedia universalis*, XVI, 943-948, Paris, in which he sketched a history of the problem (38).

4. Viktor Frankl, *Man's Search for Meaning*. New York: Pocket Books, Inc., 1980. (38).

5. Gabriel Marcel, *Creative Fidelity*. New York: Crossroad, 1982. (41).

Chapter Four

1. Rudolf Otto, *Idea of the Holy*. New York: Oxford University Press, 1950. (60).

PART IV

Chapter Three

1. Ricoeur's involvements in and contributions to education are so extensive as to require a lengthy study in themselves. For decades he provided leadership in France in the structuring of university education. In 1969-1970 as Dean of the School of Letters of the University of Paris-X at Nanterre, Ricoeur was instrumental in implementing educational reforms, but he was then overwhelmed at the violence of society and of the student/worker revolts. He resigned and published a letter in which he called the work of reform not that of a day, or a year, but of a century (195).

PART V

Chapter Two

1. Roland Dalbiez, *La méthod psychanalytique et la doctrine freudienne*. Paris: Desclée de Brouwer, 1936. Cited by Ricoeur in *Freud and Philosophy*, xii. (223).

2. Ricoeur will later broaden his concept of hermeneutics. (224).

3. Ricoeur here footnotes (FP, 24, n. 8) the extensive
    study: Henri de Lubac, *Exégèse médiévale*, I-IV.
    Paris: Aubier, 1959-1964. Ricoeur recommends that
    philosophers give more attention to the theory elabo-
    rated there which includes the distinction of analogy,
    allegory, and symbol. A comparison of Ricoeur's her-
    meneutics with that of medieval exegesis as described
    by de Lubac was published in 1968: Michel Van
    Esbroeck, *Herméneutique, structuralisme, et exégèse*.
    Paris: Desclée, 1968. (225).

PART VI

Chapter One

1. M.-D. Chenu, *Nature, Man, and Society in the Twelfth
    Century*. Chicago: The University of Chicago Press,
    1968. The French referred to by Ricoeur is: *La
    théologie au xii siècle*. Paris: Vrin, 1957. It is
    discussed by Ricoeur on p. 339 in "Contribution d'une
    réflexion sur le langage à une théologie de la
    parole." (266).

Chapter Two

1. R. Polzin, *Biblical Structuralism*. Philadelphia:
    Fortress Press and Missoula: Scholars Press, 1977,
    202. (274).

Chapter Three

1. I originally presented most of the following material
    in *Semeia* 19. Listed editor: John Dominic Crossan,
    "The Book of Job and Ricoeur's Hermeneutics." *Semeia*
    19, 1981. Copyright by The Society of Biblical Liter-
    ature. (279).

Chapter Four

1. Amos Wilder, "Semeia, An Experimental Journal for
    Biblical Criticism: An Introduction." *Semeia* 1:1-16.
    (285).

2. Norman Perrin, *Jesus and the Language of the Kingdom*.
    Philadelphia: Fortress Press, 1980. (285).

3. This volume also includes my "Symbolic Systems and the
    Interpretation of Scripture: An Introduction to the
    Work of Paul Ricoeur" and "Paul Ricoeur and Biblical
    Interpretation: A Selected Bibliography." A con-
    densed version of the first was published in *Theology
    Digest*, 24:2, 1976. (285).

PART VII

Chapter One

1. Ricoeur published in 1972 an article on "Ontology" in
    Encyclopaedia universalis, XII, 94-102, Paris, in
    which he surveyed some of the major developments and
    questions. (312).

Chapter Three

1. Unpublished transcript of a Seminar with Ricoeur at
    Emory University, 1977. I wish to thank Joan Leonard
    for a copy. (328).

2. Under the French title, *La narrativité*, the French
    chapters are: I. "L'histoire comme récit"; II. "Le
    récit de fiction"; III. "La fonction narrative"; IX.
    "Récit fictif--récit historique." (332).

3. In the remaining references to TN,I, and TR,I, if two
    page references are given, the translation is mine
    from TR,I, the second reference. (334).

4. The translators of the English version use the forms:
    "mimesis$_1$, mimesis$_2$, mimesis$_3$." I prefer to keep the
    original form. (336).

5. Ricoeur's references in the following pages include:

    William Dray, *Laws and Exploration in History*.
    London: Oxford University Press, 1957.

    George Henrik von Wright, *Exploration and Under-
    standing*. Ithaca: Cornell University Press, 1971.

    _____. *Norm and Action*. London: Routledge and
    Kegan Paul, 1963.

    _____. *An Essay in Deontic Logic and the General
    Theory of Action*. Amsterdam: North Holland, 1968.

    Arthur C. Danto, *Analytical Philosophy of History*.
    New York: Cambridge University Press, 1965.

W. B. Gallie, *Philosophy and the Historical
Understanding*. New York: Schoken Books, 1964.

Louis O. Mink, "The Autonomy of Historical
Understanding" in *History and Theory*, V/1, 1965,
24-47.

Hayden White, *Metahistory: The Historical
Imagination in Nineteenth-Century Europe*.
Baltimore: The Johns Hopkins University Press,
1973.

Paul Veyne, *Comment on écrit l'histoire*. Paris:
Éditions du Seuil, 1971.

Hayden White. *Tropics of Discourse*. Baltimore:
The Johns Hopkins University Press, 1978.

Frank Kermode, *The Sense of an Ending*. New York:
Oxford University Press, 1966. (339).

Chapter Four

1. Alphonse De Waelhens, "Pensée mythique et philosophie
    du mal," *Revue philosophique de Louvain*, LIX, 1961,
    316. (356).

2. Dirk Vansina, "Esquisse, orientation et signification
    de l'entreprise philosophique de Paul Ricoeur," *Revue
    de métaphysique et de morale*, LIX, July-Oct., 1964,
    319. (356).

3. S. C. Hackett, "Philosophical Objectivity and
    Existential Involvement in the Methodology of Paul
    Ricoeur," *International Philosophical Quarterly*, IX,
    March, 1969, 39. (357).

4. Among these is my own: Dornisch, Loretta, *A
    Theological Interpretation of the Meaning of Symbol in
    the Theory of Paul Ricoeur*. Ann Arbor: University
    Microfilms, 1974. Paperback edition available.
    (358).

5. Ricoeur's sense of humor does not appear obvious in
    most of his writing, but a conversation quickly makes
    clear an on-going humorous perception of the
    incongruities of the human condition, as well as a
    gentleness and conviviality which make for good con-
    versation (363).

SELECTED BIBLIOGRAPHY

An abbreviation is supplied for each title for simplicity of reference within the book.

Works by Ricoeur are listed first by books, then by articles; by French publication date unless only the English version is listed. References, however, are ordinarily to the English.

BOOKS--ABBREVIATIONS

CI	1969b	*The Conflict of Interpretations*
CFH	1980a	*The Contribution of French Historiography to French History*
EBI	1980b	*Essays on Biblical Interpretation*
FM	1960a	*Fallible Man*
FP	1965a	*Freud and Philosophy*
GMKJ	1948	*Gabriel Marcel et Karl Jaspers*
HHS	1981	*Hermeneutics and the Human Sciences*
HT	1965b	*History and Truth*
Hu	1967	*Husserl*
IT	1976	*Interpretation Theory*
KJ	1947	*Karl Jaspers*
MTP	1979	*Main Trends in Philosophy*
N	1980c	*La narrativité*
PPR	1978	*The Philosophy of Paul Ricoeur*
PSE	1974	*Political and Social Essays*
RSA	1969a	*The Religious Significance of Atheism*
RHP	1984a	*The Reality of the Historical Past*
RM	1975	*The Rule of Metaphor*
SA	1977	*La sémantique de l'action*
SE	1960b	*The Symbolism of Evil*
TN	1984–198 ?	*Time and Narrative* I, II, III
TR	1983–1985	*Temps et récit* I, II, III
TWB	1973	*Tragic Wisdom and Beyond*
VI	1949	*Le volontaire et l'involontaire*
FNVI or VI	1966	*Freedom and Nature: The Voluntary and the Involuntary*

(Translations are from the English unless otherwise indicated. Ordinarily VI indicates the English.)

ARTICLES--ABBREVIATIONS

(The first word or words in the title are
supplied for help in identification)

BH	1975a	"Biblical Hermeneutics . . ."
BI	1980a	"The Bible and the Imagination . . ."
CC	1977d	"Construing . . ."
CL	1973b	"Creativity in Language."
CRLTP	1968a	"Contribution d'une reflexion . . ."
C-VV	1969a	"Conclusions."
DCC	1971f	"Du conflit à la convergence . . ."
DRC	1948	"Dimensions d'une recherche . . ."
EC	1971a	"Esquisse . . ."
ES	1971b	"Evénément . . ."
ESTC	1979e	"Epilogue."
F-BD	1979a	"Foreword." *Book of Daniel.*
FEPL	1973a	"From Existentialism . . ."
FFSR	1979f	"The Function . . ."
F-HP	1971c	"Foreword." *Hermeneutic Phenomenology.*
HCI	1973e	"Herméneutique . . ."
HFD	1978a	"The Hermeneutical Function . . ."
HH	1976a	"History and . . ."
HIR	1977a	"Hermeneutic of the Idea . . ."
HTe	1979g	"Hermeneutics . . ."
I-CT	1975b	"Introduction." *Les cultures* . . .
IDA	1978i	"Imagination in Discourse . . ."
ILP	1978h	"Image and Language . . ."
IPE	1968b	"Interrogation philosophique . . ."
I-TP	1978f	"Introduction." *Le temps* . . .
IUCI	1976c	"Ideology . . ."
LJLG	1979b	"Logic of Jesus . . ."
LP	1974e	"Listening . . ."
MP	1974c	"Manifestation . . ."
MPCH	1972	"La métaphore . . ."
MPCIF	1978c	"The Metaphorical . . ."

MRHP	1978b	"My Relation . . ."
MT	1971d	"Model of the Text . . ."
NDPF	1967	"New Developments in Phenomenology . . ."
NF	1978d	"The Narrative Function . . ."
NG	1979c	"Naming God."
NT	1980b	"Narrative Time."
NTh	1980c	"Narrative Theology."
PEMR	1955	"La parole . . ."
PFMP	1979d	"The Problem . . ."
PH	1975d	"Phenomenology and . . ."
PHBH	1978e	"Philosophical Hermeneutics . . ."
PHTH	1975c	"Philosophical Hermeneutics and Theological . . ."
PMV	1974d	"Psychiatry . . ."
PR	1978ee?	"Practical . . ."
PRL	1974a	"Philosophy and . . ."
PWA	1976b	"Psychoanalysis . . ."
RBR	1979-1980	"Response . . ."
RJPR	1957	"The Relation of Jaspers . . ."
SDP	1959	"Le symbole . . ."
SEG	1971g	"Sur l'exégèse . . ."
SFT	1960	"The Symbol . . ."
SH	1977c	"Schleiermacher's . . ."
SI	1974b	"Science et . . ."
SN	1977e	"Seminar: Narrative . . ."
SSL	1968c	"Structure et . . ."
TH	1973c 1978g	"The Task of Hermeneutics . . ."
THIR	1977b	"Toward a Hermeneutic . . ."
WD	1976d	"What Is Dialectical?"
WEE	1964	"Wonder . . ."
WT	1971e	"What Is a Text?"

BOOKS

1947   KJ   Joint author with Mikel Dufrenne, *Karl Jaspers*.
                Paris: Éditions du Seuil.

1948   GMKJ   *Gabriel Marcel et Karl Jaspers*. Paris: Éditions du
                Temps Présent.

1949+   *Philosophie de la volonté* (projected three volumes).

1949   VI   I.   *Le volontaire et l'involontaire*. Paris:
                         Aubier.
                         Trans. Erazim V. Kohak,
        FNVI   *Freedom and Nature: The Voluntary and the*
        or VI   *Involuntary*. Evanston: Northwestern Uni-
                         versity Press, 1966.

                    II. *Finitude and culpabilité*.

1960a   I.   *L'homme faillible*. Paris: Aubier.
                             Trans. Charles Kelbley,
        FM   *Fallible Man*. Chicago: Henry Regnery
                             Company, 1967.

1960b   II. *La symbolique du mal*. Paris: Aubier.
                             Trans. Emerson Buchanan,
        SE   *The Symbolism of Evil*. Boston: Beacon
                             Press, 1967.

                    III. Ricoeur projected volume III as The Poetics.
                         This is discussed in the last chapter of the
                         book.

1965a   *De l'interpretation*. Paris: Éditions du Seuil.
                Trans. Denis Savage,
        FP   *Freud and Philosophy*. New Haven and London: Yale
                University Press, 1970.

1965b   HT   *History and Truth*. Trans. Charles Kelbley.
                Evanston: Northwestern University Press.

1967   Hu   *Husserl. An Analysis of His Phenomenology*. Trans.
                Edward G. Ballard and Lester E. Embree. Evanston:
                Northwestern University Press.

1969a   RSA   Joint author with Alasdair Macintyre, *The Religious*
                Significance of Atheism. New York and London:
                Columbia University Press.

1969b   *Le conflit des interprétations*. Paris: Éditions du
                Seuil. Trans. ed. Don Ihde,
        CI   *The Conflict of Interpretations*. Evanston: North-
                western University Press, 1974.

1973   TWB   Joint author with Gabriel Marcel. *Tragic Wisdom and Beyond. Including Conversations between Paul Ricoeur and Gabriel Marcel*. Trans. Stephen Jolin and Peter McCormick. Evanston: Northwestern University Press.

1974   PSE   *Political and Social Essays*. Eds. D. Stewart and J. Bien. Athens: Ohio University Press.

1975   *La métaphore vive*. Paris: Éditions du Seuil. Trans. R. Czerny

        RM   *The Rule of Metaphor*. Toronto: The University of Toronto Press, 1977.

1976   IT   *Interpretation Theory: Discourse and the Surplus of Meaning*. Fort Worth: Texas Christian University Press.

1977   SA   *La sémantique de l'action*. Collection prepared under the direction of Dorian Tiffeneau. Paris: Éditions du Centre National de la Recherche Scientifique.

1978   PPR   *The Philosophy of Paul Ricoeur: An Anthology of His Work*. Eds. C. E. Reagan and D. Stewart. Boston: Beacon Press.

1979   MTP   Ed. *Main Trends in Philosophy*. New York: Holmes and Meier.

1980a   CFH   *The Contribution of French Historiography to French History*. Oxford: Oxford University Press.

1980b   EBI   *Essays on Biblical Interpretation*. Ed. Lewis S. Mudge. Philadelphia: Fortress Press.

1980c   N   *La narrativité*. Collection prepared under the direction of Dorian Tiffeneau. Paris: Éditions du Centre National de la Recherche Scientifique.

1981   HHS   *Hermeneutics and the Human Sciences*. Ed. John Thompson. New York: Cambridge University Press.

1983   TR-I   *Temps et récit*. I. Paris: Éditions du Seuil. Trans. Kathleen McLaughlin and David Pellauer,
        TN-I   *Time and Narrative*. Chicago and London: The University of Chicago Press, 1984.

1984a   RHP   *The Reality of the Historical Past*. Milwaukee: Marquette University Press, 1984.

1984b   TR-II   *Temps et récit. II. La configuration dans le récit de fiction.*   Paris: Éditions du Seuil.

1985   TN-II   *Time and Narrative.*   Chicago and London: The University of Chicago Press.   .

1985   TR-III *Temps et récit. III. Le temps raconté.* Paris: Éditions du Seuil.

1988   TN-III *Time and Narrative.*   Chicago and London: The University of Chicago Press.

ARTICLES

1948   DRC   "Dimensions d'une recherche commune." *Esprit* 16, 837–846.

1955   PEMR   "La parole est mon royaume." *Esprit* 23, 192–205.

1957   RJPR   "The Relation of Jaspers' Philosophy to Religion." In *The Philosophy of Karl Jaspers*. Ed. Paul A. Schilpp. New York: Tudor.

1959   SDP   "Le symbole donne à penser." *Esprit* 27:60–76.

1960   SFT   (English translation) "The Symbol . . . Food for Thought." *Philosophy Today* 4:196–207.

1964   WEE   "Wonder, Eroticism, and Enigma." *Cross Currents* 34:133–141.

1967   NDPF   "New Developments in Phenomenology in France: The Phenomenology of Language." *Social Research* 34:1–30.

1968a   CRLTP   "Contribution d'une réflexion sur le langage à une théologie de la parole." *Revue de théologie et de philosophie* 18:333–348.

1968b   IPE   "Interrogation philosophique et engagement." In *Pourquoi la philosophie?* Ed. Georges Leroux. Montreal: Les Éditions de Sainte-Marie.

1968c   SSL   "Structure et signification dans le langage." In *Pourquoi la philosophie?* Ed. Georges Leroux. Montreal: Les Editions de Sainte-Marie.

1969a   C-VV   "Conclusions." In *Vérité et vérification. Wahrheit und Verifikation.* Ed. H. L. Van Breda. The Hague: Nijhoff.

1971a   EC   "Esquisse de conclusion." In *Exégèse et herméneutique.* Ed. X. Léon-Dufour. Paris: Seuil.

1971b   ES   Evénément et sens." In *Révélation et histoire.* Paris: Aubier-Montaigne.

1971c   F-HP   "Foreword." In D. Ihde, *Hermeneutic Phenomenology.* Evanston: Northwestern University Press.

1971d   MT   "Model of the Text: Meaningful Action Considered as a Text." *Social Research* 38:529–562.

1971f   WT   "What Is a Text? Explanation and Interpretation."
                In *Mythic-Symbolic Language and Philosophical
                Anthropology*. Ed. David Rasmussen. The Hague:
                Martinus Nijhoff.

1971g   DCC   "Du conflit à la convergence des méthodes en exégèse
                biblique." In *Exégèse et herméneutique*. Paris:
                Éditions du Seuil.

1971h   SEG   "Sur l'exégèse de Genèse 1,1-2,4a." In *Exégèse et
                herméneutique*. Paris: Éditions du Seuil.

1972   MPCH   "La métaphore et le problème central de
                l'herméneutique." *Revue philosophique de Louvain*
                70:93-112.

1973a   FEPL   "From Existentialism to the Philosophy of Language."
                Philosophy Today 17:88-96.

1973b   CL   "Creativity in Language." *Philosophy Today* 17:97-
                111.

1973c   TH   "The Task of Hermeneutics." *Philosophy Today*
                17:112-128.

1973d   HFD   "The Hermeneutical Function of Distanciation."
                Philosophy Today 17:129-141.

1973e   HCI   "Herméneutique et critique des idéologies." In
                Démythisation et idéologie. Ed. E. Castelli. Paris:
                Aubier.

1974a   PRL   "Philosophy and Religious Language." *The Journal of
                Religion*: 54/3:71-85.

1974b   SI   "Science et idéologie." *Revue philosophique de
                Louvain* 72:328-356.

1974c   MP   "Manifestation et proclamation." In *Le sacré,
                Études et recherches*. Ed. E. Castelli. Paris:
                Aubier-Montaigne. ("Manifestation and
                Proclamation." *Journal of the Blaisdell Institute*
                12, 1978, 13-35).

1974d   PMV   "Psychiatry and Moral Values." In *American Handbook
                of Psychiatry*, 2nd ed. 1: *The Foundations of
                Psychiatry*. Ed. Silvano Ariete. New York: Basic
                Books.

1974e   LP   "Listening to the Parables: Once More Astonished."
                Criterion 13, Spring, 18-22. (*Christianity and
                Crisis* 34, 1975:304-308).

1975a BH   "Biblical Hermeneutics." *Semeia* 4:27-148.

1975b I-CT "Introduction." In *Les cultures et le temps*.
             Paris: Les Presses de l'UNESCO.

1975c PHTH "Philosophical Hermeneutics and Theological·
             Hermeneutics: Ideology, Utopia, and Faith." In
             *Protocol of the 17th Colloquy of the Center for
             Hermeneutical Studies*. Ed. W. Wuellner. Berkeley,
             CA.

1975d PH   "Phenomenology and Hermeneutics." *Nous* 9:85-102.

1976a HH   "History and Hermeneutics." *The Journal of
             Philosophy* 73:683-695.

1976b PWA   "Psychoanalysis and the Work of Art." *Psychiatry
             and the Humanities*. Ed. J. Smith. New Haven: Yale
             University Press.

1976c IUCI "Ideology and Utopia as Cultural Imagination."
             Philosophic Exchange 2:17-28.

1976d WD   "What Is Dialectical?" In *Freedom and Morality*.
             Ed. J. Bricke. Lawrence: University of Kansas
             Press.

1977a HIR   "Hermeneutic of the Idea of Revelation." In
             *Protocol of the 27th Colloquy of the Center for
             Hermeneutical Studies*. Ed. W. Wuellner. Berkeley,
             CA.

1977b THIR "Toward a Hermeneutic of the Idea of Revelation."
             Harvard Theological Review. 70:1-37.

1977c SH   "Schleiermacher's Hermeneutics." *Monist* 60:181-197.

1977d CC   "Construing and Constructing: Review of E. D.
             Hirsch, *The Aims of Interpretation*." *Times Literary
             Supplement*. Feb. 25, 216.

1977e SN   "Seminar: Narrative." Unpublished transcript.
             Emory University.

1978a HFD   "The Hermeneutical Function of Distanciation." In
             Exegesis. Eds. F. Bovon and G. Rouiller.
             Pittsburgh: The Pickwick Press.

1978b MRHP "My Relation to the History of Philosophy." *The
             Iliff Review*. November: 5-12.

1978c MPCIF "The Metaphorical Process as Cognition, Imagination,
              and Feeling." *Critical Inquiry* 5:143-159.

1978d NF   "The Narrative Function." *Semeia* 13:177-202.

1978e PHBH   "Philosophical Hermeneutics and Biblical
              Hermeneutics." In *Exegesis* Ed. F. Bovon and G.
              Rouiller. Pittsburgh: The Pickwick Press.

1978ee? PR   "Practical Reason." Unpublished ms. Trans.
              R. Czerny.

1978f I-TP   "Introduction." *Le Temps et les Philosophies*.
              Paris: Les Presses de l'UNESCO.

1978g TH   "The Task of Hermeneutics. In *Exegesis*. Ed. F.
              Bovon and G. Rouiller. Pittsburgh: The Pickwick
              Press.

1978h ILP   "Image and Language in Psychoanalysis." In
              *Psychiatry and Language: Psychiatry and the Humani-
              ties* 3. Ed. J. H. Smith. New Haven: Yale Univer-
              sity Press.

1978i IDA   "Imagination in Discourse and Action." In *The Human
              Being in Action*. Ed. A.-T. Tymieniecka. Boston:
              Reidel.

1979a F-BD   "Foreword." (Trans. David Pellauer) In André
              Lacocque, *The Book of Daniel*. Atlanta: John Knox
              Press.

1979b LJLG   "The Logic of Jesus, the Logic of God." *Criterion*
              18/2:4-6. (*Christianity and Crisis* 39/20:324-327).

1979c NG   "Naming God." *Union Seminary Quarterly Review*
              34:215-227. (Trans. David Pellauer: "Nommer Dieu."
              Études Théologiques et Religieuses 52, 1977:
              489-508).

1979d PFMP   "The Problem of the Foundation of Moral Philosophy."
              Philosophy Today 22:175-192.

1979e ESTC   "Epilogue: The Sacred Text and the Community." In
              The Critical Study of Sacred Texts. Ed. W.
              O'Flaherty. Los Angeles: University of California
              Press.

1979f FFSR   "The Function of Fiction in Shaping Reality." *Man
              and World* 12:123-141.

1979g   HTe   "The Hermeneutics of Testimony."   *Anglican*
                    Theological Review   61:435-461.

1979-
1980   R-BR   "Response." *Biblical Research*   24/25:70-80.

1980a   BI   "The Bible and the Imagination."   In *The Bible*
                    as a Document of the University. Ed.   H. D.
                    Betz.   Chico: Scholars Press.

1980b   NT   "Narrative Time."   *Critical Inquiry*   7:169-190.

1980c   NTh   "Narrative Theology."   Paper presented at the
                    Annual Meeting of the American Academy of
                    Religion, New York. November, 1979

1981   KPJ   "The 'Kingdom' in the Parables of Jesus."
                    Anglican Theological Review   63:165-169.

1984   PN   "From Proclamation to Narrative."   *The Journal of*
                    Religion   64:501-512.

1985   RI   "Le récit interprétatif: exégèse et théologie dans
                    les récits de la passion."   *Recherches de*
                    Science Religieuses 73:17-38.

1988   CP   "La crise: un phénomène spécifiquement moderne?"
                    Revue de Théologie et de Philosophie   120:1/1-19.

1989   EPT   "Entre philosophie et théologie: la Règle d'Or en
                    question." *Revue d'Histoire et de Philosophie*
                    Religieuses 69: 1/3-9.

BIBLIOGRAPHIES

The most comprehensive published bibliographies of Ricoeur's works
are:

Vansina, Dirk
    1962   "Bibliographie de Paul Ricoeur." *Revue philosophique de
            Louvain* 60:394-414.

    1968   "Bibliographie de Paul Ricoeur. Complements." *Revue
            philosophique de Louvain* 66:85-101.

    1974   (Frans D.) "Bibliographie de Paul Ricoeur.
            Complements." *Revue philosophique de Louvain*
            72:156-181.

Lapointe, Francois H.
    1972   "A Bibliography on Paul Ricoeur." *Philosophy Today*
            16:28-33. This was updated in *Philosophy Today*
            17:176-182 (1973).

Revised and updated editions of bibliographies by Vansina and
Lapointe are given in *Studies in the Philosophy of Paul Ricoeur.*
Ed. C. Reagan. Athens: Ohio University Press, 1979.

I am also grateful to H. Frederick Reisz, Jr. and to David
Pellauer for unpublished bibliographies of Ricoeur's works.

I have previously published selected bibliographies in *Semeia* 4
and in *Semeia* 19.

GENERAL INDEX

Index: Quotations from and References to Ricoeur's Works

PROBLEMS IN CONTEMPORARY PHILOSOPHY